The Explanation of Crime

Integration of disciplines, theories, and research orientations has assumed a central role in criminological discourse yet it remains difficult to identify any concrete discoveries or significant breakthroughs for which integration has been responsible. Concentrating on three key concepts: context, mechanisms, and development, this volume aims to advance integrated scientific knowledge on crime causation by bringing together different scholarly approaches. Through an analysis of the roles of behavioral contexts and individual differences in crime causation, *The Explanation of Crime* seeks to provide a unified and focused approach to the integration of knowledge. Chapter topics range from individual genetics to family environments and from ecological behavior settings to the macro-level context of communities and social systems. This is a comprehensive treatment of the problem of crime causation which will appeal to graduate students and researchers in criminology and be of great interest to policymakers and practitioners in crime policy and prevention.

Per-Olof H. Wikström is Professor of Ecological and Developmental Criminology at the University of Cambridge.

Robert J. Sampson is Henry Ford II Professor of the Social Sciences at Harvard University.

Pathways in Crime

The Explanation of Crime

Series Editor
Per-Olof H. Wikström

Pathways in Crime aims to advance knowledge of the interactions between individual characteristics and social contexts in producing offending behavior, and to assist in the development of improved public policies, reducing criminality and enhancing individuals' life chances. Each book in the series will identify central problems and key issues in a topic by examining pathways in crime in relation to contexts and mechanisms, methods and analytical techniques, innovative research, and policy implications. This series will appeal to students, researchers, and scholars of sociology, psychology, criminology, and social and public policy.

The Explanation of Crime

Context, Mechanisms, and Development

Edited by

Per-Olof H. Wikström

and

Robert J. Sampson

CAMBRIDGE
UNIVERSITY PRESS

CAMBRIDGE UNIVERSITY PRESS
Cambridge, New York, Melbourne, Madrid, Cape Town, Singapore, São Paulo, Delhi

Cambridge University Press
The Edinburgh Building, Cambridge CB2 8RU, UK

Published in the United States of America by Cambridge University Press, New York

www.cambridge.org
Information on this title: www.cambridge.org/9780521119054

First published 2006
This digitally printed version 2009

A catalogue record for this publication is available from the British Library

ISBN 978-0-521-85707-9 hardback
ISBN 978-0-521-11905-4 paperback

Contents

Figures

Tables

Contributors

SIR ANTHONY BOTTOMS has been Wolfson Professor of Criminology at the University of Cambridge since 1984, served as Director of the Cambridge Institute of Criminology from 1984 to 1998, and is currently a Visiting Professor at the University of Sheffield (1999–) and at Queen's University Belfast (1999–). His two principal research interests lie in the fields of penology and environmental criminology, but he has a growing interest in theoretical criminology. At the University of Sheffield, he is currently directing a research project on "Urban Crime in Sheffield 1999–2001," with funding from the Barrow Cadbury Trust. This project has direct links to his earlier research in environmental criminology in the same city (*The Urban Criminal* with J. Baldwin [1976] and several subsequent articles). Professor Bottoms was elected Fellow of the British Academy in 1997 and was awarded the Sellin–Glueck Prize of the American Society of Criminology in 1996. He is a Fellow of Fitzwilliam College, Cambridge and was President (= Vice-Master) of the College from 1994 to 1998.

MARIO BUNGE was born in Buenos Aires. He obtained his PhD in physico-mathematical sciences from the Universidad Nacional de La Plata in 1952. He served as a professor of theoretical physics at the Universidad de Buenos Aires from 1956 to 1966 and at the Universidad Nacional de La Plata from 1956 to 1959 and a professor of philosophy at the Universidad de Buenos Aires from 1957 to 1963. He is currently Frothingham Professor of Logic and Metaphysics and Head, Foundations and Philosophy of Science, McGill University, Montreal, which he joined in 1966. He has authored more than 80 books and over 400 articles on theoretical physics, applied mathematics, systems theory, foundations of physics, foundations of sociology and psychology, philosophy of science, philosophy of technology, semantics, epistemology, catology, value theory, ethics, science policy, etc.

AVSHALOM CASPI is Professor of Psychology at the Institute of Psychiatry, King's College, London, and in the Department of Psychology at the University of Wisconsin-Madison. His major research interests include life-span developmental psychology, life-course sociology, development and psychopathology, personality assessment, behavioral genetics and longitudinal research methods. He is currently involved in several longitudinal studies concerned with the causes and consequences of continuity and change in behavioral development. In 1995 Professor Caspi won both the American Psychological Association Distinguished Scientific Award for Early Career Contributions to Psychology, and the American Psychological Foundation Robert L. Fantz Award. More recently, in 1998, he was elected a Fellow of the Center for Advanced Study in the Behavioral Sciences.

MARC LE BLANC is Professor in the School of Psycho-Education and the School of Criminology at the University of Montreal. He is also Director of Research for Boscoville 2000, a research and development center for adolescents with problem behavior. Professor Le Blanc has been involved in fundamental and applied research concerning juvenile delinquency for the last thirty-five years, and has been instrumental in promoting a developmental approach to the study of crime. His publications describe the extent and nature of individual delinquency and problem behavior and their development from childhood through adulthood, the etiology of self-reported and official adolescent delinquency and adult criminality, and present models of family, school, peer, constraints, self-control, and general control. His theoretical work covers four main areas: (i) the formalization and reformulation of Hirschi's social control theory; (ii) the formulation of a theory of the development of offending and of the developmental paradigm for criminology (with R. Loeber); (iii) the development of a social and personal control theory; and (iv) the formulation of a generic control theory that can apply to the commission of a crime, criminality, and individual offending. Professor Le Blanc was elected to the Social Sciences Academy of the Royal Society of Canada and is a Beccaria, Killam and deToqueville-Beaumont Fellow.

ROLF LOEBER is Professor of Psychiatry, Psychology, and Epidemiology at the Western Psychiatric Institute and Clinic, School of Medicine, University of Pittsburgh, and Professor of Juvenile Delinquency and Social Development at the Free University, Amsterdam. He is co-director of the Life History Program and is principal investigator of three longitudinal studies: the Pittsburgh

Youth Study, the Developmental Trends Study, and the Pittsburgh Girls Study. He has published over 130 peer-reviewed papers and over 90 book chapters and other papers in the fields of juvenile antisocial behavior and delinquency, substance use, and mental health problems.

TERRIE MOFFITT is Professor of Psychology at the Institute of Psychiatry, King's College London, and in the Department of Psychology at the University of Wisconsin-Madison. She is also Associate Director of the Dunedin Multidisciplinary Health and Development Research Unit at the University of Otago Medical School. Her research interests include the natural history of antisocial behavior from childhood to adulthood, domestic violence, longitudinal research methodology, measurement of abnormal behavior, neuropsychological assessment, intelligence, and behavioral genetics. In 1999 Professor Moffitt was elected Fellow of the British Academy of Medical Sciences and was a finalist for editorship of the *Journal of Abnormal Psychology* and the *Journal of Child Psychiatry & Psychology*. She has won several awards during her academic career including the Mid Career Award from the University of Wisconsin in 1997 and the Distinguished Scientific Award for Early Career Contribution to Psychology from the American Psychological Association in 1993.

ROBERT J. SAMPSON is Chairman of the Department of Sociology and the Henry Ford II Professor of the Social Sciences at Harvard University where he was appointed in January 2003 after a sabbatical in 2002–2003 at the Center for Advanced Study in the Behavioral Sciences in Stanford, California. Formerly he was the Fairfax M. Cone Distinguished Service Professor in Sociology at the University of Chicago and Senior Research Fellow at the American Bar Foundation. Professor Sampson's main research interests include crime, law, deviance, and stigmatization; and neighborhood effects and the sociology of the modern city. His current focus is race/ethnicity and sociological mechanisms of ecological inequality, the subjective meanings of disorder, spatial dynamics, the comparative network structure of community influence, collective civic engagement, and other topics linked to the general idea of community-level social processes. Much of this work stems from the Project on Human Development in Chicago Neighborhoods, for which Sampson serves as Scientific Director. His recent honors include the Michael J. Hindelang Book Award in 2004 for *Shared Beginnings, Divergent Lives: Delinquent Boys to Age 70* (2003).

N. Wim Slot is Director of PI Research, a research center for youth care and education in the Netherlands, and a professor at the Free University in Amsterdam. His research focuses on child protection and juvenile delinquency. He has co-authored a number of articles in journals such as the *Journal of Clinical Child and Adolescent Psychology* and *Child Psychiatry and Human Devlopment*.

Magda Stouthamer-Loeber is Associate Professor of Psychiatry and Psychology at the University of Pittsburgh. She obtained her master's degree in clinical psychology from the Free University in Amsterdam. Her doctorate in clinical psychology is from Queen's University, Kingston, Ontario. Her career has been in the study of antisocial behavior in children, and she has been involved in the Pittsburgh Youth Study and the Pittsburgh Girls Study, both longitudinal studies of large samples. Her interest is in mental health help for children, desistance in delinquency, and risk and protective factors. In addition, she is an expert on conducting longitudinal studies with a high participation rate and high data completion.

Per-Olof H. Wikström is Professor of Ecological and Developmental Criminology, University of Cambridge, and a Fellow of Girton College, Cambridge. He is the Director of the ESRC Cambridge Network for the Study of the Social Contexts of Pathways in Criminality (SCoPiC; see www.scopic.ac.uk for further information). This major research network spans four research sites in the UK (Cambridge, Sheffield, London, and Huddersfield) and collaborates internationally with Harvard University, the University of Pittsburgh, the University of Montreal, and the University of Zurich. Professor Wikstrom's main research interests are in the causes of crime, urban crime, adolescent offending, criminal careers, crime prevention, and cross-national comparative research. In 1994 he received the Sellin–Glueck Award for outstanding contributions to international criminology from the American Society of Criminology, and in 2002 he was elected a Fellow of the Center for Advanced Study in the Behavioral Sciences, Stanford. He has recently served as Deputy Director of the University of Cambridge Institute of Criminology and Ph.D. Program Director.

Acknowledgments

The SCoPiC network is financed by a grant from the UK Economic and Social Research Council (ESRC). We gratefully acknowledge the ESRC's important contribution in providing funding for the conference and workshop of which this book is an outcome. We would like to recognize the indirect contributions to this volume of Professors David Farrington (University of Cambridge) and John Laub (University of Maryland), who acted as discussants. Their insightful comments and criticisms have helped sharpen many of the arguments put forward in this book. We would also like to thank Charlotte Christie (the then SCoPiC administrator) and Kyle Treiber (current PhD student at Cambridge) for their invaluable assistance in helping us with all the practical matters in putting together this volume.

Introduction: Toward a unified approach to crime and its explanation

Per-Olof H. Wikström and Robert J. Sampson

"Integration" has assumed a central role in criminological discourse. There are at least four types of integration – of theories (e.g., social learning and social control), methods (e.g., qualitative and quantitative), levels of analysis (e.g., neighborhood and individual), and disciplines (e.g., psychology and sociology). The majority of integrative efforts in criminology have aimed at the first type, the integration of theoretical models derived from classical schools of thought on the causes of crime – almost always sociological. Some oft-cited attempts at theoretical integration in this realm include Elliott, Ageton, & Canter (1979), Messner, Krohn, & Liska (1989), and Braithwaite (1989). In recent years the multi-level integration of data across levels of analysis has also come on strong, especially in the form of contextual analyses that purport to estimate "neighborhood effects" on individual behavior (for a review, see Sampson, Morenoff, & Gannon-Rowley 2002).

Despite the seeming consensus that integrative modes of inquiry are important, there is still no consensus approach and it is hard to identify concrete new discoveries or significant breakthroughs in criminology that have been made in the name of integration. Put simply, the benefits for knowledge remain largely a promissory note.[1] Why is this so? A main reason, of course, is that the task is enormously difficult. Even in the so-called "hard sciences" integration is hard to come by – it takes lots of time and effort so there is no reason to expect a fast payoff. Indeed, efforts to create research collaborations that are truly interdisciplinary in practice are notoriously fraught with conflict. Another and perhaps more fundamental reason, however, is conceptual: criminology lacks an accepted and general theoretical structure for guiding integrative inquiry into the causes of crime. By this we do not simply mean adding up

[1] A number of independent observers have come to the same conclusion on the general lack of progress with respect to integration in criminology, especially of the theoretical variety. See, for example, Kornhauser (1978), Hirschi (1979), Reiss (1986), Laufer & Adler (1989), Farrington (1993), and Jensen & Akers (2003).

theories "end to end," formulating a specific hypothesis that combines prior theories, or even the implementation of an integrative method. Consider the increasing attention to "multi-level" integration. Most efforts in this area have simply taken the form of combining data across ecological levels and performing (often sophisticated) hierarchical statistical analyses rather than making concerted theoretical attempts to link individual behavior to higher-order contexts. Or take the more common approach to theoretical integration that consists of setting out to combine theories of delinquency that invoke contradictory assumptions. As Hirschi (1979) has astutely noted, it is not clear that we have advanced if we pretend to integrate what is fundamentally incompatible.

Recognizing these pitfalls, we seek to advance knowledge by providing a unified and focused approach to the integration of knowledge. Rather than attempting a Noah's Ark theory that integrates anything and everything on the one hand, or that operates within the confines of a specific discipline or level of analysis on the other, we decided to concentrate intently on three key concepts – *context, mechanisms*, and *development*. We specifically argue that criminology lacks a coherent conceptual structure that systematically links social context and individual development with a theory of causal mechanisms.[2] As explicated further in the pages to follow, we view a causal mechanism as explaining *why* a putative cause brings about an effect. Explicating mechanisms is largely a theoretical task because it involves positing a plausible process (often unobservable) that connects cause and effect through social action (Coleman, 1986; Bunge, 2004). According to a mechanism-based approach most correlates (or "risk factors") of crime are in fact spurious associations that denote markers rather than represent mechanisms that actually cause a particular social action. It follows that an important task, one undertaken in this volume, is to evaluate known correlates for their potential as representing causal mechanisms in relation to the production of crime. As motivation, consider that the correlation of contextual characteristics (such as the concentration of poverty) with levels of criminal offending has been documented in criminological research for at least 300 years. Yet the causal mechanisms that link contextual features to the development of acts of criminal offending are poorly understood.

In short, this volume aims to advance integrated scientific knowledge on crime causation by bringing together scholarly approaches to causal mechanisms that operate across multiple social contexts and individual

[2] However, the Editors have recently conducted some tentative work with this aim (Wikström & Sampson, 2003; Wikström, 2004, 2005).

development. Eschewing the preset and typically rigid analytic boundaries that dominate most criminological studies, the contributions to follow range all the way from genetics at the level of individuals to family environments to situations to ecological behavior settings to the macro-level context of communities and social systems. The disciplinary backgrounds of authors include not just the usual suspects like sociology and criminology, but also neuro-psychology, theoretical physics, and the philosophy of science. Rather than a cacophony of incompatible sounds, however, the contributors attempt, each in their own way, to come to terms with how their approaches contribute to our understanding of the causal mechanisms that link social context to individual development. Before describing this threefold approach and its manifestation in the individual chapters, we turn to a brief description of the volume's intellectual backdrop, followed by its organizational structure.

Intellectual background

The intellectual origins of this book can be traced to a pair of conferences held in Sweden in 1992 (Farrington, Sampson, & Wikström, 1993) and 1994 (Wikström, Clarke, & McCord, 1995) that posed as their main problematic the integration of levels of explanation in criminology (i.e., the linking of knowledge about individuals and their environments to the explanation and study of crime). The fundamental idea was to bring together scholars from different disciplines and research orientations within disciplines in order to promote interaction and thinking outside the box, with the hope of stimulating advances in cross-level theory and research on the causes of crime. In particular, it was felt that there was a need for greater interpersonal interaction and intellectual debate among scholars representing approaches that typically do not converse.

This idea was carried forward in 2002 with the establishment of the Cambridge-based international research network SCoPiC ("Social Context of Pathways in Crime"; see http://www.scopic.ac.uk/). The network includes researchers with an unusually diverse set of disciplinary backgrounds. SCoPiC finances new research, aims to stimulate cross-disciplinary collaboration among the members, and organizes workshops and conferences to address both theoretical and methodological problems in the integration of knowledge about crime and its causes. There is a strong continuity between the Swedish conferences and the work of the SCoPiC network. Indeed, many of the international scholars who participated in the two Swedish conferences are also part of the core group of the SCoPiC network, and some of them are in turn represented in this book.

Organization of the book

The chapters commissioned for this volume were asked to address one or more of the three key themes introduced above: the role of (i) social context, (ii) individual development, and (iii) the mechanisms (processes) by which social context and individual development interact to explain acts of crime. In Chapter 1, Bunge begins with a general approach to social context by criticizing the dominant individualistic and holistic approaches to the explanation of social phenomena such as acts of crime. He demonstrates their respective philosophical underpinnings and shortcomings and advances instead a systemic perspective that may serve as a fruitful basis for cross-level knowledge integration. Bunge also deals with the important problem of establishing causal mechanisms and as such provides an important philosophical background to some of the more specific discussions of the problem of causation and explanation dealt with by many of the other contributors. As an "outsider" to criminology we believe Bunge brings a fresh perspective to systemic thinking about mechanisms and explanation in the study of crime.

Bunge's orienting framework is followed by three chapters that focus on a particular level of explanation and its role in crime causation – the *community context* (Sampson), *situations* (Wikström), and *genetics* (Moffitt and Caspi). Sampson (Chapter 2), building on his Theory of Collective Efficacy, explicates the social mechanisms that link community context to its level of crime. He specifically argues that to understand the impact of community context on individuals we first have to understand community social processes – and develop measurement schemes thereof – on their own terms. He also advocates a "counterfactual" approach to establishing causation.

In Chapter 3, Wikström presents advances in his Situational Action Theory of Crime Causation and discusses the situational mechanisms that link individuals and settings to their action, by engaging the literature on theories of action. He argues that without a proper understanding of situational mechanisms we cannot fully explain the influences of social context and development on moral actions like acts of crime. He champions an analytical approach to the identification of causal mechanisms and experimentation as the principal method of establishing causation.

Moffitt and Caspi (Chapter 4) address the disentanglement of genetic and environmental effects on behavior, promoting the study of their interaction, and focusing particularly on behavioral genetics as a method to establish environmental effects on antisocial behavior. They argue that without a proper consideration of the influence of genetic factors it is difficult to prove conclusively the existence of environmental causation. It is rare that criminologists interested in social context consider genetics, much less a behavioral genetic design as a way to improve our estimation of the pathways through which social context operates.

The following two chapters focus on the role of individual development. In Chapter 5, Loeber, Slot, and Stouthamer-Loeber present a new strategy for organizing knowledge about key correlates of antisocial behavior by age and domain. They advocate the importance of the development of cumulative risk and promotive factors in the explanation of developmental pathways in antisocial behavior and crime. In doing so, they stress the significance of dose–response relationships and the relative proportions of risk versus promotive factors for behavioral outcomes. They present a technique to visualize the relationship between cumulative risk and promotive factors and developmental pathways, which they argue has promise for the understanding of how antisocial behavior unfolds in different environmental contexts.

Le Blanc (Chapter 6) builds on his Integrative Multilayered Control Theory, and presents an approach to the problem of developmental mechanisms that draws heavily on the chaos order paradigm. He specifically argues that this perspective, described in detail in his Chapter, offers new ways of thinking about the probabilistic nature of development and its relationship to deviance. He also integrates self- and social control theory across multiple levels of analysis and links them to the developmental mechanisms implied by chaos theory.

One of the most topical, but under-researched, areas in developmental criminology is that of desistance. In the final chapter of the book, Bottoms takes on this important problem. He engages with some key literature on agency and explores how this concept can add to our understanding of processes of persistence and desistance in crime involvement. Bottoms' engagement with some theoretical approaches on agency goes well beyond the traditional terrain of criminology and points to new insights on adult offending.

Coda

Although the SCoPiC network has the common agenda of promoting cross-level knowledge integration in the study of crime, members of the network clearly differ in their analytical approaches to how to theoretically and methodologically best achieve this goal. In the end, however, it is only through critical discussion of these different analytical approaches and the empirical testing of competing ideas that we will learn more about the causes of crime – precisely what the Network aims to encourage.

Similarly, the contributors to this volume do not all necessarily agree, nor do we as Editors necessarily agree with the arguments in each and every chapter. Our overarching motivation is to stimulate new thinking and interdisciplinary engagement around the common intellectual goal shared by all authors and, we hope, readers – the need to better understand the linkage of context, mechanisms, and development. As Karl Popper (1983: 7) reminded us, what matters most in scholarly debate and ultimately scientific progress is not shared initial content but *the shared wish to know and the readiness to learn from criticism.* It is our hope that the fruits of this process, as reflected in the Swedish and SCoPiC conferences, and the published contributions herein, will push the boundaries of future research in unanticipated and novel ways.

References

Braithwaite, J. (1989). *Crime, Shame and Reintegration.* Cambridge: Cambridge University Press.

Bunge, M. (2004). "How does it work? The search for explanatory mechanisms." *Philosophy of the Social Sciences* 34: 1–29.

Coleman, J. S. (1986). "Social theory, social research, and a theory of action." *American Journal of Sociology* 91: 1309–1335.

Elliott, D., Ageton, S., & Canter, R. (1979). "An integrated theoretical perspective on delinquent behavior." *Journal of Research in Crime and Delinquency* 16: 3–27.

Farrington, D. (1993). "Have any individual, family, or neighborhood influences on offending been demonstrated conclusively?" In D. Farrington, R. Sampson, & P.-O. Wikström (eds.), *Integrating Individual and Ecological Aspects of Crime.* Stockholm: Allmaana Forlaget.

Farrington, D., Sampson, R., & Wikström, P.-O. (eds.) (1993). *Integrating Individual and Ecological Aspects of Crime.* Stockholm: Allmaana Forlaget.

Hirschi, T. (1979). "Separate and unequal is better." *Journal of Research in Crime and Delinquency* 16: 34–37.

Jensen, G. & Akers, R. (2003). "Taking social learning theory global: micro–macro transitions in criminological theory." In R. L. Akers & G. F. Jensen (eds.), *Social Learning Theory and the Explanation of Crime. Advances in Criminological Theory* 11. New Brunswick, NJ: Transaction.

Laufer, W. & Adler, F. (1989). "Introduction: the challenges of advances in criminological theory." In W. S. Laufer & F. Adler (eds.), *Advances in Criminological Theory,* vol. I. New Brunswick, NJ: Transaction.

Kornhauser, R. (1978). *Social Sources of Delinquency.* Chicago: University of Chicago Press.

Messner, S. F., Krohn, M. D., & Liska, A. E. (1989). *Theoretical Integration in the Study of Deviance and Crime: Problems and Prospects*. New York: State University of New York Press.

Popper, K. (1983). *Realism and the Aim of Science*. London and New York: Routledge.

Reiss, A. J. (1986). "Why are communities important in understanding crime?" In A. J. Reiss & M. Tonry (eds.), *Communities and Crime*, Crime and Justice: A Review of Research, vol. VIII. Chicago: University of Chicago Press.

Sampson, R., Morenoff, J., & Gannon-Rowley, T. (2002). "Assessing neighborhood effects: social processes and new directions in research." *Annual Review of Sociology* 28: 443–478.

Wikström, P.-O. H. (2004). "Crime as alternative. Towards a cross-level situational action theory of crime causation." In J. McCord. (ed.), *Beyond Empiricism: Institutions and Intentions in the Study of Crime*. Advances in Criminological Theory 13. New Brunswick, NJ: Transaction.

(2005). "The social origins of pathways in crime. Towards a developmental ecological action theory of crime involvement and its changes." In D. P. Farrington (ed.), *Integrated Developmental and Life-Course Theories of Offending*. Advances in Criminological Theory 14. New Brunswick, NJ: Transaction.

Wikström, P.-O. H., Clarke, R., & McCord, J. (1995). *Integrating Crime Prevention Strategies: Propensity and Opportunity*. Stockholm: Allmaana Forlaget.

Wikström, P-O. H. & Sampson, R. J. (2003). "Social mechanisms of community influences on crime and pathways in criminality." In B. Lahey, T. Moffitt & A. Caspi (eds.), *Causes of Conduct Disorder and Serious Juvenile Delinquency*. New York: Guilford Press.

1 A systemic perspective on crime

Mario Bunge

Crime is the most harmful and yet the least understood of any kind of deviant behavior. A possible reason for this is that it comes in very many shapes, from plagiarism to fraud, from deception to betrayal, from shoplifting to corporate swindle and from homicide to mass murder. Another reason for our limited understanding of crime is the traditional view that it is a sin to be punished rather than prevented. This retributive attitude, rooted in the primitive desire for revenge, blocks both the search for crime mechanisms and the design of effective prevention and rehabilitation programs. Furthermore, it makes crime an exclusive subject for psychology, the law, morals, or religion, and thus it isolates criminology from the social sciences and technologies instead of placing it squarely in their midst.

The social sciences, in particular anthropology, social psychology, sociology, and history, teach us several important lessons about crime. One of them is that there are many types of crime besides theft and homicide. For instance, there are environmental crimes such as pollution, political crimes such as the suppression of dissent, and cultural crimes such as ideological censorship. Another lesson is that whoever is really interested in reducing the delinquency rate, instead of waging vociferous but ineffective "wars on crime," should try and uncover the causes of crime with a view to redesigning social policies instead of focusing on punishment, particularly since the traditional jail has proved to be a school of crime. That is, we should try and unveil the crime mechanisms. And there must be several such mechanisms since there are several kinds of crime.

In the following I shall sketch the systemic alternative to the traditional social philosophies, suggest a typology of crimes, comment on some criminological hypotheses, and propose a model to explain the differences in the rates of small-scale crimes across cultures. It will also be noted that, fortunately, criminology is quickly becoming half

I thank Per-Olof Wikström and Michael Kary for helpful advice, as well as Dedos Brujos, the pickpocket with whom I shared a Peronist jail, and who taught me that some criminals are better men than their judges.

inter-science and half social technology. Whether policymakers will take this progress into account remains to be seen.

Systemic alternative to the traditional social philosophies

Since crimes involve at least two persons, they are social facts. And all social facts involve people embedded in social networks that are in turn included in society at large. These are of course platitudes, yet they are at variance with the two traditional social philosophies, namely individualism and holism. Indeed, the individualists, like Max Weber, insist rightly that social facts result directly or ultimately from individual action. But they regard institutions only as placing constraints on such action: they deny the very existence of the social systems where every social fact happens. By contrast, the holists, like Emile Durkheim, regard individual action as only a reaction to pressures exerted by society as a whole: they are right in stressing the social embeddedness of individual action. But they deny personal initiative and responsibility, and they minimize the effectiveness of agency. Thus, as has been said, whereas the individualist person is under-socialized, the holist one is over-socialized. Hence individualists and holists are bound to regard social deviance, in particular crime, in very different lights. Indeed, whereas individualists tend to blame exclusively the offender, his character, education, or perhaps even his genes, holists tend to blame only society, and to regard the victimizer as only a victim.

The consequences of these two philosophies for social policy design are quite different: whereas the individualist criminologist will recommend correction exclusively, the holist is likely to propose social reforms with disregard for personal problems and habits. I submit that, while each of these two extreme social philosophies has a grain of truth, both miss the central truth, namely, that every individual, even the hermit, belongs at once to several social systems, such as family, network of friends and acquaintances, firm, club, gang, school, religious congregation, political party, or what have you. This explains why every social action elicits some reactions that propagate along several networks: "with the complex interaction that constitutes society, action ramifies. Its consequences are not restricted to the specific area in which they are intended to center and occur in interrelated fields explicitly ignored at the time of the action" (Merton, 1976: 154).

In other words, an individual's actions cannot be understood without considering the systems of which he is a part, just as these cannot be understood except as being composed of individuals who maintain, reinforce, or weaken the bonds that keep them and others in their systems. In other words, individual and society, or agency and structure, are simply two faces of the same social coin. In particular, the lawbreaker is both victimizer and victim. Hence crime management should involve social reform and rehabilitation programs as well as social control, both formal and informal. In short, there are neither stray individuals nor social systems towering above individuals.

Regrettably, talk of social systems evokes some embarrassing memories, namely the holistic excesses and verbal acrobatics of Hegel and, closer to us, those of Talcott Parsons and his followers, in particular Niklas Luhmann, Jürgen Habermas, David Easton, and Erwin Laszlo. Therefore, I hasten to clarify that I favor a non-holistic notion of a system. This is the clear concept used in mathematics, the factual ("empirical") sciences, and engineering. In all of these fields, a system is conceived of as a complex object, concrete or abstract, composed of interrelated items, and possessing some (systemic or emergent) properties absent from its constituents. A classical example is that of a body of liquid water, whose macro-properties, such as fluidity and transparency, are not possessed by its constituent molecules. Likewise, a nuclear human family consists of the spouses and their children, and it possesses the emergent properties of cohesiveness and harmony, of being a household and the primary locus of child-rearing and socialization, and of counting as a single entity for others.

Given the large number of kinds of system, as well as the dense fog surrounding much of the systems-theoretic literature, it will be convenient to adopt a general and fairly clear model of a system.

The CESM model of a system

When faced with the task of describing a system, one starts by asking the following four questions. What is it made of (*composition*)? What surrounds it (*environment*)? Which are the bonds that hold it together (*structure*)? How does it work (*mechanism*)? This is why the simplest model of a concrete system *s*, whether atom, cell, family, or what have you, is what I call the CESM sketch:

$\mu(s) = \langle C(s), E(s), S(s), M(s) \rangle$, where
$C(s)$ = Composition = Collection of the parts of *s*;
E(s) = Environment = Collection of items, other than those in *s*, that act or on are acted upon by some or all components of *s*;
S(s) = Structure = Collection of relations, in particular bonds, between components of *s* or between these and things in the environment;

M(s) = Mechanism = Collection of processes that allow *s* to perform its specific function(s).

Every one of the components of this ordered quadruple is bound to change over time, as does every concrete thing. Yet some components of CESM are likely to be more lasting than others. Thus, the membership and environment of an army in wartime change rapidly, whereas its structure (command chain) and mechanism (combat) remain rather constant. Criminal gangs are parallel. For example, the composition of a Mafia "family" at any given time is the collection of its members; its environment, the society in which it operates; its structure, the relations that preserve its physical integrity and the fear and obedience of its victims; and its mechanism consists of all of the criminal activities in which the particular "family" specializes, from intimidation of jury members and enforcement of the *omertà* norm to racketeering and murder. This example alone should suggest that success in fighting organized crime cannot be attained by focusing on a single aspect, such as composition: it also requires gaining control over the environment of the organization, in particular its victims, clients, and accomplices, as well as its suppliers of guns and drugs.

The environment of an organism should not be regarded as an unchanging context, but rather as partially constructed by the organism itself. Niche construction, an important if usually neglected ecological and evolutionary feature (Odling-Smee, Laland, & Feldman, 2003), is even more important in human society. For example, the refugee from a community in a process of disorganization, such as an inner-city slum, may be tempted to join or organize another social system, whether lawful or criminal, to provide himself with a favorable habitat. This dissolves the apparent paradox that social *dis*organization is a major source of *organized* crime: the two processes do not occur at the same time in the same system. Social geography, urban sociology, and environmental criminology have emphasized for decades the importance of place and, in particular, of local ties, their dissolution, and their reconstitution in new ways (e.g., Bottoms, 1994). In particular, the weakening of interpersonal (social) bonds and informal social control (society–individual bonds) is conducive to deviant behavior, which in turn further weakens those ties (Thornberry, 1987; Sampson & Laub, 1993).

Structure is sometimes confused with composition, and at other times with system, but it is neither. The structure of a system is the set of all the relations, in particular the bonds (or relations that make a difference), that keep a system whole. Another somewhat problematic

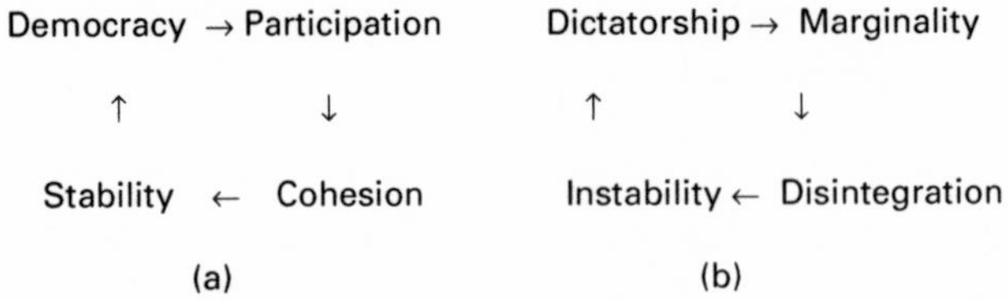

Figure 1.1. Feedback loops involving four social mechanisms: (a) constructive (b) destructive

concept is that of a mechanism, particularly because the word evokes the works of a clock or some other mechanical system. As used in contemporary physics, chemistry, biology, sociology, and engineering, the mechanism of a system is the collection of processes that keep it going. Obvious examples are metabolism in a cell, learning in a school, and work in a factory (see Bunge, 1999, 2004).

Social mechanisms have two peculiarities: they are purposeful, and they are linked. For example, democracy may be regarded as a mechanism for favoring participation; the latter is a mechanism for reinforcing social cohesion; in turn, cohesion favors stability, which reinforces democracy. The four mechanisms are thus linked in a self-sustaining causal chain – and so are their duals (Figure 1.1).

Criminologists are particularly interested in three mechanisms: those of criminogenesis, crime perpetration, and crime control. Criminogenesis is a society-wide mechanism: it is the set of pathways leading some people to habitual law-breaking, that is, to the life stories that, in a given society and under certain circumstances, push people to earning their livelihoods at the expense of other people's property or life. The second mechanism is the process individual delinquents and criminal gangs face. It can be summarized as follows: Problem (e.g., how to get the next meal ticket?) → Alternatives (e.g., work, borrow, steal, murder with intent to steal) → Evaluation (e.g., expected gains and risks) → Choice (e.g., decision to pick a pocket) → Action (e.g., picking a pocket and fleeing). This mechanism is the object of Situational Action Theory (Wikström, 2004a). Finally, there is the set of crime-management mechanisms, both formal and informal, that occupy not only law-enforcers but also community leaders, legislators interested in crime prevention and correction, and the people who build, manage, or supply jails.

The view that the concept of a system is central to social science and technology and, indeed, to all sciences and technologies, may be called *systemism*. Systemism has two components: ontological and

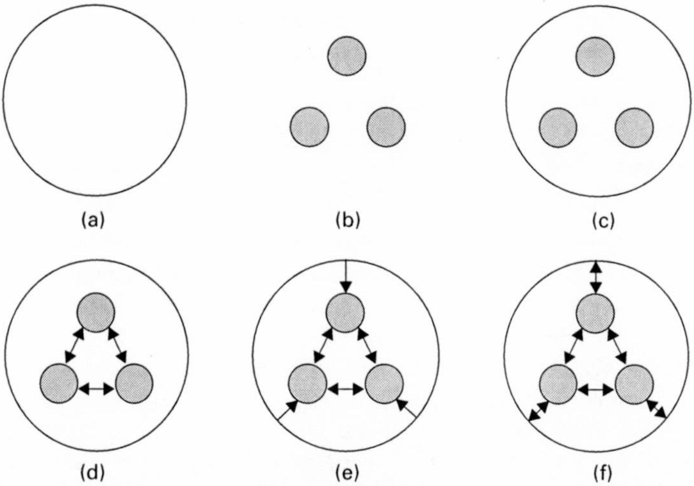

Figure 1.2. (a) Holism: the individual is just a drop in the social sea (e.g., Marx) (b) radical individualism: individuals, who are free and mutually independent, are the source of everything social (c) institutional individualism: individuals are constrained by institutions (e.g., Weber) (d) internalist systemism: structure prevails over environment (e) environmentalist systemism: system embedded in environment (f) full-fledged systemism: the constituents interact both among themselves and with their environment

methodological. Ontological systemism holds that the world is a system rather than either a collection of individuals or a solid block. Its methodological partner is the view that wholes are best understood through analysis (top-down), and individuals through synthesis (bottom-up). I have developed these views starting from a study of social structure (Bunge, 1974, 1979a; Bunge & García-Sucre, 1976). These led to a systemic ontology (Bunge, 1979b), where every item is either a system or a component of one. In turn, this ontology leads to a systemic epistemology (Bunge, 1983a, 1983b), where the knower is both creative and a child of his place and time, and where every bit of genuine knowledge belongs to at least one conceptual system, and every research field overlaps partially with at least one other such field. The ontology underlying the structurism of Anthony Giddens (1984) is akin, though restricted to social matters as well as far less precise because he makes no use of formal tools (see also Lloyd, 1991).

Figure 1.2 suggests some of the peculiarities of the social ontologies in question – from holism and individualism to systemism in the case of a three-component system such as a water molecule, a married couple with a child, or a political triumvirate.

The NBEPC schema and the crime spectrum

According to the idealist, in particular neo-Kantian and neo-Hegelian, schools in the philosophy of social studies, a fact is either natural or cultural, never both (see, e.g., Dilthey, 1883; Geertz, 1973; Weber, 1976). Such alleged dichotomy is the ontological basis of the partition of the sciences into natural and cultural (or spiritual). For example, Searle (1995: 27) holds that there are two categories of fact: brute, such as a sunrise, and institutional, such as a conversation. However, since conversing, trading, warring, and all other social facts involve live persons, those facts are biosocial rather than purely social. This is why there are biosocial sciences such as biogeography, demography, epidemiology, anthropology, psychology, and social medicine. The mere existence of these inter-sciences falsifies the natural/cultural dichotomy. What is true is that, for analytical purposes, one may seize on certain features and pretend that the others do not exist or are less important. For instance, in making, studying, or applying criminal law one may disregard international relations – unless of course the event in question happens to be criminal in the light of international law.

I have argued elsewhere (Bunge, 2003) that every social fact has five different but closely linked features: environmental (N), biopsychological (B), economic (E), political (P), and cultural (C). I have also suggested that a social change may originate in either of these sources, so that there is no single prime social mover, not even "in the last analysis." The conjunction of these two theses is represented in Figure 1.3. I submit that Ibn Khaldûn, Alexis de Tocqueville, Karl Marx, the mature Max Weber, and Fernand Braudel might have concurred.

The same figure also suggests the multi-causation thesis that in society there is no first motor, since the N, B, E, P, and C factors can be ordered in $5! = 120$ different ways. For example, a military aggression (P) can kill and injure many people (B), disrupt the economy (E) and the culture (C), and destroy natural resources (N): $P \rightarrow B \& E \& C \& N$. And a profound cultural innovation, such as the computer revolution, can have strong economic effects, with the consequent environmental, biological, and political consequences: $C \rightarrow E \rightarrow N \& B \& P$.

Let us now look at crime in the light of the NBEPC schema. Before doing so, however, we should remember that there are two different concepts of crime: the moral and the legal. The former coincides with

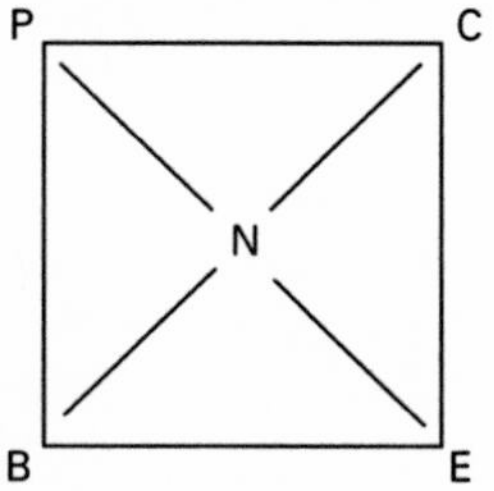

Figure 1.3. The five factors of a social fact. The edges represent actions and fluxes of various kinds, from energy flows and information transfers to more or less subtle social actions and signals, from wink and poster to greeting and shoving

that of antisocial behavior, whether or not it is sanctioned by the law of the land. By contrast, the legal (and legal-positivist) concept of crime is the same as "law-breaking behavior." The extensions of the two concepts overlap partially: every society condones some moral crimes, such as lying, while it condemns some virtuous actions, such as that of breaking unfair laws. For instance, some societies condemn small-scale murder but not mass murder. Moreover, some societies accept legal murder to the point that hanging judges are respected although they are literally serial killers. In the rest of this section we shall deal only with antisocial (hence immoral) behavior. Moreover, for our purposes we need not distinguish, as Moffitt (1993) rightly does, between youthful crimes, the vast majority of offences, and persistent antisocial behavior. We shall distinguish two or more species in each genus. Occasionally a crime species, such as military aggression, will be included in two different genera, which is why we shall propose a typology rather than a classification. (In the latter any two classes on the same rank, such as that of species, are disjoint.)

1. *Environmental*: against the natural or social environment
   1.1 Pollution
   1.2 Wanton destruction of non-renewable resources or public goods

2. *Biological*: against health or life
   2.1 Medical quackery ("alternative medicine")
   2.2 Sale of harmful products
   2.3 Assault
   2.4 Torture

  2.5 Murder
  2.6 Sexism
  2.7 Racism
  2.8 Ethnic "cleansing"
  2.9 War

3. *Economic*: against property
   3.1 Small-scale theft
   3.2 Vandalism
   3.3 Corporate swindle
   3.4 Embezzlement
   3.5 Conquest

4. *Political*: against political enemies
   4.1 Electoral fraud
   4.2 Coercion of innocent people
   4.3 Group-sponsored terrorism
   4.4 State terrorism
   4.5 War

5. *Cultural*: against knowledge or art
   5.1 Plagiarism and fraud
   5.2 Charlatanism (e.g., postmodernism)
   5.3 Pseudoscience (e.g., Creation "science")
   5.4 Deceptive advertising
   5.5 Hate propaganda
   5.6 Ideological censorship
   5.7 Attack on cultural heritages or organizations

These are only analytical distinctions. In real social life every crime of a certain type (i.e., with a certain goal) is usually accompanied by crimes of other types. For instance, murder is sometimes committed as a means for theft or for political power. Most wars have been initiated with the aim of grabbing land, natural resources, or trade routes. And military aggression for any purpose is the ultimate crime, for it has all the five features noted above.

The epistemological problem

How should crime be investigated? The contemporary philosophy of social science is divided into two main camps with regard to the optimal strategy to investigate social facts: realism and anti-realism, in particular hermeneuticism. Realists hold that social facts, being real, should be investigated just like physical facts, namely, objectively. By contrast, the hermeneuticists claim that the investigation of social facts should start by unveiling the intentions of the individuals that cause them. For example, most anthropologists and archeologists start by trying to find out how their subjects make a living. By contrast, the young Max Weber, who investigated the situation of the agricultural laborers in East Prussia, tried to discover what those individuals felt. In particular, he wished to know whether they were satisfied with their lives. He did not bother to investigate their objective living conditions, because at that time he believed that social facts are basically spiritual facts (see Lazarsfeld & Oberschall, 1965). Likewise Geertz (1973) focuses on the so-called symbolic activities, such as conversation and ritual, and overlooks the way people procure the essentials to survive.

The realism–subjectivism cleavage has a philosophical source, namely, the materialism–idealism ontological splitting. Indeed, idealists hold that ideas rule the world; consequently they look for the ideas lurking behind every fact. By contrast, materialists deny the autonomous existence of ideas, and regard the latter as brain processes; consequently they search for material factors behind every cultural item – and, if they are vulgar materialists, they minimize or even ignore the function of ideas. Idealism is the academic's ideal philosophy because it can be practiced in a library, whereas materialism calls for exploring the dangerous extramural world.

Now, social facts happen outside people's minds: they are objective and consequently they must be studied as objectively as possible, as Durkheim (1901) insists. But all such facts are partly consequences of mental processes in the actors. Consequently the social relations, unlike the purely physical ones, are mediated by brains. For example, it is important but not enough to know that during the 1990s the homicide rate in the United States fell by 44 percent, whereas the decline in the burglary rate was 42 percent (Rosenfeld, 2004). We must also ask why this happened, but we will not learn why unless we also ask, among other things, what, in addition to the increased opportunities for service jobs that emerged during that period, made potential offenders change their mind and reject the crime option. Likewise, we still do not understand adequately the recent proliferation of suicide bombings: further research in the borders of psychology, sociology, and political science is needed in this case (Atran, 2003; Sagemore, 2004).

Some types of explanation of crime

The methodological correlate of the idealism–materialism cleavage in social science and technology is this. The idealist will focus on the state of mind of his subjects, whereas the materialist will concentrate on their material circumstances. This is why the former will be satisfied with circulating questionnaires asking for self-reports, whereas the latter will insist on checking first-hand the living conditions. The costs and benefits of both methods are well known.

Yet the two methods are complementary rather than mutually exclusive, and this for two reasons. One is that, as the so-called Thomas theorem has it, people react not to social facts but to the way they perceive them, whence the need for self-reports in addition to socio-economic statistics. The second reason is that we need to find out the distal as well as the proximate causes of behavior. And for this we need to study not only how the actors of interest are living right now, but also what led them to choose their lifestyle, in particular the course of their childhood socialization (or its failure), the state of their neighborhood and of the job market at the time they chose their career, and so on. This is particularly obvious in the case of juvenile and youthful delinquency.

Why does antisocial behavior increase tenfold during adolescence (Moffitt, 1993)? And why do offences of all kinds peak sharply at age 17 and not, say, at 14 or 22, or why do they not remain constant for all ages past childhood? The answer of social control theory, namely "crime occurs because of the weakening of social bonds," will not fully persuade the developmental psychologist. He knows that the adolescent brain undergoes profound transformations: it becomes awash in hormones, while its prefrontal cortex, the seat of decision-making and in particular self-control, is still under-developed. Consequently the adolescent experiences strong new drives, and has new aspirations, at about the same time that the parental and social rules begin to relax. That is also the time when a person gets to know and befriend individuals outside family and school, as social learning theory emphasizes. All the necessary conditions, some neurophysiological and others social, are in place for committing antisocial actions in the pursuit of instant gratification.

In short, the famous *mens rea* of the jurist starts forming in the brain of a rapidly developing youngster embedded in an unfavorable surrounding. Furthermore, frontal lobe damage is associated with impaired moral judgment and social behavior. Such impairment is particularly severe when the lesion occurs in infancy, before the patient has had an opportunity to learn and internalize social and moral norms (Anderson *et al.*

1999). However, "no study has reliably demonstrated a characteristic pattern of frontal network dysfunction predictive of violent crime" (Brower & Price, 2001: 720). Fortunately, further development of the brain, which attains maturity at about 22, along with lessons from negative experiences, leads to marked desistance. So, crime is not in our genes. (See Lewontin, 2000 for a criticism of genetic determinism.) The methodological moral is clear: understanding the making of offenders calls for the convergence of psychology and sociology (see, e.g., Agnew, 1992; Moffitt, 1993; Loeber, 1996; Robinson, 2004; Wikström, 2004).

However, that is not the take of the methodological individualist: he starts from the adult mind, and regards the delinquent's social environment as only a collection of potential victims. In particular, the self-styled economic imperialists are radical individualists, and favor utilitarian (or rational-choice) models of crime. According to these, everyone is a free, smart, and selfish individual in a social vacuum (e.g., Becker, 1970; Wilson & Herrnstein, 1985; Dahlbäck, 2003). These models may certainly explain a few crimes, particularly the dumbest and the smartest, in terms of calculations or miscalculations of expected utilities, or rather rough estimates of risks and benefits. But they do not explain (a) why the vast majority of delinquents are male, young, poor, and rather unintelligent; and (b) what circumstances in his life course may lead an individual to envisage a career in crime. In other words, the "rationality" postulate does not help identify the "turning point" in the potential delinquent's life (see Sampson & Laub, 1993). Nor does the rational-choice approach help discover the social setting (objective situation) and the perception of it which leads an individual to commit a particular offence (see Bottoms, 1994; Wikström, 2004).

Consequently, the "rationality" dogma does not help design effective crime-prevention policies and programs. The successful projects of this kind owe nothing to the economic or rational-choice approach, and much to the psycho-socio-economic approach. Let us consider briefly two of the best-known crime prevention projects. Operation Ceasefire (Braga *et al.*, 2001), conducted in Boston, was a frontal attack on the problem of youth gang violence. However, its goal was not repressive but preventive: specifically, it attempted to help law-enforcers identify and diagnose violent gangs with the help of sociograms, as well as to discover their gun sources – which the police had wrongly assumed to have been purchased mostly in the Southern states of the United States. Another exemplary project was the Project on Human Development in Chicago Neighborhoods (Sampson, Raudenbush, & Earls, 1997). This was an indirect attack on the problem of the increasing criminality found in disintegrating communities. Its aim was to strengthen informal social control through decreasing residential mobility. To attain this goal, a decaying and crime-ridden neighborhood around the University of Chicago was redesigned and rebuilt. Both the Boston and the Chicago projects regard the offender as a member of more than one social system, embedded in turn in society at large. And both projects involve not only academics but also professionals and public servants.

Systemists can make use of the genuine findings of all schools, whether individualist or holist, because they are just as interested in the micro level as in the macro level. In particular, the systemic view of social facts sketched in the first two sections is one of multiple and frequent reciprocal causation: at any one time, every person and every social system is both recipient and effector of a large number of stimuli of many different types and intensities. However, when viewed synchronically, one of the aspects of the event in question is likely to be, or appear to be, more salient than the others. In this case the concomitant features may be legitimately neglected to a first approximation, so that unidisciplinarity may succeed partially. However, when attention shifts from point events to long-term processes, it is often seen that variables of several kinds are relevant and take turns in initiating changes (Braudel, 1969). When this happens, synchronicity and unidisciplinarity fail, and diachronicity and cross-disciplinarity are called for. Evolutionary developmental biology (Wilkins, 2002), developmental criminology (Loeber & Le Blanc, 1990; Farrington, 1996), the *Annales* school of historiography (Braudel, 1969), and Trigger's (2003) account of the early civilizations, are clear examples of the convergence of disciplines required to understand complex and long-drawn processes. So are biochemistry, cognitive neuroscience, and social psychology.

I submit that the preceding piece of methodological advice applies in particular to criminology. Indeed, it suggests that unifactorial models of crime are unlikely to be completely true because there may be as many crime mechanisms as types of crime. This may in turn explain why so many different explanations of crime are proposed and why some of them, even though one-sided, hold a grain of truth. Let us take a quick look at two such models.

Multi-factorial and multi-level models of crime

In a holistic perspective, individual action results exclusively from social pressures: we are passive products of the socialization process. That is, the causal arrow starts at the macro level: Structure → Agency. By contrast, the individualist starts at the micro level: he tries to account for social facts in a bottom-up fashion, exclusively in terms of individual features, such as disregard for moral norms. That is, the causal arrow starts at the micro level: Agency → Structure. Instead, the systemist may start at either level but he will eventually involve the other one as well: his will be a multi-level account. Of course, sometimes more than two levels must be distinguished. For instance, one may have to refer to the national or even international levels, which count as mega levels; or one may have to introduce a meso level such as the one constituted by governments and international corporations. However, small-scale crimes, such as truancy, tax evasion, theft, assault, rape, and murder with intent to steal, seldom require the consideration of more than two levels: individual and society. We shall restrict our attention to small-scale offences.

We need two models to account for such offences: one for individual behavior, and the other to account for criminality as a regular feature of a whole social group, such as the proverbial inner-city inhabitants of the industrialized world, and of the shanty town of the third world. In other words, we need one model for the proximate causes of crime, and a different one for its distal causes: those that drive an individual to commit repeated offences, or even to adopt crime as a career. I adopt Wikström's model for the former case. Figure 1.4 exhibits a simplified version of it.

The individual's dispositions that play a role in antisocial behavior are not necessarily genetic or inborn. Indeed, genetic predisposition has been shown in only a tiny percentage of delinquents. Moreover, one of the best studies of this problem (Caspi *et al.*, 2004) concludes that maltreated children with a certain gene are less likely to develop into antisocial persons. This is just one instance of the well-known regularity in behavioral genetics: genes propose, environment disposes. More precisely, genes are necessary but insufficient, because they are activated or inactivated by environmental stimuli.

Nor does ethnicity count as a disposition to antisocial behavior. For instance, it is true that African Americans, as a group, are about seven times more likely than Caucasian Americans to commit crime, or rather of being caught and punished. But this can be explained in sociological terms. Hence it is fallacious to conclude that a particular African American man, with no criminal record, is seven times more likely to commit crimes than his Caucasian American employer. And yet law-enforcers, jurors, and even judges have been known to be prejudiced against African Americans. The statistical approach to crime detection and control is methodologically wrong, because statistics is about

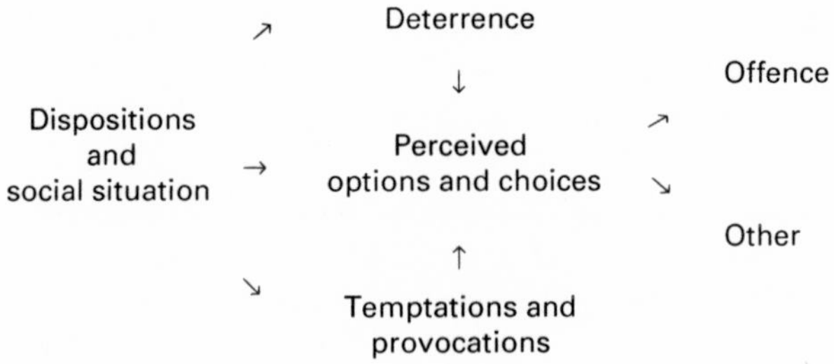

Figure 1.4. Proximate causal factors of unlawful acts
Source: Modified from Wikström & Sampson, 2003: 122.

groups, not individuals. Individual behavior can only be forecast on the basis of a study of individual characteristics.

I propose to supplement the above model with my own of distal causes of crime. The basic idea is this:

> Marked inequality generates unhappiness, low-esteem, envy, greed, dishonesty, anomie, dissatisfaction with the social order, and their social manifestations: uncooperativeness, violence, and eventually rebellion and its bloody sequels. The more marginal the individual, the less bound he feels to observe the prevailing moral and legal codes. For example, where gypsies are discriminated against, they feel free to steal from members of the ethnic majority, whom they rightly regard as aliens, although they would not dream of stealing from one another (Bunge, 1989: 180).

But of course morals and self-control are only regulators. One must look elsewhere for crime mechanisms, because people act from habit, need, or desire, not from restraint. The analogy with the car is obvious: what moves the car is the engine, not the brakes.

Most adult delinquents are not pathological. They are biologically normal people who break the law because they cannot or will not meet their needs and satisfy their desires through honest work, and are not stopped by either moral scruples or external constraints. In fact, social statistics point to social rather than purely psychological sources of crime. They tell us that small-scale theft and violence increase with unemployment and its concomitants, poverty and segregation, both social and spatial (e.g., Massey, 2001).

However, I submit that unemployment and segregation are just two aspects of a more comprehensive and widespread social malady, namely marginality. This is, in turn, a consequence of marked and rigid social stratification and the concomitant low degree of social mobility, as well as its psychological counterpart, namely low expectations. Marginality

Macro level	Marginality	↔	Criminality	*Ostensive variables*
	↓		–↑	
Micro level	Anomie	↔	Solidarity	*Hypothetical variables*

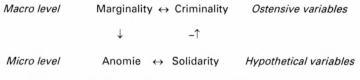

Figure 1.5. Distal causal factors of unlawful acts
Source: Modified from Bunge, 2003: 209.

may be defined as exclusion of the individual from at least one of the main social systems: economy, polity, and culture. Economic marginality may be measured by the unemployment rate; political marginality, by the rate of voter abstention; and cultural marginality, by the rate of functional illiteracy. Besides, there are two further micro-variables that must be reckoned with: anomie, the psychological counterpart of marginality, and solidarity, which compensates to some extent for anomie. I assume that these four variables are related as shown in the Boudon–Coleman diagram in Figure 1.5.

The upper-level variables are observable or nearly so, whereas the lower-level ones are hypothetical constructs on a par with chemical valence, propensity to violence, and price elasticity. The simple arrow symbolizes causation, and the double arrow interaction. In all cases but the last, an increase in one of the features causes an increase in the dependent one. In two cases the variables reinforce each other. For instance, the more marginal a person, the more likely he is to break the law; and, having once broken the law, the harder it gets for him to get a job and associate with non-offenders. By contrast, stronger solidarity, in the form of either community support or a welfare state, discourages criminality – hence the minus sign attached to the upward arrow. (For the trade-off between marginality and group solidarity in a Mexican shanty town, see Lomnitz, 1977. For the buffer effect of the welfare state, see Sutton, 2004). Both models fit in with the systemic approach, because they embed the actor in his social environment, and regard the latter as being in turn modifiable by agency. An attempt is made to quantify them in the appendix to this chapter.

Concluding remarks

The study and prevention of delinquency, like that of other social anomalies, has been approached in three different ways: holistic or top-down, individualist or bottom-up, and systemic or multi-level (Figure 1.6).

Macro level	Social anomaly	Social anomaly	Social anomaly
	↓	↑	↓↑
Micro level	Deviant behavior	Deviant behavior	Deviant behavior
	(a)	(b)	(c)

Figure 1.6. Three approaches to the study and prevention of delinquency: (a) holistic (b) individualist (c) systemic

The first approach treats the delinquent as a victim of his social milieu, the second as a source of social disruption, and the third as both victim and victimizer. The first two approaches can be fruitful if implemented scientifically: witness, for example, the insights (and limitations) of both control theory and strain theory. But the systemic approach is the more realistic, and therefore the more likely to bear important fruit, because every person belongs at once to several social systems, all of which shape him or her and which, at the same time, he or she maintains or alters. This is why "all types of social problems tend to be interrelated, making it difficult to know what causes what, and when and how it is best to intervene" (Farrington, 1996: 70). And that is the same reason that good criminology is interdisciplinary (Robinson, 2004).

Because social anomalies come in bundles or systems, the criminologist faces a large set of entangled variables. The worst strategy is to declare the tangle hopelessly complex, hence beyond the reach of science, though perhaps within the reach of intuition, empathetic understanding, or *Verstehen*, whatever this slippery word may be taken to mean. The next worst strategy is to deny complexity and assume that everything social boils down to either the genome (sociobiology) or self-interest ("economic imperialism"). Actually the best way to understand a tangle is to analyse it, to identify the most salient variables, and to build increasingly complex and deep theoretical models that interrelate those variables. How do we know that this is the best approach? Because it gave us modern science.

Appendix: Two quantitative models

Wikström (2004b) suggests that what moves an individual to commit a criminal act is the nature of his "intersection" with a setting (environment, opportunity, temptation, etc.). Change the individual or the setting, and a different action is likely to result. Here is a possible simple-minded formalization of this powerful intuitive idea.

Let us suppose that individuals are moved by causes, reasons, and valuations of causes as well as of reasons. And suppose further that the critical variables are: family status, unemployment, deficient socialization, estimate of the efficiency of an action, and valuation of its outcome. Finally, suppose that all five factors can be quantified as variables taking values in the [0,1] real interval, and that they combine multiplicatively, so that their product is zero if any of them vanishes, and maximal if all of them are maximal. In symbols, the likelihood (not probability!) that an individual will commit a particular crime is

$C = f.u.s.e.v$, where
f (family status) $= 0$ if the individual is married; 1 if he is unmarried;
u (unemployment) $= 0$ if the individual has a steady job; $= 1$ if otherwise;
s (deficient socialization) = percentage of individual's antisocial actions;
e (prior estimated efficiency of action) = (benefit − cost) / benefit;
v (prior estimated value of action) = degree to which action satisfies needs and wants.

It might be objected that u should not be a dichotomous variable, since there is such a thing as a part-time job. However, recent empirical studies show that, at least among youths and young adults, who make up the bulk of the criminal class, occasional employment is not a crime deterrent. The other four variables, particularly e, are far more problematic. Still, they are important enough to justify a serious effort at further investigation.

I submit that the above formula exhibits the situational character of crime. And it also makes room for individual development. Indeed, in most cases the value of C decreases with age, as the individual becomes more firmly inserted in society (e.g., by getting married), and learns to better estimate the costs and benefits of crime. And, even if the formula were not empirically validated, it might help hone some key concepts and focus the discussion.

Let us finally try to quantify my own model of the distal causes of criminality (Figure 1.5). Assume that, to a first approximation, the criminality rate is a linear function of marginality. In obvious symbols, $C = \alpha + \beta M$, where α is the crime rate at full integration (full employment and no segregation), and β is the rate of increase of C with M. However, even if this empirical generalization is basically correct, it calls for explanation, particularly since there are large variations in delinquency rates among countries. For instance, the crime rate is much higher in the United States than in countries, such as India and Turkey, characterized by endemic high unemployment and underemployment, but by far more cohesion in the lower social strata. In general, criminality is higher in divided societies, where everyone is expected to fend for themselves, than in homogeneous societies, where everyone is expected to help and control others. It is also higher in cities where the poor and the immigrant (both internal and foreign) are geographically isolated in slums. This suggests that the clues to such differences in criminality are anomie (or mismatch between expectations and accomplishments) and solidarity. Let us finally combine these hypotheses into a single formula.

Though quantitative, the four variables occurring in Figure 1.5 are somewhat problematic. Criminality rate is the best known but not the least troublesome. Indeed, whereas in some countries certain misdemeanors count as crimes, in others they are overlooked, and conversely; besides, the quality of social statistics varies greatly across countries. These two factors taken together render international comparisons problematic. As for marginality, it does not even occur in social statistics, partly because the experts in social indicators are not acquainted with the index of social participation, the dual of marginality (Bunge & García-Sucre, 1976). And yet it is quite simple: the degree P of social participation of the social group G in the activities in a given society S equals the cardinality (numerosity) of the intersection of G with S divided by the size of G. That is, $P = |G\ S| \ / \ |G|$. The corresponding marginality M is just the complement of P to unity, i.e., $M = 1 - P$. One may thus estimate the economic, political, and cultural marginalities of a social group in a given society. Adding up the three sectoral marginalities one obtains the total marginality of G in S. As for anomie, it may be taken to be the average ratio of unfulfilled desiderata (or expectations) to the total number of desiderata. (In obvious symbols, $A = 1 - (|C| \ / \ |D|)$, where C = Consummata, and D = Desiderata.) Finally, solidarity may be measured by the rate of participation in volunteer work, both formal and informal. One may hope that further work in both social indicators and social statistics will eventually clear these problems. Setting methodological scruples aside, we proceed to stating our model.

To a first approximation, the four variables in question are related by the following linear equations:

$C = aA$ (criminality is proportional to anomie) (1)

$$A = bM - cS \text{ (trade-off between marginality and solidarity)} \quad (2)$$

$$S = d + eM \text{ (solidarity increases linearly with marginality)} \quad (3)$$

Substituting (2) and (3) into (1), we retrieve the initial hypothesis:

$$C = \alpha + \beta M \quad (4)$$

where now the macro-social parameters α and β are analysed in micro-social terms:

$$\alpha = -acd \text{ and } \beta = a(b - ce) \quad (5)$$

Linearity and the occurrence of too many empirical parameters are surely the most objectionable features of this model. However, methodologists tell us that, when the database is overwhelming, as it is in sociology, economics, and medicine, a crude mathematical model is better than none. This is because such a model involves fairly clear ideas and it may point to main trends, and its assumptions are so transparent that it may provoke constructive criticism and thus advance knowledge. And even if it does not, it may have a mind-honing effect.

References

Agnew, Robert (1992). "Foundation for a general strain theory of crime and delinquency." *Criminology* 30: 47–87.

Anderson, Steven W., Bechara, Antoine, Damasio, Hanna, Tranel, Daniel, & Damasio, Antonio R. (1999). "Impairment of social and moral behavior related to early damage in human prefrontal cortex." *Nature Neuroscience* 2: 1032–1037.

Atran, Scott (2003). "Genesis of suicide terrorism." *Science* 299: 1534–1539.

Becker, Gary (1970). "Crime and punishment: an economic approach." *Journal of Political Economy* 76: 211–233.

Bottoms, Anthony E. (1994). "Environmental criminology." In M. Maguire, R. Morgan, & R. Reiner (eds.), *The Oxford Handbook of Criminology*. Oxford: Clarendon Press.

Braga, Anthony A., Kennedy, David M., Waring, Elin J. & Piehl, Anne Morrison (2001). "Problem-oriented policing, deterrence, and youth violence: an evaluation of Boston's Operation Ceasefire." *Journal of Research in Crime and Delinquency* 38: 195–225.

Braudel, Fernand (1969). *Ecrits sur l'histoire*. Paris: Flammarion.

Brower, M. C. & Price, B. H. (2001). "Neuropsychiatry of frontal lobe dysfunction in violent and criminal behavior: a critical review." *Journal of Neurology and Neurosurgical Psychiatry* 71: 720–726.

Bunge, Mario (1974). "The concept of social structure." in W. Leinfellner and W. Köhler (eds.), *Developments in the Methodology of Social Science*. Dordrecht: Reidel.

(1979a)."A systems concept of society: beyond individualism and holism." *Theory and Decision* 10: 13–30.

(1979b). *A World of Systems*. Treatise on Basic Philosophy, vol. IV. Dordrecht: Reidel.

(1983a). *Exploring the World.* Treatise on Basic Philosophy, vol. V. Dordrecht: Reidel.

(1983b). *Understanding the World.* Treatise on Basic Philosophy, vol. VI. Dordrecht: Reidel.

(1989). *Ethics: The Good and the Right*. Treatise on Basic Philosophy, vol. VIII. Dordrecht: Reidel.

(1999). *The Sociology–Philosophy Connection*. New Brunswick, NJ: Transation.

(2003). *Emergence and Convergence: Qualitative Novelty and the Unity of Knowledge.* Toronto: University of Toronto Press.

(2004). "How does it work?" *Philosophy of the Social Sciences* 34: 182–210.

Bunge, Mario & García-Sucre Máximo (1976). "Differentiation, participation, and cohesion." *Quality and Quantity* 10: 171–178.

Caspi, Avshalom, McClay, Joseph, Moffitt, Terrie E., Mill, Jonathan, Martin, Judy, Craig, Ian W., Taylor, Alan, & Poulton, Richie (2004). "Role of genotype in the cycle of violence in maltreated children." *Science* 297: 851–854.

Dahlbäck, Olof (2003). *Analyzing Rational Crime – Models and Methods*. Dordrecht: Kluwer.

Dilthey, Wilhelm (1959) [1883]. "Einleitung in die Geisteswissenschaften. In *Gesammelte Schriften*, vol. I. Stuttgart: Teubner; Göttingen: Vanderhoeck und Ruprecht.

Durkheim, Emile (1988) [1901]. *Les règles de la méthode sociologique*, 2nd edn. Paris: Flammarion.

Farrington, David P. (1996). "The explanation and prevention of youthful offending." In J. David Hawkins (ed.), *Delinquency and Crime: Current Theories*. Cambridge: Cambridge University Press.

Geertz, Clifford (1973). *The Interpretation of Cultures*. New York: Basic Books.

Giddens, Anthony (1984). *The Constitution of Society*. Berkeley: University of California Press.

Hawkins, J. David, ed. (1996). *Delinquency and Crime: Current Theories*. Cambridge: Cambridge University Press.

Lazarsfeld, Paul F. & Oberschall, Anthony R. (1965). "Max Weber and empirical social research." *American Sociological Review* 30: 185–199.

Lewontin, Richard (2000). *It Ain't Necessarily So*. New York: New York Review of Books.

Loeber, Rolf (1996). "Developmental continuity, change, and pathways in male juvenile delinquency problem behaviors and delinquency." In J. David Hawkins (ed.), *Delinquency and Crime: Current Theories*. Cambridge: Cambridge University Press.

Loeber, Rolf & Le Blanc, Marc (1990). "Toward a developmental criminology." In M. Tonry & N. Morris (eds.), *Crime and Justice* vol. XII. Chicago: University of Chicago Press.

Lomnitz, Larissa (1977). *Networks and Marginality: Life in a Mexican Shantytown*. San Francisco: Academic Press.

Lloyd, C. (1991). "The methodologies of social history: a Critical survey and defense of structurism." *History and Theory* 30: 180–219.

Massey, Douglas S. (2001). "Segregation and violent crime in Urban America." In E. Anderson & D. S. Massey (eds.), *Problems of the Century: Racial Stratification in the United States*. New York: Russell Sage.

Merton, Robert K. (1976). *Sociological Ambivalence and other Essays*. New York: The Free Press.

Moffitt, Terrie E. (1993). "Adolescence-limited and life-course-persistent antisocial behavior: a developmental taxonomy." *Psychological Review* 100: 674–701.

Odling-Smee, F. John, Laland, Kevin N. & Feldman, Marcus W. (2003). *Niche Construction: The Neglected Process in Evolution*. Princeton: Princeton University Press.

Robinson, Matthew B. (2004). *Why Crime? An Integrated Systems Theory of Antisocial Behaviour*. Upper Saddle River, NJ: Pearson/Prentice Hall.

Rosenfeld, Richard (2004). "The case of the unsolved crime." *Scientific American* 290 (2): 82–89.

Sagemore, Marc (2004). *Understanding Terror Networks*. Philadelphia: University of Pennsylvania Press.

Sampson, Robert J. & Laub, John H. (1993). *Crime in the Making: Pathways and Turning Points through Life*. Cambridge, MA: Harvard University Press.

Sampson, Robert J., Raudenbush, Stephen W., & Earls, Felton (1997). "Neighbourhoods and violent crime: a multilevel study of collective efficacy." *Science* 277: 918–924.

Searle, John (1995). *The Construction of Social Reality*. New York: The Free Press.

Sutton, John R. (2004). "The political economy of imprisonment in affluent Western democracies, 1960–1990." *American Sociological Review* 69: 170–189.

Thornberry, Terence P. (1987). "Toward an interactional theory of delinquency." *Criminology* 25: 863–891.

Trigger, Bruce G. (2003). *Understanding Early Civilizations*. Cambridge: Cambridge University Press.

Weber, Max (1976) [1922]. *Wirtschaft und Gesellschaft: Grundriss der Verstehende Soziologie*, 5th edn., 3 vols. Tübingen: J. C. B. Mohr (Paul Siebeck).

Wikström, Per-Olof H. (2004a). "Crime as alternative." In J. McCord (ed.), *Beyond Empiricism: Institutions and Intentions in the Study of Crime*. Advances in Criminological Theory 13. New Brunswick, NJ: Transaction.

(2004b). "The social origins of pathways in crime." In D. P. Farrington (ed.), *Integrated Developmental and Life Course Theories of Offending*. Advances in Criminological Theory 14. New Brunswick, NJ: Transaction.

Wikström, Per-Olof H. & Sampson, Robert J. (2003). "Social mechanisms of community influences on crime and pathways in criminality." In Benjamin B. Lahey, Terrie E. Moffitt, & Avshalom Caspi (eds.), *Causes of Conduct Disorder and Serious Juvenile Delinquency*. New York: Guilford Press.
Wilkins, Adam S. (2002). *The Evolution of Developmental Pathways*. Sunderland MA: Sinauer Associates.
Wilson, James Q. & Herrnstein, Richard J. (1985). *Crime and Human Nature*. New York: The Free Press.

2 How does community context matter? Social mechanisms and the explanation of crime rates

Robert J. Sampson

The idea of "community" is at once compelling and frustrating. Indeed, few would disagree that at some fundamental level a community's social context matters for crime. Yet the concept is sufficiently vague that it risks becoming meaningless – if community context is all things to all people then it is simply a metaphor with no real explanatory power. What is a community? Neighborhood? Even if we can agree on the unit of analysis, what exactly about the community is doing the explaining? Do communities act? What is the mechanism at work?

In this chapter I shall attempt to make some explanatory progress by setting out a conceptual framework for thinking about community social context and crime. In its pure form my claim is not only that communities matter but also that we need not have to explain individual criminal behavior. Multi-level integration is all the rage these days, but to demonstrate a causal effect of community does not necessarily require individuals as units of analysis. As I shall elaborate, a theory of crime rates, especially one that aims to explain how neighborhoods fare as units of social control over their own public spaces in the here and now, is logically not the same theoretical enterprise as explaining how neighborhoods exert long-term or developmental effects that ultimately translate into individual crime (Wikström & Sampson, 2003). Both sets of mechanisms may be at work, but one does not compel the other. By way of analogy, consider that a comparative theory of between-society variations in crime is not required to explain between-individual differences within a society to be considered valid, just as individual differences should not be invalidated just because they fail to explain crime (and possibly even to vary) across societies. What matters is the causal question being asked.

However, I still believe macro–micro theoretical integration is the ultimate (if misunderstood) goal, and so shall not pursue the argument in its pure form. Logically, the present approach can potentially inform individual-developmental and situational-level theories of crime, in addition to integrative attempts to spell out the mechanisms by which individual social actions create emergent community systems (Coleman, 1986). I return to this point in the Conclusion.

In short, because of the imbalance in prior research that favors individual-level theory, my major focus in this chapter is on neighborhood-level variations in rates of crime. There is a strong tradition of ecological research to build upon, of course, but the limits of our knowledge are none the less apparent. By focusing primarily on correlates of crime at the level of community social composition – especially poverty and race – prior research has tended toward a risk-factor rather than an explanatory approach. In this chapter I move from these community-level correlations, or markers, closer to the underlying *social mechanisms* theoretically at work. I conceptualize a social mechanism as a theoretically plausible (albeit typically unobservable) contextual process that accounts for or explains a given phenomenon (Sorensen, 1998; Bunge, 2004), in this case crime rates. In the ideal case a mechanism links putative causes and effects.

Another move I make is to draw on counterfactual reasoning to set forth principles for establishing causality. Counterfactual reasoning draws from the experimental tradition to define a causal effect as the difference in outcome between the world in which the subject, typically an individual, receives a treatment and the "counterfactual" world in which the same individual does not (Winship & Morgan, 1999). Obviously the same person cannot simultaneously serve as treatment and control, and so experimental research has proceeded by estimating causal effects by comparing treatment and control groups that are randomly assigned and thus presumed to be equivalent on all but the experimental manipulation. As I shall discuss, the counterfactual strategy may be usefully applied to the neighborhood-effects literature. Specifically, although I do not demonstrate causation empirically, my goal is to aim at a preliminary understanding of community-level social mechanisms that explain crime from the perspective of causal reasoning.

Definitions and background facts

At the outset it is necessary to set forth some ground rules for exploration. The first is that I take a spatial framework in defining neighborhood or community contexts. Although there are many types of communities that one could define in terms of shared values or primary group ties, I define neighborhoods and local communities ecologically, letting the properties of social organization vary. Thus, for example, sometimes neighborhoods make a community in the traditional sense of shared values, but often they do not – neighborhoods are *variable* in the nature and content of social ties. Like Tilly, then, I make territoriality define neighborhoods and leave the extent of solidarity (or "felt community") problematic (1973: 212).

The ecological underpinning of neighborhood has a venerable history. Robert Park and Ernest Burgess laid the foundation for urban sociology by defining local communities as "natural areas" that developed as a result of competition between businesses for land use and between population groups for affordable housing. A neighborhood, according to this view, is a sub-section of a larger community – a collection of both people and institutions occupying a spatially defined area influenced by ecological, cultural, and sometimes political forces (Park, 1916: 147–154). Suttles (1972) later refined this view by recognizing that local communities do not form their identities only as the result of free-market competition. Instead, some communities have their identity and boundaries imposed on them by outsiders, such as the state. Suttles (1972) also argued that the local community is best thought of not as a single entity, but rather as a hierarchy of progressively more inclusive residential groupings. In this sense, we can think of neighborhoods as ecological units nested within successively larger communities.

In practice, most social scientists and virtually all empirical studies resort to "statistical" neighborhoods that depend on geographic boundaries defined by the central government (e.g., census) or other administrative agencies (e.g., school districts, police districts). Although administratively defined units such as census tracts or political wards are reasonably consistent with the notion of overlapping and nested ecological structures, they offer imperfect operational definitions of neighborhoods for research and policy. Researchers have thus become increasingly interested in strategies to define neighborhoods that respect the logic of street patterns and the social networks of neighbor interactions (e.g., Grannis, 1998).

Neighborhood stratification

Modern neighborhood research has used an ecological approach to study first and foremost the so-called "structural" dimensions of disadvantage, especially the geographic isolation of the poor, and, especially in the United States, the racial isolation of African Americans in concentrated poverty areas (Wilson, 1987). The range of outcomes associated with concentrated disadvantage extends well beyond crime and violence to include infant mortality, low birth weight, teenage childbearing, dropping out of high school, and child maltreatment (Brooks-Gunn, Duncan, & Aber, 1997). The weight of evidence suggests that there are geographic "hot spots" for crime and problem behaviors, and that such hot spots are characterized by the concentration of multiple forms of disadvantage.

To a lesser extent, the social-ecological literature has considered aspects of neighborhood differentiation other than concentrated disadvantage, including life-cycle status, residential stability, home ownership, population density, and ethnic heterogeneity. The evidence on these factors is mixed, especially for population density and ethnic heterogeneity (Brooks-Gunn, Duncan, & Aber, 1997; Morenoff, Sampson, & Raudenbush, 2001). There is no consistent body of evidence confirming that density or ethnic heterogeneity, *per se*, are direct predictors of crime and violence. Perhaps the most extensive area of ecological inquiry after disadvantage, dating back to the early Chicago School, concerns residential stability and home ownership. There is research showing that residential instability and low rates of home ownership are durable correlates of many problem behaviors (Brooks-Gunn, Duncan, & Aber, 1997), but recent inquiry suggests that residential stability in particular interacts with poverty. In contexts of severe deprivation and poverty, residential stability has been shown to correlate with negative rather than positive outcomes (e.g., Ross, Reynolds, & Geis, 2000), which is not surprising if long-term exposure to concentrated disadvantage is a risk factor.

A more recent but understudied object of inquiry is concentrated *affluence* (Massey, 1996). Brooks-Gunn *et al.* (1993) argue that it is the positive influence of concentrated socio-economic resources and educated neighbors, rather than the presence of low-income neighbors, that matters most for adolescent behaviors. The common tactic of focusing on disadvantage may thus obscure the potential protective effects of affluence and education.

In short, empirical research on social-ecological differentiation has established a reasonably consistent set of "neighborhood facts" relevant to crime.

(1) There is considerable social inequality between neighborhoods in terms of socio-economic and racial/ethnic segregation. There is also evidence on the connection of concentrated disadvantage with the geographic isolation of minority or immigrant groups.

(2) A number of social problems tend to come bundled together at the neighborhood level, including, but not limited to, crime, adolescent delinquency, social and physical disorder, low birth weight, infant mortality, school dropout and child maltreatment.

(3) These two sets of clusters are themselves related. Neighborhood predictors common to many child and adolescent outcomes include the concentration of poverty, racial isolation, single-parent families, and to a lesser extent rates of home ownership and length of tenure.

(4) Empirical results have not varied much with the operational unit of analysis. The place stratification of local communities by factors such as social class, race, and family status is a robust phenomenon that emerges at multiple levels of geography, whether local community areas, census tracts, political wards or other "neighborhood" units.

(5) The ecological concentration of poverty appears to have increased significantly during recent decades, as has the concentration of affluence at the upper end of the income scale.

Neighborhood stratification and ecological differentiation thus remain persistent. The next logical question is: *how* does neighborhood context matter for crime? The cumulative facts on neighborhood concentration show that crime and other seemingly disparate outcomes are none the less linked together empirically across neighborhoods and are predicted by similar community characteristics (Sampson, Morenoff, & Gannon-Rowley, 2002). It follows there may be general underlying causes, or mechanisms. I now assess this possibility with respect to crime rates, and follow this with a number of challenges to theories that posit the existence of neighborhood effects.

Beyond poverty: social processes and mechanisms

During the 1990s, a number of scholars moved beyond the traditional fixation on concentrated poverty and began to explicitly theorize and directly measure how neighborhood social processes bear on the well-being of children and adolescents. Unlike the more static features of socio-demographic composition (e.g., race, class position), social processes or mechanisms provide accounts of *how* neighborhoods bring about a change in a given phenomenon of interest (Sorensen, 1998: 240; Wikström & Sampson, 2003). Although concern with neighborhood mechanisms goes back at least to the early Chicago School of sociology, only recently have we witnessed a concerted attempt to theorize and empirically measure the social-interactional and institutional dimensions that might explain how neighborhood effects are transmitted. Elsewhere, my colleagues and I reviewed this "process turn" in neighborhood effects research (Sampson, Morenoff, & Gannon-Rowley, 2002). Our assessment led to the following synthesis.

"Ecometrics" – advances in research design and measurement

One of the most important "first-order" findings from recent research is that community-based surveys can yield reliable and valid measures of neighborhood social and institutional processes. However, unlike individual-level measurements, which are backed up by decades of psychometric research into their statistical properties, the methodology needed to evaluate neighborhood mechanisms is not widespread. Raudenbush and Sampson (1999) thus proposed moving toward a science of ecological assessment, which they call "ecometrics," by developing systematic procedures for directly measuring neighborhood mechanisms, and by integrating and adapting tools from psychometrics to improve the quality of neighborhood-level measures. Leaving aside statistical details, the important *theoretical* point is that neighborhood processes can and should be treated as ecological or collective phenomena rather than as stand-ins for individual-level traits. I believe this distinction is crucial for the advancement of research.

There is very little consistency in the way neighborhood social and institutional processes are operationalized or theoretically situated in criminological research. Nevertheless, and at the risk of oversimplification, I believe that at least four classes of neighborhood mechanisms, while interrelated, appear to have independent ecometric validity for community-level theory.

Density of social networks/interaction: One of the driving forces behind much of the research on neighborhood mechanisms has been the concept of social capital, which is generally conceptualized as a resource that is realized through social relationships (Coleman, 1988). The studies we reviewed included a number of measures that tap dimensions of interpersonal relations, such as the level or density of social ties between neighbors, the frequency of social interaction among neighbors, and patterns of "neighboring." Social capital is generally thought to inhibit crime through mechanisms of information exchange and interlocking ties, especially intergenerational closure between adults and children, which in turn enhance social control.

Norms and collective efficacy: Although social ties are important, the willingness of residents to intervene on behalf of community safety may depend, in addition, on conditions of mutual trust and shared expectations among residents. One is unlikely to intervene in a neighborhood context where the rules are unclear and people mistrust or fear one another. It is the linkage of mutual trust and the shared willingness to intervene for the public good that captures the neighborhood context of what Sampson, Raudenbush, & Earls (1997) term *collective efficacy*. Sampson and colleagues constructed a measure of collective efficacy by combining the capacity for informal social control with social cohesion. Other measures related to the idea of shared expectations for social control include informal surveillance or guardianship (Bellair, 2000) and the monitoring of teenage peer groups (Veysey & Messner, 1999; Bellair, 2000). The key mechanism in collective efficacy theory is control, thereby forging a link with classical deterrence theory with the important exception that the idea of efficacy rests on citizen-induced or informal action and not externally imposed or proactive official sanctions.

Organizational infrastructure refers to the quality, quantity, and diversity of institutions, especially non-profit and civic community-based organizations that provide public services, such as libraries, schools and other learning centres, child care, organized social and recreational activities, medical facilities, family support centres, and employment opportunities (Tripplet, Gainey, & Sun, 2003). A community's organizational infrastructure is linked to but not the same thing as the density of civic participation in local organizations. In practice, however, empirical measures have focused on the presence of neighborhood institutions based on survey reports (Elliott *et al.*, 1996; Coulton, Korbin, & Su, 1999) and archival records (Peterson, Krivo, & Harris, 2000). A few studies have used surveys to tap levels of actual participation in neighborhood organizations (Veysey & Messner, 1999; Morenoff, Sampson, & Raudenbush, 2001). Organizational participation and institutional density have both traditionally been seen as key foundations for anti-crime efforts in neighborhood settings.

Just because an organization is located in a particular community does not mean that its interests mesh with that community, however. McRoberts' (2003) recent study of the religious ecology of churches in Boston shows that the density of organizations is hardly sufficient, especially when the constituents of the organization (in his case, parishioners) come from *outside* the community. In thinking about institutions theoretically, we thus need to be careful not to conflate organizational density with coordinated *action* for local interests. Recent research has begun to examine the link between organizational density, civic membership in organizations, and the actual mobilization of action for collective pursuits (Sampson, Morenoff, & Raudenbush, 2005).

Routine activities: A concern for institutions suggests a fourth, often overlooked factor in discussions of neighborhood effects: how land use patterns and the ecological distribution of daily routine activities impact crime. Wikström and Sampson (2003) refer to ecologically structured routines as "behavior settings." The location of schools, the mix of residential with commercial land use (such as strip malls and bars), public transportation nodes, and large flows of night-time visitors, for example, are relevant to organizing how and when children come into contact with their peers, adults, and non-resident activity. Like studies of institutions, however, direct measures of social activity patterns and behavior settings are relatively rare. More common in studies of routine activities are simple measures of land use in the neighborhood, such as the presence of schools, stores and shopping malls, motels and hotels, vacant lots, bars, restaurants, gas stations, industrial units, and multi-family residential units (Sampson, Morenoff, & Gannon-Rowley, 2002). In theory, routine activities are important insofar as they provide opportunities for predatory crime and lubricate the sorts of social interactions that underlie disputatious encounters.

To date, most research on neighborhood interactional and institutional processes has focused on police records of homicide, robbery, and stranger assault, and survey reports of violent and property victimization. This focus is not surprising given the influence of "social disorganization" theory in criminology, motivating research on crime rates and neighborhood mechanisms. Overall, crime rates have been found to be significantly related to neighborhood ties and patterns of interaction, informal social control, institutional resources, and routine activity patterns – especially mixed land use and proximity to schools and malls (for a review see Sampson, Morenoff, & Gannon-Rowley, 2002). There is evidence, however, suggesting that "strong" social ties and intergenerational ties may not be as critical for crime as the shared expectation that neighbors will intervene on behalf of the neighborhood. One can imagine situations where strong ties may impede efforts to establish social control, as when dense local ties foster the growth of gang-related networks (Pattillo-McCoy, 1999). Moreover, "weak ties" – less intimate connections between people based on more infrequent social interaction – may be essential for establishing social resources, such as job referrals, because they integrate the community by bringing together otherwise disconnected subgroups (Granovetter, 1973; Bellair, 1997; Warner & Rountree, 1997). Two general research findings support this line of thinking. First, some studies have shown that the association of ties with crime is largely mediated by informal social control and social cohesion (Elliott *et al.*, 1996; Morenoff, Sampson, & Raudenbush, 2001). Second, other studies have qualified the relationship between ties and crime by suggesting that crime is related only to certain patterns of neighborhood ties and social interaction, such as social ties among women (Rountree & Warner, 1999) or moderate frequency of social interaction among neighbors (Bellair, 1997).

A further look at collective efficacy theory

These findings suggest that the activation of social ties to achieve shared expectations for action, or what my colleagues and I (Sampson, Raudenbush, & Earls, 1997) propose is a general construct of "collective efficacy," may be a critical ingredient for understanding neighborhood crime and more general aspects of community well-being. One reason I believe cohesion and support are important in generating social control is that they are fundamentally about *repeated* interactions and thereby expectations about the future. There is little reason to expect that rational agents will engage in sanctioning or other acts of social control or support in contexts where there is no expectation for future contact or where residents mistrust one another. The argument of collective efficacy theory is thus that repeated interactions may signal or generate shared norms outside the "strong tie" setting of friends and kin.

Another conceptual move of collective efficacy theory is its emphasis on *agency*. Moving away from a focus on private ties, use of the term collective efficacy is meant to signify an emphasis on shared beliefs in a neighborhood's capability for action to achieve an intended effect, coupled with an active sense of engagement on the part of residents. Some density of social networks is essential, to be sure, especially networks rooted in social trust. But the key theoretical point is that networks have to be activated to be ultimately meaningful. Collective efficacy therefore helps to elevate the "agentic" aspect of social life (Bandura, 1997) over a perspective centered mainly on the accumulation of stocks of social resources as found in ties and memberships (i.e., social capital). This conceptual orientation is consistent with the redefinition by Portes and Sensenbrenner (1998) of social capital in terms of "expectations for action within a collectivity." Distinguishing between the resource potential represented by personal ties, on the one hand, and the shared expectations for action among neighbors represented by collective efficacy on the other, therefore helps clarify the dense networks paradox: *social networks foster the conditions under which collective efficacy may flourish, but they are not sufficient for the exercise of control.* The theoretical framework I propose recognizes the transformed landscape of modern urban life, holding that, while community efficacy may depend on working trust and social interaction, it does not require that my neighbor or local police officer be my friend.

My colleagues and I tested the theory of collective efficacy in a survey of 8,782 residents of 343 Chicago neighborhoods in 1995. Applying ecometric methods, a five-item Likert-type scale was developed to measure shared expectations about social control. Residents were asked about the likelihood that their neighbors could be counted on to take action if: (i) children were skipping school and hanging out on a street corner, (ii) children were spray-painting graffiti on a local building, (iii) children were showing disrespect to an adult, (iv) a fight broke out in front of their house, and (v) the fire station closest to their home was threatened with budget cuts. Our measurement relied on vignettes because of the fundamental unobservability of the capacity for control; the act of intervention is only observed under conditions of challenge. If high collective efficacy leads to low crime, then at any given moment no intervention will be observed *precisely because of the lack of need.* Like Bandura's (1997) theory of self-efficacy, the argument is that expectations for control will increase behavioral interventions when necessary, but the scale itself taps shared expectations for social action – in our case ranging from informal intervention to the mobilization of formal controls. The emphasis is on actions that are generated "on the ground" rather than top-down. (Again, however, we should not make the mistake of artificially separating informal from formal control – the act of calling the police may be conceived as informal or citizen-induced mobilization of formal resources.)

The "social cohesion/trust" part of the measure taps the nature of community relationships and was measured by coding whether residents agreed that "People around here are willing to help their neighbors"; "People in this neighborhood can be trusted"; "This is a close-knit neighborhood"; "People in this neighborhood generally get along with each other"; and "People in this neighborhood share the same values." As hypothesized, social cohesion and social control proved to be strongly related across neighborhoods and thus combined into a summary measure of collective efficacy, yielding an aggregate-level reliability in the high eighties.

In our research we found that collective efficacy is associated with lower rates of violence, controlling for concentrated disadvantage, residential stability, immigrant concentration, and a comprehensive set of individual-level characteristics (e.g., age, sex, SES, race/ethnicity, home ownership) as well as indicators of dense personal ties and the density of local organizations (Sampson, Raudenbush, & Earls, 1997; Morenoff, Sampson, & Raudenbush, 2001). Whether measured by official homicide events or violent victimization as reported by residents, neighborhoods high in collective efficacy consistently have significantly lower rates of violence. This finding holds up controlling for prior neighborhood violence, which is negatively associated with collective efficacy. This pattern suggests a reciprocal loop where violence depresses later collective efficacy (e.g., because of fear). Nevertheless, a two-standard-deviation elevation in collective efficacy was associated with a 26 percent reduction in the expected homicide rate (Sampson, Raudenbush, & Earls, 1997: 922).

Another finding is that the association of disadvantage and stability with violence is reduced when collective efficacy is controlled, suggesting a potential causal pathway at the community level. This pathway is presumed to operate over time, wherein collective efficacy is undermined by the concentration of disadvantage, racial segregation, family disruption, and residential instability, which in turn fosters more crime (Sampson, Raudenbush, & Earls, 1997; Sampson & Raudenbush, 1999). Morenoff, Sampson, and Raudenbush (2001) also show that the density of personal ties and organizations is associated with higher collective efficacy and hence lower crime, even though the former does not translate directly into lower crime rates. These findings are consistent with, although do not prove, the hypothesis that collective efficacy mediates the effect of both structural resources (e.g., affluence, home ownership, organizations) and dense systemic ties on later crime.

What about evidence from beyond Chicago? Rather than provide a narrative review of the evidence on collective efficacy theory that might be biased by my priors, I rely on an independent assessment. Recently, Pratt and Cullen (2005) have undertaken a painstaking review of more than 200 empirical studies from 1960 to 1999 using meta-analysis. The bottom line is that collective efficacy theory fares well, with an overall correlation of −0.303 with crime rates across thirteen relevant studies (95 percent confidence interval of −0.26 to −0.35). By meta-analysis standards this is a robust finding, and the authors rank collective efficacy fourth when weighted by sample size, ahead of traditional suspects such as poverty, family disruption, and race. Although the number of studies and hence empirical base is limited, and while there is considerable variability in operationalization across studies, the class of mechanisms associated with social disorganization theory and its offspring, collective efficacy theory, shows a robust association with lower crime rates (see also reviews in Sampson, Morenoff, & Gannon-Rowley, 2002, and Kubrin & Weitzer, 2003).

Spatial and cross-community networks

Social networks play a major role in the theoretical conceptualization of community social mechanisms. However, networks need not be conceptualized only in personal terms, the typical approach considered thus far. I would argue that neighborhoods are themselves nodes in a larger network of spatial relations. Contrary to the common assumption in criminology of analytic independence, neighborhoods are interdependent and characterized by a functional relationship between what happens at one point in space and what happens elsewhere.

Consider first the inexact correspondence between the neighborhood boundaries imposed by census geography and the ecological properties that shape social interaction. One of the biggest criticisms of neighborhood-level research to date concerns the artificiality of boundaries; for example, two families living across the street from one another may be arbitrarily assigned to live in different "neighborhoods" even though they share social ties. From the standpoint of a theory of mechanisms, it is thus important to account for social and institutional ties that link residents *across* neighborhoods. Allowing for spatial dependence challenges the assumption that neighborhoods represent intact social systems, functioning as islands unto themselves.

Second, spatial dependence is implicated by the fact that homicide offenders are disproportionately involved in acts of violence near their homes (Block, 1977; Reiss & Roth, 1993). From a routine activities perspective, it follows that a neighborhood's "exposure" to homicide risk is heightened by geographical proximity to places where known offenders live (see also Cohen, Kluegel, & Land, 1981). Moreover, to the extent that the risk of becoming a homicide offender is influenced by contextual factors such as concentrated poverty, concentrated affluence, and collective efficacy, spatial proximity to such conditions is also likely to influence the risk of homicide victimization in a focal neighborhood.

A third motivation for studying spatial dependence relates to the notion that interpersonal crimes such as homicide are based on social interaction and thus subject to diffusion processes (Morenoff & Sampson, 1997; Cohen & Tita, 1999; Messner *et al.*, 1999; Rosenfeld, Bray, & Egley, 1999; Smith, Frazee, & Davison, 2000). Acts of violence may themselves instigate a sequence of events that leads to further violence in a spatially channelled way. For example, many homicides, not just gang-related ones, are retaliatory in nature (Block, 1977; Black, 1983). Thus a homicide in one neighborhood may provide the spark that eventually leads to a retaliatory killing in a nearby neighborhood. In addition, most homicides occur among persons known to one another (Reiss & Roth,

1993), usually involving networks of association that follow geographical vectors.

There are good reasons, then, to believe that the characteristics of surrounding neighborhoods are crucial to understanding violence in any given neighborhood. The idea of spatial dependence challenges the urban village model, which implicitly assumes that neighborhoods represent intact social systems, functioning as islands in themselves. Our findings support the spatial argument by establishing the independent effects of spatial proximity and the inequality of neighborhood resources that are played out in citywide dynamics (Morenoff, Sampson, & Raudenbush, 2001). Specifically, controlling for all measured characteristics internal to a neighborhood, both the collective efficacy and the violence in a given neighborhood are significantly and positively linked to the collective efficacy and violence rates of surrounding neighborhoods, respectively (Sampson, Morenoff, & Earls, 1999; Morenoff, Sampson, & Raudenbush, 2001). This finding suggests a diffusion or exposure-like process, whereby violence and collective efficacy are conditioned by the characteristics of spatially proximate neighborhoods, which in turn are conditioned by adjoining neighborhoods in a spatially linked process that ultimately characterizes the entire metropolitan system. The mechanisms of racial segregation are a major force in such spatial inequality, explaining why it is that despite similar income profiles, black middle-class neighborhoods are at greater risk of violence than white middle-class neighborhoods (Sampson, Morenoff, & Earls, 1999).

Despite advances in spatial-analysis techniques and spatial thinking, it remains the case that most neighborhood-level research remains focused on *intra*-neighborhood processes. The unit of analysis is the neighborhood and the various processes (e.g., collective efficacy, exchange) going on either within the neighborhood or in adjacent neighborhoods. The ways in which neighborhoods are tied into the larger social system of cities, regions, and indeed the national or global economy are not well understood. The early work of Park and Burgess (1925) in *The City* talks about the ecological *system* whereby neighborhoods are pieces of a social or larger "whole" of the city. Yet the overwhelming legacy of the Chicago School has been the community study, with its attendant focus on the intra-community system, *or* the between-neighborhood study of variations in internal controls and other neighborhood processes (e.g., as seen in the body of work stemming from the social disorganization tradition).

What is needed is a truly systemic approach that seeks to theorize and study empirically the "articulation" function of the local community

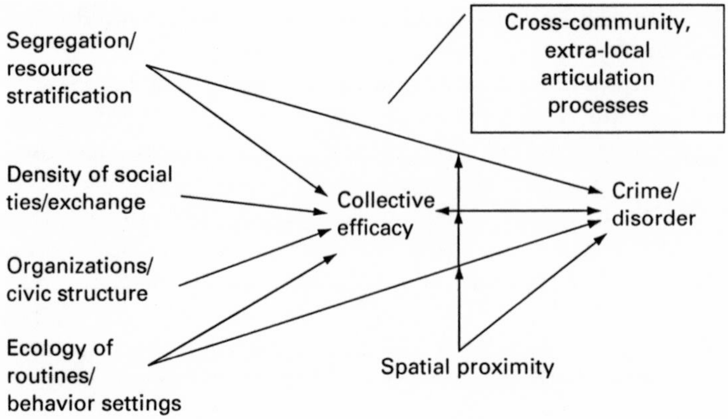

Figure 2.1. Theory of neighborhood stratification, social-spatial mechanisms, and crime rates

vis-à-vis the larger social world – how organizations and social networks differentially connect local residents to the cross-cutting institutions that organize much of modern economic, political, and social life (Janowitz, 1975; Marwell, 2005). Here the unit of analysis would be relations *across* neighborhoods – not merely as a function of geographical distance (e.g., ties in adjacent neighborhoods) but of the actual networks of connections that cross-cut neighborhood and even metropolitan boundaries.

Summary

A sketch of the major argument made to this point is shown in Figure 2.1. This portrays the importance of structural background (resource stratification), organizations, the ecology of routines, and spatial dynamics (with both conditioning and direct effects), along with the mediating role of a hypothesized community mechanism in the form of collective efficacy (which can itself be influenced by crime) and cross-community mechanisms of articulation. I do not claim this representation to be exhaustive, and in future work I plan to augment the model to include missing ingredients (e.g., subcultural intensity; networks of organizational ties). But parsimony does have its benefits in the way of surfacing key theoretical points and assumptions.

For example, the model makes clear that collective efficacy theory is not merely an attempt to push the burden of social control or support onto residents, "blaming the victim" as some have claimed. Inequality in resources matters greatly for explaining the production of collective efficacy. Indeed, although some studies show that social and institutional processes mediate the association of neighborhood structural factors with crime and other aspects of well-being, in many cases they do not explain all or even most of the traditional correlations. Factors such as concentrated disadvantage, affluence, immigration, and residential stability remain direct predictors of many outcomes (Peterson, Krivo, & Harris, 2000; South & Baumer, 2000; Morenoff, Sampson, & Raudenbush, 2001). Moreover, neighborhood mechanisms are not produced in a vacuum; key social processes, particularly those related to the idea of collective efficacy, appear to emerge mainly in environments with a sufficient endowment of socio-economic resources and residential stability (Sampson, Raudenbush, & Earls, 1997). In Chicago, for example, concentrated disadvantage and lack of home ownership predict lower levels of later collective efficacy, and the associations of disadvantage and housing instability with violence are significantly reduced when collective efficacy is controlled (Sampson, Raudenbush, & Earls, 1997). These patterns are consistent with the inference that neighborhood resources influence crime and violence in part through the mediating role of neighborhood efficacy. The capacity to exercise control under conditions of trust is thus seen as the most proximate to explaining crime, but certainly collective efficacy is at some fundamental level an endogenous social process.

In theoretical terms, Figure 2.1 also posits that organizations and institutional strength represent a mechanism that can sustain capacity for social action in a way that transcends traditional personal ties (cf. Tripplet, Gainey, & Sun, 2003). In other words, civic organizations are at least in principle able to foster collective efficacy, often through strategic networking of their own. Whether garbage removal, choosing the site of a fire station, school improvements, or police responses, a continuous stream of challenges faces modern communities, challenges that no longer can be met (if they ever were) by relying solely on individuals. Action depends on connections among organizations that are not necessarily dense or reflective of the structure of personal ties in a neighborhood. Our research supports this position, showing that the density of local organizations and voluntary associations predicts higher levels of collective efficacy, net of prior crime, poverty, and social composition of the population (Morenoff, Sampson, & Raudenbush, 2001).

Figure 2.1 further places in context the "broken windows" debate over whether disorder is an explanatory mechanism, outcome, or both.

Much of the interest in disorder was stimulated by the theory of "broken windows" (Wilson & Kelling, 1982), which suggests that physical signs of disorder – such as broken windows, public drinking, and graffiti – signal the unwillingness of residents to confront strangers, intervene in a crime, or call the police. However, there is evidence that the mechanism linking disorder and crime is not as strong as broken windows theory would suggest, and that disorder is predicted by the same characteristics as crime itself, inducing a spurious relationship (Sampson & Raudenbush, 1999; Markowitz *et al.*, 2001; Taylor, 2001). This does not necessarily mean that disorder is irrelevant. Because signs of disorder are stark visual reminders of neighborhood deterioration, they may trigger institutional disinvestment, out-migration, and a general malaise among residents, serving as a feedback loop with respect to neighborhood well-being (Sampson & Raudenbush, 2004).

Finally, the conceptual orientation of Figure 2.1 is meant to emphasize both spatial proximity and cross-cutting articulation processes that characterize the entire set of relationships. Articulation processes, in other words, apply to the entire set of what are typically considered intra-neighborhood factors. Structural constraints like neighborhood poverty, for example, are determined in part by city and federal housing policies, and social mechanisms like collective efficacy presumably are determined in part by the extra-local political and organizational resources that communities can bring to bear on local issues. How communities are tied to the larger social, political, economic, and moral order of the city is thus a system-wide process, albeit one I acknowledge has few exemplars in extant research.

Challenges to community-level theory

Despite the progress that has been made in recent research, a number of major challenges exist to making firm inferences about the causal role of neighborhood ecology and social mechanisms. In addition there are key misunderstandings on how to properly assess neighborhood effects. In this section I tackle six major issues that I believe require focused attention and that provide sufficient traction to make progress. Although methodological in part, resolution of these issues bears directly on the advancement of community-level theory.

Selection bias and experimental logic

Although a full discussion is beyond the scope of this chapter, the issue of "selection bias" is the biggest challenge traditionally put to neighborhood-level research (see e.g., Farrington, 1993; Mayer & Jencks, 1989). Many ask how we know that the area differences in any outcome of interest, such as adolescent delinquency, are the result of neighborhood factors rather than the differential selection of adolescents or their families into certain neighborhoods.

A recent body of research has directly taken up this issue by examining an ongoing housing program in five major cities across the United States. The Moving to Opportunity (MTO) demonstration was a US Department of Housing and Urban Development project in Boston, Baltimore, New York City, Chicago, and Los Angeles (Goering & Feins, 2003) where families were moved from inner-city, high poverty areas to low poverty areas. The MTO program utilized an experimental design by randomly assigning eligible applicants to one of three "groups," two receiving a "treatment" in the form of government vouchers or certificates, and the third a control group that received no experimental treatment. This process of random assignment provides a rather unique opportunity to separate the role of neighborhood context from the selection bias that may arise from residential mobility decisions. Because not all subjects take up the experimental treatment, the MTO Treatment-on-Treated (TOT) analysis compares the outcomes of families who actually received the treatment (those who actually move, whether in the location-restricted or unrestricted groups) to the outcomes of control-group families who would have accepted the treatment had it been offered. The Intent-to-Treat (ITT) analysis compares the average outcomes for either treatment group with those of the control group, estimating the effect of being offered the treatment, regardless of whether the family decides to accept the certificate/voucher and move (Katz, Kling, & Liebman, 2001).

The evidence is generally positive for the outcomes of movers to low-income areas, at least in the initial follow-ups. Generally, families that moved to low poverty areas experienced improved outcomes *vis-à-vis* overall health (physical and mental), safety, boys' problem behavior, and well-being (Goering & Feins, 2003). A reduction in behavior problems among boys was found in Boston (Katz, Kling, & Liebman, 2001) as well as in Baltimore (Ludwig, Hirschfield, & Duncan, 2001). The large reduction in juvenile arrests for violent offences in Baltimore was accompanied by an increase in juvenile arrests for property offences, although the latter finding pertains only to the intent-to-treat specification. Also, there is emerging evidence that moving, for boys, may in the long term lead to an increase in behavioral problems, whereas, for girls, moving seems to be a protective factor.

Despite the obvious importance of the MTO experiments, we should not lose sight of their research design and consequently the questions that can and cannot be addressed. Most important, the random assignment of housing vouchers *does not address causal processes of why neighborhoods matter*. When MTO families move from one neighborhood to another, entire bundles of variables change at once, making it difficult to disentangle the change in neighborhood poverty from simultaneous changes in social processes (Katz, Kling, & Liebman, 2001: 621). The clear tendency has been to interpret MTO results in terms of the effects of changing concentrated poverty, but for the reasons noted above, such an assertion is arbitrary; any number of changes in social processes associated with relocating out of poverty may account for the result – perhaps, most importantly, moving itself. Note also that MTO does not randomly allocate neighborhood conditions to participants; voucher recipients can choose to live in any number of "middle class" neighborhood conditions.

The MTO-type experiments can therefore be seen to offer an excellent answer to the general question: does moving matter? Or, in particular, should a family move out of high poverty areas to improve the lives of its children? But whereas the MTO may provide policymakers with evidence on whether offering housing vouchers can improve the lives of poor children, they are less satisfactory to social scientists interested in explaining the mechanisms of neighborhood effects. If we really want to learn about the causal effects of neighborhoods in an experimental design, the proper intervention is to randomly assign at the level of *neighborhoods* or other social units, not individuals (see Boruch & Foley, 2000).

One can imagine, for example, an experiment that randomly assigns neighborhoods to receive some treatment, such as community policing or an effort to mobilize local collective efficacy. Because of random assignment, neighborhoods would be presumed equivalent on all "individual-level" selection factors, rendering the latter irrelevant as confounders. If crime rates are significantly reduced after the randomized intervention we may then speak of a causal neighborhood-level effect of the theoretical mechanism on crime without recourse to individual-level considerations. That is to say, only individuals commit crimes, but a neighborhood intervention that demonstrates a reduction in crime rates may still make causal claims absent an individual-level theory that connects the intervention to the specific actors responsible for acts of crime. Such neighborhood- or population-level interventions are relatively more common in the public health arena (for an interesting example see Sikkema, 2000), and from a public policy perspective may even be more cost-effective than individual interventions. Regardless, my point is that we do not have to intervene at the level of an individual to demonstrate a causal effect of neighborhoods, or neighborhood mechanisms. Our research designs to date have been limited, based on theoretical predilections and lack of imagination rather than scientific logic.

Over-control and indirect pathways

Even if we were to accept the individual explanation mandate, much research on neighborhoods is inconsistent with the logical expectations set forth by contextual theories that stress enduring effects of context on developmental pathways. The most common strategy in multi-level neighborhood research is to estimate a "direct effects" model whereby a host of individual, familial, peer, and school variables are entered as controls alongside *current* neighborhood characteristics of residence. But this strategy confounds the potential importance of both long-term community influences and mediating developmental pathways regarding children's personal traits and dispositions, learning patterns from peers, family socialization, school climate, and more. Put differently, static models that estimate the direct effect of current neighborhood context on a particular outcome (e.g., delinquency, level of academic achievement) may be partitioning out relevant variance in a host of mediating and developmental pathways of influence. A recent study, for example, showed that current neighborhood context was relatively unimportant once the role of early neighborhood disadvantage was taken into account (Wheaton & Clarke, 2003). Early neighborhood disadvantage had cumulative developmental effects on childhood stressors, which then influenced later adolescent outcomes in a life course sequence. If neighborhood mechanisms exert their primary causal influence in childhood, as in this study, then the current practice of controlling for individual risk factors is flawed, as is the common practice of looking at the concurrent effects of neighborhood context.

Event-based models

Another disconnect between theory and design is tied to the common practice in neighborhood-effects research of looking solely at the characteristics of an individual's place of residence. Although seemingly natural, a problem with this approach is that many behaviors of interest (e.g., stealing, smoking, taking drugs) unfold in places (e.g., schools, parks, city centre areas) *outside* of the residential neighborhoods in which the individuals involved in these behaviors live. Logically, then, we may have a theory that accurately explains variation of crime event rates across neighborhoods regardless of who commits the acts (residents or otherwise), and another that accurately explains how neighborhoods influence the individual behavior of residents no matter where they are. In the latter case neighborhoods have developmental or enduring effects as noted above (e.g., Wheaton & Clarke, 2003); in the former, situational effects. The logical separation of explanation is reinforced by considering the nature of routine activity patterns in modern cities, where residents traverse the boundaries of multiple neighborhoods during the course of a day. Urbanites occupy many different neighborhood contexts outside of home, especially when it comes to adolescents in the company of peers (Wikström & Ceccato, 2004).

In short, it is possible for the prevalence of participation in some crimes to be spread fairly evenly across individuals living in many neighborhoods, even as crime events are highly concentrated in relatively few neighborhoods. This sort of neighborhood effect on *events* (typical of drug markets, for example, where buyers often come from afar) is obscured in current practice. It thus pays to take seriously contextual theories that focus more on behavior settings and events than individual differences (Wikström & Sampson, 2003); for example, how neighborhoods fare as units of guardianship or socialization over their own public spaces.

Interestingly, it turns out that recent research on the Chicago PHDCN data finds that collective efficacy does not in fact predict individual rates of self-reported violence based on the residence of the subjects (Sampson, Morenoff, & Raudenbush, 2005). It is hard to know whether this finding is partly due to the way violence was measured (self-reports), but if we set this issue aside, it appears that whereas collective efficacy predicts the event rate of violence in a neighborhood, it does not necessarily predict rates of offending by neighborhood youth which may occur anywhere in the city. Put differently, collective efficacy may be more situational than even the original theory suggests, with little "staying power" once residents are outside its purview.

Discriminant validity and the role of theory

Another problem that is at once theoretical and methodological turns on the discriminant validity of the concept of collective efficacy. Thomas

Cook and his colleagues (1997) have argued that researchers of community need to pay increased attention to the "lumping" together of social processes. In its simplest form, the question is whether there is just one big factor that underlies the correlations among seemingly disparate social processes. A similar point was made about the lumping together of structural covariates by Land and McCall (1990); disentangling and estimating independent effects within a set of highly collinear predictors is a recipe for methodological confusion. More recently, Taylor (2002) has correctly pointed out the strong empirical overlap among many indicators of social disorganization, informal social control, and collective efficacy.

Unfortunately, resolution of this legitimate issue is not easy. The critics are right that many community concepts overlap empirically, but that does not mean they tap the same concept or that statistical methods necessarily help to resolve the problem. It is instructive to recall the debate between Bernard Lander and his critics some fifty years ago. In using factor analysis, Lander (1954) identified a concept he called anomie, which carries high loadings for home ownership, percent black, and crime, among others. As Kornhauser (1978) argues, however, Lander includes in the explanatory factor (anomie) the outcome itself: crime. From Lander's perspective the indicators could not be separated empirically (there was a lack of "discriminant validity"), but from a theoretical perspective we would not want to say that crime is the same construct as home ownership. Rather they are ecologically intertwined in a social process.

Fast forwarding to the present, ecological scholars are well aware that percent black typically loads on a factor defined by poverty. We can complicate this even more by adding in violent crime, reminiscent of Lander. As a simple exercise, I entered the percent poverty, unemployment, percent black and the violent crime rate in a principal components analysis for Chicago neighborhoods in 1990 and 2000. Only one factor emerged! Surely we would not want to interpret this factor as saying crime is the same concept as race or poverty. What the factor taps is the empirical entwinement of the multiple indicators; the factor tells us nothing about causality, sequential order, mediation, or anything else of ultimate interest. The same goes for social processes. If we throw in a series of indicators from the PHDCN Community Survey, it turns out disorder loads with collective efficacy (negatively). Again, does this mean they are the same construct? As earlier, I would argue no – I believe disorder is a marker for low collective efficacy, like crime, but my argument derives from logic and theory, not simply from the data. All this goes to say that ecological mechanisms of allocation and segregation create groupings of variables that are difficult to interpret and even harder to study with respect to crime. *No statistical method can solve what is fundamentally a theoretical issue about causal mechanisms.*

Although resolution of this complex issue is surely beyond this chapter, I should like to emphasize one point, however, that speaks in favor of collective efficacy theory. As I have been at pains to argue, one of the distinguishing features of collective efficacy theory is its insistence that agency and control are not redundant with dense personal ties. In point of fact, this assertion is supported despite the otherwise lumpy nature of the data when it comes to factor or principal components analysis. Specifically, indicators of control and cohesion (and yes, disorder) consistently load together on a separate factor from density of personal and friendship ties. This finding has recently been confirmed with a repeated cross-sectional replication of the 1995 Chicago Community Survey in 2002. There is also evidence that collective efficacy is highly stable over time, as is the separate construct of dense ties. Based on theory and empirical evidence, then, we have some confidence to maintain the core analytical distinction between efficacy (social action) and dense ties, all the while recognizing that the correlations among social processes, just as among structural covariates, are high. The larger point is that neither fancy statistical methods nor the correlations among social processes and structural features of the city ("the data") speak for themselves – an organizing theoretical model is needed.

Comparative studies

A final concern I have about extant community research is its seeming disregard for the establishment of generality in causal mechanisms. The prime example is that most of our knowledge has been gained from US cities and only a few of them at that. Yet nothing in the logic of collective efficacy is necessarily limited to specific cities, the United States, or any country for that matter. Just how far can we push collective efficacy theory? Is it applicable in societies like France, where republican values and strong norms of state intervention rather than individual responsibility might conflict with the notion of neighbors intervening? Does it hold in welfare states where concentrated disadvantage is less tenacious, or in former Soviet states where public spiritedness is allegedly on the wane? Our comparative knowledge base is unfortunately limited. Very few multi-level studies have been carried out with the explicit goal of cross-national comparison of crime rates and community social mechanisms.

An exception is found in a recent comparison of leading cities in Sweden and the United States. Although Chicago and Stockholm differ significantly in their social structure and levels of violence, this does not necessarily imply a difference in the processes or mechanisms that link communities and crime. In fact, Sampson and Wikström (2005) show that rates of violence are significantly predicted by low collective efficacy in Stockholm as in Chicago. Furthermore, collective efficacy is fostered by housing stability and undermined by concentrated disadvantage, again similarly in both cities. These findings are rather remarkable given the vast cultural and structural differences between the countries in question. Sweden is a modern welfare state with residential communities that are highly planned. "Race" groups are nonexistent and immigration comes primarily from Turkey and Morocco. Chicago is the quintessential American city, rank with inequality and the segregation of African Americans, and with neighborhoods that are emblematic of unplanned market sorting. Immigration flows are also very different, coming primarily from Mexico rather than Europe or Africa.

That the data show an almost invariant pattern despite these differences is thus consistent with the general theoretical emphasis in this paper on neighborhood inequality in social resources and the contextual conditions that foster the collective efficacy of residents and organizations. But this is only one study. The empirical application of neighborhood studies to other societal contexts is badly needed if we are to make further progress in understanding the generalizability of the link between community social mechanisms and crime rates.

Conclusion and implications

It is by now apparent that there are two big, and dominant, questions that have been asked about community context and crime. As Wikström and Sampson (2003) summarize, the first is about contextual effects *on individual development*. This perspective starts with individuals as the unit of analysis and looks to see if neighborhood characteristics influence their course of human development. Selection bias in different contexts is the main concern in this genre of research. In the counterfactual paradigm, the key question is whether the same individual, growing up in one neighborhood, would follow a different course of development if he/she had in fact grown up in another neighborhood.

Randomly assigning individuals to different contexts is the scientifically approved way to answer this question directly, and answers are now forthcoming. As the nascent experimental literature has demonstrated, when randomization *at the individual level* is invoked we still find evidence for the apparent influence of place on individuals and their course of development. It remains unclear, however, what mechanisms account for the change.

A second question asks how to explain variations in crime *rates* across *communities*. Here the counterfactual is not about individuals but neighborhoods, leading to experiments (even if only thought experiments) where neighborhoods are randomly allocated to treatment and control conditions and some macro-level intervention introduced. In this scenario individual selection is irrelevant to the evaluation of the causal effect. The basic argument uniting this chapter is that the community-level causal question is an interesting and compelling one, equal in intellectual integrity to the developmental one. It follows that research needs to take seriously the measurement and theoretical analysis of neighborhoods as important units of analysis *in their own right*, especially with regard to social-interactional and institutional processes. Neighborhood-level experiments provide a crucial lever for causal explanation at this level.

A further implication of a community-level systems approach is to acknowledge and begin the hard work of investigating *cross-cutting* community networks. The traditional emphasis on intra-neighborhood processes has yielded important fruit, but we know that neighborhoods are embedded in much larger social systems. One of the fundamental insights of Wilson (1987) was to recognize how the social organization of local communities, especially in the segregated ghettoes of American cities, was deeply intertwined with the large-scale changes taking place in society, such as de-industrialization and the transition to a service economy. How community organizations, local networks, culture, and collective efficacy depend on these extra-community processes remains poorly understood. As Marwell (2005) has argued, taking a truly social-ecological approach to the city as a system was envisioned but never realized by Park and Burgess (1925). Analysing between-community variations in intra-neighborhood processes, even including their spatial proximity effects, does not fully get at the larger question of how local neighborhoods are articulated within the metropolis. To do so means widening our focus from internal neighborhood dynamics to the truly relational aspects of cross-cutting neighborhood ties. I see this as a cutting-edge issue in the future of neighborhood research.

Finally, let us return to the distinction I raised at the beginning and reconsider the nature of individual and community "multi-level" integration. Although beyond the scope of this chapter, there is a third big question that turns tables on the dominant "top-down" approach to integration in criminology and examines the effect of context *on* individuals. As the late James Coleman argued eloquently in articulating a social theory of action, individual actions can also, perhaps more importantly, be seen as moving *up* to create emergent properties of the system – what he termed "type 3" relations (1986: 1322). In the present case, this form of theoretical integration would seek not to explain individual criminal behavior as a function of neighborhood context, but rather how the interdependent and purposive actions of individuals, such as their social exchanges, control actions, civic memberships, and everyday routines *combine to produce an emergent neighborhood context that in turn creates constraints on the actors who make up the social system of explanation.* From this perspective the very idea of a "hierarchical model" of explanation and even of a "level" of analysis begins to break down, for individuals constitute and are interdependent with social structure rather than simply "nested" within structures.

Some twenty years later, Coleman's (1986) vision of a truly integrated system of macro- and micro-level causal explanation remains unfulfilled. One hopes that criminology has the theoretical and empirical tools to crack the case, which if nothing else would have the desirable effect of retiring the biased notion, one I confess having succumbed to, that taking individuals seriously means treating neighborhood context as a trait of the individual, and individual actions (read "selection") as the enemy of contextual-level or social mechanisms. By the same token, and even accepting the principles of methodological individualism, taking communities seriously as units of analysis in their own right can proceed without theoretical guilt.

References

Bandura, Albert (1997). *Self Efficacy: The Exercise of Control.* New York: W. H. Freeman.

Bellair, Paul E. (1997). "Social interaction and community crime: examining the importance of neighbour networks." *Criminology* 35: 677–703.

(2000). "Informal surveillance and street crime: a complex relationship." *Criminology* 38: 137–167.

Black, Donald (1983). "Crime as social control." *American Sociological Review* 48: 34–45.

Block, Richard (1977). *Violent Crime: Environment, Interaction, and Death.* Lexington, MA: Lexington Books.

Boruch, Robert & Foley, Ellen, (2000). "The honestly experimental society: sites and other entities as the units of allocation and analysis in randomised trials." In L. Bickman (ed.), *Validity and Social Experimentation: Donald T. Campbell's Legacy*. Thousand Oaks, CA: Sage.

Brooks-Gunn, Jeanne, Duncan, Greg, & Aber, Lawrence, eds. (1997). *Neighbourhood Poverty*, vol. II: *Policy Implications in Studying Neighbourhoods*. New York: Russell Sage.

Brooks-Gunn, Jeanne, Duncan, Greg, Klebanov, Pamela, & Sealand, Naomi (1993). "Do neighborhoods influence child and adolescent development?" *American Journal of Sociology* 99: 353–395.

Bunge, Mario (2004). "How does it work? The search for explanatory mechanisms." *Philosophy of the Social Sciences* 34: 1–29.

Cohen, Jackie & Tita, George (1999). "Diffusion in homicide: exploring a general method for detecting spatial diffusion processes." *Journal of Quantitative Criminology* 15: 451–493.

Cohen, Lawrence, Kluegel, James, & Land, Kenneth (1981). "Social inequality and predatory criminal victimization: an exposition and test of a formal theory." *American Sociological Review* 46: 505–524.

Coleman, James S. (1986). "Social theory, social research, and a theory of action." *American Journal of Sociology* 91: 1309–1335.

(1988). "Social capital in the creation of human capital." *American Journal of Sociology* 94: S95–120.

Cook, Thomas, Shagle, Shobha, & Degirmencioglu, Serdar (1997). "Capturing social process for testing mediational models of neighborhood effects." In Jeanne Brooks-Gunn, Greg Duncan, & Lawrence Aber (eds.), *Neighbourhood Poverty*, vol. II: *Policy Implications in Studying Neighbourhoods*. New York: Russell Sage.

Coulton, Claudia J., Korbin, Jill E., & Su, M. (1999). "Neighbourhoods and child maltreatment: a multi-level study." *Child Abuse and Neglect* 23: 1019–1040.

Elliott, Delbert, Wilson, William J., Huizinga, David, Sampson, Robert, Elliott, Amanda, & Rankin, Bruce (1996). "The effects of neighborhood disadvantage on adolescent development." *Journal of Research in Crime and Delinquency* 33: 389–426.

Farrington, David P. (1993). "Have any individual, family, or neighborhood influences on offending been demonstrated conclusively?" In David P. Farrington, Robert Sampson, & Per-Olof Wikström (eds.), *Integrating Individual and Ecological Aspects of Crime*. Stockholm: Allmaana Forlaget.

Goering, John & Feins, Judith, eds. (2003). *Choosing a Better Life? Evaluating the Moving to Opportunity Experiment*. Washington, DC: Urban Institute Press.

Grannis, Rick (1998). "The importance of trivial streets: residential streets and residential segregation." *American Sociological Review* 103(6): 1530–1564.

Granovetter, Mark S. (1973). "The strength of weak ties." *American Journal of Sociology* 78: 1360–1380.

Janowitz, Morris (1975). "Sociological theory and social control." *American Journal of Sociology* 81: 82–108.

Katz, Lawrence F., Kling, Jeff, & Liebman, Jeff (2001). "Moving to opportunity in Boston: early results of a randomised mobility experiment." *Quarterly Journal of Economics* 116(2): 607–654.

Kornhauser, Ruth (1978). *Social Sources of Delinquency*. Chicago: University of Chicago Press.

Kubrin, Charis E. & Weitzer, Ronald (2003). "New directions in social disorganization theory." *Journal of Research in Crime and Delinquency* 40: 374–402.

Land, Kenneth, McCall, Patricia, & Cohen, Lawrence (1990). "Structural covariates of homicide rates: are there any invariances across time and space?" *American Journal of Sociology* 95: 922–963.

Lander, Bernard (1954). *Toward an Understanding of Juvenile Delinquency*. New York: Columbia University Press.

Ludwig, Jens, Hirschfield, Paul, & Duncan, Greg J. (2001). "Urban poverty and juvenile crime: evidence from a randomised housing-mobility experiment." *Quarterly Journal of Economics* 116(2): 665–679.

Markowitz, Fred, Bellair, Paul, Liska, Allen & Liu, Jianhong (2001). "Extending social disorganization theory: modelling the relationships between cohesion, disorder, and fear." *Criminology* 39: 293–319.

Marwell, Nicole (2005). "Beyond neighborhood social control: from interaction to institutions." Unpublished paper, Department of Sociology, Columbia University.

Massey, Douglas S. (1996). "The age of extremes: concentrated affluence and poverty in the twenty-first century." *Demography* 33: 395–412.

Mayer, Susan & Jencks, Christopher (1989). "Growing up in poor neighborhoods: how much does it matter?" *Science* 243: 1441–1445.

McRoberts, Omar (2003). *Streets of Glory: Church and Community in a Black Urban Neighbourhood.* Chicago: University of Chicago Press.

Messner, Steven, Anselin, Luc, Baller, Rob, Hawkins, Darnell, Deane, Glenn, & Tolnay, Stewart (1999). "The spatial patterning of county homicide rates: an application of exploratory spatial data analysis." *Journal of Quantitative Criminology* 15: 423–450.

Morenoff, Jeffrey & Sampson, Robert J. (1997). "Violent crime and the spatial dynamics of neighborhood transition: Chicago, 1970–1990." *Social Forces* 76: 31–64.

Morenoff, Jeffrey D., Sampson, Robert J. & Raudenbush, Stephen (2001). "Neighbourhood inequality, collective efficacy, and the spatial dynamics of homicide." *Criminology* 39: 517–560.

Park, Robert (1916). "Suggestions for the investigations of human behavior in the urban environment." *American Journal of Sociology* 20: 577–612.

Park, Robert & Burgess, Ernest (1925). *The City*. Chicago: University of Chicago Press.

Pattillo, Mary (1999). *Black Picket Fences: Privilege and Peril Among the Black Middle Class*. Chicago: University of Chicago Press.

Peterson, Ruth D., Krivo, Lauren J., & Harris, Mark A. (2000). "Disadvantage and neighborhood violent crime: do local institutions matter?" *Journal of Research in Crime and Delinquency* 37: 31–63.

Pratt, Travis & Cullen, Frances (2005). "Assessing macro-level predictors and theories of crime: a meta-analysis." In Michael Tonry (ed.), *Crime and Justice: A Review of Research,* vol. XXXII. Chicago: University of Chicago Press.

Portes, Alejandro & Sensenbrenner, Julia (1993). "Embeddedness and immigration: notes on the social determinants of economic action." *American Journal of Sociology* 98: 1320–1350.

Raudenbush, Stephen W. & Sampson, Robert J. (1999). " 'Ecometrics': toward a science of assessing ecological settings, with application to the systematic social observation of neighborhoods." *Sociological Methodology* 29: 1–41.

Reiss, Albert J. & Roth, Jeff, eds. (1993). *Understanding and Preventing Violence,* vol. I. Washington, DC: National Academy Press.

Rosenfeld, R., Bray, T. M., & Egley, A. (1999). "Facilitating violence: a comparison of gang-motivated, gang-affiliated, and nongang youth homicides." *Journal of Quantitative Criminology* 15(4): 495–516.

Ross, Catherine, Reynolds, J. R., & Geis, K. J. (2000). "The contingent meaning of neighborhood stability for residents' psychological well-being." *American Sociological Review* 65: 581–597.

Rountree, Pamela & Warner, Barbara (1999). "Social ties and crime: is the relationship gendered?" *Criminology* 37: 789–813.

Sampson, Robert J., McAdam, Doug, MacIndoe, Heather, & Weffer, Simón (2005). "Civil society reconsidered: the durable nature and community structure of collective civic action." *American Journal of Sociology,* 111: 673–714.

Sampson, Robert J., Morenoff, Jeffrey, & Earls, Felton (1999). "Beyond social capital: spatial dynamics of collective efficacy for children." *American Sociological Review* 64: 633–660.

Sampson, Robert J., Morenoff, Jeffrey D., & Gannon-Rowley, Thomas (2002). "Assessing neighborhood effects: social processes and new directions in research." *Annual Review of Sociology* 28: 443–478.

Sampson, Robert J., Morenoff, Jeffrey D., & Raudenbush, Stephen (2005). "Social anatomy of racial and ethnic disparities in violence." *American Journal of Public Health* 95: 224–232.

Sampson, Robert J. & Raudenbush, Stephen (1999). "Systematic social observation of public spaces: a new look at disorder in urban neighborhoods." *American Journal of Sociology* 105: 603–651.

(2004). "Seeing disorder: neighborhood stigma and the social construction of broken windows." *Social Psychology Quarterly* 67: 319–342.

Sampson, Robert J., Raudenbush, Stephen, & Earls, Felton (1997). "Neighbourhoods and violent crime: a multilevel study of collective efficacy." *Science* 277: 918–924.

Sampson, Robert J. & Wikström, Per-Olof (2005). "The social order of violence in Chicago and Stockholm neighborhoods." In Stathis Kalyvas, Ian Shapiro, and Tarek Masoud (eds.), *Order, Conflict, and Violence.* New York: Cambridge University Press.

Sikkema, K. J., Kelly J. A., Winett, R. A., Solomon, L. J., Cargill, V. A., Roffman, R. A., McAuliffe, T. L., Heckman, T. G., Anderson, E. A.,

Wagstaff, D. A., Norman, A. D., Perry, M. J., Crumble, D. A. & Mercer, M. B. (2000). "Outcomes of a randomised community-Level HIV prevention intervention for women living in 18 low-income housing developments." *American Journal of Public Health* 90: 57–63.

Smith, W. R., Frazee, S. G., & Davison, E. L. (2000). "Furthering the integration of routine robbery as a diffusion process." *Criminology* 38: 489–523.

Sorensen, Aage B. (1998). "Theoretical mechanisms and the empirical study of social processes." In Peter Hedström & Richard Swedberg (eds.), *Social Mechanisms: An Analytical Approach to Social Theory*. Cambridge: Cambridge University Press.

South, Scott J. & Baumer, Eric P. (2000). "Deciphering community and race effects on adolescent premarital childbearing." *Social Forces* 78: 1379–1407.

Suttles, Gerald (1972). *The Social Construction of Communities*. Chicago: University of Chicago Press.

Taylor, Ralph B. (2001). *Breaking Away from Broken Windows: Baltimore Neighbourhoods and the Nationwide Fight Against Crime, Grime, Fear, and Decline*. Boulder, CO: Westview.

(2002). "Fear of crime, local social ties, and collective efficacy: maybe masquerading measurement, maybe déjà vu all over again." *Justice Quarterly* 19: 773–792.

Tilly, Charles (1973). "Do communities act?" *Sociological Inquiry* 43: 209–240.

Triplett, Ruth A., Gainey, Randy R., & Sun, Ivan Y. (2003). "Institutional strength, social control and neighborhood crime rates." *Theoretical Criminology* 7: 439–467.

Veysey, B. M. & Messner S. F. (1999). "Further testing of social disorganization theory: an elaboration of Sampson and Groves's 'Community Structure and Crime'." *Journal of Research in Crime and Delinquency* 36: 156–174.

Warner, Barbara & Rountree, Pamela (1997). "Local social ties in a community and crime model: questioning the systemic nature of informal social control." *Social Problems* 44: 520–536.

Wheaton, Blair & Clarke, Philippa (2003). "Space meets time: integrating temporal and contextual influences on mental health in early adulthood." *American Sociological Review* 68: 680–706.

Wikström, Per-Olof & Ceccato, Vania (2004). "Crime and social life: a space-time budget study." Paper presented at the Annual Meeting of the American Society of Criminology, Nashville, TN, November.

Wikström, Per-Olof & Sampson, Robert J. (2003). "Social mechanisms of community influences on crime and pathways in criminality." In Benjamin B. Lahey, Terrie E. Moffitt & Avshalom Caspi (eds.), *Causes of Conduct Disorder and Serious Juvenile Delinquency*. New York: Guilford Press.

Wilson, James Q. & Kelling, George (1982). "The police and neighborhood safety: broken windows." *Atlantic Monthly* 127: 29–38.

Wilson, William Julius (1987). *The Truly Disadvantaged: The Inner City, the Underclass, and Public Policy*. Chicago: University of Chicago Press.
Winship, Christopher & Morgan, Stephen (1999). "The estimation of causal effects from observational data." *Annual Review of Sociology* 25: 659–706.

3 Individuals, settings, and acts of crime: situational mechanisms and the explanation of crime

Per-Olof H. Wikström

The questions, "Why do people commit crime?" and "What can we do about it?" are central to any society. The answers to these questions require a basic understanding of what causes crime. I submit that criminological theory, by and large, has not been able to fully address the problems of causation and explanation. I argue that a major reason for this is that criminological theory generally suffers from *a lack of a theory of action, a poor integration of levels of explanation* and *an unclear definition of crime* (Wikström, 2004).

Without a clear conception of

(1) what crime is (what the theory should explain),
(2) what moves people to commit acts of crime (a theory of action), and
(3) how individual characteristics and experiences and environmental features interact in this process (integration of levels of explanation),

we cannot fully address the *causes* of crime. Moreover, without addressing these points in depth we lack the necessary theoretical foundation to evaluate fully the role of individual development and change (Wikström, 2005) and the role of systemic factors and their changes over time (Wikström & Sampson, 2003) in the explanation of crime.

Crimes are acts of moral rule-breaking. To explain crime is to explain why individuals *break moral rules* defined as crime in law. Crimes are acts committed by individuals. To explain acts of crime is to explain *what moves individuals* to break moral rules defined in law.

The fundamental argument of the Situational Action Theory of Crime Causation is that people are moved to action (including acts of crime) by how they *see their action alternatives* and *make their choices* when *confronted with the particularities of a setting* (Wikström, 2004).

People differ in what alternatives they see and what choices they make in a particular setting depending on *who they are* (i.e., their knowledge and skills, experiences, and morality) and the *characteristics of the setting* (e.g., opportunities and frictions and their moral context). To explain crime we need to *identify* the key individual characteristics and experiences (*crime propensities*) and the environmental features (*crime inducements*) that *influence* whether an individual tends to see crime as an alternative and tends to act upon it. Moreover, we also need to explain how individual propensity *interacts* with environmental inducement in moving people to engage in acts of crime. In other words, to explain acts of crime we need to understand the *situational mechanisms* that link individual and setting to acts of crime.

People are different and they operate in different environments. While *systemic factors* (features of social structure and organization) and their related social processes, *do not* explain what moves individuals to commit acts of crime, they help to explain (i) *why individuals become different* and (ii) *why they come to operate in different environments* (activity fields)[1] and, hence, help explain why they *develop* different individual (crime) propensities and why they *face* different environmental (crime) inducements in their daily lives (Wikström, 2005). In other words, (relevant) systemic factors (and individuals' life histories), rather than being causes of acts of crime, may be regarded as the "causes of the causes."[2]

I submit that without an in-depth understanding of the situational mechanisms that create acts of crime we cannot fully understand the important (but *indirect*) role of systemic factors (e.g., inequality, segregation, and social and moral norms) and their changes over time in crime causation. Neither can we fully understand the important (but *indirect*) role of individual development and change in crime causation. This chapter focuses on the understanding of the situational mechanisms in crime causation and presents advances in the Situational Action Theory of Crime Causation (Wikström, 2004, 2005).

What is crime? What a theory of crime causation should explain

Current theories of the causes of crime (and criminological risk factor research more generally), by and large, pay surprisingly little attention to *the conceptualization of crime*, that is, what a theory of *crime* causation

[1] An activity field is the specific configuration of settings with their particularities in which the individual operates.
[2] A phrase borrowed from Elster (1999: 30).

should explain.[3] This is an important oversight because without a clear conception of what is to be explained (what crime is) it is difficult to build an adequate theory of its causes (and to assess empirically its value as an explanation).

The key argument in the Situational Action Theory of Crime Causation is that crime, fundamentally, is an act of breaking a moral rule. *Moral rules* prescribe what is right and wrong to do (or not to do) in a particular circumstance. *Criminal law* is essentially a set of moral rules (but far from all moral rules are regulated by criminal law). *Crime* may be defined as *an act of breaking a moral rule defined in criminal law.*[4]

However, acts in which individuals are unaware that they are breaking a moral rule defined in law (*mistakes*) are not covered by the proposed theory (even if the act constitutes a crime in the legal sense). In addition to this, the theory does not cover unintentional activity (*accidents*) nor the acts of children under the age at which they have developed a clear sense of morality (an age which may be difficult to pinpoint exactly and which is likely to show some individual variation).

I suggest that the concept of moral rule-breaking is preferable to concepts like "antisocial behaviour," "conduct disorder" and "delinquency" because it is more precise and clearly indicates that what we aim to explain is the breaking of (moral) rules that can be changed and that vary by place and over time. It puts the emphasis on the *breaking* of a rule (to smoke when it is illegal to do so) rather than the act itself (to smoke).[5] This is what should be explained by a theory of *crime* causation.

The answer to the question "Why do people commit crime?" is fundamentally the answer to the question "*why do people break moral rules (as defined in law)?*" A theory of why people commit crime (a theory of crime causation) may be viewed as a *special case* of a more general theory of why people break moral rules (a theory of moral rule-breaking).

[3] A commendable but, in my judgment, not entirely successful attempt to address this problem is made by Gottfredson and Hirschi (1990: 3–16) in their General Theory of Crime.

[4] A common type of definition of crime is acts defined in and punishable by law. The definition I propose here is consistent with the "lexical" definition of crime but specifically stresses that acts of crime are acts of moral rule-breaking. What generally differentiates crime and other moral rules is the greater *formality* with which the rules are generated (the legislative procedure), enforced (policing), and sanctioned (courts).

[5] The concept of crime does not imply the commission of any particular type of act, just the commission of an act that constitutes a rule-breaking.

What the theory does not imply

To argue that a theory of crime causation is a theory of why individuals break moral rules as defined in law *does not imply any acceptance of existing laws as necessarily legitimate or morally justified* based on higher-order moral principles. The question raised here is not whether the laws are legitimate or morally justified, but why individuals (follow or) break them. For example, part of the reason why an individual breaks a particular law may very well be that he or she does not find the law legitimate or morally justified (i.e., the law does not *correspond* to his or her moral values).

To argue that a theory of crime causation is a theory of why individuals break moral rules as defined in law *does not imply that laws, necessarily, are moral norms*, that is, that most people in a jurisdiction necessarily need to agree with or find particular laws legitimate and morally justified. Some laws may be moral norms, others not. The question of whether a particular law (moral rule), in a particular society at a particular time, is also a moral *norm* is an empirical question. The question raised here is not why people (follow or) break generally accepted laws, just why they (follow or) break laws.

To argue that a theory of crime causation is a theory of why individuals break moral rules as defined in law *does not imply any specific assumptions about why certain acts are regulated by law and others not.* Although it may be plausible that at least some core laws have a grounding in human nature or emerge from human efforts to deal with the problem of maintaining social order, there is no need to take a standpoint on whether or not this is the case in order to argue that a theory of crime causation is a theory of why individuals break moral rules as defined in law. The question raised here is not why we have the laws we have, but why people (follow or) break them.

Advancing knowledge about why we have the laws we have (their origins and foundations), and whether they are normative (in a particular jurisdiction), and making principled evaluations of their moral justification and legitimacy (with regard to higher-order moral principles) are all important topics in themselves in the broader treatment of the phenomenon of crime, but not ones that specifically need to be addressed in order to explain why people commit acts of crime (or abide by the law).

A general theory

The Situational Action Theory of Crime Causation is a general theory of crime. A general theory of crime is a theory that aims to explain all kinds of acts of crime. Defining crime as the breaking of moral rules defined in law has the great advantage of putting the emphasis on what all crimes (in all places at all times) have in common. Moreover, this definition gives a clear focus to what is to be explained: the causal mechanisms (processes) that move people to break moral rules defined in law. A *general theory of crime* is thus *a theory that can identify the causal mechanisms through which individuals are moved to break the moral rules defined in law.*

Objections to a general theory of crime

It is sometimes argued that a general theory of the causes of crime is difficult or impossible to achieve because crime *covers so many different types of acts that have little in common.* For example, Wilson and Herrnstein (1985) state, regarding crime, "that it is difficult to provide a true and interesting explanation for actions that differ so much in their legal and subjective meaning" (p. 21).[6] This objection is correct if one focuses on explaining the many different *acts* that constitute crime (e.g., rape, tax fraud, drunken driving), but if the focus rather is on explaining the *rule-breaking* (that is common to all crimes) this objection becomes less of a problem.

Another objection against a general theory of crime is the fact that crimes are *socially defined*, and hence that, in principle, *what is a crime one day can be legal the next* (and the reverse) and therefore it is meaningless to try to *explain* crime. Again, this objection is less of a problem if we focus on explaining the *rule-breaking* rather than the particular act.

It is true, however, that if the law were abolished (which, in principle, is possible) there would be no crimes and no need for a specific theory of *crime* causation. But, as I have argued previously, if a theory of crime causation is regarded as a special case of a more general theory of *moral rule-breaking*, the fundaments of the theory (i.e., the basic mechanisms operating) will stay the same even if "defined in law" is dropped from the definition of what is to be explained. Laws are moral rules and crimes are moral rule-breakings. Human beings are rule-guided actors and human societies are based on rules (social and moral norms). It is therefore not conceivable that moral rule-breaking could be eradicated by abolishing morality (as technically crime can be eliminated by abolishing the law). In other words, *the foundation of a general theory of*

[6] They choose to focus their explanation on "why some persons commit serious crimes at a high rate and others not" (Wilson & Herrnstein, 1985: 21). However, it is difficult to see how restricting the scope of explanation to "serious crimes at a high rate" would solve their stated problem.

crime is not the law but the existence of moral rules (of which laws are a special case).[7]

A general theory does not need to fit all known facts about crime

It is often claimed that *a general theory of crime has to fit known facts about crime*. For example, Braithwaite (1989: 44) talks about "facts a theory of crime ought to fit" and he states, in reference to some key correlates of crime, that "any credible theory would at least have to be consistent with these findings, and preferably offer an explanation for most of them." Recently, Agnew (2005: 2) has made a similar claim, saying "a general theory must list those factors or variables that have a large, direct effect on crime." These are basically arguments that a general theory of crime has to account for the non-random patterns of correlation (and predictions) demonstrated in empirical research on crime. I disagree. There is no reason why a general theory of crime *has* to account for all patterns of correlation (or even account for all of the strongest and the most stable correlates) since most of the correlates are likely to be only *markers* or *symptoms* rather than causes of crime. What is needed is that the theory is consistent with known patterns of (strong and stable) correlations *relevant* to the theoretical statements made in the theory.

A scientific approach

The Situational Action Theory of Crime Causation aims at a scientific approach to explanation. A *scientific approach* could be defined as one that focuses on answering *why questions* (establishing causal processes or mechanisms) by means of theory *and* empirical research and thereby on providing proper explanation (e.g., Salmon, 1998: 125–141).

Empirical research can establish *correlations*, allow us to make *predictions*, and sometimes demonstrate *causes* by manipulation (experimentation). However, only theory can provide *explanation* by answering *why* questions (Why does *X* cause *Y*?), and, thereby, specifying *how* the studied outcome is produced by the putative cause (e.g., Bunge, 1999: 51). A *scientific explanation* may be defined as a theory (hypothesis) that (i) is consistent with relevant (statistical) correlates and predictions, (ii) is supported, as far as possible, by demonstrated changes in hypothesized causal relationships by manipulation (experimentation), and

7 The special significance (in most cases) of the fact that a moral rule is defined in law cannot be underestimated because this fact often has implications for the importance of the rule in moral education and its level of monitoring and sanctioning.

(iii) provides explanation by suggesting plausible causal processes (mechanisms) that link the putative causes and the effect and thereby tells us how the outcome is produced. I would argue that no theory in criminology even comes close to fulfilling the above stated criteria for a scientific explanation. However, this is what we should aim to accomplish, difficult as it may be.

The need to address the problem of correlation and causation

The problem of confusing correlation and causation is well discussed in the philosophical literature on causation and explanation. As Salmon puts it, "the main danger in confusing statistical correlation with genuine causation is the danger of confusing symptoms with causes" (1998: 45). This problem is also clearly acknowledged by some leading researchers within the risk factor paradigm in the study of crime: "a major problem with the risk factor paradigm is to determine which risk factors are causes and which are merely markers or correlated with causes" (Farrington, 2000: 7).

Criminological research has demonstrated numerous correlates and predictions of crime involvement (sometimes utilizing advanced statistical modeling).[8] Although demonstrating non-random patterns of correlation and making predictions are important activities, they are rather pointless if at the same time there is no conception that the findings represent causation and therefore can be subject to explanation.[9] Put bluntly, to demonstrate correlation and make predictions may (in most instances)[10] not be very useful knowledge if there is no

[8] Sometimes the use of statistical modeling to predict crime is wrongly equated with explaining crime.

[9] Ideally, the variables researchers include in statistical models should be variables they have grounds to believe are potential causes, although I suspect that in many cases (including some analyses I have conducted myself) there is a tendency to include a lot of standard variables without much thought about their potential causal status. It is questionable whether some types of standard variables can be potential causes at all. I think there are good reasons to believe that attributes like sex and race cannot cause actions. Unless one assumes that people can be, for example, more or less male, or more or less white, which in my view would be highly dubious (see discussion in Holland, 1986: 954–955). Attributes are merely symptoms and as such they can be helpful in identifying social problems but not in explaining them.

[10] Exceptions may be in cases where predicting concentrations of events helps us identify the existence of problems (symptoms), which may be an important starting point for thinking about their causes and explanation or for policy-oriented interventions (although the latter require knowledge about causation to be effective).

underlying causation. However, the central problems of differentiating between causation and correlation and of providing explanation of findings are not always dealt with very well in criminological research. One consequence of this is that there are, so to speak, *too many* potential causes (correlates, predictions) of which we struggle to make sense (Wikström, 2004). The risk factor approach to the study of crime is a good illustration of the problems that neglecting to address the issues of causation and explanation properly may generate.

The concept of *risk factors* is rarely well defined in criminological research (e.g., a risk factor being defined as a factor that increases risk). In practice, it often refers to a stable correlate (and the possibility of making predictions). To be meaningfully different from the concept of correlates the concept of risk factors has to imply some form of causation.[11] That causation is often implied is clear when policy recommendations are made based on the findings of risk factor studies.[12] Typically, the policy advice is that one should aim to reduce risk factors. To be valid, such advice has to imply that the concept of risk factors involves causation and is not just another word for correlation. Successful policy is based on targeting causes, i.e., the ability to manipulate the causes of the problem. Confusing correlation and causation may lead to wrongful policy decisions. However, causation is rarely tested through experimentation, and explanation is rarely offered by demonstrating plausible causal mechanisms. This means that the basis from which to evaluate whether suggested risk factors are causes is often limited.

I submit that, in order to advance knowledge about crime causation, we need to move from the current focus on mapping out non-random patterns of correlation and making predictions (a risk factor approach), to concentrate on the task of establishing causation and providing explanation (an explanatory approach).[13]

How do we move beyond demonstrating correlations and making predictions to establishing causation and providing explanation? I suggest that there are two *complementary* approaches to tackling this problem:

[11] It seems to me that what is often implied by the concept of risk factor is some kind of probabilistic causation.

[12] The same reasoning obviously also holds when so-called protective factors are discussed.

[13] This is not to say that establishing correlation and making predictions are unimportant activities. On the contrary, they are important starting points in the search for causation and explanation. Moreover, this is not to argue that there is no consideration of causation and explanation in criminology, just that the prime focus is on demonstrating correlation and making predictions.

(1) *empirically*, by conducting more experimentation with the aim of establishing causal relationships (i.e., demonstrating that if A is manipulated, B will change in predicted ways);
(2) *theoretically*, by carrying out more analytical work with the aim of establishing credible causal mechanisms (i.e., making plausible that A causes B *because* <specification of mechanism>).

Preferably, the latter (identified credible mechanisms) should guide the former (experimentation);[14] that is, the focus should be on testing causation through experimentation in cases where credible causal mechanisms have been analytically identified. However, it is acknowledged that experimentation, for ethical and practical reasons, may not always (perhaps rarely) be a realistic option. Therefore, advancing knowledge about crime causation will, in the first instance, be a question of more extensive analytical work which aims to sort causes from correlates by identifying plausible causal mechanisms (ideally supported where possible by experimentation).

The importance of having a theory of action

Contemporary theories of crime are rarely based on an explicit theory of action. This is surprising since crimes are *acts*, or more precisely a special class of acts (acts that constitute moral rule-breakings), carried out by *individuals*. To explain acts of crime we ultimately need to explain what *moves individuals* to break moral rules defined in law.[15] However, few criminological theories focus on explaining acts of crime; rather they aim to explain[16] *individual differences* in the extent of crime involvement (e.g., Gottfredson & Hirschi, 1990; Farrington, 1992; Agnew, 2005) or *area and place variation* in crime (or offender) rates[17] (e.g., Sampson & Groves, 1989; Brantingham & Brantingham, 1993; Bursik & Grasmick,

[14] We could, of course, apply the reverse strategy, i.e., focus on experimentation to establish causation and then look for explanation (identifying causal mechanisms). However, I believe that this would be a highly uneconomical strategy since we would have little guidance to which correlates would be plausible candidates as causes (and we have hundreds of demonstrated correlates). Moreover, experimentation may be easier to justify in cases where we have a strong analytical argument that causation is plausible.

[15] To emphasize the fact the crimes are acts by individuals does not mean disregarding the important (but indirect) role systemic factors play in the explanation of crime. It only implies that to understand the role of systemic factors in the explanation of crime we need to explain *how* systemic factors impact on factors causing individual action (Wikström & Sampson, 2003).

[16] In some cases it appears that it is prediction rather than explanation that is on offer.

[17] Sometimes crime rates are measured by victim rates (through victim surveys), but that is not of immediate importance for the point being made here.

1993). If criminological theories refer at all to theories of action they mostly make general reference to the importance of choice without giving any more developed account of its role within the theory, typically alluding to self-interest, pleasures and pain, cost and benefits and similar grounds for action (e.g., Wilson & Herrnstein, 1985; Hirschi, 1986; Braithwaite, 1989; Farrington, 1996).

Why is a theory of action important? I submit that it is important because *it can help specify the causal mechanisms that link the individual, and the environment, to action.* In fact, I would claim that a proper theory of action is a theory that specifies the causal processes that link the individual's characteristics and experiences (predispositions) and the features of his environment (inducements and constraints) to his acts.

Without a theory of action that explains *how* individual characteristics and experiences, and environmental features, move individuals to break moral rules defined in law, it is difficult to come up with credible explanations of *why* there are individual differences in crime involvement and area and place variations in crime rates. A theory of action, by telling us what moves people to commit acts of crime, gives guidance to *what* individual and environmental factors are important in causing acts of crime, and thereby helps to determine which individual and environmental correlates may operate as causes and which are merely symptoms.

Features of social organization and its related social processes (systemic factors) and patterns of individual development and change *do not* cause action but may be important as causes of the causes of action, i.e., as causes of individual characteristics and experiences and environmental features conducive to individuals acting in breach of moral rules defined in law. For example, if individuals' moral perceptions and moral choices are key factors in the causation of acts of crime, this fact directs our attention to the importance of explaining the role of systemic factors and individual development in causing differential moral perception and choice. Schick (1997: 15) puts it well when he claims, "the background is frequently cited, what people do being traced back to their childhood, to a strict or slack education, often to poverty, to abuse, to bad parenting. Matters of that sort can't be ignored, but their bearing is indirect. The background at most predisposes."

Classic action theory

There is an extensive literature on what may be called *classic action theory* and its problems (e.g., Aristotle, *Nicomachean Ethics*; Bunge, 1999: 87–101; Davidson, 1980, 2004: 101–134; Schick, 1991, 1997; Searle,

1983, 2001). It is not my intention to review this literature here, but simply to bring out and examine some key themes I believe give important background to the discussion of advances in the Situational Action Theory of Crime Causation.

Classic action theory is generally concerned with *voluntary* and *intentional* action that is *outcome* oriented. An individual's desires and beliefs are generally seen as the *reason* for his actions, and the reason for action is often seen as its *cause*. Davidson (1980: 4) claims that "the primary reason for an action is its cause." The idea that reasons causes action implies that human beings have *agency*, that is, powers to make things happen intentionally.

The basic idea of classic action theory reads something like: if an individual *wishes* (desires) to do something, and *believes* that he can do it, and he *intends* to do it, and if he *acts* upon his intention (i.e., carries out an intentional act), his desires and beliefs *explain* why he did it. In the words of Aristotle, "man is the source of his actions" (*Nicomachean Ethics*, p. 62).

Evaluating key themes in classic action theory

There are many contentious issues relating to classic action theory. Commentators differ in their take on various problems relating to the meaning and role of, and the relationship between, key concepts. What follows in this section is my evaluation of, and conclusion about, these debates in the context of my aim to advance the Situational Action Theory of Crime Causation.

Desires and beliefs

The concepts of desire and belief are not easily defined and their usage appears to vary somewhat in the literature. It seems clear that a *desire* generally refers to a wish directed towards an end (a desire-satisfaction), for example, a desire to smoke, where the smoking constitutes the desire-satisfaction. It is not always clear whether a feeling of pleasure needs to be part of the desire-satisfaction, but it probably need not. *Beliefs* normally have to do with assessments of whether, and how, a desire can be satisfied. They are typically based on knowledge, experiences, and perceptions. To have a belief is to have some degree of confidence in having the *capability* (e.g., having the skills, know-how, etc. of how to smoke) and the *means* available (the opportunity to smoke, e.g., cigarettes and a lighter) to carry out an act that will satisfy the desire in question (to smoke). Beliefs may be true or false; for example, it may turn out that the agent forgot that he had left his cigarettes at home and therefore his belief that he could smoke was false.

Motivation and intention

It seems clear that desire–belief pairs are generally seen as motivators. If I want to smoke and I believe I can do this I may be considered *motivated* to smoke. However, being motivated to smoke is not always the same as having the *intention* to smoke (i.e., being committed to it). For example, there may be many different conflicting desire–belief pairs (motivations) at the same time among which I have to choose. A *choice* is often seen as forming an intention by *deliberation*, that is, making a decision by assessing the pros and cons of the various action alternatives (although, as I will discuss later, many actions may be an expression of habits in which the choice is automatic rather than based on deliberation).

Even after forming an intention it is not necessary that the individual will actually perform the intended act. This is particularly so if there is a time lapse between the formation of the intention and the performance of the act; for example, "other things" may happen and "circumstances" may change making the agent *change his mind* (the intention is never carried out). For example, after I have decided to smoke a cigarette, I may get a sudden chest pain, or my wife, who does not like me to smoke, may unexpectedly arrive, causing me to change my mind about smoking the cigarette.

Intentional action

Intentional actions are generally seen as bodily movements, or sequences of bodily movements (e.g., walking, talking, hitting, singing, lifting, smoking), under the guidance of the individual. The fact that they are performed under the monitoring of the individual implies that they can be *interrupted* at any time before completion. For example, when trying to light my cigarette it suddenly starts to rain causing me to decide to stop my attempts to light the (now wet) cigarette.

Consequences of action

Intentional actions may *succeed or fail* in accomplishing the intended outcome. They have *consequences*. "The consequences of an action are ... effects of its result." (von Wright, 1971: 88). The consequences may be *intended or unintended*, or both. For example, the intended consequence of smoking may be the enjoyment I get from smoking and an unintended consequence may be that I annoy other people present by exposing them to cigarette smoke. Individuals' future actions may be influenced by the successes and failures and the observed consequences of their previous actions (*cumulative experiences*). Past experiences are likely to be an important source of an individual's current beliefs.

The picture of the action process I have given so far, based on themes treated in classic action theory and discussions thereof, describes how individual motivations (desire–belief pairs), through deliberation, may cause intentions (commitment to action), which, in turn, may (or may not) be carried out in actions, which, in turn, have consequences. But this is not the whole story; there are some, more contentious issues that need to be treated before we move on.

Commitments as motivation

There is more to motivation than desires and beliefs. Not all motivations are outcome-oriented. Searle has made a strong argument about the importance of *desire-independent reasons* in human action. Searle (2001: 7) talks about two kinds of reasons for action, desire-dependent and desire-independent reasons, in which the former refers to "what you want to do or what you have to do in order to get what you want" and the latter to "what you have to do regardless of what you want." Desire-independent reasons are according to Searle essentially *commitments*.[18] Desire-independent reasons "do not require any extra pleasure, desire or satisfaction. The motivation for performing the action is precisely the motivation for wanting to perform the action" (Searle, 2001: 191). That is, the commitment is the motivation. For example, if I have promised my wife that I will clean the ashtray in our garden this commitment may be reason enough for me to clean the ashtray in our garden. I do not need to take any particular pleasure in cleaning the ashtray in order to be motivated to do it.

Intentional inaction

A particular problem not very much discussed in action theory is that of *intentional inaction*. Intentional inaction may be defined as the choice (intention) *not* to perform specific bodily movements, or sequences thereof. Just as with intentional actions, intentional inactions may be

[18] I shall later on argue that another important class of desire-independent reasons is provocations.

caused by desires, beliefs, and commitments. The reason for inaction may be a desire to reach a particular outcome by *not* acting in a particular way (e.g., not providing a friend who asks for a cigarette with a cigarette because I do not want him to smoke) or having made a commitment *not* to act in a particular way (e.g., I have promised my heart surgeon to try not to smoke). Just as with intentional actions, intentional inactions may succeed or fail and have consequences and thereby may also be an important part of what creates individuals' *experiences* and as such have implications for future processes of choice regarding taking action or inaction in particular circumstances.

Moral rule-guidance

If desires, beliefs, and commitments are seen as motivators creating reasons for (causing) intentional action and inaction, there is still something important missing in the understanding of what moves people to action. Schick (1991, 1997) has convincingly highlighted the important role for motivation of how we see our options and in that respect the importance of the circumstances (psychological context) in which we make choices, "our conceivings and labellings of the facts understood" (Schick, 1997: 23). He talks about an individual's *understandings* of an action alternative as "his seeing it as something he wants to be doing" (Schick, 1997: 18). He further claims that "people's understandings are a major factor of what it is that moves them, that how they see their options and prospects plays a central causal role" (Schick, 1991: 7–8). One of Schick's examples illustrating his key point, that is particularly criminologically relevant, is the following.

> The man who rapes and the man who doesn't are the same in their beliefs and desires. They both believe that a show of force might frighten some women into having sex with them, and they both want sex. They differ in their understandings. The rapist sees rape as raw, rough sex, as tough-guy sex, the way he likes it. The other sees rape as a violation. He wants sex, but not the violation, and so the way he understands rape doesn't connect with what he wants, which means that he isn't moved to rape. (Schick, 1997: 19)

It seems clear (to me) that Schick's concept of understandings basically relates to the individual's *morality* (i.e., his moral rules) in that it has to do with the individual's values regarding whether particular action alternatives are the right or wrong thing to do in order to fulfill a particular desire (or make and keep a particular commitment) in a particular circumstance.

I suggest that what *action alternatives* an individual *perceives* and which he *acts upon* to fulfill a particular desire,[19] and what commitments he is prepared to enter into and meet – in addition to the role played by his beliefs – are *guided* by his views on what actions (or inactions) are the right or wrong things to do (or not to do) in the particular circumstance. Also the individual's evaluation of the success or failure and the consequences of his actions (inactions) are guided by his moral values. In other words, an individual's intentional actions (or inactions) are guided by his moral values as applied to the particularities of the circumstance. A moral value is fundamentally a moral rule.[20] A moral rule, as previously defined in this chapter, is a prescription for what is right and wrong to do (or not to do) in a particular circumstance.[21]

Not all intentional actions (inactions) have a moral dimension (i.e., a right and wrong dimension). However, I believe that many (if not most) types of intentional actions (or inactions) of any significance, at least in some circumstances, do. For example, even simple acts such as switching on a light may be guided by whether it is the right or wrong thing to do in a certain circumstance (e.g., not switching on a light in daytime or making sure the lights are out in unoccupied rooms). Acts that are carried out under moral rule-guidance may be referred to as *moral actions*, defined as *intentional acts that are performed under the guidance of rules prescribing what is right or wrong to do in a particular*

[19] Davidson (1980) includes both desires and moral values and principles under the concept of pro-attitudes, which in his view, together with beliefs, are the reasons for action. Davidson defines the concept of pro-attitudes in the following way: "desires, wantings, urges, promptings, and a great variety of moral views, aesthetic principles, economic prejudices, social conventions, and public and private goals and values in so far as these can be interpreted as attitudes of an agent directed towards action of a certain kind" (1980: 4). In other words, pro-attitudes may be thought of as individual predispositions (propensities) to engage in certain kinds of action. I would argue that there is a clear advantage in separating desires and morality in the explanation of human action. For example, morality may play an important role in how an individual evaluates action alternatives to fulfill particular desires and in controlling their expression.

[20] I shall use these two concepts interchangeably.

[21] It is important to stress here that I use the concept of moral rule as a concept stating what is the right or wrong thing to do (or not to do) in a particular context. For example, if you play chess there are rules specifying what moves you are allowed to make; if you drive your car there are rules specifying which side of the road you should drive on; and if you shop there are rules stating that you have to pay for the things you take from the shelves, etc. The concept of moral rule, as applied here, does not mean that a particular moral rule necessarily has to be judged the right thing to do (or not to do) by some independent (higher-order) criterion of what is good and bad to do (or not to do) in a particular circumstance. If an individual subscribes to a moral rule he holds this moral rule; if he does not, he does not hold this moral rule. One obvious implication of this is that individuals may differ in what actions (and inactions) they consider to be morally right or wrong to do (or not to do) in a particular circumstance, regardless of the moral norm.

circumstance. When explaining acts of crime, we are explaining moral actions.

Just as *experiences* of success or failure and consequences of intentional actions (or inactions) may lead to changes in an individual's beliefs (e.g., he may gain or lose confidence in his ability to pull off certain actions or achieve certain goals), they may also have implications for developments and changes in his moral values (e.g., he may come to see particular actions or inactions in a different moral light depending on the observed consequences of his particular actions or inactions).

Interferences

Not all factors that influence an action process are known to or under the control of the individual. It has been suggested that individual action may be viewed as "trying" (O'Shaughnessy, 1997). Things may happen and circumstances may change during the course of an action. This may include anything from a sudden illness (e.g., a heart attack) to external interventions (e.g., being told off for smoking), and they may be referred to as interferences.

Interferences may be defined (from the individual's point of view) as unforeseen or unexpected events or interventions that force the agent to change a course of action (inaction) or that change the outcome and consequences of the action (inaction). Interferences may happen at any step of the process (i.e., at the stage of motivation, intention, action (inaction), or consequence).

Interferences are more likely to occur in prolonged than in instant action processes. For example, if I want to smoke and decide to go and buy some cigarettes in order to be able to satisfy my desire I may fall over and break my leg on the way to the convenience store, which would stop me from carrying out the intended action and thereby prevent me from satisfying my desire as planned.

The process of choice

Making a choice is forming an intention (commitment) to carry out a particular action (or to refrain from a particular action). The starting point for the process of choice is motivation (desires and beliefs, or commitments)[22] and its end the resulting action (or inaction) and its consequences. The process is guided by the individual's moral rules and may be subject to interferences at each stage (see Figure 3.1).

[22] I will later argue that provocations are also an important class of motivations.

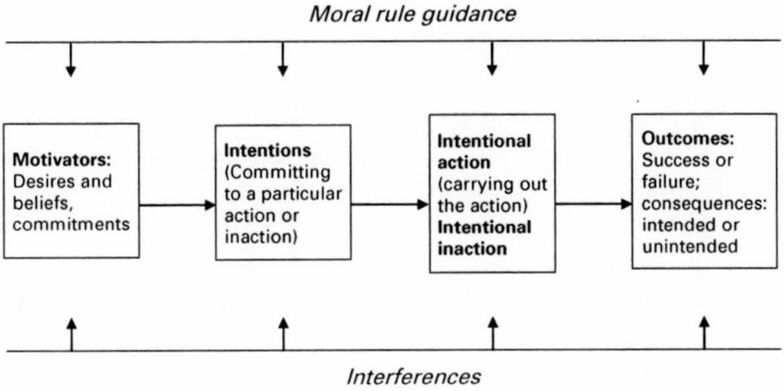

Figure 3.1. The basic steps of the process of choice and its outcomes

Free will, rational choices, and self-control

Three aspects of the process of choice that have attracted particular attention are the roles played in human choice by free will, rational choices, and self-control. In other words, to what extent is human choice characterized by free will, rational choices, and self-control. I suggest that the simple answer to this complex question is that they all are part of human choice but *only* when deliberation is part of the process of choice. Only when an individual's choice is the outcome of a deliberation over different action alternatives can he be said to have exercised *free will.* That is so because (i) deliberation implies that there is no causally sufficient preconditions for selecting one of the alternatives and (ii) the act of choosing among the alternatives may therefore be defined as an act of free will. Searle (2001: 50) talks about "the gap" as representing free will and defines "the gap" as "the phenomenon that we do *not* normally experience the stages of our deliberations and voluntary actions as having causally sufficient conditions or as setting causally sufficient conditions for the next stage."

Rational choices also require deliberation because to choose the best alternative requires that the agent identify action alternatives from which to choose. Davidson (1980: 113) states that "in order for x to engage in rational decision making, he has to assume he has a genuine choice." It seems highly plausible to argue that *when an agent deliberates* he aims to choose from the options he perceives the one he judges to be the best course of action based on his knowledge, experiences, and morality.

Finally, only when the agent deliberates is it possible for him to exercise *self-control*, because "exercises of self-control oppose something in support of something else" (Mele, 2001: 64). In other words, without perceived action alternatives there is nothing to "fight against" and hence no room for employing self-control. In this context "*weakness of the will*" (failed self-control) may be defined as occurring when the individual does not succeed in acting upon the option that appears the most rational to him (i.e., the best or morally correct option). For example, the individual has decided that it is best for his health not to smoke but he smokes anyway, or he does not think he should smoke in front of his toddler but does it anyway.

If this argument is correct, the importance of free will, rational choices, and self-control in the explanation of crime is dependent on the extent to which acts of crime are preceded by deliberation.

Two types of choice process: deliberation and habit

Most presentations and discussions of classic action theory concern action arising out of processes of choice that involve deliberation. However, as pointed out by several authors, not all intentions and actions are preceded by deliberation. Davidson (2004: 107) states that, "Most of our actions are not preceded by any conscious reasoning and deliberation. We don't usually 'form' intentions, we just come to have them." Searle (2001: 45), on a similar note, claims that "Not all actions are premeditated. Many of the things I do, I do quite spontaneously."

In fact, it may be argued that a lot of (perhaps most) human actions (inactions) may be viewed as expression of habits. A *habit* may be defined as *a tendency to intentionally act (or not act) in a certain way as a response to particular familiar circumstances*. For example, the tendency to light a cigarette when having coffee after lunch, without much deliberation on whether or not to smoke before the act of smoking. The idea that action arises either out of habit or after deliberation fits well with the idea that there are two basic systems of *cognitive processing* that guide action; the experiential (associative) and the rational (deliberative) systems (e.g., Carver & Scheier, 1998; Kahneman, 2002).

Dewey (2002: 49) suggests, in discussing habits as *tendencies*, that, "the word 'tendency' is an attempt to combine two facts, one that habits have a certain causal efficacy, the other that their outworking in any particular case is subject to contingencies, to circumstances which are unforeseeable and which carry an act one side of its usual effect." For example, my *habit* of having a cigarette with coffee after lunch may be interfered with by the fact that an American visitor, who hates smoke, accompanies me, which (after some deliberation) makes me *decide* not to smoke that day with coffee after lunch. In other words, even if my normal tendency is to smoke with coffee after lunch, occasionally atypical things may happen at coffee after lunch that break the habit (automatic choice) and promote deliberation that may (or may not) cause an action (inaction) differing from the usual. If changes in a familiar circumstance have a more permanent character (i.e., the American visitor stays for a long period and regularly accompanies me to lunch) this may instigate a change in my habit of smoking whilst having coffee after lunch. In other words, *habits depend for their continued expression on a stable and unchanging circumstance to which they are an acquired response*.

Habits may be seen as being caused by *repetition* of particular actions (individual habituation) *in response* to particular circumstances (environmental habituation). "Given enough repetition, an activity may drop out of consciousness altogether. Having reached that point, the activity is now under the management of the experiential system" (Carver & Scheier, 1998: 336). "With repetition of behavior in stable contexts, actions become automatic in the sense that deliberation about behavior becomes unnecessary. These well-practised behaviors represent habits" (Wood & Quinn, 2005: 55).

In contrast to processes of choice involving deliberation, habits involve the perception of only *one* causally effective alternative for action (inaction),[23] and therefore *habitual action (inaction) does not involve the exercise of free will, rational choices, or self-control.*

Whether one should call action based upon seeing only one causally effective alternative for action (or inaction) a process of choice or not could be debated. However, I believe one can make a sound argument that expressing a habit is in fact making a choice. The difference between deliberation and habit is *how* the choice emerges (by consideration of pros and cons or more or less automatically), not that a choice is made (i.e., that an intention is formed). While a choice after deliberation is a case of decision-making, a habit is a case of making an automatic choice. Habits are, however, different from pure *reflexes* in that they are intentional (i.e., they have a direction and conditions of satisfaction).[24]

[23] To say that habits only involve seeing one alternative for action does not imply a total unawareness of other action alternatives; it is just to say that the preconditions for choosing the particular alternative are so strong that no other alternative comes into contention.

[24] Searle states that "intentionality is that property of many mental states and events by which they are directed at or about or of objects and states of the affairs in the world" (1983: 1), and he further claims that "intentional states such as beliefs, desires, and intentions, have conditions of satisfaction and directions of fit" (2001: 37).

While deliberations are oriented toward the *future* – in the words of Aristotle, "deliberation does not refer to the past but only to the future and what is possible" (1999: 149)[25] – habits are oriented toward the *past*, they refer to past experiences of actions (inactions) that are "automatically" enacted without much thought as a response to the exposure to a familiar circumstance. As such, habits (when enacted) may be viewed as actions (inactions) brought about by causally sufficient preconditions (i.e., a particular response to a particular familiar environmental circumstance based on a predisposition to react in this way to the particular circumstance).

A process of choice involving deliberation is most likely in response to new, unexpected or unfamiliar circumstances, while automatic choices (habits) are most likely in response to familiar circumstances that do not involve anything new or unexpected. Habits grow out of an individual's dealings with repeated exposure to particular circumstances. They are the formation of automatic responses (choices) based on the recurring experiences (and evaluations) of successes and failures and the consequences of actions (and inactions) in particular circumstances.

An important point to keep in mind here is that what currently are actions (inactions) expressing a habit may previously have been actions (inactions) involving deliberation. For example, if I start a new job I may be uncertain whether and where it is acceptable to smoke, and therefore I may initially deliberate over whether or not to smoke and where to smoke. Eventually, however, I will come to know through experience when and where it is acceptable to smoke and then just automatically (without deliberation) smoke in these circumstances. It is a plausible assumption that the more an individual acts, and the longer period of time for which he has acted, in particular and stable environments, the more his actions are likely to be an expression of habits. Developing habits is a way to economize with effort when operating in familiar circumstances.

A question of particular interest, when dealing with the topic of crime, is the extent to which acts of crime reflect deliberate choices or are expressions of habits. I suspect that many individual acts of moral rule-breaking (and crime), rather than being manifestations of deliberate choices, may essentially be caused by habit. I will return to this topic and deal with it in greater depth later.

[25] This does not imply, however, that an actor does not draw upon the past in deliberating about the future.

Perception of alternatives

Classic action theory, and decision-making theory more generally, appear to focus mainly on how individuals make choices among a set of action alternatives. Less attention is given to the question of *why* individuals see certain (and not other) action alternatives in the first place. This, I would argue, is a crucial question to address in the explanation of intentional action (inaction) because the alternatives for action that we perceive *set boundaries* for the kind of choices we may make. For example, it would be rather pointless to study what influences the *choice* to smoke or not to smoke, among individuals who do not see smoking as an option. Rather the main question here would be why some individuals *perceive* smoking as an option and others not. It is important to stress in this context that not perceiving a particular alternative for action is very different from intentional inaction. In other words, a choice to smoke (intentional action) or not to smoke (intentional inaction) is different from not seeing smoking as an alternative altogether, because in the latter case there is no choice involved (i.e., no intention is formed). I suspect that in many cases (perhaps most) law-abiding behavior is a reflection of the individual not perceiving acts of crime as an action alternative and hence law abidance does not generally involve a process of choice (e.g., a choice of intentional inaction). That is, we generally *do not choose not to* commit crime; we just *do not perceive* crime as an option.

Perception

Perception is the information we get from our senses (e.g., seeing, hearing, and feeling) *and* our knowledge- and experience-based interpretation, and moral evaluation, of this information. Dretske (2000: 116) argues that "perceptual awareness of facts is a mental state or attitude that involves the possession and use of concepts, the sort of cognitive or intellectual capacity involved in thoughts and belief." He further claims that, "one *learns* to perceive (i.e., recognize, identify, classify) those things that, even before learning takes place, one can see" (100). For example, I may learn that what my father does when he lights up a cigarette is that he smokes (I come to recognize, identify, and classify the action as smoking).

However, perception is not only about seeing and classifying objects and events, but also involves an important *moral dimension*. That is, an evaluation of what the individual can see, hear, and feel in terms of his morality (moral rules), which defines (i) the moral significance (if any) of the setting in which he takes part (i.e., is there a question of what is the right or wrong thing to do) and (ii) the moral appropriateness of perceived action alternatives (i.e., what is the right or wrong thing to do). Blum (1994: 37) has made a strong argument that "perception depends on the agent's already possessing certain moral categories." Schick (1997: 51), on a similar note, states that "our seeings enlist certain values we have, different seeings tapping different values, and the values so tapped or enlisted enter the reasons that move us."

Perception is what links the individual to his environment

The individual is linked to his environment through perception and deals with his environment through his choice of actions (inactions). Searle (1983: 139) points out that "our most fundamental ways of coping with the world are through action and perception, and these ways essentially involve intentional causation." Perception has been described by Maund as "a means by which someone navigates their way through their environment" (2003: 25), in that perceptions "are guides to action," "are connected with perceptual thoughts and beliefs," and "form the basis of judgements" (2003: 50).

What we perceive is dependent on (i) the setting in which we take part (which determines what we can see, hear, and feel) and (ii) who we are (our past experiences, knowledge, and morality, through which what we see, hear, and feel is filtered). Perception is thus an outcome of the *interaction* between the individual and the setting.

Perception creates motivation and defines action alternatives

It is through his encounters with the circumstances of a particular setting and his interpretation and evaluation of these circumstances that an individual comes to have specific motivations and to define his action alternatives. What action alternatives an individual perceives are crucial for what choices he may make and, based upon this, what kind of actions (inactions) he may take in the particular setting.

In this context it is important to recall, as previously argued, that motivation is (i) to have a desire *and* a belief – not just a desire (want, need) – or (ii) to have made a commitment.[26] Individuals do not get moved to action (inaction) just by wanting something; they also have to believe that they can get (or at least have a remote possibility of getting) what they want by some action (inaction). The latter (beliefs) are

[26] I will later argue that provocations are also an important class of motivations.

strongly dependent on how they perceive their circumstances, and hence motivation is dependent on perception. The same reasoning also holds for commitments; the individual has to perceive the circumstances as being relevant to a commitment made for the commitment to act as a motivator. For example, if I have made a commitment not to smoke in my house, this commitment does not act as a motivator for my actions (inactions) when I am out walking the dog.

Perception precedes the process of choice

Perception precedes the process of choice and is therefore more fundamental in the explanation of action (inaction) than is the process of choice. Blum (1994: 37) argues that "perception occurs prior to deliberation, and prior to taking the situation to be one in which we need to deliberate. It is precisely because the situation is seen in a certain way that the agent takes it as one in which he feels moved to deliberate." I suggest that the same order of events (i.e., first perception, then choice) also holds for habitual choices; it is through the perception of familiar circumstances that environmental stimuli may enact habitual responses (automatic choices).

Perception of alternatives and process of choice: the situational mechanisms linking individual and setting to action

On the basis of what has been discussed above, I submit that *perception of alternatives* and the *process of choice* may be regarded as the *situational mechanisms* that link the individual and the setting (environment) to his action.

Perceptions are the external inputs (seeing, hearing, feeling), filtered through an individual's knowledge, experiences, and morality, that bring about motivation and define action alternatives; *choice* (through deliberation or habit) is the internal process that deals with the inputs and causes intention; *action* (inaction) is the bodily movements (withheld bodily movements) brought about by intention, and its *consequences* the external effects (Figure 3.2).

To explain the roles of individual differences and the environment in the causation of acts of crime we need to explain how individuals' characteristics and experiences and the environmental inducements and constraints they face in their daily lives interact in affecting their perception of alternatives and their process of choice. Specifically, I shall argue that when considering the explanation of moral rule-breakings like

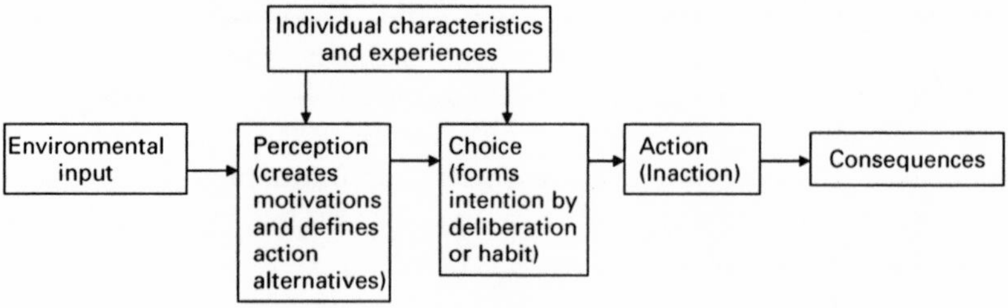

Figure 3.2. The basic steps of the action process and its outcome

crime, what ultimately needs to be explained is *how* individuals' morality (and executive capabilities),[27] and the moral context of the environments in which they operate, *interact* in influencing their moral perceptions and moral choices (moral judgments and moral habits).

The role of individual differences

An individual is defined by his body and characterized by his particular biological and psychological make-up, experiences, and agency (powers to make things happen). Individual differences are *differences* between individuals in their biological and psychological make-up, experiences, and agency. Individual development is *changes* in an individual's biological and psychological make-up, experiences, and agency. The idea that individual differences are important in the explanation of action is essentially the idea that different individuals would act differently when faced with the same setting. For example, some individuals may habitually smoke whilst drinking coffee after lunch, while others may never consider smoking whilst having coffee after lunch.

Individual differences are important in the explanation of intentional action (inaction) because they represent differences in the evaluation and processing of particular environmental input. Individual characteristics (whether genetic or acquired) and experiences *do not* in themselves instigate particular actions (e.g., acts of rape, theft, or speeding). However, they are an important part of what causes an individual to act in a particular way, through their impact on the individual's perception of action alternatives and process of choice *in response to* specific environmental stimuli (e.g., certain opportunities or frictions and their moral context). In other words, while it may be argued that intentional action (inaction) is always environmentally

[27] I shall deal with the role of executive capabilities later when I briefly return to treat the topic of self-control in crime causation.

instigated (by what we see, hear, and feel in a particular setting) it is also true that *action (inaction) is always an outcome of an individual's evaluation and processing of the environmental input.*

Action theories generally acknowledge that individuals are different but this fact does not figure much in the discussion of these theories. The main reason for this is that action theories generally focus on what causes action, not what causes individual differences in action (or how these differences emerge). When individual differences are mentioned they are generally referred to as the background. Searle (2001: 25), for example, states that "in real life there will be restrictions set by my Background, by my biological limits and by the culture that I have been brought up in. The Background restricts my sense of the possibilities that are open to me at any given time."

Individuals have certain knowledge and skills, experiences, and moral values that influence their perceptions of alternatives and their processes of choice in the particular setting in which they take part. As such they are an important part of the factors that bring an individual to act in a particular way in a particular setting. The *developmental question* is how these differences emerge. The findings of developmental research *do not* explain why individuals commit acts of crime, but rather the findings may explain why individuals *come to have* certain knowledge, experiences, and moral values that are important in the explanation of their moral actions.

I submit that there is a need to better integrate the developmental question with that of what causes action (action theory). This is because the latter (action theory) would guide developmental research into crime *to focus more clearly on aspects of development relevant to the emergence of individual characteristics and experiences that are important in the causation of acts of crime*. As previously discussed, we currently have hundreds of individual correlates (and predictions) that we struggle to make sense of, most of which are likely to be *irrelevant* to the explanation of crime in that they are symptoms or markers rather than causes. Moreover, some standard correlates are by their very nature, i.e., by being *attributes*, not even possible candidates as causes of action, for example, sex and race (see, e.g., Holland, 1986: 954–955). Their inclusion in the explanation of crime may sometimes obscure rather than enlighten our understanding of the causes of acts of crime.[28] It is, for example, difficult to

[28] However, I do acknowledge that sometimes knowledge about individual differences in crime involvement by attribute (e.g., by sex and race) may be important in directing our attention to the existence of social conditions that cause (other) individual differences that may act as causes of crime. For example, the fact that males are more often involved in crimes may be because more males have been subjected to social conditions

see how the fact that someone is male or Asian, *in itself*, would cause him to see certain action alternatives or make certain choices. This is not the same as saying that being male or Asian cannot have any impact on how an individual develops certain knowledge and skills, experiences, and morality relevant to their perceptions of alternatives and processes of choice. For example, being male may have some consequences, depending on the cultural context in which they live, such as how they are brought up and thereby come to develop certain characteristics and experiences. However, the point is that *it is the characteristics and experiences they have* (that will vary among males) that influence their actions rather than the fact that they are male. The same reasoning will, in principle, hold for any biological difference that does not have a one-to-one relationship with a particular attribute (of which I can think of none). For example, males vary significantly in their testosterone levels.

If developmental research into crime was based on a clear conception of what factors cause an individual to commit acts of crime – which it rarely is – my guess is that the contribution of developmental research to the *explanation* of crime would be much more significant than it is currently.

Individuals are not only different in their knowledge and skills, experiences, and morality but also in the environments in which they operate and have developed. The role of the environment in individual development is generally a neglected topic in developmental research (Wikström, 2005). I suggest that it is essential to address this topic better if we want to advance our understanding of how individual differences in knowledge and skills, experiences, and morality relevant to moral actions like crime emerge.

The environment instigates action processes

An individual's environment is all that is external to the individual and that with which he comes into contact. The individual's environment may be conceptualized as his activity field. An *activity field* may be defined as *the configuration of the settings in which the individual takes part during a particular period of time* (e.g., his daily activity field or his annual activity field). A *setting* may be defined as *the social and physical*

that promote moral values that permit them to see crime as an option and to act upon this, a fact that may raise important questions as to why that is the case. In this context, it is important to bear in mind that when addressing the question of why there are individual differences, the individual difference is the outcome (that which is to be explained) rather than the cause.

environment (objects, persons, and events) that the individual, at a particular moment in time, can access with his senses (e.g., what he can see, hear, and feel). This also includes everything he can see, hear, and feel through the exposure to and use of various *media* (e.g., television, radio, telephone, computers, newspapers, books, etc.) present in the setting. Settings exist independently of the individual. The idea that the environment is important in the explanation of action is equivalent to saying that an individual acts differently depending on what kind of setting he faces. For example, I may habitually smoke while having coffee after lunch, but never even consider smoking while teaching a class of students.

The environment is important for action because it instigates the action process. If we take seriously the fact that individuals' actions (inactions) are outcomes of how they perceive action alternatives and make choices, and acknowledge that *what* action alternative an individual perceives, and *what* he chooses (by deliberation or habit) to do (or not to do) in a particular setting is *dependent on the characteristics of the setting*, the implication is that an individual's environment (activity field) is crucial for what kind of actions (inactions) he will take. In other words, not only are individual differences in knowledge and skills, experiences, and morality important for an individual's actions (inactions), but also individual differences in the environments in which they operate. Individuals' knowledge and skills, experiences, and morality are always *applied* to the particularities of the setting in which they take part. It is the *interaction* between an individual and his environment that determines his course of actions (inactions).

In this context it is important to keep in mind that an individual's current knowledge and skills, experiences, and morality depend on his previous pattern of interactions with particular environments.

The problematic notion of selection effects

A particularly intriguing question concerns the extent to which an individual is able to *select* the environments in which he operates, and hence how much he affects the environmental influences to which he is subjected. It is obvious that at the time of birth (and before birth) an individual has no influence on his environment, but it is equally clear that he will increasingly (with age) be able to have (at least) some influence on his environment, at each stage within the (perceived and real) constraints set by his current situation.

There is no question that individuals (some much more than others) have an influence on the environmental conditions to which they are exposed. Further, there is no question that individual characteristics and experiences are an important factor in what causes individuals to select one over others of the environments accessible to them.

However, it does not make much sense to regard environmental influences on action (or development, for that matter) as essentially an individual characteristic (*selection effect*) purely on the grounds that the individual has selected to be in a particular environment. The questions (i) why individuals are *exposed to* certain environmental influences (regardless of whether this is by their choice or not), and (ii) what is the *effect on* their actions (inactions) of the environmental influences to which they are subjected, are *two different questions*. One cannot be reduced to the other. For example, we can explain why someone who likes to visit prostitutes of his own choice is *exposed to* the environment of red-light districts, but this does not explain the *effect on* his actions of being in the environment of a red-light district.

Some key features of settings

Individual action (inaction) always takes place in a setting. Settings vary in the kind of opportunities they provide for action, the type of frictions they generate, and the moral contexts in which these opportunities and frictions occur. An individual's activity field can, in principle, be characterized by the set of opportunities and frictions that the individual encounters and the moral contexts in which they occur. Depending on the preferences, knowledge and skills, experiences, and morality of the individual who engages with a particular setting, its opportunities may cause temptations and its frictions may cause provocations, while the moral context in which these opportunities and frictions occur will guide any action (inaction) that the individual may take in response to any perceived temptations or provocations.

Opportunities and temptations

Action depends on *opportunity*. "In order for an act to be performable, there must be an opportunity for its performance" (von Wright, 1971: 125). If there are no cigarettes or no matches or lighters available there is no opportunity to smoke, regardless of whether I desire to do so or not. If I have made a commitment to go and buy some cigarettes for a friend but find out that all shops that sell cigarettes have closed there is no opportunity for me to keep my commitment.

A particular setting will provide particular opportunities for action (inaction) and hence determine the range of actions (inactions) that are *possible* (or not possible) in the particular setting. Some kinds of action opportunities are almost ever present (e.g., to destroy an object). Others are limited to specific, and sometimes even rare, settings (e.g., to have a swim or play golf). Settings generally include plentiful opportunities although most are likely to be irrelevant to a particular individual. What types of opportunity are *relevant* to a particular individual is dependent on his desires (and commitments).

Opportunities that are relevant to the individual may cause temptations (i.e., inducements to action). A *temptation* may be defined as a *perceived opportunity to satisfy a particular desire*. The individual making a *connection* between an opportunity and a desire in a particular setting *causes* a temptation. That is, the individual comes to *believe* that he can satisfy a particular desire in a particular setting. For example, if I have a desire to smoke and someone offers me a cigarette (i.e., provides an opportunity), this will tempt me to smoke. In other words, while individuals have desires and the setting provides opportunities, temptations are an outcome of the individual's *interaction* with the setting and as such it is a situational concept. An implication of this is that *motivation is always situational* (i.e., desires do not cause motivation and neither do opportunities, but their interaction does). The sometimes voiced question of whether motivations are individually *or* environmentally caused is therefore wrongly put.

The same basic line of reasoning also applies to *commitments* as motivators. Commitments can only be met when there is an opportunity to do so. Therefore a commitment will only motivate an individual to action when the individual makes a *connection* between a commitment he has made and an opportunity to honor the commitment.

Frictions and provocations

A particularly interesting aspect of motivation – when considering moral actions like crime – is the role of *negative emotions* (e.g., irritations or rage) generated by *unwanted external interferences* in the individual's course of action or directed against his self-defined sphere of influence (e.g., his property or significant others). In this case the motivation does not emerge out of a *belief* that a desire can be satisfied, or that a commitment can be met, but rather out of an *emotional reaction* (e.g., annoyance or anger) directed toward external obstacles or unwanted third-party interventions. As Forgas and Laham (2005: 169) note: "It is ... clear that many affective states arise prior to elaborate cognitive processing, and that such precognitive reactions may in turn function as directional input to motivate behavior."

Unwanted external interferences may be labeled frictions. A *friction* may be defined as *an obstacle to an intended action, or a third-party unwanted intervention in an individual's course of action or directed against his self-defined sphere of influence.*

The individual may see a friction as a provocation *if* he interprets the perceived source of friction as antagonistic. In other words, if an individual connects a friction with a perceived antagonistic intent this *causes* him to be provoked (e.g., to become annoyed or angry with the perceived source of the friction). A *provocation* may be defined as *an emotional inducement to respond aggressively toward the perceived source of a friction or toward someone or something representing the source of friction.* Aggression is here defined as any action (inaction) carried out with intent to harm another living being or destroy an object. A perceived source of friction may be an individual or an abstract entity such as "the state" or "the neighbors."

Whether the individual interprets a source of a friction as antagonistic will depend on his knowledge, experiences, and morality. Provocation is a situational concept because provocations are an outcome (interpretation of antagonistic intent) of the interaction between the individual (his knowledge, experiences, and morality) and the setting (the encountering of a friction). In other words, *only* when a friction is seen as caused by an antagonistic intent will it cause a provocation.

In the same way as a commitment, a provocation may be considered a *desire-independent reason.* That is so because provocations do not require any "extra pleasure, desire, or satisfaction" to motivate action. The provocation is the motivation. The fact that individuals may sometimes take great pleasure in the consequences of their actions (inactions) in response to a provocation does not change this fact.

Settings as moral contexts

Settings do not only vary in the opportunities they provide and the frictions they generate but crucially also in the moral context in which these opportunities and frictions occur. Settings vary in (i) what moral rules apply to them (e.g., whether you are allowed to smoke or not), (ii) the level of their enforcement (e.g., if compliance with a non-smoking rule is effectively monitored or not), and (iii) the severity of sanctioning of breaches of specific moral rules (e.g., the consequences that will follow if caught smoking). The *moral context of a setting* may be defined as *the moral rules that apply to the setting and their levels of enforcement and sanctioning.* Some moral rules are specific to particular settings, whilst others have a more global reach. However, even when a rule is global in nature there are nearly always some circumstances in which it may not apply (e.g., even the moral rule that says that you should not kill – and the corresponding law – sometimes makes exceptions to the general rule in which a killing is regarded as morally justified).

The moral context of a setting is *independent* of the individual (his knowledge, experiences, and morality) although his *perception* of the moral context of a setting is not. Individuals may more or less correctly identify the moral rules that apply to a setting, and their levels of enforcement and sanctioning. If an individual operates in a familiar setting his perception of the moral context is more likely to be accurate than if he maneuvers in an unfamiliar setting. For example, an individual who regularly shop-lifts cigarettes in his local shopping mall may have a more accurate picture of his risk of getting caught and of the consequences of being caught than an individual who steals cigarettes for the first time in the same shopping mall.

Which aspects of the moral context of a setting are *relevant* to the actions (inactions) of a particular individual depend on his motivations (temptations, commitments, and provocations). For example, rules regulating smoking in a particular setting are likely to be irrelevant to the actions of non-smokers because they may not be tempted to smoke (even when there is an opportunity to do so). On the same account, the levels of enforcement and sanctioning of breaches of a non-smoking rule are also irrelevant because they will have no influence on whether a non-smoker smokes or not. In other words, it is *not* because he fears the consequences of his actions (deterrence) that the non-smoker will not smoke in a non-smoking area. It is because he does not see smoking as an action alternative and therefore he will not be tempted to smoke. It is only when an individual is motivated to commit a particular action (inaction) that would constitute a breach of a moral rule that *deterrence* (i.e., the anticipated risk of detection and sanctioning if carrying out the action) may play a role in guiding his actions.

The individual will *evaluate* (habitually or through deliberation) the moral context he faces based on his knowledge, experiences, and morality. Whether he will act upon action alternatives that breach moral rules (or constitute acts of crime) in pursuing a temptation, honoring a commitment or responding to a provocation will be *guided* by his moral evaluations of the setting (his moral habits or moral judgments) based upon his moral values and his perception of the moral context of the setting. For example, if I desire to smoke and someone offers me a cigarette (a temptation), I may still out of habit (moral habit) or after some deliberation (moral judgment) refrain from smoking because of being in an area where smoking is not permitted (the moral context).

However, if I am really desperate to smoke and I disagree with the legitimacy of the non-smoking rule (moral values), or I believe the risk of being detected is low or the consequences of being caught are mild (the moral context), I may out of habit (moral habit) or after some deliberation (moral judgment) smoke even though I am in an area where smoking is not permitted. In other words, the individual's moral values and (his perception of) the moral context in which he takes part will guide whether his motivations are expressed in actions (inactions) that breach a moral rule (violate a law).

The Situational Action Theory of Crime Causation

The Situational Action Theory of Crime Causation aims to explain how individual characteristics and experiences and environmental features interact in moving individuals to break moral rules defined in law (or moral rules more generally). Its cornerstone, which I have developed at some length in this chapter, is that individuals' actions (and inactions) ultimately are a consequence of how they perceive their action alternatives and make their choices when confronted with the particularities of a setting.

Perception of action alternatives and the process of choice are the suggested key *situational mechanisms* that link an individual and his environment (settings) to his actions (inactions). They are the basic mechanisms through which the influences on action of the individual's characteristics and experiences and the features of the environment (settings) in which he operates can be *integrated.*

An individual's actions (inactions) can never be explained by individual characteristics (genetic or acquired) and experiences alone. No particular individual characteristic or experience (or combination thereof, for that matter) causes an individual to take a certain action (inaction). Actions are never taken in an environmental vacuum. On the contrary, they are the individual's way of dealing with his environment. Motivations arise, action alternatives are perceived, and choices are made in response to the environmental conditions an individual faces.

Intentional actions (inactions) can never be explained solely by environmental conditions. There are no particular environmental conditions that cause all individuals that are exposed to them to act in the same specific way.[29] What motivations an individual has, what action

[29] With the main exception of reflexes, which are not the topic of this chapter.

alternatives he will perceive, and what choices he will make in a particular setting are dependent on his individual characteristics and experiences in that they will act as a filter in his processing and evaluation of the environmental input.

The action a particular individual takes is always a result of the features of the settings in which he takes part and his processing and evaluation of the environmental input. Specific combinations of individuals and settings will cause particular actions (inactions). The challenge is to specify the *individual–setting matrices* (the causal interactions) that are likely to produce particular types of acts (e.g., acts of crime). In other words, in which kinds of circumstance are which kinds of individual likely to act in a particular way?

Explaining acts of crime

If, as I have argued, an act of crime is essentially the breaking of a moral rule defined in law, to explain acts of crime is to explain why an individual is moved to break a moral rule defined in law. If, as I have further argued, moral rule guidance plays an essential role in what moves an individual to act (or not act) in a particular way based upon a particular motivation, the individual's morality, and the moral context in which he acts, will play a key role in determining (i) whether the individual *perceives* a moral rule-breaking (crime) as an action alternative and (ii) whether he, out of moral habit or after a moral judgment (deliberation), will *choose* to act upon such an alternative. Individuals' acts of crime (moral rule-breaking) are ultimately a consequence of their moral perceptions and moral choices.

While motivations (temptations, commitments, and provocations) have *a general directional influence* on what kinds of action (inactions) an individual may consider (and hence what kinds of acts of crime he may consider), it is the moral rule guidance based on an individual's morality, and the moral context in which he operates, that will determine whether specific motivations are expressed in action alternatives that constitute acts of crime (moral rule-breaking). What motivates an individual is important for *what particular kinds of crime he may commit*, while the moral rule guidance is important for *whether he commits a crime* as a consequence of a specific motivation. For example, an individual *may* steal a particular CD because he wants it (and have an opportunity to steal it). However, of all individuals who want to have a particular CD, many will not consider (or dare) getting it through an act of theft (even if they have an opportunity to do so).

There are no particular motivations that cause acts of crime. Acts of crime are committed for endless reasons. An individual may steal a mobile telephone because he wants it and thinks he can get it by an act of theft (temptation). He may beat up a stranger because he spilled some beer on his clothes (provocation). He may rob a bank because he has an obligation to do so as a member of a gang (commitment).

There are no particular motivations that cause particular acts of crime. The same act of crime may be committed for different reasons. An individual may kill another person because he wants to kill someone, because the victim has insulted him, or because he has made a promise to a friend to do so because the victim has cheated his friend of money.

The crucial question in explaining an act of crime is to explicate why an individual comes to see an act of moral rule-breaking as an action alternative and why he chooses to act upon it in order to realize a particular motivation.

Acts of crime as a result of an individual's moral engagement with a moral context

According to the Situational Action Theory of Crime Causation, an individual's moral actions (and acts of crime) can be viewed as an outcome of the individual's moral engagement with the moral context of a particular setting.

When an individual (with his particular knowledge and skills, experiences, and morality) encounters a setting (with its particular opportunities and frictions and moral context) this may (i) give rise to certain motivations (temptations, commitments, and provocations) and (ii) define certain action alternatives and their moral qualities to deal with these motivations (moral perceptions).

On the basis of moral perceptions, an individual will either (i) out of habit (moral habit) or (ii) after some deliberation (moral judgment), form an intention (make a moral choice). Whether the moral choice is made out of moral habit or involves a moral judgment will depend on the familiarity of the setting and its circumstances. Familiar settings and circumstances (and consistent motivations) will tend to favor choices based upon moral habit while unfamiliar settings or circumstances (and conflicting motivations) will tend to favor choices based on moral judgment. If the individual deliberates over his action alternatives (makes a moral judgment) free will, rational choice, and self-control will be part of the process of choice; otherwise it will not. Crucially, when making moral judgments, individuals will vary in their capability to exercise self-control (based on their executive capabilities).

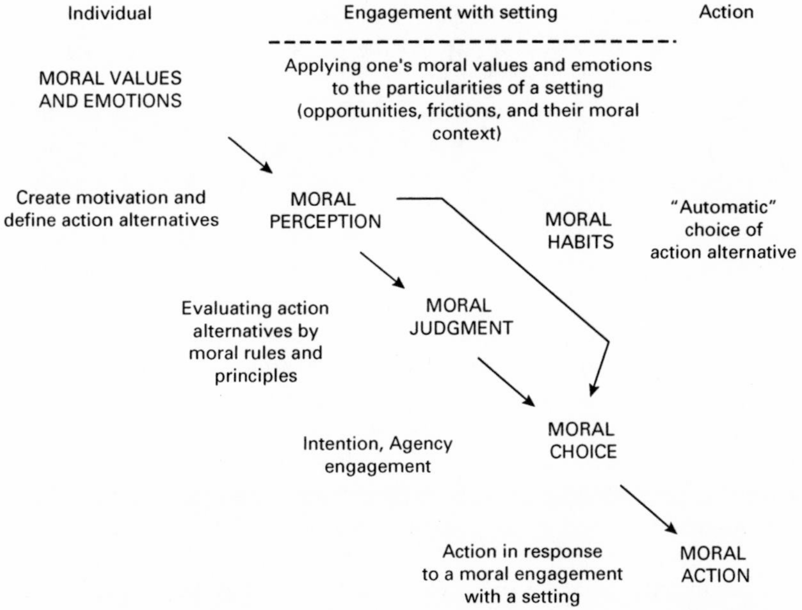

Figure 3.3. The basic steps of the individual's moral engagement with a moral setting

A moral choice made will result in the intended moral action if there are no external interferences that prevent the action (inaction) being carried out. An individual's capability to carry out a particular moral action successfully (i.e., to accomplish the intended consequence) will also depend on his agency in a particular context. An individual's agency (powers to make things happen) is context-dependent. That is, it varies between the settings in which he takes part. For example, a chief executive may have a strong agency at his office, but much less so at his golf club.

The basic steps of the individual's moral engagement with a moral setting are illustrated in Figure 3.3. Let's consider in some more detail certain key features of this process.

Individual morality

At any given time, individuals will vary in their moral values (moral rules) as will the strength of particular moral values they hold. The strength of an individual's particular moral values may be regarded as the degree to which he will feel guilt or shame (*moral emotion*s) if violating a certain moral rule. Since individuals vary in their moral rules and how much they care about abiding by particular moral rules, individuals may be thought of as having different *moral thresholds* (or tipping points) for breaking particular moral rules (or, for that matter, moral rules more generally). It seems plausible that the higher the moral threshold an individual has the stronger the environmental inducement needed to move him to break a moral rule.

Moral perceptions

An individual will always enter a setting (a moral context) having certain moral categories (moral values and their attached emotions). The individual may be said to *engage* with a setting when his interaction with the setting causes him to have particular motivations and perceive certain action alternatives. When individuals engage with a setting they *apply* their moral categories to the moral context of the setting causing particular moral perceptions. Moral perception helps create motivation. Moral perception defines the action alternatives and their moral qualities in the particular setting. *Moral perception* may be defined as *the identification of action alternatives and their moral qualities in response to particular motivations in a particular setting*. This is the basis upon which an individual (after some deliberation or out of habit) will make a moral choice.

To the extent that an individual's moral values (and their strength) correspond to the moral rules of the settings in which he takes part he will be unlikely to see a moral rule-breaking as an action alternative. In other words, an individual who operates in an environment in which there is a high *correspondence* between his moral rules and those of the settings in which he takes part will rarely *perceive* breaching moral rules as an action alternative.

I suggest that a main reason for *moral rule-following* is that individuals' moral values (which they care about) correspond to the moral rules of the settings in which they operate causing them not to see moral rule-breaking as an action alternative when faced with particular motivations. To the extent that the *rules of law* correspond to an individual's moral rules, and the moral rules of the settings in which he operates, he will not tend to see crime as an action alternative.

This is an important argument because, as pointed out earlier, in this case abiding by moral rules (laws) is *not a question of choice*, but rather a question of perception of action alternatives (moral perceptions). That is, it is a question of *not seeing* the breaking of a moral rule (law) as an action alternative, rather than making a choice not to break a moral rule (commit an act of crime). Choice does not come into the process. One notable implication of this is that in these cases, fear of consequences (deterrence) plays no role in influencing whether an individual will or will not abide by the law. Other significant implications are that abiding by the law in these cases is not a result of making rational choices or exercising self-control.

An intriguing question in this context is to what extent law-abiding conduct is caused by the fact that individuals do not see acts of crime as an alternative. I suspect it is a rather important cause of law abidance, particularly (but not exclusively) as regards crimes that are generally considered more serious moral violations in a particular culture context. Most people will normally *not see as an action alternative* the killing of another person or the theft of a car, regardless of how angry they are with another person, or how much they want a particular car. At the other extreme, many people may without much deliberation exceed the speed limit, smoke cannabis, or steal office supplies from work – in these cases, I suspect, mostly out of habit.

Moral habits

Aristotle stresses the important role of habit in human morality: "Moral virtue ... is formed by habit"; "none of the moral virtues is implanted in us by nature, for nothing which exists by nature can be changed by habit"; "the virtues are implanted in us neither by nature nor contrary to nature: we are by nature equipped with the ability to receive them, and habit brings this ability to completion and fulfilment" (*Nicomachean Ethics*, p. 33).

Much of human behavior is habitual. Individuals may follow or break moral rules (laws) out of habit. A *moral habit* may be defined as *a tendency intentionally to act, or not act, in accordance with a moral rule in a particular moral context.* As previously argued, a habit is an "automatic" response to familiar settings and circumstances (in which there are no conflicting motivations); an individual's moral perception will cause him to see only one causally effective action alternative[30] and to choose without much deliberation this alternative for the action (inaction). Wood and Quinn (2005: 57) argue that "habits are guided by minimal or sporadic cognitive monitoring" and that "habits tend to be repeated through associative mechanisms without conscious decisions to act"

[30] Although an individual may be loosely aware of other action alternatives they lack any causal efficacy for his process of choice (see note 23).

(59). When acting habitually, the perception–choice process is quick and unreflective, even largely unconscious. Another way to put this is to say that in this case an individual's thought process leading up to action (inaction) primarily is one of intuition. Kahneman (2002: 452) argues that "a defining property of intuitive thoughts is that they come to mind spontaneously, like percepts."

It has been maintained that "the more emotionally charged a situation is, the more a person's thinking is dominated by the experiential system" (Carver & Scheier, 1998: 333, referring to a theory by Epstein). If this is true, moral habits may play a particularly important role when an individual responds to provocation.

The idea that much human behavior is guided by an individual's *experiences of past consequences* of actions (inactions) is vital when considering moral habits. Habits grow out of repeated experiences (successes and failures and observed consequences of previous actions and inactions) and therefore the experiences of the outcomes of following or breaking particular moral rules in particular settings will be a significant source in the development of moral habits. The moral habit an individual has at any given time is dependent on his history of moral experiences (his interactions with particular moral contexts). If the individual tends to operate in familiar settings and circumstances his moral actions (inactions) are likely to predominantly express his moral habits (i.e., reflect an acquired tendency to react in a particular way to specific environmental cues in a particular environment based upon repeated experiences of outcomes arising from acting in that particular environment). It is essential to note in this context that this holds both for the habit of following as well as for the habit of breaking certain moral rules in a particular setting.

A key feature of habitual action (inaction) is that it does not involve much deliberation, and therefore that rational choice, fear of consequences (deterrence), and self-control do not play any great role in the process of choice leading up to action (inaction).

An intriguing question is the extent to which individuals' law abidance or law-breaking is a result of moral habituation. I suspect that moral habits may play a crucial role in crime causation, particularly (but not exclusively) as regards what sometimes is referred to as everyday crime (common acts of crime that are generally considered not very serious moral rule violations in a particular cultural context). I also suspect that *processes* of individual and environmental habituation are important in the explanation of criminal career features such as increases over time in the frequency and seriousness of offending (escalation), as well as decreases over time in the frequency and seriousness of offending (de-escalation). Why individuals embark on persistent offending and why they eventually may desist from constant offending may, to an important extent, be related to moral habits and their changes.

Moral judgments

An individual will have to make a moral judgment (deliberate over the moral qualities of perceived action alternatives) when there is no single causally effective action alternative (moral habit) that will guide his moral choice in response to particular motivations in a particular setting. The need to make moral judgments is greatest when an individual encounters unfamiliar settings or circumstances. The key action alternatives when deliberating about moral action (and crime) are those of *whether (i) to act or not to act, or (ii) to act in a particular way* upon a particular motivation, when the action (or inaction), if carried out, would involve the breaking of a moral rule (or the commission of an act of crime). A *moral judgment* may be defined as *the deliberation over the moral implications of acting, or not acting, or acting in a particular way, upon a particular motivation in a particular setting.*

In contrast to action based upon habits, the thought process preceding action based upon judgments is slower and more reflective. The individual is aware (conscious) of making a choice and he is likely to actively monitor carrying out his actions. He generally aims to select the best alternative for action of those perceived (making a rational choice). His executive capability to exercise self-control and the deterrent qualities of the setting in which he takes part and his sensitivity to deterrence are crucial parts of the process (see further below).

Although the *initiation* of a particular moral action may primarily be caused either by a moral habit or by making a moral judgment, when carrying out the action (particularly if it is a prolonged action process) *interferences* may cause the individual to switch the mode of the thought process. The most likely type of switch caused by interference is one from habitual into deliberative guidance of action. For example, the driver who speeds out of habit may suddenly be aware of a police car (speed camera, a group of small children playing at the roadside, etc.) that may cause him to deliberate over whether or not to continue to speed. In other words, certain *morally charged environmental cues* might cause a break in the carrying out of habitual action (inaction) and transform it into deliberative action.

The role of self-control

One of the currently most popular theories of crime causation is that of Gottfredson and Hirschi (1990) in which they stress the crucial role of self-control. They view self-control as an individual trait that develops early in life and thereafter remains stable over the life course. They argue that individuals with poor self-control are more likely to engage in acts of crime. I shall argue that self-control is *not* a trait and that exercising self-control is *only* possible in cases where an individual deliberates over action alternatives.

Self-control is an important part of the process of making a moral judgment.[31] An individual exercises self-control when he acts in accordance with his morality when faced with motivations that involve action alternatives which *conflict* with his morality. Self-control may be viewed as the successful moral management of responses to particular motivations. Bernstein (1999: 191), in a discussion of the philosophies of Pierce and Dewey, emphasizes that "there can be no self-control of conduct or self-criticism unless there are norms by which we can distinguish the true from the false, the right from the wrong, the correct from the incorrect. All reasoning exists in a logical space of norms."

Self-control is a situational (rather than individual) concept in that it refers to an individual's dealings with his environment (i.e., it deals with the question of whether to act or not to act, or act in a particular way, upon a particular motivation in a particular setting). *Self-control* may be defined as *the successful inhibition of perceived action alternatives, or interruption of a course of action, that conflict with an individual's morality*. Self-control, as a successful interruption of a course of action, may occur when the execution of a moral habit is subjected to an interference, which switches a habitual process into one of deliberation, and thereby brings self-control into play (as in the example of speeding given above).

Self-control is only activated when (i) an individual deliberates among action alternatives and (ii) identifies a conflict between acting upon a particular motivation in a particular way and his morality. If breaking a moral rule (or committing a crime) does not involve a conflict between an individual's morality and acting upon a particular motivation, (a poor capability to exercise) self-control plays no part in the causation of the act. In other words, in this case *the moral rule-breaking is a question of morality rather than of poor self-control*. For example, for smokers who do not see it as a moral issue whether to smoke or not in the presence of a

[31] In processes of deliberation where there is no moral issue (right and wrong issue), self-control does not enter into the process of choice.

newborn child, their act of smoking in front of a newborn child is a question of their morality rather than of their poor self-control.

Some individuals will have a greater ability than others to exercise self-control when faced with the judgment of whether or not to act upon temptations and provocations in ways that would conflict with their morals. They will have better *cognitive tools* to manage the expression of their motivations in ways that would not conflict with their morality. These tools may be referred to as *executive capabilities* (or executive functions) and crucially involve abilities of gathering, holding, and effectively processing and evaluating relevant information when deliberating over action alternatives. In other words, the quality of individual deliberation is dependent on their executive capabilities (see further Wikström & Treiber, 2006).

Individuals with strong executive capabilities have a greater ability to control expressions of motivations that would conflict with their morality. They are more likely to be able to combat motivational forces to act in particular ways that conflict with their morals. It is probable that genetic factors and biological factors (e.g., effects of head injuries) may play an important part, interacting with cumulative experiences particularly during childhood, in the *development* of the executive functions that forms the basis for an individual's potential to exercise self-control. Alcohol and drug intoxication may affect an individual's executive capabilities *momentarily*[32] and thereby his potential to exercise self-control.

Although (poor) self-control is presented as the key cause of acts of crime in some theories of crime causation, I submit that morality is a more basic factor in the causation of acts of crime. It is only when an individual *perceives* an action alternative that involves breaking a moral rule, and when he *deliberates* over whether to act upon this alternative or not, that his potential for self-control (based on his executive capabilities) will play a causal role in his choice of actions (inactions).

The role of deterrence

An important part of the moral context of a setting is its deterrent qualities. If there is an *effective monitoring* of and an *effective sanctioning* of moral rule-breakings the setting has strong *deterrent qualities*. The deterrent qualities of a setting are independent of an individual's perception of the setting's deterrent qualities. For example, there seems to

[32] There may also be long-term influences on executive capabilities from alcohol and drug abuse.

be a tendency for some individuals to overestimate the deterrent qualities of a setting (particularly among those who are not regularly involved in breaking moral rules and committing crimes). *Deterrence* may be defined as *the avoidance of breaking a moral rule (committing an act of crime) in a particular setting because of the fear of consequences,*[33] the fear of consequences being dependent on the perceived risk of intervention (*certainty*) and associated risk of sanction (*severity*) if breaking a particular moral rule (committing an act of crime) in a particular setting.

There is no doubt that fear of consequences may influence an individual's choice of actions (inactions). However, if an individual does not see crime as an action alternative (*deterrence irrelevant*), or he commits an act of crime out of habit (*makes no moral judgment*), deterrence does not enter as a factor influencing his choice of actions (inactions). It is only when he sees crime as an action alternative *and* he deliberates over whether to commit the crime or not (*makes a moral judgment*) that the fear of consequences may affect his choice (Wikström, 2006).

However – in a prolonged process of action – the unexpected or sudden appearance of a strong deterrent cue (an interference) may act as a *habit-breaker* (i.e., may turn a habitual process into one of deliberation). Again, the example of speeding out of habit and then suddenly encountering a police car (deterrent cue) is a good illustration of this point.

An individual's potential to exercise self-control may have an important influence on his *sensitivity* to the deterrent qualities of a setting. I submit that individuals with weaker executive capabilities may be less sensitive to the deterrent qualities of a setting. That is, their *threshold* for what levels of monitoring and sanctioning of a particular moral rule-breaking would affect their action choice is higher.

The argument is simple: those who have weaker executive capabilities and thus less potential to exercise self-control (i.e., to control the expression of perceived action alternatives which conflict with their morals) are also, for this very reason, less likely to take into account in their decision-making the risks of intervention and of facing negative consequences (the setting's deterrent qualities). Only when deterrent cues are imminent and strong are they likely to override the motivational forces that prompt individuals (with weaker executive capabilities) to act contrary to their moral values.

[33] I shall use fear of consequences throughout the chapter although concepts like worry and anxiety may often better describe the active emotion in deterrence.

MORAL PERCEPTION	CHOICE: THOUGHT PROCESS	ACTION GUIDANCE	INTENTIONAL MORAL ACTION
	MORAL JUDGMENT		
No causally effective alternative	**Deliberation** (Rational choice, self-control, deterrence)	**Self-monitoring** (conscious)	Rule-following or rule-breaking
One causally effective alternative	**Intuition** (Experiential, inherent*)	**Habitual** (unconscious)	Rule-following or rule-breaking
	MORAL HABIT		

Figure 3.4. Two basic processes of choice and action guidance. *Some habits may have a basis in inherent tendencies to react in particular ways to particular environmental stimuli. Carver and Scheier (1998: 336) talk about two sources of automaticity: (i) inherent, primitive in-built tendencies; and (ii) repetition.

Although the impact of deterrence on an individual's choice of action may be limited to cases in which that individual deliberates (makes a moral judgment), an individual's *cumulative experiences* of operating in settings with particular deterrent qualities may be an important factor in his development of moral habits. It is probable that repeated exposure to settings with strong deterrent qualities promote the development of habits of moral rule-following, while repeated exposure to settings with weak deterrent qualities encourages the development of habits of moral rule-breaking. Experiences of monitoring and sanctioning of moral rule-breakings is an important part of an individual's moral education and moral habit formation.

Moral choices

To make a moral choice is to form an intention to carry out a particular moral action (i.e., an action [inaction] that is carried out under the guidance of what is the right or wrong thing to do). There are, as discussed above, two principal ways of arriving at a moral choice – out of moral habit or based on a moral judgment (Figure 3.4). Only when making a moral judgment does rational choice, self-control, and deterrence play a central role in the process of choice. On the basis of their moral choices individuals will take moral action, which may, or may not, constitute acts of moral rule-breaking (acts of crime).

Explaining individual differences in crime involvement, area and place differences in crime rates, and crime trends

Explaining why an individual commits an act of crime is *different* from explaining why there are individual differences in crime involvement, why areas and places vary in their crime rates, and why there are changes over time in the crime rate of a geographical location. However, I submit that without a proper understanding of what moves individuals to commit acts of crime (break moral rules) it is difficult to come up with credible explanations of individual differences in crime involvement, area and place variations in crime rates, and changes over time in the crime rate of a geographical location.

If individuals' acts of crime are fundamentally caused by their moral perceptions and moral choices (intentional causation), which, in turn, are based on the interaction between their morality and the moral context in which they operate, explaining individual differences, area and place variations, and changes over time in crime all come down to explaining individual differences, spatial variation, and temporal changes in the morality of individuals and the moral contexts in which they operate.

Explaining *individual differences* in crime involvement is fundamentally a question of explaining *why* individuals come to differ (i) in their morality (and their supporting executive capabilities) and (ii) in the moral contexts in which they operate. It is a question of identifying *what* developmental processes – under the influence of *what* systemic factors and their related social processes (e.g., inequality and segregation) – will *form and shape* the morality of individuals (and their executive capabilities) and affect their *exposure* to particular moral contexts.

Explaining *area and place variation* in crime rates is fundamentally a question of explaining *why* areas or places differ (i) in the morality of people who reside or visit the area or place, and (ii) in their moral context. It is a question of addressing how systemic factors and their related social processes influence the distribution in space of individuals with different morality and how they create spatially different moral contexts (settings).

Explaining *crime trends* is fundamentally a question of explaining *why* there are changes over time in a specific geographical unit (i) in the morality of individuals present, and (ii) in the moral contexts in which they operate. It is a question of addressing what social processes cause change in the social conditions of a particular geographical unit that influence the moral characteristics of the settings in which individuals develop (lagged effects on action) and act (instant effects on action).

References

Agnew, R. (2005). *Why Do Criminals Offend? A General Theory of Crime and Delinquency*. Los Angeles: Roxbury.

Aristotle, *Nicomachean Ethics*. Translated by Martin Ostwald (1999). *Library of Liberal Arts*. Englewood Cliffs, NJ: Prentice Hall.

Bernstein, R. J. (1999). *Praxis and Action. Contemporary Philosophies of Human Activity*. Philadelphia: University of Pennsylvania Press.

Blum, L. A. (1994). *Moral Perception and Particularity*. Cambridge: Cambridge University Press.

Braithwaite, J. (1989). *Crime, Shame and Reintegration*. Cambridge: Cambridge University Press.

Brantingham, P. J. & Brantingham, P. L. (1993). "Environment, routine and situation. Toward a pattern theory of crime." In R. V. Clarke & M. Felson (eds.), *Routine Activity and Rational Choice*. New Brunswick, NJ: Transaction.

Bunge, M. (1999). *The Sociology–Philosophy Connection*. New Brunswick, NJ: Transaction.

Bursik, R. J. & Grasmick, H. G. (1993). *Neighborhoods and Crime*. New York: Lexington Books.

Carver, C. S. & Scheier, M. F. (1998). *On The Self-Regulation of Behavior*. Cambridge: Cambridge University Press.

Davidson, D. (1980). *Essays on Actions and Events*. Oxford: Clarendon Press.

(2004). *Problems of Rationality*. Oxford: Clarendon Press.

Dewey, J. (2002). *Human Nature and Conduct*. Amherst, MA: Prometheus.

Dretske, F. (2000). *Perception, Knowledge and Belief. Selected Essays*. Cambridge: Cambridge University Press.

Elster, J. (1999). *Alchemies of the Mind. Rationality and the Emotions*. Cambridge: Cambridge University Press.

Farrington, D. P. (1992), "Explaining the beginning, progress and ending of antisocial behavior from birth to adulthood." In J. McCord (ed.), *Facts, Frameworks, and Forecasts: Advances in Criminological Theory*, vol. III. New Brunswick, NJ: Transaction.

(1996). "The explanation and prevention of youthful offending." In J. D. Hawkins (ed.), *Delinquency and Crime*. Cambridge: Cambridge University Press.

(2000). "Explaining and preventing crime: the globalization of knowledge – The American Society of Criminology 1999 Presidential Address." *Criminology* 38(1): 1–24.

Forgas, J. P. & Laham, S. M. (2005). "The interaction between affect and motivation in social judgement and behavior." In J. P. Forgas, K. D.

Williams, & S. M. Laham (eds.), *Social Motivation. Conscious and Unconscious Processes*. Cambridge: Cambridge University Press.

Gottfredson, D. C. & Hirschi, T. (1990). *A General Theory of Crime*. Stanford: Stanford University Press.

Hirschi, T. (1986). "On the compatability of rational choice and control theories of crime." In D. B. Cornish & R. V. Clarke (eds.), *The Reasoning Criminal*. New York: Springer Verlag.

Holland, P. W. (1986). "Statistics and causal inference." *Journal of the American Statistical Association* 81: 945–960.

Kahneman, D. (2002). "Maps of bounded rationality: a perspective on intuitive judgement and choice." Nobel Prize Lecture, Stockholm, December 8.

Maund, B. (2003). *Perception*. Montreal and Kingston: McGill–Queen's University Press.

Mele, A. R. (2001). *Autonomous Agents. From Self-Control to Autonomy*. Oxford: Oxford University Press.

O'Shaughnessy, B. (1997). "Trying (as the mental 'pineal gland')." In A. R. Mele (ed.), *The Philosophy of Action*. Oxford: Oxford University Press.

Salmon, W. C. (1998). *Causality and Explanation*. New York: Oxford University Press.

Sampson, R. J. & Groves, W. B. (1989). "Community structure and crime: testing social disorganization theory." *American Journal of Sociology* 94: 774–802.

Schick, F. (1991). *Understanding Action. An Essay on Reasons*. Cambridge: Cambridge University Press.

(1997). *Making Choices. A Recasting of Decision Theory*. Cambridge: Cambridge University Press.

Searle, J. R. (1983). *Intentionality. An Essay in the Philosophy of Mind*. Cambridge: Cambridge University Press.

(2001). *Rationality in Action*. Cambridge, MA: MIT Press.

Von Wright, H. G. (1971). *Understanding and Explanation*. London: Routledge & Kegan Paul.

Wood, W. & Quinn J. M. (2005). "Habits and the structure of motivation in everyday life." In J. P. Forgas, K. D. Williams, & S. M. Laham (eds.), *Social Motivation. Conscious and Unconscious Processes*. Cambridge: Cambridge University Press.

Wikström, P.-O. H. (2004). "Crime as alternative: towards a cross-level situational action theory of crime causation." In J. McCord (ed.), *Beyond Empiricism: Institutions and Intentions in the Study of Crime*. Advances in Criminological Theory 13. New Brunswick, NJ: Transaction.

(2005). "The social origins of pathways in crime: towards a developmental ecological action theory of crime involvement and its changes." In D. P. Farrington (ed.), *Integrated Developmental and Life Course Theories of Offending*. Advances in Criminological Theory 14. New Brunswick, NJ: Transaction.

(2006). "Deterrence and deterrence experiences: preventing crime through the threat of punishment." In S. G. Shoham (ed.), *International Penology Textbook*. Eastbourne: Sussex Academic Press.

Wikström, P.-O. & Sampson, R. J. (2003). "Social mechanisms of community influences on crime and pathways in criminality." In B. B. Lahey, T. E. Moffitt, & A. Caspi (eds.), *Causes of Conduct Disorder and Serious Juvenile Delinquency*. New York: Guilford Press.

Wikström, P.-O. & Treiber, K. (2006). "The role of self-control in crime causation: beyond Gottfredson and Hirschi's General Theory of Crime." Unpublished paper.

Wilson, J. Q. & Herrnstein, R. J. (1985). *Crime and Human Nature*. New York: Touchstone Books.

Wrong, D. H. (1994). *The Problem of Order. What Unites and Divides Society?* New York: The Free Press.

4 Evidence from behavioral genetics for environmental contributions to antisocial conduct

Terrie Moffitt and Avshalom Caspi

Despite assiduous efforts to eliminate it, antisocial behavior is still a problem. Approximately 20 percent of people in the developed world experience victimization by perpetrators of violent and non-violent illegal behavior each year (US Bureau of Justice Statistics, 2002). The *World Report on Violence and Health* (World Health Organization, 2002) tallies the staggering burden of mortality, disease, disability, and compromised well-being brought about by perpetrators of family violence and other violent crimes. Behavioral science needs to achieve a more complete understanding of the causes of antisocial behavior to provide an evidence base for effectively controlling and preventing it. A new wave of intervention research in the last decade has demonstrated clear success for a number of programs designed to prevent antisocial behavior (http://www.preventingcrime.org/; Heinrich, Brown, & Aber, 1999; Sherman *et al.*, 1999; Weissberg, Kumpfer, & Seligman, 2003). Nevertheless, the reduction in antisocial behavior brought about by even the best prevention programs is, on average, modest (Olds *et al.*, 1998; Wasserman & Miller, 1998; Heinrich, Brown, & Aber, 1999; Wilson, Gottfredson, & Najaka, 2001; Dodge, 2003; Wandersman & Florin, 2003). The best-designed intervention programs reduce serious juvenile offenders' recidivism by only about 12 percent (Lipsey & Wilson, 1998). This modest success of interventions that were theory-driven, well-designed, and amply funded sends a clear message that we do not yet understand the causes of antisocial behavior well enough to prevent it.

Why look for causes of antisocial behavior in the family?

Simultaneous with the new wave of research evaluating interventions is a wave of research pointing to the concentration of antisocial behavior in families. In the 1970s, the astounding discovery that fewer than 10 percent of individuals perpetrate more than 50 percent of crimes (Wolfgang, Figlio, & Sellin, 1972) prompted researchers to investigate individual career criminals (Blumstein & Cohen, 1987) and examine the childhood origins of such persistent reoffenders (Moffitt, 1993). This research constructed the evidence base supporting the new wave of preventive intervention trials (Yoshikawa, 1994). Recently journalists have drawn public attention to certain families who across several generations seem to contain far more than their share of criminal family members (Butterfield, 1996, 2002). This familial concentration of crime has been confirmed as a characteristic of the general population (Farrington, Barnes, & Lambert, 1996; Rowe & Farrington, 1997; Farrington *et al.*, 2001). In general, fewer than 10 percent of the families in any community account for more than 50 percent of that community's criminal offences. The family concentration of antisocial behavior could be explained by a genetic influence on antisocial behavior, but it might just as easily be explained by non-genetic social transmission of antisocial behavior within families. Again, causation is not well understood. Studies that cannot disentangle genetic and environmental influences cannot help.

Antisocial behavior research is stuck in the risk-factor stage

Influential reviewers have concluded that the study of antisocial behavior has been stuck in the "risk-factor" stage (Farrington, 1988, 2003; Hinshaw, 2002; Rutter, 2003a, 2003b) because so few studies have used designs that are able to document causality (Rutter *et al.*, 2001). A variable is called a "risk factor" if it has a documented predictive relation with antisocial outcomes, whether or not the association is causal. The causal status of most risk factors is unknown; we know what statistically predicts psychopathology outcomes, but not how or why (Kraemer *et al.*, 1997; Kraemer, 2003). There are consequences to the field's failure to push beyond the risk-factor stage to achieve an understanding of causal processes. Valuable resources have been wasted because intervention programs have proceeded on the basis of risk factors, without sufficient research to understand causal processes. Mentoring programs are based on evidence that poor adult–child bonding is a risk factor for antisocial outcomes. Family preservation programs are based on evidence that family dissolution is a risk factor. Peer-group skills programs are based on evidence that peer delinquency is a risk factor. Mentoring programs and family preservation have not worked (Wasserman & Miller, 1998), and peer-group programs have been shown to exacerbate adolescent offending (Klein, 1995; Dishion, McCord, & Poulin, 1999). Similarly, Drug Abuse Resistance Education (DARE), gun buybacks, boot camps, Outward Bound type programs, after-school leisure-time programs, youth job programs, and neighborhood watch programs were all originally designed to correct known risk factors for delinquent offending, but formal evaluation has revealed that none of these interventions works to reduce antisocial behavior, and some of them have marked iatrogenic effects (Sherman *et al.*, 1999). Simply put, the cost of getting causation wrong is not trivial.

A central barrier to interpreting an association between an alleged environmental risk factor and an antisocial outcome as a cause–effect association is, of course, the old bugbear that correlation is not causation. Some unknown third variable may account for the association, and that third variable may well be heritable. For example, does the cycle of violence from abusive parent to aggressive child arise from environmental transmission, or genetic transmission (DiLalla & Gottesman, 1991)? More than a hundred studies have addressed the question of genetic influence on antisocial behavior, and reviews and meta-analyses of this literature conclude that genes influence 40 to 50 percent of its variation in the population (Miles & Carey, 1997; Rhee & Waldman, 2002). Perhaps the most pragmatic implication from this evidence of genetic influence for antisocial behavior is that we can no longer blithely assume environmental causation, but rather we must re-examine each putative environmental risk factor for antisocial behavior, one by one, while using research methods that are capable of applying explicit controls for genetic effects (Rutter *et al.*, 2001). Because much research on intergenerational transmission continues without genetic controls (Serbin & Karp, 2003), this point cannot be made too often. Without control for genetic variation, further risk-factor research remains ambiguous if not uninformative.

During the 1990s, the assumption that "nurture" influences behavior came under fire. Traditional socialization studies of antisocial behavior, which could not separate environmental influences from their correlated genes, were challenged by four important empirical discoveries: (i) ostensible environmental measures are influenced by genetic factors (Plomin & Bergeman, 1991); (ii) parents' heritable traits influence the environments they provide for their children (Plomin, 1994; Kendler, 1996); (iii) people's genes influence the environments they encounter (Plomin, DeFries, & Loehlin, 1977; Kendler, 1996); and (iv) environmental influences did not seem to account for the similarity among persons growing up in the same family (Rowe, 1994).

It was said that although non-behavioral-genetic studies might show that certain rearing experiences predict young people's antisocial outcomes, theories of causation based on findings from such designs are guilty of a fundamental logical error: mistaking correlation for causation (Scarr, 1992). These challenges culminated in admonishments that so far the evidence for genetic influences outweighed the evidence for environmental influences within the family (Rowe, 1994; Harris, 1998). Many social scientists responded to this claim, reasserting evidence for environmental influences (Collins *et al.*, 2000; Vandell, 2000; Reid, Patterson, & Snyder, 2002). However, the reason there is all this controversy about the importance of the family environment in the first place is that the evidence base was not decisive enough to compel both camps. The best way forward to resolve the debate is to use research designs that can provide leverage to test environmental causation.

Ordinary studies cannot test whether a risk factor is causal, and it would be unethical to assign children to experimental conditions expected to induce aggression. Fortunately, researchers can use three other methods for testing causation: natural-experiment studies of within-individual change (Cicchetti, 2003; Costello *et al.*, 2003); treatment experiments (Howe, Reiss, & Yuh, 2002); and, the focus of this review, behavioral-genetic designs. None of the three alone can provide decisive proof of causation, but if all supply corroborative evidence by ruling out alternative non-causal explanations about a risk factor, then a strong case for causation can be made.

How can behavioral-genetic research help?

Behavioral-genetic designs are a useful addition to a toolkit for testing environmental causation. It is somewhat counterintuitive to think about using behavioral-genetic designs to control for and rule out genetic influences while highlighting environmental influences in bas-relief, but paradoxically, this is one of their strongest applications. Behavioral genetics disentangles genetic from non-genetic aspects of familial transmission, and thereby can rule out one of the most serious challenges to environmental causation: a heritable third variable that accounts for the correlation between a putative environmental risk factor and antisocial outcome. Behavioral genetics also has methods to put genetic and non-genetic influences back together again in a systematic and controlled way, to work out how they jointly cause behavior. Behavioral genetics has been rapidly moving beyond the initial question of heritability (Kendler, 2001; Dick & Rose, 2002), to apply its methods to a broad array of causal questions (Moffitt, 2005). Concurring evidence from behavioral-genetic methods, natural experiments of within-individual change, and treatment experiments will move the study of antisocial behavior beyond the risk-factor stage where it has been stuck, to inform strong causal theory about how antisocial behavior develops.

Testing hypotheses about environmental causation

Before reviewing studies that have applied behavioral-genetic designs to testing environmental causation, we address two often-voiced reservations about behavioral-genetic studies. One reservation is about whether effect sizes from studies of twins and adoptees can be generalized to the population. The other reservation is about whether assumptions limit inference from twin studies or adoption studies.

How well do twins and adoptees represent the population?

An important issue is whether the prevalence rates and distributions of antisocial behaviors among twins and adoptees represent antisocial behaviors among ordinary people (Rutter, 2002). This issue is relevant to the question of whether estimates of environmental influence from behavioral-genetic samples apply to the general population. Although this has been assumed more than it has been examined, the assumption is probably defensible for twin studies because twin-versus-singleton comparisons have not found differences in the prevalence rates of antisocial behavior or antisocial personality traits (Gjone & Novik, 1995; van den Oord *et al.*, 1995; Levy *et al.*, 1996; Simonoff *et al.*, 1997; van der Valk *et al.*, 1998; Moilanen *et al.*, 1999; Johnson *et al.*, 2002). Adoptees, on the other hand, tend to show elevated rates of antisocial outcomes, although the skewed distribution of these outcomes has the same shape within adoptee samples as in the general population (Hutchings & Mednick, 1973; Sharma, McGue, & Benson, 1998). Importantly, the effect sizes for *associations between* risk factors and psychopathology outcomes have been found to be similar across behavioral-genetic and non-genetic studies. For instance, in our own Environmental Risk Longitudinal Twin Study (The E-risk Study; Moffitt *et al.*, 2002), associations between children's behavior and maternal depression, exposure to domestic violence, maternal warmth and negativity, maternal smoking during pregnancy, socio-economic status, and neighborhood deprivation are all comparable to these associations in the wider literature.

Inference from different types of behaviorial-genetic designs

Antisocial behavior has been studied in twins reared together, adoptees, and twins reared apart. Behaviorial-genetic research is not limited to exotic samples; researchers also examine ordinary families whose members vary in genetic relatedness (e.g., full siblings, half-siblings, step-siblings, cousins, and unrelated children reared in the same family) (Rowe, Almeida, & Jacobson, 1999). This variety of research designs offers a special advantage for inference, because comparing their estimates tells us that the environmental effect sizes for antisocial behavior are robust across different designs; they are not biased by the limitations and flaws peculiar to one design.

A number of potential flaws are unique to adoption studies. First, adoption agencies may attempt to maximize similarity between the adoptee's biological and adoptive families to increase the child's chance of fitting in with the new family (this is called "selective placement"). Related to this, biological mothers who intend to give their baby away may neglect prenatal care and continue to abuse substances during pregnancy, and many unwanted babies experience institutionalization before they are adopted. If adoptive homes, prenatal care, and institutional care are selectively worse for the babies given up by antisocial biological mothers, this could bias estimates of heritability upward and estimates of environmental effects downward, by misattributing the criminogenic influences of these three unmeasured non-genetic factors to any criminogenic influence of genes (Mednick *et al.*, 1986).

Second, both adoptees and twins reared apart are likely to be reared in home environments that are unusually good for children because adoptive parents are carefully screened. Adoption breaks up the association between genetic risk and environmental risk naturally occurring in ordinary families by removing genetically at-risk children from damaging homes and placing them in salutary homes. As a result, interactions between environmental adversity and genetic vulnerability that exacerbate behavior problems in ordinary children (and twins) are uncommon among adoptees (Stoolmiller, 1999). The restricted range of rearing environments resulting from screening of adoptive parents could suppress estimates of environmental effects and thus bias heritability estimates upward (Fergusson, Lynskey, & Horwood, 1995; Stoolmiller, 1999). However, this flaw of adoption studies is offset by studies of national twin registers (e.g., Cloninger & Gottesman, 1987) or stratified high-risk twin samples (e.g., Moffitt *et al.*, 2002), because such sampling frames represent the complete population range of environmental and genetic backgrounds.

Studies of twins avoid the potential flaws of adoption studies, but they suffer several potential flaws of their own. First, the logic of the twin design assumes that all of the greater similarity of monozygotic (MZ), compared to dizygotic (DZ), twins can safely be ascribed to MZ twins' greater genetic similarity. This "equal environments assumption" requires that MZ twins are not treated more alike than DZ twins on the causes of antisocial behavior (Kendler *et al.*, 1994). Because MZ twins look identical they might be treated more similarly than DZ twins in some way that promotes antisocial behavior, and as a result, estimates of heritability from studies of twins reared together could be biased upward, and estimates of environmental effects could be biased downward, relative to the correct population value (DiLalla, 2002). In fact, we found that young MZ twins receive somewhat more similar discipline than DZ twins (Jaffee *et al.*, 2004a). However, studies of adoptees do not suffer this flaw, and neither do studies of twins reared apart, because MZ twins reared apart do not share environments (unless their genetically influenced behaviors evoke similar reactions from care-givers in their separate rearing environments, which is a genetic effect).

Second, in studies of twins, MZ twins differ more than DZ twins in prenatal factors affecting intrauterine growth; for example, MZ twins sharing the same chorion appear to suffer more foetal competition for nutrients. These intrauterine factors also violate the assumption that environments are equal for MZ and DZ twins, but intrauterine differences tend to make MZ twins less alike than their genotypes and thus would bias heritability estimates downward and environmental effects upward (Rutter, 2002).

Third, genomic factors that make some MZ twin pairs' genotypes less than perfectly identical (such as random inactivation of genes on one of each girl's two X chromosomes; Jorgensen *et al.*, 1992) could in theory affect twin-study estimates, but so far no evidence shows that these processes influence behavior.

Fourth, parental assortative mating can bias heritability estimates. Coupled partners are known to share similarly high or low levels of antisocial behaviors (Krueger *et al.*, 1998; Galbaud du Fort *et al.*, 2002). When parents of twins mate for similarity this should increase the genetic similarity of DZ twins, but MZ twins' genetic similarity cannot increase beyond its original 100 percent, and as a result heritability estimates will be biased downward and environmental estimates upward relative to the correct population value. The implication of biological-parent assortative mating for adoption studies is the opposite; biological-parent similarity for antisocial behaviors would bias adoptees' heritability upward relative to the correct population value (because adoptee/

biological-parent correlations would represent a double-dose of parental genes).

Fifth, twin studies using adult reports to measure behavior sometimes suffer from rater artefacts; for example, adults may mix up or conflate the behavior of MZ twins and they may exaggerate differences between DZ twins. Such a rater artefact does not afflict adoption studies (nor twin studies using the twins' self-reports, as twins do not confuse themselves).

In any case, comparisons between designs have revealed that studies of twins reared together yield estimates that are more similar than different to the estimates from studies of twins reared apart or of adoptees (Rhee & Waldman, 2002). On the one hand, this is because any bias arising from factors such as selective adoptee placement, violations of the equal-environment assumption, intrauterine twin differences, or assortative mating, is only very small (Miles & Carey, 1997; Rutter, 2002). On the other hand, these factors bias estimates upward as often as they bias them downward, canceling each other out. The bottom line is that it is important for tests of environmental risk to exploit a variety of behavioral-genetic designs, as well as experimental designs and studies of within-individual change.

Behavioral-genetic studies of parenting effects on children's aggression

To illustrate how behavioral-genetic designs are helping to move the study of antisocial behaviors from the risk-factor stage to causal understanding, we next review research investigating one risk factor, parents' "bad parenting" of their children, and one antisocial outcome, "children's physical aggression." We have construed "bad parenting" broadly; this review includes risk factors from mothers' smoking heavily during pregnancy, to inconsistent or unskilled discipline, to frank child neglect and abuse. The outcome, "children's physical aggression" includes hitting, fighting, bullying, cruelty, and so forth. It is already known that "bad parenting" statistically predicts children's aggression, and bad parenting plays a central causal role in leading theories of antisocial behavior (Thornberry, 1996; Lahey, Moffitt, & Caspi, 2003). The aim of the research reviewed here is to determine whether the relation between bad parenting and children's aggression is a true cause–effect relation, such that interventions that stop bad parenting can reasonably be expected to prevent aggression from emerging. This aim is fundamental because studies of adoptions have documented the dispiriting fact that aggression emerges in adopted children despite the fact that they were separated from their at-risk biological parents at birth and reared by skilled and loving adoptive parents.

Our research review systematically tackles six questions in turn. (1) Is there evidence that children's aggression cannot be wholly explained by genetic factors, and must have non-genetic environmental causes as well? (2) Do parents' genes influence bad parenting? (3) Does a genetic effect on parents' bad parenting confound a cause–effect interpretation of the association between bad parenting and children's aggression? (4) Does a genetic "child effect" evoke bad parenting to further confound a cause–effect interpretation of the association between bad parenting and children's aggression? (5) After all genetic confounds are controlled, does bad parenting have an environmentally mediated causal effect on children's aggression? (6) Does bad parenting interact with genetic risk, such that the effects of bad parenting are even stronger among genetically vulnerable children? Each question is presented in a separate section below, with the research designs that can answer each question being described first, and the findings so far being reviewed next. The research designs covered here are not intended to be exhaustive, but are intended to illustrate what kinds of studies could be done, using the logic of behavioral-genetic methods.

Question 1: Is children's aggression wholly accounted for by genetic factors, or does it have non-genetic causes as well?

More than a hundred twin, adoption, and sibling studies have been carried out to answer this question. This work has revealed that genetic causal processes account for only about half of the population variation in antisocial behavior, thereby unequivocally proving that environmental influences account for the other half. This fact constitutes a remarkable contribution to the understanding of causation (Plomin, 1994). In addition, it is now recognized that the heritability coefficient indexes not only the direct effects of genes, but also the effects of interactions between genes and family-wide environments (Purcell 2002; Rutter & Silberg, 2002). In such interactions the effect of an environmental risk may be even larger than previously reported, among the subgroup of individuals having a vulnerable genotype. This is likely to be the case for antisocial behaviors.

One useful feature of behavioral-genetic research designs is that they offer two powerful methods for documenting the importance of environmental effects (Plomin *et al.*, 2001). One of these methods of detecting environmental influence tests whether any of the family members in a study sample are more similar than can be explained by the proportion of genes they share. For instance, MZ twins' genetic similarity is twice that of DZ twins. Therefore, if nothing but genes influenced antisocial behavior MZ twins' behavior ought to be at least twice as similar as that of DZ twins. If not, then something environmental has influenced the twins and enhanced their similarity. For almost all human behavioral traits studied so far, environmental factors shared by family members (variously labeled the "family-wide," "common," or "shared" environment) have not been found to make family members similar. In other words, the estimated influence of shared environment has been found to be almost nil for most human behavioral traits (Rowe, 1994). Antisocial behavior is a marked exception. A comparison of shared-environment effects across ten psychiatric disorders revealed that such effects were stronger for antisocial personality and conduct disorder than for affective, anxiety, or substance disorders (Kendler *et al.*, 2003). Estimates of shared-environment effects on population variation in antisocial behavior are about 15 to 20 percent as reported by meta-analyses and reviews (Miles & Carey, 1997; Rhee & Waldman, 2002). The small size of this shared-environment estimate should not be too surprising, because the twin-study coefficient indexing the shared environment does not include environmental effects involved in gene–environment interactions. We can think of the shared-environment coefficient as the residual effects of shared environments that remain after controlling for gene–environment interactions. As most human behavior involves nature–nurture interplay, it is remarkable that as much as 20 percent of the population variation in antisocial behavior can be attributed to direct environmental effects not conditional on genetic vulnerability.

The second method of detecting the presence of environmental influence is to test whether any family members are less similar than expected from the proportion of genes they share (Plomin & Daniels, 1987). For instance, if a pair of MZ twins, despite sharing all their genes, are not perfectly identical in antisocial behavior, this indicates that experience has reduced their behavioral similarity. After estimates of the influences of heritability (50 percent) and shared family environment (20 percent) on antisocial behavior are calculated, the remainder of population variation, 30 percent, is assumed to reflect environmental influences not shared by family members (variously labelled "unique," "person-specific," or "non-shared" experiences). These experiences might include criminogenic experiences unique to the individual and not shared with his sibling, such as a head injury, being the unique target of sexual abuse, living with an antisocial spouse, or serving a prison sentence. There are two caveats about estimates of the effect of non-shared environments. First, measurement error inflates these estimates because random mistakes in measuring behavior will result in scores that look different for twins in an MZ pair, and it is not easy to differentiate such faux MZ differences from true MZ differences caused by the twins' non-shared experiences. The second caveat is that the coefficient for non-shared environmental effects indexes not only the direct effects of non-shared experiences, but also the effects of interactions between non-shared environments and genes (Purcell, 2002; Rutter & Silberg, 2002). Thus, some portion of the non-shared environment effect may be attributable to error or genes, and the size of this portion is unknown.

It would be highly unlikely that any behavior disorder is wholly determined by genes, but it is important to begin any program of research into causal processes by ascertaining what effect sizes we can expect for both genetic and environmental influences under natural conditions, in the absence of intervention. For overall population variation in antisocial behavior, these effects are 50:50. Therefore, because behavioral-genetic studies have shown that the answer to question 1, 'Does children's aggression have any non-genetic causes?' is a definite yes, there is strong evidence that environmental causes must exist.

Question 2: Do parents' genes influence bad parenting?

It is important to know the size of the contribution of parents' genotypes to their bad parenting, because if parenting is substantially influenced by parents' genotype, then its correlation with children's aggression cannot be confidently interpreted as a cause–effect relation. But how much do people's genes influence their parenting? Answering this question requires researchers to treat parenting as a phenotype in behavioral-genetic research.

What research designs can be used to answer this question? We can study *adoptions* to test if biological parents' bad parenting (of the children they did not give up for adoption) predicts that their adopted-away child will also engage in bad parenting when she becomes a parent. Such a study would show that bad parenting is genetically transmitted, in the absence of social transmission. However, this study has not been conducted, because of the difficulty of obtaining parenting data from two generations of adults separated by adoption.

We can study *adult MZ twins reared apart* to test whether they are similar in providing bad parenting to their children. The Swedish Adoption Twin Study of Aging carried out this design, by asking fifty pairs of adult MZ twins reared apart to report their own parenting styles using the Moos Family Environment Scale (Plomin *et al.*, 1989). Results indicated that 25% of the variation in parenting was genetically influenced.

We can study *adult twin parents* to ascertain how much variation in their bad parenting is attributable to genetic versus environmental sources. The aforementioned Swedish twin study carried out this design, studying 386 adult twin pairs, and again results indicated that 25% of the variation in the Family Environment Scale was genetically influenced (Plomin *et al.*, 1989). In another study, 1,117 pairs of mid-life twin volunteers who had on average reared three children reported their own parenting styles. The heritability estimate for an overall measure of parenting, called "care," was 34 (Perusse *et al.*, 1994). A Virginia sample of 262 pairs of adult twin mothers reported their own parenting styles, and the heritability estimates were 21% for "physical discipline," 27% for "limit-setting," and 38% for "warmth" (Kendler, 1996; Wade & Kendler, 2000). An Oregon sample of 186 pairs of adult twin mothers and adoptee mothers reported their own parenting styles, and the heritability estimates ranged from 60% for "positive support" to 24% for "control" (Losoya *et al.*, 1997). These findings were echoed by a study of 236 pairs of adult twin mothers reporting their own parenting, in which genetic effects were found for "positivity" and "monitoring" (Towers, Spotts, & Niederhiser, 2001; Niederhiser *et al.*, 2004). Finally, a study of 1,034 adult twin mothers found a heritability estimate of more than 50% for self-reported smoking during pregnancy, which is a known prenatal parenting risk factor for children's aggression (D'Onofrio *et al.*, 2003).

What research is needed? This very small literature is a good beginning, but a number of limitations need to be overcome. First, the studies have relied on the twin design, and twin-design weaknesses ought to be complemented by the strengths of the adoption design (see Deater-Deckard, Fulker, & Plomin, 1999). Second, measurement has relied on parents' self-reports, and thus the findings are a mix between genetic influences on actual parenting behavior and genetic influences on self-perception and self-presentation (Plomin, 1994; Kendler, 1996). As a third limitation, studies have tended to focus on mothers and have excluded fathers, for the obvious reason that fathers' non-participation in research disproportionately characterizes families of aggressive children. However, fathers' antisocial behavior in the home is a central aspect of bad parenting that predicts children's aggression (Jaffee *et al.*, 2003). Fourth, and most serious for our purposes of investigating antisocial behavior, the samples under-represent families at serious risk, and the parenting measures do not address the most powerful bad-parenting risk factors for children's aggression, such as exposure to domestic violence, child neglect, maternal rejection, and child abuse. These serious forms of bad parenting themselves constitute antisocial acts, and as a result we should anticipate that the influence of parents' genes on them is much stronger than the genetic influences found for parenting styles within the normative range, such as spanking, monitoring, or limit-setting. Because serious bad parenting is antisocial, it is not unreasonable to expect genetic influence on serious bad parenting to resemble genetic influence on other antisocial behaviors (50%).

The answer to question 2, "Do parents' genes influence bad parenting?," seems to be "probably." It may be surprising that so little research has been done into the question of a genetic contribution to bad parenting. The question has been neglected because parenting has not often been viewed by behavioral-genetic researchers as a phenotypic outcome variable. Moreover, developmental researchers who are interested in parenting as an outcome almost never adopt behaviorial-genetic research methods. It is quite likely that bad parenting is under some amount of genetic influence because parenting styles are known to be associated with parents' personality traits (Belsky & Barends, 2002; Spinath & O'Connor, 2003) and personality traits are known to be under genetic influence (Plomin & Caspi, 1999). Bad parenting should be treated as a phenotype in future behavioral-genetic research (McGuire, 2003).

Question 3: Does an effect of parents' genes on bad parenting confound a cause–effect interpretation of the association between bad parenting and children's aggression?

The technical term for this question is "passive" correlation between genotype and an environmental measure, often abbreviated as "rGE" (Plomin, DeFries, & Loehlin, 1977). A passive rGE confound occurs when a child's behavior and the environment his parents provide are correlated because they have the same origins in his parents' genotype (i.e., not because bad parenting itself causes children's aggression). Parents may transmit to their child a genetic liability for aggression, and simultaneously provide an environment of violent, abusive maltreatment that is symptomatic of the parent's genetic liability for aggression. To the extent that such parenting is under genetic influence, then the observed association between bad parenting and child aggression could be a spurious artefact of a third variable that causes both: genetic transmission. This is why it is important to study passive rGE.

It is important to note that the mere evidence that bad parenting is under the influence of parents' genes (question 2) is not sufficient to conclude that this genetic influence goes on to mediate the connection between bad parenting and children's aggression. Rutter and Silberg (2002) make this point, explaining that genes influence which mothers have low birth-weight babies but that babies' birth-weights are wholly determined by environmental conditions, not by any genes inherited from their mothers. To take this point to an extreme, genes influence which breeds of dog bite readily, but once a dog bites, injury to the unfortunate victim is wholly environmentally mediated. Therefore, despite the fact that antisocial behavior is concentrated in families and this concentration is known to be under the influence of parental genes, it remains possible that the pathway from bad parenting to children's aggression is wholly environmentally mediated. For this reason it is important to disentangle (i) the genetic origins of bad parenting from (ii) the genetic and environmental mechanisms by which bad parenting produces children's aggression.

None the less, the pairing of bad parenting with children's aggression as risk-factor-and-outcome intuitively raises the question of genetic mediation. The reason behind this intuition is that bad parenting and children's aggression both bear a relation to the antisocial trait. Bad parenting and juveniles' aggression both violate the rights and safety of victims, and both are criteria for antisocial personality disorder (American Psychiatric Association, 1994). Moreover, aggressive children followed up to adulthood are found to be bad parents (Fagot *et al.*, 1998; Jaffee *et al.*, 2001; Serbin & Karp, 2003). If bad parenting and children's aggression are age-heterotypic expressions of the same genetically influenced trait, this could constitute an rGE that rules out any causal status for bad parenting.

What research designs can be used to answer this question? There are at least four appropriate research designs, but to our knowledge none of them has been carried out. We can study *adoptions* to test if the biological parents' bad parenting predicts the adopted-away children's aggression, even if parent and child never have contact. This study has not been conducted, because of the difficulty of obtaining parenting data from adopted children's biological parents. We can compare correlations between bad parenting and children's aggression in natural families versus adoptive families. If the correlation is stronger in natural families (which have both genetic and environmental processes of transmission) than in adoptive families (which have only environmental transmission), then genetic transmission is taking place (Plomin, 1994). However, this design is biased toward finding evidence of an rGE confound, because there is more variation in bad parenting among natural than adoptive families, which could produce larger correlations with children's aggression in natural families (Stoolmiller, 1999). To avoid such bias, we can conduct a study *within adoptive families* to test if rearing parents' bad parenting is more strongly correlated with their natural children's aggression than with their adoptive child's aggression (Rutter & Silberg, 2002). The within-family design holds constant the variation in bad parenting across natural versus adoptive parent–child pairs, but requires a sample of families having both an adopted and a natural child, not too far apart in age. We are not aware of a study that has compared the correlations between bad parenting and natural children's aggression versus adoptive children's aggression. However, a study was conducted of 667 adoptive families, which found adoptive parents' reports of "family functioning" were more strongly correlated with self-reported antisocial behavior in their natural child than in their adopted child (McGue, Sharma, & Benson, 1996).

A particularly promising method studies the families of adult MZ twins who are mothers to test if MZ aunts' bad parenting predicts their nephews' aggression. In this twin-mothers design, both MZ sisters are genetic mothers to each others' birth children. However, the MZ aunt does not provide the rearing environment for her nieces and nephews; only the children's birth mother is an environmental mother to them. If the MZ aunts' and the MZ mothers' parenting predicts the children's aggression to the same extent, this would be strong evidence of a complete rGE confound. But, if the MZ mother's parenting predicts the children's aggression better than does the MZ aunt's parenting, this would show that bad parenting has an environmental effect. This elegant design offers unprecedented capacity to disentangle sources of bad parenting from mechanisms of risk for the children of bad parents, particularly when DZ twin mothers as well as MZ twin mothers are sampled (D'Onofrio *et al.*, 2003; Silberg & Eaves, 2004). This children-of-twins design is newly being applied to the question of causes of children's aggression by Silberg (2002) and colleagues, but findings were not available at the time of this writing.

The aforementioned methods test the hypothesis that genetic transmission explains the observed association between bad parenting and child aggression by looking for an effect of parenting on behavior over and above genetic influence on behavior. Another method is to compare the effect size of the association between bad parenting and children's aggression before versus after genetic influences are controlled. Any shrinkage estimates the extent to which the association is mediated by genetic transmission. This method is an instance of the familiar test for mediation (Baron & Kenny, 1986). In their meta-analysis of studies of differential treatment of siblings, Turkheimer and Waldron (2000, see their Table 3) showed that the effect sizes for associations between risk factors and behavior outcomes tended to shrink by at least half when genetic confounds were controlled. However, this meta-analysis compared effect sizes across two groups of studies, those with versus those without genetic designs, and the groups of studies differed on design features such as sample composition or sample size. Comparisons of the effect sizes for bad parenting predicting children's aggression before and after genetic controls within the same sample would be more informative.

What research is needed? A close reading of the literature reveals that researchers have neglected the questions of whether genes contribute to bad parenting and whether genetic transmission confounds environmental interpretations of the link between bad parenting and children's aggression. The field seems to have presupposed affirmative answers to these questions but not built a conclusive evidence base. As such, research applying any of the designs described here to parenting is needed. However, a comparison of effect sizes in studies with versus without genetic controls suggests genetic transmission might explain as much as half the connection. The answer to question 3, "Are cause–effect interpretations of the connection between bad parenting and children's aggression confounded by genetic transmission?," seems to be "probably."

Question 4: Does a genetic "child effect" evoke bad parenting to confound a cause–effect interpretation of the association between bad parenting and children's aggression?

The technical term relevant to this question is "evocative" correlation between genotype and an environmental measure, and it is also abbreviated as "rGE" (Plomin, DeFries, & Loehlin, 1977). Evocative rGE occurs when a child's behavior and the parenting he receives are correlated because they have the same origins in his own genotype (i.e., not because bad parenting itself causes children's aggression). The evocative rGE is a conceptual extension of the "child effect" discussed by Bell (1968), who pointed out that children influence their parents' behavior. The child-effect hypothesis has been shown to apply to the question at hand here; namely, children's aggression can elicit bad parenting (e.g., Lytton, 1990). Behavioral geneticists add the hypothesis that the child's parent-provoking behaviors may be under genetic influence. Like passive rGE, evocative rGE confounds interpretation of the association between parenting and children's aggression. To the extent that bad parenting is elicited by a child's genetically influenced behavior, then the observed association between bad parenting and child aggression could be a spurious artefact of a third variable that causes both: the child's genotype.

What research designs can be used to answer this question? A large number of studies have ascertained *twins' recollections of how they were treated by their parents* during childhood, and found that MZ twins' ratings of their parents' child-rearing are more similar than DZ twins' ratings, suggesting an influence of childrens' genotype on parents' parenting (Rowe, 1983; Hur & Bouchard, 1995; Kendler, 1996). This literature has been reviewed elsewhere (e.g., Plomin & Bergeman, 1991; Plomin, 1994). There is a basic difficulty with this literature, however. Although it seems reasonable to interpret the findings as evidence for a child effect on bad parenting, studies of twins' self-reports about their parents' treatment of them do not rule out the alternate interpretation of a genetic effect on perceptual bias, according to which MZ twins are more alike than DZ twins in how they interpret their parents' treatment or how they revise their childhood memories (Krueger, Markon, & Bouchard, 2003). None the less, the body of studies is generally interpreted as evidence for genetic child effects on parenting because several other studies have shown genetic child effects using adoption and sibling family designs instead of twins, and by using observational or multi-informant measures of parenting instead of twins' self-reports (Braungart, Plomin, & Fulker, 1992; Rende *et al.*, 1992; O'Connor *et al.*, 1995; Deater-Deckard *et al.*, 1999; Reiss *et al.*, 2000; Niederhiser *et al.*, 2004). These numerous studies decidedly demonstrated that a genetic child effect on parenting exists, but they did not demonstrate what it is that children do to provoke bad parenting. In other words, these studies did not include children's aggression as a measured variable.

Another research design is to study *adoptions*, to test if adoptees' aggression predicts their adoptive parents' bad parenting, while establishing that the adoptees' aggression has a genetic basis (i.e., that it is predicted by their biological parents' antisocial behavior). Three studies have used this compelling design (Ge *et al.*, 1996; O'Connor *et al.*, 1998; Riggins-Caspers *et al.*, 2003). The first study examined forty-one adolescent adoptees, defined genetic risk as the biological parent's official diagnosis, measured adoptee antisocial behaviors via multiple sources, and measured adoptive parents' hostility, warmth, nurturant involvement, and harsh-inconsistent parenting via multiple sources, including observations (Ge *et al.*, 1996). The second study examined fifty-six to eighty child adoptees (depending on the analysis), defined genetic risk via biological mother's self-report, and measured adoptee antisocial behaviors and adoptive parents' negative control via adoptive parent self-report (O'Connor *et al.*, 1998). The third study examined 150 adult adoptees, defined genetic risk as biological parent's diagnosis, measured adoptee conduct problems via adoptees' retrospective self-reports, and measured adoptive parents' harsh discipline via adoptee's retrospective reports (Riggins-Caspers *et al.*, 2003). All three studies reported that adoptees who are at high genetic risk for psychopathology receive more discipline and control from their adoptive parents than adoptees who are at low genetic risk. Furthermore, unlike prior research, the three studies demonstrated that the link from a child's genetic risk to adoptive parent's parenting is mediated by the child's genetically influenced aggressive behavior problems. Individual studies in this threesome were limited by a small sample, or by single-source retrospective data, but as a set the three studies provide robust evidence for a genetically mediated child effect in which the causal arrow runs from children's aggression to parenting. However, adoption samples are not well suited to ascertaining whether the child effect applies to parenting outside the normal range. As a result of self-selection by older, better-educated, higher-income applicants and subsequent screening by adoption agencies, adoptive parents are better prepared for parenting than ordinary parents. Moreover, they tend to have unusually high motivation for parenting, and responsibility for few children (Stoolmiller, 1999). Designs other than adoption designs are needed to test whether the evocative genetic child effect extends to the sorts of bad parenting (e.g., child neglect, psychological abuse, physical maltreatment) found in families whose members exhibit serious, persistent antisocial outcomes.

A third design for testing genetic child effects is to study *twin children*, asking whether twin *A*'s aggression predicts the bad parenting received by twin *B*, and vice versa. This is an application of bivariate twin modeling. Its basic logic is that if the correlation between twin *A*'s aggression and twin *B*'s experience of bad parenting is higher among MZ pairs than DZ pairs, this would indicate that the same set of genetic influences causes children's aggression and provokes bad parenting. Bad parenting must be measured separately for each twin, so that it can be used as a phenotype, like each twin's aggression. Two studies of several hundred sibling pairs taking part in the study of Nonshared Environment in Adolescent Development (NEAD), have applied variations of this bivariate approach, using multi-source measures of adolescents' and parents' behavior. A genetic child effect accounted for most of the correlation between adolescents' antisocial behavior and parents' negativity assessed cross-sectionally (Pike *et al.*, 1996), and longitudinally after accounting for the continuity of adolescent antisocial behavior (Niederhiser *et al.*, 1999).

As noted earlier, it is important to know whether the genetic child effect for ordinary parenting (as indicated by previous adoption studies and the NEAD study) also applies to extreme forms of bad parenting associated with serious, persistent antisocial behavior. We applied the bivariate modeling approach to this question in our "E-risk" longitudinal study of 1,116 British families with young twins (Jaffee *et al.*, 2004a). To do this, the E-risk study incorporated two innovations (Moffitt *et al.*, 2002). First, it assessed a birth cohort in which one-third of families were selected to over-sample families who were at high risk (findings are weighted back to represent the population of British families having babies in the 1990s). Second, the study interviewed mothers about parenting that was beyond normal limits (physical maltreatment: neglectful or abusive care resulting in injury, sexual abuse, registry with child protection services) as well as about parenting in the normative range (frequency of corporal punishment: grabbing, shaking, spanking). Children's genes influenced which children received corporal punishment, explaining 24 percent of the variation in the cohort, but children's genes were unrelated to becoming a victim of maltreatment. Bivariate twin modeling of the cross-twin, cross-phenotype correlations revealed that children's genes accounted for almost all of the correlation between corporal punishment and children's aggression, indicating that most of the observed association between this form of parenting and children's aggression is a genetic child effect. However, children's genes did not account for the correlation between physical maltreatment and children's aggression, indicating that extreme, seriously bad parenting causes children's aggression for reasons that are not genetic. Although difficult children can and do provoke their parents to use frequent corporal punishment in the normal range, factors leading to injurious maltreatment lie not within the child, but within the family environment or the adult abuser. There are limits to child effects.

What research is needed? Taken together, the adoption and twin studies reviewed in this section provide evidence to answer question 4.

Yes, the observed association between normative parenting and child aggression is in large part a spurious artefact of a third variable that causes both: the child's genotype. The child-to-parent effect strongly outweighed any parent-to-child effect in five of the six studies (Ge *et al.*, 1996; Pike *et al.*, 1996; Niederhiser *et al.*, 1999; Riggins-Caspers *et al.*, 2003; Jaffee *et al.*, 2004a). A provocative deduction from this group of studies is that Scarr (1991) may have been correct when she argued that improving parenting in the normal range of environments will not produce significant changes in children's outcomes because the associations between ordinary parenting and child outcome are not causal. "There is no evidence that family environments, except the worst, have any significant effect on the development of conduct disorders, psychopathy, or other common behavior disorders" (Scarr, 1991: 403). Scarr (1992) further argued that damaging environmental conditions outside the expected range will have causal influences on children quite apart from genetic influences, and in keeping with this notion, one study showed maltreatment makes children aggressive apart from any influence of their genotypes. This distinction between normative and extreme forms of parenting has implications for future research. Most of the genetically informative studies to date have assessed parenting using omnibus measures (e.g., "family functioning," "negativism," "control") because the goal was to ascertain whether or not genetic child effects existed at all. However, parenting intervention programs try to change specific well-defined forms of parental behavior. To inform these interventions, research is needed to query genetic versus environmental mediation of specific features of parenting. Furthermore, the aspects of parenting that correlate with children's aggression are probably quite different in early childhood, later childhood, and adolescence. Genetically informative studies of samples at different ages are needed to inform parenting interventions tailored to developmental stages.

We have looked here at the specific question of whether children's genotype evokes bad parenting, but it is useful to note that the evocative type of rGE is a subset of a larger class referred to as active rGE. Active rGE encompasses at least three different processes, when people's genetically influenced behavior leads them to "(1) create, (2) seek, or (3) otherwise end up in environments that match their genotypes" (Rutter & Silberg, 2002: 473). Restated, environments are provoked by a person's genetically influenced behavior, or a person chooses environments consonant with her genotype, or a person's genotype results in him selectively finding himself in certain environments. Antisocial behavior can bring about each of these three processes at any point in the life course (Scarr & McCartney, 1983). Antisocial behavior creates social reactions from others when aggressive toddlers evoke harsh discipline, when child bullies are rejected by peers, when teenagers who fight are expelled from schools, when young shoplifters are convicted by courts, or when abusive husbands are divorced by their wives. Antisocial individuals seek environmental settings consonant with their proclivities when antisocial children gravitate toward a delinquent peer group, when antisocial men and women mate assortatively, when people who like to fight, frequent certain bars, or attend soccer games, when paedophiles seek volunteer work with children, or when psychopaths infiltrate retirement communities for easy access to fraud victims. People who have behaved antisocially selectively find themselves in criminogenic environments when troubled children are tracked into special classes for disturbed pupils, when troubled teenagers are recruited by gangs, when violent young men are incarcerated in prisons, or when parolees find nothing but unsavoury, unskilled jobs available to them. These active rGE processes are of enormous importance in understanding the continuity of antisocial behavior across the entire life course (Caspi & Moffitt, 1995; Laub & Sampson, 2003). Once genetically influenced behavior has brought a person into contact with an environment, the environment may have unique causal effects of its own, cutting off opportunities to develop alternative prosocial behaviors, promoting the persistence of antisocial behavior, and exacerbating its seriousness (Moffitt, 1993). Research is needed to test for active rGE processes involved in antisocial behavior at developmental stages across the life course.

Question 5: After all genetic confounds are controlled, does bad parenting have any environmentally mediated effect on children's aggression?

The new generation of research designs that can evaluate whether a risk factor has an environmentally mediated effect on children's aggression has three key features. First, the studies must employ a genetically sensitive design to control for the confounding effects of parents' genes or children's genes on putative environmental measures. As we have seen, these confounding effects are at least small to moderate, and in the case of child effects they may be large, so they must be controlled.

The second key feature is that designs must employ an observed measure of the construct alleged to have environmental effects on children; in the case here, bad parenting. Traditional behavioral-genetic studies have reported latent environmental variance components, but not observed measures. This has been problematic because even very large twin studies are underpowered to detect environmental influence on twin similarity as a latent variance component, whereas statistical power to detect such influence is increased if a putative environmental variable is measured so its effects can be estimated empirically (Kendler, 1993). In keeping with this, significant effects for a measured variable have been found even despite the presence of a nonsignificant shared-environment variance component (Kendler *et al.*, 1992). In this section we abandon the distinction between "shared" and "non-shared" environmental variance components because shared and non-shared effects are not features of a measured environmental risk; one form of bad parenting, such as maltreatment, can exert either shared or non-shared effects, or both (Turkheimer & Waldron, 2000; Rutter & Silberg, 2002).

The third key feature is that genetically informative samples must accurately represent the full range of families' environmental circumstances. Many behavioral-genetic samples suffer substantial biases in recruitment and attrition, inadvertently restricting their range of participating families to primarily the middle class. Contemporary theories of psychopathology implicate experiences outside the normal range such as exposure to domestic violence or child maltreatment, which are generally concentrated in the poorest segment of the population, the segment not sampled by most behavioral-genetic studies. (Scandinavian national twin registers of psychiatric hospital and court records accurately represent variation in the population, but such register studies have been unable to measure children's environments directly.) Newer studies are striving to provide a strong and fair test of the hypothesis that rearing environments influence behavior disorders in a causal manner.

What research designs can be used to answer this question? Four basic behavioral-genetic methods can be used to rule out gene–environment correlation confounds while testing causation by putative environmental risk factors. As mentioned before, natural experiments and intervention experiments can also assess environmental causation but here we focus on genetically sensitive designs.

We can study *adoptions* to test if the adoptive parents' bad parenting increases adoptees' aggression, over and above the genetic influence from the biological parents' aggression. The large adoption studies of antisocial behavior that emerged from Scandinavia and the United States in the 1970s and 1980s were primarily cited for their innovation of demonstrating genetic influences; they showed that adoptees' criminal offending was significantly associated with the antisocial behavior of their biological parents, although these parents did not rear the adoptees. However, some of these same studies asked whether adoptees' criminal offending was also associated with the antisocial behavior of the adoptive parents who did rear them (Mednick & Christiansen, 1977; Bohman *et al.*, 1982; Cadoret, Cain, & Crowe, 1983). Rates of antisocial behavior in adoptive parents were extremely low (because of adoption agency screening), and the adoptive-parent effects were very small and often non-significant, but these studies constituted the first real empirical attempts to test if bad parental behavior exerts a non-genetic effect on children's aggression.

To our knowledge, an adoption study of antisocial behavior was the first ever in the behavioral sciences to apply behavioral-genetic methods to control for genetic confounds while testing an environmental hypothesis (VanDusen *et al.*, 1983). It was well established that low socio-economic status is a risk factor for offending, but Mednick and colleagues were concerned that some dysfunctional genetic susceptibilities transmitted within families might account for the coincidence of fathers' low-status occupations with sons' antisocial activities. As such, they used the Danish Adoption Study data to disentangle the socio-economic status that adoptees were conceived in (their biological father's occupational status) from the socio-economic status in which they were reared (adoptive father's status). Results demonstrated that biological inheritance could not explain the majority of the class–crime connection; the social class in which people grew up had a direct causal environmental effect on their probability of criminal offending (VanDusen *et al.*, 1983).

A recent update of this approach measured marital problems, legal problems, and psychopathology in adoptive parents (Cadoret *et al.*, 1995). Although these problems initially appeared to be correlated with adoptees' antisocial outcomes, the study detected an interaction between genetic and environmental risk, which indicated that adoptive parents' problems had no effect of their own, in the absence of genetic risk. This finding that adoptive parenting has no effect of its own apart from in interaction with pre-existing genetic risk has been reported by other adoption studies (Mednick, Gabrielli, & Hutchings, 1984). However, it may be difficult to detect parenting effects using adoptive parents, because their parenting tends to be restricted to the normal range (Stoolmiller, 1999). It is possible that mildly bad parenting in the normal range has such weak effects that it only makes a difference if the child is already at genetic risk.

We can study the *children of adult MZ twin mothers*. As described earlier in this article, in this children-of-twin-mothers design, the MZ aunt constitutes a genetic mother to the child, but not an environmental mother (Silberg & Eaves, 2004). Thus, if a MZ mother – son correlation is larger than its companion MZ aunt – nephew correlation, this provides evidence that environmental mothering influences children, over and above genes. Such research is underway (Silberg, 2002; D'Onofrio *et al.*, 2003).

We can study *twin children* to test if the shared experience of bad parenting makes children more similar in their levels of aggression than would be predicted based on their degree of genetic relationship. A basic approach is to conduct ordinary behaviorial-genetic modeling that apportions genetic versus environmental effects on child behavior (denoted ACE), and then add a measured putative environmental risk factor (denoted M-ACE) to test whether the children's shared experience of that risk factor can account for any of the shared environmental variation in their behavioral phenotype. The first twin study to apply this approach to problem behavior reported that living in a deprived neighborhood explained a significant 5 percent of the shared-environment variation in two-year-olds' behavior problems (Caspi *et al.*, 2000). Another study applied this approach to examine five-year-old's exposure to their mothers' experience of domestic violence (Jaffee *et al.*, 2002). This study shows that exposure to domestic violence over the first five years of their lives is particularly relevant for children who develop both externalized and internalized problems simultaneously; such co-occurring problems are associated with poor prognosis. Domestic violence exposure explained a significant 13.5 percent of the shared-environment variance in children's co-morbid outcome. A third, unpublished study reported that measured parental monitoring accounted for 15 percent of the shared-environment variance in behavior problems in a large sample of eleven- to twelve-year-old Finnish twins (described in Dick & Rose, 2002). A caveat about this approach is in order. Inference of environmental causation is compromised if parent and child share genes that simultaneously influence both the measure of parenting and the measure of child aggression.

The basic twin design can be improved upon by adding indicators of mothers' and fathers' behavioral phenotype to the usual indicators of twin behavior. This approach, called the "extended twin-family design" (Kendler, 1993), estimates the effect of the putative environmental risk factor on child behavior while controlling for genetic effects on both parents and children. An assumption of the design is that the parental phenotype measures carry genetic information parallel to that in the child phenotype measures. (Although this assumption is seldom fulfilled perfectly it seems not an unreasonable one to make about antisocial behavior, which has strong child-to-adult continuity.) The first twin study to apply this approach to parenting was reported by the Virginia Twin Study of Adolescent Behavioral Development (Meyer *et al.*, 2000). Antisocial conduct problems were assessed for adolescent twins and their parents in 1,350 families. The measured parenting variables were called "marital discord" and "family adaptability." No effect was found for marital discord, but measured family adaptability accounted for 4 percent of the variance in adolescents' conduct problems.

A complementary approach to testing whether a risk factor has a causal (versus non-causal) role in the origins of antisocial behavior has been used by studies that rule out passive rGE through statistical controls for parental antisocial behavior. This approach does not differentiate whether the risk factor is influenced at the genotype versus phenotype level of parental antisocial behavior. However, it does offer the advantage that it can be employed in non-twin samples, if phenotypic data are collected for all family members. In the above-mentioned E-risk longitudinal twin study of 1,116 families, we examined the effects of fathers' bad parenting on young children's aggression (Jaffee *et al.*, 2003). Mothers' antisocial behavior was statistically controlled, to make clear that the findings applied specifically to fathers' behavior. As expected from the literature on single mothers, a prosocial father's absence predicted more aggression by his children. But the study revealed a new finding: an antisocial father's *presence* predicted more aggression by his children, and this harmful effect was exacerbated the more years a father lived with the family and the more time each week he spent taking care of the children. Inference of environmental causation was supported because the finding for conventional fathers (less involvement predicts more child aggression) was contrary to that for antisocial fathers (more involvement predicts more child aggression), and the latter association held after ruling out passive rGE by statistically controlling for both parents' antisocial histories. Obtaining data from fathers is challenging (Caspi *et al.*, 2001), but because fathers are often a target of social policies, a better evidence base about their parenting is needed.

In another report, the E-risk study evaluated the hypothesis that maternal depression promotes children's aggression (Kim-Cohen *et al.*, in press). Research has shown that the children of depressed mothers are likely to develop conduct problems. However, it has not been clear that this correlation represents environmental transmission, because women's depression is under genetic influence (Kendler *et al.*, 1992), it often co-occurs with a girlhood history of antisocial conduct, which is also under genetic influence (Moffitt *et al.*, 2001), and depressed women often mate assortatively with antisocial men (Moffitt *et al.*, 2001). We controlled for antisocial behavior in the twins' biological father, and for the mothers' own antisocial history. Although the connection between mothers' depression and children's conduct problems decreased after this stringent control for familial liability, it remained statistically significant. It concerned us that depressed women might exaggerate ratings of their children's problem behaviors, but the pattern of findings remained the same when teachers' ratings of child behavior were substituted as the outcome measure. A temporal analysis showed that the effect of maternal depression on children's aggression depended on the timing of the depression episodes (a type of natural experiment design). If E-risk mothers experienced depression, but only before their children's birth and not after, the children were not unusually aggressive. In contrast, only if mothers suffered depression while rearing their children were the children likely to develop aggression. Finally, the possibility that a child effect (in which children's aggression provoked mothers' depression) explained the association was ruled out by documenting within-individual change. After controlling for each child's aggression up to age 5, the children exposed to an episode of maternal depression between ages 5 and 7 became more aggressive by the age 7 assessment. Taken together, these four results are not consistent with a genetic account of the association between maternal depression and children's aggression.

The E-risk study also examined the effects of physical maltreatment on young children's aggression (Jaffee *et al.*, 2004b), using twin-specific reports of maltreatment. This study satisfied six conditions that together supported the hypothesis that physical maltreatment has an environmentally mediated causal influence on children's aggression: (i) children's maltreatment history prospectively predicted aggression; (ii) the severity of maltreatment bore a dose–response relation to aggression; (iii) the experience of maltreatment was followed by increases in aggression from prior levels, within individual children; (iv) there was no child effect provoking maltreatment; (v) maltreatment predicted aggression while mothers' and fathers' antisocial behaviors were statistically controlled; and (vi) modest but significant effects of maltreatment on aggression remained present after controlling for genetic transmission of liability to aggression in the family. A similar analytic approach using twin-specific measures of risk was taken by the Minnesota Twin Family Study (Burt *et al.*, 2003), which studied 808 eleven-year-old twin pairs. Models revealed that measured parent–child conflict accounted for 12 percent of the variance in the externalizing syndrome of oppositional, conduct, and attention-deficit-hyperactivity disorders (23 percent of the common-environment variation in this syndrome).

A potential challenge to the findings from the aforementioned studies of parenting effects on twin children is that some of the findings may arise from child effects provoking bad parenting. The finding about parental monitoring is susceptible to this challenge because parental monitoring is known to be subject to strong child effects (Kerr & Stattin, 2000). However, it seems less plausible that children provoke their mothers' domestic violence experience, or their fathers' antisocial history. Ill-behaved children might provoke maternal depression but the study took this into account by showing that children exposed to maternal depression subsequently developed new antisocial behavior. Finally, the possibility that an environmental child effect accounted for the observed influence of maltreatment or parent–child conflict on children's aggression was ruled out by modeling twins-specific measures.

As a final design, we can study *MZ twin children*, to test if differences between siblings in their exposure to bad parenting makes them different on aggression. The fact that MZ twins are not perfectly concordant for aggression opens a window of opportunity to uncover if a non-genetic cause specific to one twin has produced the behavioral difference. A number of studies have tested if differential parental treatment can account for differences in antisocial behavior between siblings and cousins within a family (e.g., Conger & Conger, 1994; Rodgers, Rowe & Li, 1994; Reiss, 2000). Most of these studies have already been reviewed by Turkheimer and Waldron (2000). However, comparing the parenting experiences of discordant MZ twins allows the least ambiguous interpretation of results. Three studies have reported that MZ-twin differences in bad parenting are correlated with MZ-twin differences in antisocial behavior (Pike *et al.*, 1996; Asbury, Dunn, Pike & Plomin, 2003; Caspi *et al.*, 2004).

The E-risk study reported that within 600 MZ twin pairs, the twin who received relatively more maternal negativity and less maternal warmth developed more antisocial behavior problems (Caspi *et al.*, 2004). Negativity and warmth were measured by coding voice tone and speech content in mothers' audiotaped speech about each of their twins separately, according to the well-known "expressed emotion" paradigm. This study provided the strongest evidence to date that the effect of mothers' emotional treatment of children causes aggression, by ruling out five alternative explanations of the finding. (i) Using MZ twin pairs ruled out the possibility that a genetically transmitted liability explained both the mother's emotion and her child's antisocial behavior. (ii) Using MZ twins also ruled out the possibility that a genetic child effect provoking maternal emotion accounted for the finding. (iii) The study used the longitudinal natural experiment approach to rule out that any non-genetic child effect provoking maternal emotion accounted for the finding, by controlling for prior behavior that could have provoked maternal negative emotion and showing that individual children whose mothers were negative toward them at age 5 evidenced a subsequent increase of antisocial behavior between age 5 and age 7. (iv) The study controlled for twin differences in birth weight in an effort to rule out the possibility that twins with neuro-developmental difficulties had more behavior problems and elicited more negative emotion from mothers. (v) The study measured the children's behavior using teacher reports to rule out the possibility that a mother's negativity toward a child led her to exaggerate her report of the child's behavior problems. Effect sizes for the influence of maternal emotion on children's aggression ranged from large ($r = 0.53$) to small ($r = 0.10$), depending on how many controls were applied.

Not all tests of putative environmental risk factors confirm environmental effects. Lest readers assume that application of behavioral-genetic methods to a putative environmental risk factor will necessarily affirm that its effects are environmentally mediated, it is useful to mention that some known risk factors do not appear to be causal. First, as noted above, we found that children's genes accounted for virtually all of the association between their corporal punishment (i.e., spanking) and their conduct problems. This indicated a "child effect," in which children's bad conduct provokes their parents to use more corporal punishment, rather than the reverse (Jaffee *et al.*, 2004a). Second, studies have reported that mothers' smoking during pregnancy is correlated with children's conduct problems, but pregnancy smoking is known to be concentrated among mothers who are antisocial, have mental health problems, mate with antisocial men, and rear children in conditions of social deprivation. When the family liability for transmission of psychopathology from parents to children was controlled through statistical controls for the parents' antisocial behavior, mental health, and social deprivation, the effect of even heavy smoking during pregnancy disappeared. This study suggests that although pregnancy smoking undoubtedly has undesirable effects on outcomes such as infant birth weight, it is probably not a cause of conduct problems (Maughan *et al.*, 2004).

A third finding of nil environmental influence concerned father absence. In families having absent fathers, the children are known to have more conduct problems. However, absent fathers are more antisocial on average than fathers who stay with their children, and antisocial behavior can be genetically transmitted. We controlled for mother's and father's antisocial history, and found that the association between father absence/presence and children's conduct problems disappeared. This suggests that father absence is not a direct cause of conduct problems, but rather is a proxy indicator for familial liability to antisocial behavior (Jaffee *et al.*, 2003).

What research is needed? To date, question 5, "Does bad parenting have an environmentally mediated causal effect on children's aggression?" has been answered in the affirmative by behavioral-genetic reports from several twin samples, finding such effects for family adaptability, parent–child conflict, parental monitoring, bad fathering, maternal depression, physical maltreatment, and mothers' negative expressed emotions. These studies share an Achilles' heel: because different forms of parenting risk are concentrated in the same families, the particular parenting measure targeted in a study may be a proxy for some other, correlated risk factor. Research is needed that isolates the effects of one risk factor from its correlates. Nevertheless, whatever the most influential parenting behaviors are, the studies attest that parents can have environmentally mediated effects.

All of the studies testing measured environmental variables were conducted very recently, illustrating that such testing is a new direction in behaviorial-genetic research (Kendler, 2001; Dick & Rose, 2002). In keeping with this chapter's example program of research into bad parenting and children's aggression, we reviewed only studies measuring "bad parenting." It wasn't necessary to use bad parenting to illustrate how behavioral-genetic methods can be used to study environmental causation; the methods can and should be applied to any known risk factor for antisocial behavior, from lead toxicity to unemployment. However, our choice of bad parenting allowed us to cover the majority of studies published to date that have looked at measured risk factors for antisocial behavior using genetically sensitive designs. So far, behaviorial-genetic designs have been applied to test causation for only a handful of other risk factors for antisocial behavior, namely neighborhood deprivation (Caspi *et al.*, 2000; Cleveland, 2003), school classmates' behavior (Rose *et al.*, 2003), and child sexual abuse (Dinwiddie *et al.*, 2000). This small set of studies signals the beginning of a major research initiative. We expect the list of risk factors studied with behavioral-genetic controls to grow to encompass environmental factors ranging from prenatal teratogens to prison sanctioning of adult offenders.

The environmental effects reported in studies that controlled for genetic influences were uniformly small. It may surprise some developmentalists to learn that when familial liability and child effects are controlled, parenting influences on children drop to small effect sizes. However, small effects ought to be expected, for three reasons. First, it must be remembered that these small effects reflect true environmental associations after they have been purged of the confounding influences that inflate effect sizes in non-genetic studies. Associations between risk factors and behavior outcomes tend to shrink by at least half when genetic confounds are controlled (Turkheimer & Waldron, 2000). This shrinkage suggests that the risk–outcome correlations that social scientists are accustomed to seeing are inflated to about double their true size.

Second, small effects for any particular risk factor make sense, in view of evidence that clear risk for antisocial behavior accrues only when a person accumulates a large number of risks (Rutter, Giller, & Hagell, 1998), each of which may individually have only a small effect (Daniels & Plomin, 1985).

A third reason why small effects should not be too surprising is that they represent the main effects of measured environments, apart from any environmental effects involved in gene–environment interactions. Recall that adoption studies found no effects of bad adoptive parenting in the absence of genetic liability, but bad adoptive parenting was associated with elevated antisocial outcomes for adoptees at genetic risk (Mednick *et al.*, 1984; Cadoret et al., 1995). In twin designs, when testing whether the shared experience of bad parenting enhances twin similarity in aggression over and above genetic influences on similarity, gene × environment interactions are controlled along with other genetic influences. In twin designs testing whether differential experiences of bad parenting are associated with MZ-twin differences in aggression, differential outcomes arising from gene × environment interactions are ruled out by the twins' identical genotypes. In contrast, genetic risk and bad parenting are not usually disentangled in real life as they are in behavioral-genetic studies. In ordinary lives, genetic and environmental risks often coincide. It is possible in theory that environmental effects conditional on genetic vulnerability could be quite large. We next turn to the question of gene × environment interactions influencing antisocial behavior.

Question 6: Testing the hypothesis of interaction between genes and environments

The study of gene–environment (G × E) interaction entails substantial methodological challenges. It requires measured environments that are truly environmental, measured genetic influence, some means of separating them from each other, and enough statistical power for a sensitive test of interaction (Rutter and Silberg, 2002). Despite the challenges, theory-driven hypotheses of G × E interaction are well worth testing, because where measured G × E are found to influence behavior disorders, both specific genes and specific environmental risks can conceivably have moderate-to-large effects, as opposed to the very small effects expected from prior quantitative genetic research. Specific genes revealed to be stronger in the presence of environmental risk would guide strategic research into those genes' expression, possibly leading to genetic diagnostics and improved pharmacological interventions (Evans & Relling, 1999). Specific environmental effects revealed to be stronger in the presence of genetic risk would prompt a new impetus for specific environmental prevention efforts, and would help to identify who needs the prevention programs most. The study of G × E is especially exciting in antisocial behavior research, where investigations have pioneered the way for all behavioral disorders. Studies of antisocial behavior were first to report evidence of interaction between latent genetic and latent environmental risks ascertained in adoption studies, and also first to report evidence of an interaction between a measured genetic polymorphism and a measured environmental risk. Four research designs have been used.

Adoption studies of latent G × E The first evidence that genetic and environmental risks influence antisocial behavior together in a synergistic way came from adoption studies. Among the 6,000 families of male adoptees in the Danish Adoption Study, 14% of adoptees were convicted of crime where neither their biological nor adoptive parents had been convicted, whereas 15% were convicted if their adoptive parent alone was convicted, 20% were convicted if their biological parent alone was convicted, and 25% were convicted if both biological and adoptive parents were convicted, although there were only 143 such cases (Mednick & Christiansen, 1977). This pattern of percentages did not represent a statistically significant cross-over interaction term, but it did illustrate clearly that the effects of genetic and environmental risk acting together were greater than the effects of either factor acting alone. The finding was buttressed by two studies from American and Swedish adoption registers completed about the same time (Cloninger, *et al.*, 1982; Cadoret, Cain, & Crowe, 1983).

Adoption studies of latent G × measured E In a pool of 500 adoptees from the Iowa and Missouri adoption studies, adoptees had the most elevated antisocial behaviors when they experienced "adverse circumstances" in their adoptive homes as well as having birth mothers with antisocial personality problems or alcoholism (Cadoret, Cain, & Crowe 1983). This landmark study documented that the interaction was statistically significant, and replicated across two independent samples. This finding was replicated and extended in another Iowa adoption cohort of 200 families (Cadoret *et al.*, 1995). Adoptive parents' adversity was defined according to the presence of marital problems, legal problems, substance abuse, or mental disorder and it interacted significantly with biological parents' antisocial personality disorder to predict elevated rates of childhood aggression, adolescent aggression, and diagnosed conduct disorder in the adoptees. This same Iowa adoption study was creatively analyzed to demonstrate that adversity in the adoptive home can moderate the genetic child effect in which children's aggression provokes bad parenting (Riggins-Caspers *et al.*, 2003). Adoptees' genetic liability for antisocial behavior (defined as biological parents' psychopathology) provoked more harsh discipline from the adoptive parents in homes where the adoptive parents suffered adversity (marital, legal, substance, or psychopathology problems). There is one problem with studying G × E in adoption designs, and that is that adoption itself breaks up the naturally occurring processes of rGE that characterize the non-adopted majority population, thereby precluding the possibility of G × E. This separation allows the empirical study of G × E, but, paradoxically, it probably results in an underestimate of the influence of G × E on antisocial outcomes in the general population. For this reason, adoption G × E studies should be complemented with twin studies.

A twin study of latent G × measured E Our E-risk twin study also yielded evidence that genetic and environmental risks interact (Jaffee, Caspi, Moffitt, Dodge, Rutter, Taylor, & Tully, in press). Because we already knew that conduct problems were highly heritable in the E-risk twin sample at age 5 (Arseneault *et al.*, 2003), we were able to estimate each child's personal genetic risk for conduct problems by considering whether his or her co-twin had already been diagnosed with conduct disorder, and whether he or she shared 100 percent versus 50 percent of genes with that diagnosed co-twin. This method's usefulness had been demonstrated previously in a landmark G × E study showing that the risk of depression following life-event stress depends on genetic vulnerability (Kendler *et al.*, 1995). For example, an individual's genetic risk is highest if his or her co-twin sibling already has a diagnosis of disorder and the pair is monozygotic. Likewise, an individual's genetic risk is lowest if his or her co-twin has been free from disorder and the pair is monozygotic. Individuals in dizygotic twin pairs fall between the high and low genetic risk groups. In our study an interaction was obtained such that the effect of maltreatment on conduct problem symptoms was significantly stronger among children at high genetic risk than among children at low genetic risk. (Because there was no genetic child effect provoking maltreatment, the genetic risk groups did not differ on concordance for maltreatment or the severity of maltreatment.) In addition, the experience of maltreatment was associated with an increase of 24 percent in the probability of diagnosable conduct disorder among children at high genetic risk, but an increase of only 2 percent among children at low risk.

Studies of measured G × measured E; testing a measured gene The aforementioned adoption and twin studies established that genotype does interact with bad parenting in the etiological processes leading to antisocial behavior. However, the studies did not implicate any particular genes. We conducted one study to test the hypothesis of gene × environment interaction using a measured environmental risk, child maltreatment, and an identified gene, the MAOA polymorphism (Caspi *et al.*, 2002). We selected the MAOA gene as the candidate gene for our study for four reasons (supporting research being cited in Caspi *et al.*, 2002). First, the gene encodes the MAOA enzyme, which metabolizes the neurotransmitters linked to maltreatment victimization and aggressive behavior by previous research. Second, drugs inhibiting the action of the MAOA enzyme have been shown to prevent animals from habituating to chronic stressors analogous to maltreatment, and to dispose animals toward hyper-reactivity to threat. Third, in studies of mice having the MAOA gene deleted, increased levels of neurotransmitters and aggressive behavior were observed, and aggression was normalized by restoring MAOA gene expression. Fourth, an extremely rare mutation causing a null allele at the MAOA locus was associated with aggressive psychopathology among some men in a Dutch family pedigree, although no relation between MAOA genotype and aggression had been detected for people in the general population.

We selected maltreatment for this study for four reasons (supporting research being cited in Caspi *et al.*, 2002). First, childhood maltreatment is a known predictor of antisocial outcomes. Second, not all maltreated children become antisocial, suggesting that vulnerability to maltreatment is influenced by heretofore unstudied individual characteristics. Third, our above-mentioned twin research had established that maltreatment's effect on children's aggression is environmentally mediated, i.e., the association is not an artefact of a genetic child effect provoking maltreatment nor of transmission of aggression-prone genes from parents. As such, maltreatment can serve as the environmental variable in a test of gene × environment interaction. Fourth, animal and human studies suggest that maltreatment in early life alters neurotransmitter systems in ways that can persist into adulthood and can influence aggressive behavior.

Based on this logic to support our hypothesis of G × E, we measured childhood maltreatment history (8% severe, 28% probable, 64% not maltreated) and MAOA genotype (37% low-activity risk allele, 63% high-activity risk allele) in the 442 Caucasian males of the longitudinal Dunedin Multidisciplinary Health and Development Study. We found that maltreatment history and genotype interacted to predict four different measures of antisocial outcome: an adolescent diagnosis of conduct disorder, an age-26 personality assessment of aggression, symptoms of adult antisocial personality disorder reported by informants who knew the study members well, and court conviction for violent crime up to age 26, the latest age of follow-up. Among boys having the combination of the low-MAOA-activity allele and severe maltreatment, 85% developed some form of antisocial outcome. Males having the combination of the low-activity allele and severe-to-probable maltreatment were only 12% of the male birth cohort, but they accounted for 44% of the cohort's violent convictions, because they offended at a higher rate on average than other violent offenders in the cohort.

Replication of this study was of utmost importance, because the study reported the first instance of interaction between a measured gene and a measured environment in the behavioral sciences, and because reports of connections between measured genes and disorders are notorious for their poor replication record (Hamer, 2002). One initial positive replication, and extension, has emerged from the Virginia Twin Study for Adolescent Behavioral Development (Foley *et al.*, 2004). This team studied 514 Caucasian male twins and measured environmental risk using an adversity index comprised of parental neglect, interparental violence, and inconsistent discipline. MAOA genotype and adversity interacted significantly such that 15% of boys having adversity but the high-MAOA-activity allele developed conduct disorder, in comparison to 35% of boys having adversity plus the low-activity allele. This study went a step further, controlling for maternal antisocial personality disorder to rule out the possibility that passive rGE might have resulted in the co-occurrence of environmental and genetic risk. This study thus replicated the original G × E between the MAOA polymorphism and maltreatment, extended it to other forms of parental treatment, and showed that it is not an artefact of passive rGE.

Genes as protective factors promoting resilience An intriguing finding from the two MAOA G × E studies was that, in contrast to the G × E interaction's marked effects on antisocial outcomes, the unique effects of maltreatment apart from its role in the G × E interaction were very modest. Maltreatment initially predicted antisocial outcomes in the full cohorts, but within the high-MAOA-activity genotype group its effects were reduced by more than half (Caspi *et al.*, 2002; Foley *et al.*, 2004). This pattern is in keeping with the findings from adoption and twin studies cited earlier in this section, all of which found that measured bad parenting had relatively little effect on children who were at low genetic risk (Cloninger *et al.*, 1982; Cadoret, Cain, & Crowe, 1983; Mednick *et al.*, 1984; Cadoret *et al.*, 1995; Jaffee *et al.*, in press). Taken together, these findings suggest the novel notion that genotype can be a protective factor against adversity. Some people respond poorly to adversity while others are resilient to it, and the reason for this variation has been a holy grail in developmental research. The search for sources of resilience has tended to focus on social experiences thought to protect children, overlooking a potential protective role of genes (but see Kim-Cohen *et al.*, 2004). The potential protective effect of genes deserves more attention (Insel & Collins, 2003).

In this chapter we reviewed the first studies in a new generation of research that exploits behavioral-genetic designs to address the interplay between measured environmental risks and genetic risks in the origins of antisocial behavior. This work has only recently accelerated, and more of it is needed before conclusions can be drawn. However, even the few studies so far counteract prior claims that associations between family risk factors and child antisocial outcome might be nothing more than a spurious artefact of familial genetic transmission. This argument can be subjected to empirical test, and such tests need to address both child effects on environments (involving children's genes) and gene–environment correlations (involving parents' genes). Further, although the "residual main effects" of environmental risk factors may appear small after controlling for genetic transmission, this is not the whole story. Emerging evidence about gene–environment interactions suggests that environmental risks can affect people more strongly than previously appreciated, in genetically vulnerable segments of the population. Although this chapter has argued that twin and adoption studies together can provide a good evidence base, the most compelling information about gene–environment interplay will come from converging findings from behavioral-genetic designs, treatment experiments, and longitudinal natural experiments showing within-individual change.

References

American Psychiatric Association (1994). *Diagnostic and Statistical Manual of Mental Disorders*, 4th edn. Washington, DC

Arseneault, L., Moffitt, T. E., Caspi, A., Taylor, A., Rijsdijk, F. V., Jaffee, S., Ablow, J. C., & Measelle, J. R. (2003). "Strong genetic effects on cross-situational antisocial behavior among 5-year-old children according to mothers, teachers, examiner-observers, and twins' self-reports." *Journal of Child Psychology and Psychiatry* 44: 832–848.

Asbury, K., Dunn, J., Pike, A., & Plomin, R. (2003). "Nonshared environmental influences on individual differences in early behavioral development: a monozygotic twin differences study." *Child Development* 74: 933–943.

Baron, R. M. & Kenny, D. A. (1986). "The moderator–mediator distinction in social psychological research: conceptual, strategic, and statistical considerations." *Journal of Personality and Social Psychology* 51: 1173–1182.

Bell, R. Q. (1968). "A reinterpretation of the direction of effects in socialization." *Psychological Review* 75: 81–95.

Belsky, J. & Barends, N. (2002). "Personality and parenting." In M. H. Bornstein (ed.), *Handbook of Parenting, vol. III: Being and Becoming a Parent, 2nd edn.* Mahwah, NJ: Lawrence Erlbaum Associates.

Blumstein, A. & Cohen, J. (1987). "Characterizing criminal careers." *Science* 237: 985–991.

Bohman, M., Cloninger, C. R., Sigvardsson, S., & von Knorring, A. L. (1982). "Predisposition to petty criminality in Swedish adoptees. I. Genetic and environmental heterogeneity." *Archives of General Psychiatry* 39: 1233–1241.

Braungart, J. M., Plomin, R., & Fulker, D. W. (1992). "Genetic mediation of the home environment during infancy: a sibling adoption study of the HOME." *Developmental Psychology* 28: 1048–1055.

Burt, A. S., Krueger, R. F., McGue, M., & Iacono, W. (2003). "Parent–child conflict and the comorbidity among childhood externalizing disorders." *Archives of General Psychiatry* 60: 505–513.

Butterfield, F. (1996). *All God's Children: The Bosket Family and the American Tradition of Violence*. New York: Avon.

(2002). "Father steals best: crime in an American family." *New York Times*, at http://www.nytimes.com/2002/08/21/national/21FAMI.html.

Cadoret, R. J., Cain, C. A., & Crowe, R. R. (1983). "Evidence for gene–environment interaction in the development of adolescent antisocial behavior." *Behavior Genetics* 13: 301–310.

Cadoret, R. J., Yates, W. R., Troughton, E., Woodworth, G., & Stewart, M. A. S. (1995). "Genetic–environmental interaction in the genesis of aggressivity and conduct disorders." *Archives of General Psychiatry* 52: 916–924.

Caspi, A., McClay, J, Moffitt, T. E., Mill, J., Martin, J., Craig, I., Taylor, A., & Poulton, R. (2002). "Role of genotype in the cycle of violence in maltreated children." *Science* 297: 851–854.

Caspi, A. & Moffitt, T. E. (1995). "The continuity of maladaptive behavior." In D. Cicchetti & D. Cohen (eds.), *Manual of Developmental Psychopathology*, vol. II. New York: Wiley.

Caspi, A., Moffitt, T., Morgan, J., Rutter, M., Taylor, A., Arseneault, L., Tully, L., Jacobs, C., Kim-Cohen, J., & Polo-Tomas, M. (2004). "Maternal expressed emotion predicts children's antisocial behavior problems: using MZ-twin differences to identify environmental effects on behavioral development." *Developmental Psychology* 40(2): 149–161.

Caspi, A., Taylor, A., Moffitt, T. E., & Plomin, R. (2000). "Neighborhood deprivation affects children's mental health: environmental risks identified using a genetic design." *Psychological Science* 11: 338–342.

Caspi, A., Taylor, A., Smart, M. A., Jackson, J., Tagami, S., & Moffitt, T. E. (2001). "Can women provide reliable information about their children's fathers? Cross-informant agreement about men's antisocial behavior." *Journal of Child Psychology and Psychiatry* 42: 915–920.

Cichetti, D. (2003). "Experiments of nature: contributions to developmental theory." *Development and Psychopathology* 15: 833–835.

Cleveland, H. H. (2003). "Disadvantaged neighborhoods and adolescent aggression: behavioral genetic evidence of contextual effects." *Journal of Research on Adolescence* 13: 211–238.

Cloninger, C. R. & Gottesman, I. I. (1987). "Genetic and environmental factors in antisocial behavior disorders." In S. A. Mednick, T. E. Moffitt, & S. A. Stack (eds.), *The Causes of Crime: New Biological Approaches*. New York: Cambridge University Press.

Cloninger, C. R., Sigvardsson, S., Bohman, M., & von Knorring, A. L. (1982). "Predisposition to petty criminality in Swedish adoptees. II. Cross-fostering analysis of gene–environment interaction." *Archives of General Psychiatry* 39: 1242–1247.

Collins, W. A., Maccoby, E. E., Steinberg, L., Hetherington, E. M., & Bornstein, M. H. (2000). "Contemporary research on parenting." *American Psychologist* 55: 218–232.

Conger, K. J. & Conger, R. D. (1994). "Differential parenting and change in sibling differences in delinquency." *Journal of Family Psychology* 8: 287–302.

Costello, E. J., Compton, S. N., Keeler, G., & Angold, A. (2003). "Relationships between poverty and psychopathology: a natural experiment." *Journal of the American Medical Association* 290: 2023–2029.

Daniels, D. & Plomin, R. (1985). "Differential experience of siblings in the same family." *Developmental Psychology* 21: 747–760.

Deater-Deckard, K., Fulker, D. W., & Plomin, R. (1999). "A genetic study of the family environment in the transition to early adolescence." *Journal of Child Psychology and Psychiatry* 40: 769–775.

Dick, D. M. & Rose, R. J. (2002). "Behavior genetics: What's new? What's next?" *Current Directions in Psychological Science* 11: 70–74.

DiLalla, L. F. (2002). "Behavior genetics of aggression in children: review and future directions." *Developmental Review* 22: 593–622.

DiLalla, L. F. & Gottesman, I. I. (1991). "Biological and genetic contributions to violence: Widom's untold tale." *Psychological Bulletin* 109: 125–129.

Dinwiddie, S., Heath, A. C., Dunne, M. P., Bucholz, K. K., Madden, P. A. F., Slutske, W. S., Bierut, L. J., Statham, D. B., & Martin, N. G. (2000). "Early sexual abuse and lifetime psychopathology: a co-twin control study." *Psychological Medicine* 30: 41–52.

Dishion, T. J., McCord, J., & Poulin, F. (1999). "Iatrogenic effects in interventions that aggregate high-risk youth." *American Psychologist* 54: 1–10.

Dodge, K. A. (2003). "Investing in the prevention of youth violence." *International Society for the Study of Behavioral Development Newsletter* 2: 8–10.

D'Onofrio, B. M., Turkheimer, E. N., Eaves, L. J., Corey, L. A., Berg, K., Solaas, M. H., & Emery, R. E. (2003). "The role of the children of twins design in elucidating causal relations between parent characteristics and child outcomes." *Journal of Child Psychiatry and Psychology* 44: 1130–1144.

Evans, W. E. & Relling, M. V. (1999). "Pharmacogenetics: translating functional genomics into rational therapeutics." *Science* 286: 487–491.

Fagot, B. I., Pears, K. C., Capaldi, D. M., Crosby, L., & Leve, C. S. (1998). "Becoming an adolescent father: precursors and parenting." *Developmental Psychology* 34: 1209–1219.

Farrington, D. P. (1988). "Studying changes within individuals: the causes of offending." In M. Rutter (ed.), *Studies of Psychosocial Risk: The Power of Longitudinal Data*. Cambridge: Cambridge University Press.

(2003) "Developmental and life-course criminology." *Criminology* 41: 201–235.

Farrington, D. P., Barnes, G. C. & Lambert, S. (1996). "The concentration of offending in families." *Legal and Criminological Psychology* 1: 47–63.

Farrington, D. P., Jolliffe, D., Loeber, R., Stouthamer-Loeber, M. & Kalb, L. (2001). "The concentration of offenders in families, and family criminality in the prediction of boys' delinquency." *Journal of Adolescence* 24: 579–596.

Fergusson, D. M., Lynskey, M., & Horwood, L. J. (1995). "The adolescent outcomes of adoption: a 16-year longitudinal study." *Journal of Child Psychology and Psychiatry* 36: 597–615.

Foley, D., Eaves, L., Wormley, B., Silberg, J., Maes, H., Hewitt, J., Kuhn, J., & Riley, B. (2004). "Childhood adversity, MAOA genotype, and risk for conduct disorder." *Archives of General Psychiatry* 61: 738–744.

Galbaud du Fort, G., Boothroyd, L. J., Bland, R. C., Newman, S. C., & Kakuma, R. (2002). "Spouse similarity for antisocial behavior in the general population." *Psychological Medicine* 32: 1407–1416.

Ge, X., Conger, R. D., Cadoret, R. J., Neiderhiser, J. M., Yates, W., Troughton, E. & Steward, M. A. (1996). "The developmental interface between nature and nurture: a mutual influence model of childhood antisocial behavior and parent behavior." *Developmental Psychology* 32: 574–589.

Gjone, H. & Novik, T. S. (1995). "Parental ratings of behavior problems: a twin and general population comparison." *Journal of Child Psychology and Psychiatry* 36: 121–124.

Hamer, D. (2002). "Rethinking behavior genetics." *Science* 298: 71–72.

Harris, J. R. (1998). *The Nurture Assumption.* New York: The Free Press.

Heinrich, C. C., Brown, J. L., & Aber, J. L. (1999). *Evaluating the Effectiveness of School-based Violence Prevention: Developmental Approaches* (Society for Research in Child Development Social Policy Report, 13, no. 3, pp. 1–18). Ann Arbor, MI: SRCD Executive Office.

Hinshaw, S. P. (2002). "Intervention research, theoretical mechanisms, and causal processes related to externalizing behavior patterns." *Development and Psychopathology* 14: 789–818.

Howe, G. W., Reiss, D., & Yuh, J. (2002). "Can prevention trials test theories of etiology?" *Development and Psychopathology* 14: 673–694.

Hur, Y. & Bouchard, T. J., Jr. (1995). "Genetic influences on perceptions of childhood family environment: a reared-apart twin study." *Child Development* 66: 330–345.

Hutchings, B. & Mednick, S. A. (1973). "Genetic and environmental influences on criminality in Denmark." In B. S. Brown & E. F. Torrey (eds.), *International Collaboration in Mental Health.* Rockville, MD: National Institute of Mental Health.

Insel, T. R. & Collins, F. S. (2003). "Psychiatry in the genomics era." *American Journal of Psychiatry* 160: 616–620.

Jaffee, S. R., Caspi, A., Moffitt, T. E., Dodge, K., Rutter, M., Taylor, A., & Tully, L. (in press). "Nature x nurture: genetic vulnerabilities interact with physical maltreatment to promote behavior problems." *Development and Psychopathology.*

Jaffee, S. R, Caspi, A., Moffitt, T. E., Polo-Tomas, M., Price, T., & Taylor, A. (2004a). "The limits of child effects: evidence for genetically-mediated child effects on corporal punishment, but not on maltreatment." *Developmental Psychology* 40: 1047–1058.

Jaffee, S. R., Caspi, A., Moffitt, T. E., & Taylor, A. (2004b). "Physical maltreatment victim to antisocial child: evidence of an environmentally-mediated process." *Journal of Abnormal Psychology* 113(1): 44–55.

Jaffee, S. R., Caspi, A., Moffitt, T. E., Taylor, A., & Dickson, N. (2001). "Predicting early fatherhood and whether young fathers live with their children: prospective findings and policy recommendations." *Journal of Child Psychology and Psychiatry* 42: 803–815.

Jaffee, S. R., Moffitt, T. E., Caspi, A., & Taylor, A. (2003). "Life with (or without) father: the benefits of living with two biological parents depend on the father's antisocial behavior." *Child Development* 74: 109–126.

Jaffee, S. R., Moffitt, T. E., Caspi, A., Taylor, A., & Arseneault, L. (2002). "The influence of adult domestic violence on children's internalizing and externalizing problems: an environmentally-informative twin study." *Journal of the American Academy of Child and Adolescent Psychiatry* 41: 1095–1103.

Johnson, W., Krueger, R. F., Bouchard, T. J., & McGue, M. (2002). "The personalities of twins: just ordinary folks." *Twin Research* 5: 125–131.

Jorgensen, A. L., Phillip, J., Raskind, W. H., Matsushita, M., Christensen, B., Dreyer, V., & Motulsky, A. A. (1992). "Different patterns of X inactivation

in MZ twins discordant for red–green color vision deficiency." *American Journal of Human Genetics* 51: 291–298.
Kendler, K. S. (1993). "Twin studies of psychiatric illness." *Archives of General Psychiatry* 50: 905–915.
(1996). "Parenting: a genetic epidemiologic perspective." *American Journal of Psychiatry* 153: 11–20.
(2001). "Twin studies of psychiatric illness: an update." *Archives of General Psychiatry* 58: 1005–1014.
Kendler, K. S., Kessler, R. C., Walters, E. E., MacLean, C., Neale, M. C., Heath, A. C., & Eaves, L. J. (1995). "Stressful life events, genetic liability and onset of an episode of major depression in women." *American Journal of Psychiatry* 152: 833–842.
Kendler, K. S., Neale, M. C., Kessler, R. C., Heath, A. C., & Eaves, L. J. (1992). "Childhood parental loss and adult psychopathology in women: a twin study perspective." *Archives of General Psychiatry* 49: 109–116.
(1994). "Parental treatment and the equal environments assumption in twin studies of psychiatric illness." *Psychological Medicine* 24: 579–590.
Kendler, K. S., Prescott, C. A., Myers, J., & Neale, M. C. (2003). "The structure of genetic and environmental risk factors for common psychiatric and substance use disorders in men and women." *Archives of General Psychiatry* 60: 929–937.
Kerr, M. & Stattin, H. (2000). "What parents know, how they know it, and several forms of adolescent adjustment: further support for a reinterpretation of monitoring." *Developmental Psychology* 36: 366–380.
Kim-Cohen, J., Moffitt, T. E., Caspi, A., & Taylor, A. (2004). "Genetic and environmental processes in young children's resilience and vulnerability to socio-economic deprivation." *Child Development* 75(3): 651–668.
Kim-Cohen, J., Moffitt, T. E., Taylor, A., Pawlby, S. J., & Caspi, A. (in press). "Maternal depression and children's antisocial behavior: nature and nurture effects." *Archives of General Psychiatry.*
Klein, M. W. (1995). *The American Street Gang.* New York: Oxford University Press.
Kraemer, H. C. (2003). "Current concepts of risk in psychiatric disorders." *Current Opinion in Psychiatry* 16: 421–430.
Kraemer, H. C., Kazdin, A. E., Offord, D. R., Kessler, R. C., Jensen, P. S., & Kupfer, D. J. (1997). "Coming to terms with the terms of risk." *Archives of General Psychiatry* 54: 337–343.
Krueger R. F., Markon K. E., & Bouchard T. J. (2003). "The extended genotype: the heritability of personality accounts for the heritability of recalled family environments in twins reared apart." *Journal of Personality* 71: 809–833.
Krueger, R. F., Moffitt, T. E., Caspi, A., Bleske, A., & Silva, P. A. (1998). "Assortative mating for antisocial behavior: developmental and methodological implications." *Behavior Genetics* 28: 173–186.
Lahey, B., Moffitt, T. E., & Caspi, A., eds. (2003). *The Causes of Conduct Disorder and Serious Juvenile Delinquency.* New York: Guilford Press.

Laub, J.H. & Sampson, R.J. (2003). *Shared Beginnings, Divergent Lives: Delinquent Boys to Age 70.* Cambridge, MA: Harvard University Press.

Levy, F., Hay, D., McLaughlin, M., Wood, C., & Waldman, I. (1996). "Twin-sibling differences in parental reports of ADHD, speech, reading, and behavioral problems." *Journal of Child Psychology and Psychiatry* 37: 569–578.

Lipsey, M.W. & Wilson, D.B. (1998). "Effective intervention for serious and violent juvenile offenders: synthesis of research." In R. Loeber & D. P. Farrington (eds.), *Serious and Violent Juvenile Offenders.* Thousand Oaks, CA: Sage.

Losoya, S.H., Callor, S., Rowe, D.C., & Goldsmith, H.H. (1997). "Origins of familial similarity in parenting: a study of twins and adoptive siblings." *Developmental Psychology* 33: 1012–1023.

Lytton, H. (1990). "Child and parent effects in boys' conduct disorder: a reinterpretation." *Developmental Psychology* 26: 683–697.

Maughan, B., Taylor, A., Caspi, A. & Moffitt, T.E. (2004). "Prenatal smoking and child conduct problems: testing genetic and environmental explanation of the association." *Archives of General Psychiatry* 61: 836–843.

McGue, M., Sharma, A., & Benson, P. (1996). "The effect of common rearing on adolescent adjustment: evidence from a US adoption cohort." *Developmental Psychology* 32: 604–613.

McGuire, S. (2003). "The heritability of parenting." *Parenting: Science and Practice* 3: 73–94.

Mednick, S.A. & Christiansen, K.O. (1977). *Biosocial Bases of Criminal Behavior.* New York: Gardner Press.

Mednick, S.A., Gabrielli, W.F., & Hutchings, B. (1984). "Genetic factors in criminal behavior: evidence from an adoption cohort." *Science* 224: 891–893.

Mednick, S.A., Moffitt, T.E., Gabrielli, W.F., & Hutchings, B. (1986). "Genetic factors in criminal behavior: a review." In J. Block, D. Olweus, & M.R. Yarrow (eds.), *The Development of Antisocial and Prosocial Behavior.* New York: Academic Press.

Meyer, J.M., Rutter, M., Silberg, J.L., Maes, H., Simonoff, E., Shillady, L.L., Pickles, A., Hewitt, J.K., & Eaves, L.J. (2000). "Familial aggregation for conduct disorder symptomatology: the role of genes, marital discord, and family adaptability." *Psychological Medicine* 30: 759–774.

Miles, D.R. & Carey, G. (1997). "Genetic and environmental architecture of human aggression." *Journal of Personality and Social Psychology* 72: 207–217.

Moffitt, T.E. (1993). "'Life-course-persistent' and 'adolescence-limited' antisocial behavior: a developmental taxonomy." *Psychological Review* 100: 674–701.

(2005). "The new look of behavioral genetics in developmental psychopathology: gene–environment interplay in antisocial behavior." *Psychological Bulletin* 131: 533–554.

Moffitt, T.E., Caspi, A., Rutter, M., & Silva, P.A. (2001). *Sex Differences In Antisocial Behavior: Conduct Disorder, Delinquency, and Violence in the Dunedin Longitudinal Study.* Cambridge: Cambridge University Press.

Moffitt, T. E. & the E-risk Study Team (2002). "Teen-aged mothers in contemporary Britain." *Journal of Child Psychology and Psychiatry* 43: 1–16.

Moilanen, I., Linna, S. L., Ebeling, H., Kampulainen, K., Tamminen, T., Piha, J., & Almqvist, F. (1999). "Are twins' behavioral/emotional problems different from singletons'?" *European Child and Adolescent Psychiatry* 8: 62–67.

Niederhiser, J. M., Reiss, D., Hetherington, E. M., & Plomin, R. (1999). "Relationships between parenting and adolescent adjustment over time: genetic and environmental contributions." *Developmental Psychology* 35: 680–692.

Niederhiser, J. M., Reiss, D., Pederson, N., Lichtenstein, P., Spotts, E. L., Hansson, K., Cederblad, M., & Elthammer, O. (2004). "Genetic and environmental influences on mothering of adolescents: a comparison of two samples." *Developmental Psychology* 40: 335–351.

O'Connor, T. G., Deater-Deckard, K., Fulker, D., Rutter, M., & Plomin, R. (1998). "Genotype–environment correlations in late childhood and early adolescence: antisocial behavioral problems in coercive parenting." *Developmental Psychology* 34: 970–981.

O'Connor, T. G., Heatherington, E. M., Reiss, D., & Plomin, R. (1995). "A twin-sibling study of observed parent–adolescent relations." *Child Development* 66: 812–829.

Olds, D., Henderson, C. R., Jr., Cole, R., Eckenrode, J., Kitzman, H., Luckey, D., Pettitt, L., Sidora, K., Morris, P., & Powers, J. (1998). "Long-term effects of nurse home visitation on children's criminal and antisocial behavior: 15-year follow-up of a randomized trial." *Journal of the American Medical Association* 280: 1238–1244.

Perusse, D., Neale, M. C., Heath, A. C., & Eaves, L. J. (1994). "Human parental behavior: evidence for genetic influence and potential implications for gene-culture transmission." *Behavior Genetics* 24: 327–336.

Pike, A., McGuire, S., Hetherington, E. M., Reiss, D., & Plomin, R. (1996). "Family environment and adolescent depressive symptoms and antisocial behavior: a multivariate genetic analysis." *Developmental Psychology* 32: 590–603.

Pike, A., Reiss, D., Hetherington, E. M., & Plomin, R. (1996). "Using MZ differences in the search for nonshared environmental effects." *Journal of Child Psychology and Psychiatry* 37: 695–704.

Plomin, R. (1994). *Genetics and Experience: The Interplay Between Nature and Nurture*. Thousand Oaks, CA: Sage.

Plomin, R. & Bergeman, C. S. (1991). "The nature of nurture: genetic influences on 'environmental' measures." *Behavioral and Brain Sciences* 14: 373–427.

Plomin, R. & Caspi, A. (1999). "Behavior genetics and personality." In L. A. Pervin & O. P. John (eds.), *Handbook of Personality*. New York: Guilford Press.

Plomin, R. & Daniels, D. (1987). "Why are children in the same family so different from each other?" *Behavioral and Brain Sciences* 10: 1–16.

Plomin, R., DeFries, J. C., & Loehlin, J. C. (1977). "Genotype–environment interaction and correlation in the analysis of human behavior." *Psychological Bulletin* 84: 309–322.

Plomin, R., DeFries, J. C., McClearn, G. E., & McGuffin, P. (2001). *Behavioral Genetics*, 4th edn. New York: W. H. Freeman.

Plomin, R., McClearn, G. E., Pederson, N. L., Nesselroade, J. R., & Bergeman, C. S. (1989). "Genetic influence on adults' ratings of their current family environment." *Journal of Marriage and the Family* 51: 791–803.

Purcell, S. (2002). "Variance components models for gene–environment interaction in twin analysis." *Twin Research* 5: 554–571.

Reid, J., Patterson G. R., & Snyder J. (2002). *Antisocial Behavior in Children and Adolescents.* Washington, DC: American Psychological Association.

Reiss, D., Neiderhiser, J. M., Hetherington, E. M., & Plomin, R. (2000). *The Relationship Code: Deciphering Genetic and Social Influences on Adolescent Development.* Cambridge, MA: Harvard University Press.

Rende, R. D., Slomkowski, C. L., Stocker, C., Fulker, D. W., & Plomin, R. (1992). "Genetic and environmental influences on maternal and sibling interaction in middle childhood: a sibling adoption study." *Developmental Psychology* 28: 484–490.

Rhee, S. H. & Waldman, I. D. (2002). "Genetic and environmental influences on antisocial behavior: a meta-analysis of twin and adoption studies." *Psychological Bulletin* 128: 490–529.

Riggins-Caspers, K. M., Cadoret, R. J., Knutson, J. F., & Langbehn, D. (2003). "Biology–environment interaction and evocative biology–environment correlation: contributions of harsh discipline and parental psychopathology to problem adolescent behaviors." *Behavior Genetics* 33: 205–220.

Rodgers, J. L., Rowe, D. C., & Li, C. (1994). "Beyond nature versus nurture: DF analysis of nonshared influences on problem behaviors." *Developmental Psychology* 30: 374–384.

Rose, R. J., Viken, R. J., Dick, D. M., Bates, J. E., Pulkinnen, L., & Kaprio, J. (2003). "It does take a village: nonfamilial environments and children's behavior." *Psychological Science* 14: 273–277.

Rowe, D. C. (1983). "A biometric analysis of perceptions of family environment." *Child Development* 54: 416–423.

(1994). *The Limits of Family Influence: Genes, Experience, and Behavior.* New York: Guilford Press.

Rowe, D. C., Almeida, D. M., & Jacobson, K. C. (1999). "School context and genetic influences on aggression in adolescence." *Psychological Science* 10: 277–280.

Rowe, D. C. & Farrington, D. P. (1997). "The familial transmission of criminal convictions." *Criminology* 35: 177–201.

Rutter, M. (2002). "Nature, nurture, and development: from evangelism through science toward policy and practice." *Child Development* 73: 1–21.

(2003a). "Commentary: Causal processes leading to antisocial behavior." *Developmental Psychology* (special issue on violent children) 39: 372–378.

(2003b). "Crucial paths from risk indicator to causal mechanism." In B. Lahey, T. E. Moffitt, & A. Caspi (eds.), *The Causes of Conduct Disorder and Serious Juvenile Delinquency.* New York: Guilford Press.

Rutter, M., Giller, H., & Hagell, A. (1998). *Antisocial Behavior by Young People.* Cambridge: Cambridge University Press.

Rutter, M., Pickles, A., Murray, R., & Eaves, L. (2001). "Testing hypotheses on specific environmental causal effects on behavior." *Psychological Bulletin* 127: 291–324.

Rutter, M. & Silberg, J. (2002). "Gene–environment interplay in relation to emotional and behavioral disturbance." *Annual Review of Psychology* 53: 463–490.

Scarr, S. (1991). "The construction of the family reality." *Behavioral and Brain Sciences* 14: 403–404.

(1992). "Developmental theories for the 1990's: development and individual differences." *Child Development* 63: 1–19.

Scarr, S. & McCartney, K. (1983). "How people make their own environments." *Child Development* 54: 424–435.

Serbin, L. & Karp, J. (2003). "Intergenerational studies of parenting and the transfer of risk from parent to child." *Current Directions in Psychological Science* 12: 138–142.

Sharma, A. R., McGue, M. K., & Benson, P. L. (1998). "The psychological adjustment of United States adopted adolescents and their nonadopted siblings." *Child Development* 69: 791–802.

Sherman, L. W., Gottfredson, D. C., MacKenzie, D. L., Eck, J., Reuter, P., & Bushway, S. D. (1999). *Preventing Crime: What Works, What Doesn't, What's Promising.* New York: Russell Sage. Also available from the US Department of Justice, http://www.ojp.usdoj.gov/nij.

Silberg, J. L. (2002). *Parental Effects on Depression and Disruptive Behavior in the Children of Twins: A Proposal to the US National Institute of Mental Health.* Richmond, VA: Medical College of Virginia.

Silberg, J. L. & Eaves, L. J. (2004). "Analysing the contributions of genes and parent–child interaction to childhood behavioral and emotional problems: a model for the children of twins." *Psychological Medicine* 34: 1–10.

Simonoff, E., Pickles, A., Meyer, J. M., Silberg, J., Maes, H., Loeber, R., Rutter M., Hewitt J. K., & Eaves L. J. (1997). "The Virginia Twin Study of adolescent behavioral development" *Archives of General Psychiatry* 54: 801–808.

Spinath, F. M. & O'Connor, T. G. (2003). "A behavioral genetic study of the overlap between personality and parenting." *Journal of Personality* 71: 785–808.

Stoolmiller, M. (1999). "Implications of the restricted range of family environments for estimates of heritability and nonshared environment in behavior–genetic adoption studies." *Psychological Bulletin* 125: 392–409.

Thornberry, T. P., ed. (1996). *Advances in Criminological Theory: Developmental Theories of Crime and Delinquency.* London: Transaction.

Towers, H., Spotts, E. L., & Niederhiser, J. (2001). "Genetic and environmental influences on parenting and marital relationships: current findings and future directions." *Marriage and Family Review* 33: 11–29.

Turkheimer, E. & Waldron, M. (2000). "Nonshared environment: a theoretical, methodological, and quantitative review." *Psychological Bulletin* 126: 78–108.

US Bureau of Justice Statistics (2002). *Criminal Victimization 2001*. (NCJ Report 194610). Washington, DC: US Department of Justice. Available at http://www.ojp.usdof.gov/bjs.

van den Oord, E. J. C. G., Koot, H. M., Boomsma, D. I., Verhulst, F.C., & Orlebeke, J. F. (1995). "A twin–singleton comparison of problem behavior in 2–3 year olds." *Journal of Child Psychology and Psychiatry* 36: 449–458.

van der Valk, J. C., Verhulst, F. C., Stroet, T. M., & Boomsma, D. I. (1998). "Quantitative genetic analysis of internalising and externalising problems in a large sample of 3-year-old twins." *Twin Research* 1: 25–33.

Vandell, D. L. (2000). "Parents, peer groups, and other socializing influences." *Developmental Psychology* 36: 699–710.

VanDusen, K., Mednick, S. A., Gabrielli, W. F., & Hutchings, B. (1983). "Social class and crime in an adoption cohort." *Journal of Criminal Law and Criminology* 74: 249–269.

Wade, T. D. & Kendler, K. S. (2000). "The genetic epidemiology of parental discipline." *Psychological Medicine* 30: 1303–1313.

Wandersman, A. & Florin, P. (2003). "Community interventions and effective prevention." *American Psychologist* 58: 441–448.

Wasserman, G. A. & Miller, L. S. (1998). "The prevention of serious and violent juvenile offending." In R. Loeber & D. P. Farrington (eds.), *Serious and Violent Juvenile Offenders*. Thousand Oaks, CA: Sage.

Weissberg, R. P., Kumpfer, K. L., & Seligman, M. E. P. (2003). "Prevention that works for children and youth." *American Psychologist* 58: 425–432.

Wilson, D. B., Gottfredson, D. C., & Najaka, S. S. (2001). "School-based prevention of problem behaviors: a meta-analysis." *Journal of Quantitative Criminology* 17: 247–272.

Wolfgang, M. E., Figlio, R. M., & Sellin, T. (1972). *Delinquency in a Birth Cohort*. Chicago: University of Chicago Press.

World Health Organization (2002). *World Report on Violence and Health*. Geneva.

Yoshikawa, H. (1994). "Prevention as cumulative protection." *Psychological Bulletin* 115: 28–54.

5 A three-dimensional, cumulative developmental model of serious delinquency

Rolf Loeber, N. Wim Slot, and Magda Stouthamer-Loeber

Modern criminological theories aim to explain crime, but they do so with a different emphasis on pathways to crime and ranges of explanatory factors (e.g., Thornberry & Krohn, 2002; Farrington, 2005; Wikström, 2005). Theoretical explanations of serious delinquency and violence are sometimes met with consistent empirical findings, and sometimes with equivocal results. On the one hand, meta-analyses indicate a high degree of replication of bivariate associations between explanatory/risk factors and later serious delinquency (e.g., Lipsey & Derzon, 1998; Howell, 2003). On the other hand, results from multivariate analyses based on multiple predictors vary greatly from study to study (Thornberry, 1997; Thornberry & Krohn, 2002; Farrington, 2005). This is partly caused by studies selecting relatively few of the known explanatory/risk factors of serious delinquency and underemphasizing other factors. Although theories of antisocial and delinquent behavior often have several factors in common (e.g., juveniles' relationships with parents and peers), they differ in their relative emphasis on domains, settings, and details of explanatory factors, and the ways that these factors are interrelated (see above sources and chapters in Lahey, Moffitt, & Caspi, 2003 and in Farrington, 2005).

We are greatly indebted to the following individuals for their advice: David Farrington, John Laub, Marc Le Blanc, and Dustin Pardini. Tony Glass with great enthusiasm prepared the three-dimensional drawings. Leena Augimeri, Alison Hipwell, James (Buddy) C. Howell, and Chris Koegl provided most useful comments on an earlier draft, and Debra Anthony assisted with the final preparations of the chapter. The research was supported by grant no. 96-MU-FX-0012 from the Office of Juvenile Justice and Delinquency Prevention, grant no. 50778 from the National Institute of Mental Health, and grant no. 411018 from the National Institute of Drug Abuse. Points of view or opinions in this document are those of the authors and do not necessarily represent the official position or policies of the US Department of Justice, the National Institute of Mental Health, and the National Institute of Drug Abuse.

The theories almost always share three themes with the goals of explaining (i) antisocial and delinquent behavior over the life course, particularly in terms of prevalence, frequency, and severity of delinquent acts, (ii) individual differences in antisocial/delinquent behavior and developmental changes in these differences, and (iii) non-offending or low-level offending. The key is for researchers, practitioners and policymakers to understand how the combination of (i), (ii), and (iii) explains why some individuals and not others become serious property offenders or violent offenders and understand this both on the population level (e.g., all youth in a particular city) and on the individual level (that is, a particular juvenile minor offender at risk of becoming a serious offender). Along these lines, there is a need for better life-course models that incorporate the development and accumulation of risk and protective factors. To date, the integration of these components in a model has taken place almost exclusively through the following methods. Firstly, model specification is usually visually illustrated in a two-dimensional plane of variables in boxes (representing mostly independent variables and usually a single outcome of antisocial behavior) and their interrelationships are expressed by arrows between the boxes. Secondly, virtually all model specification rests on statistical tests of the hypothesized relationships between independent measures, also called risk factors (the boxes), and an outcome, such as serious delinquency. Risk factors are defined here as events or conditions that are associated with an increased probability of serious forms of delinquency, and are distinguished from promotive factors, which are those associated with lowered risk of delinquency. Following the example of Sameroff *et al.* (1998), we distinguish between promotive and protective factors, with the former referring to main effects regarding positive outcomes (comparable to the main effects of risk factors, but then inverted), while the latter are positive factors studied in situations in which individuals are exposed to risk factors or adversity (thus, an interactive term), following the position put forward by Rutter (1985).

Theoretical approaches, buttressed by empirical, longitudinal data and multivariate statistical models developed over the past four decades, have demonstrated that antisocial behavior is explained by multiple factors, that there are linkages between independent factors (in terms of mediation and moderation), and that it is useful to control for possible confounds. However, there are at least five limitations. Firstly, the results of the multivariate models have been enormously diverse. The second disadvantage is that most models have not delineated developmental pathways to serious forms of antisocial behavior (such as violence) by the specification of developmental antecedents to such serious outcomes (e.g., aggression). We presume that such a specification is necessary to identify both homotypic and heterotypic continuity of antisocial behavior and delinquency with development. Homotypic continuity refers to the continuity of the same manifestations over time, whereas heterotypic continuity refers to different manifestations of antisocial behavior that are developmentally linked in a successive manner over time. Against this backdrop of continuity and discontinuity of antisocial behaviors, we need to better understand selection processes which influence how and why certain individuals and not others become serious offenders. The third limitation of current multivariate models is that they usually address, in a very limited fashion, changes in the saliency of risk factors and their risk domains with development. Fourthly, current models do not specify differences between individuals in their exposure to an *accumulation* of specific risk (or promotive) factors with development. A fifth disadvantage has to do with the fact that the majority of studies focus only on risk factors as a way of explaining antisocial behavior and neglect to consider either promotive factors or the combined effect of risk and promotive factors on antisocial outcomes.

Finally, two major strengths of current criminological theories are the explanation of current offending levels in populations and the risk of future offending. However, we argue that criminological theories can be enhanced in at least two other ways, firstly by incorporating past development, and secondly, by incorporating possible future development. In the first category are differences in individuals' *past history of offending* (and history of behavior problems that are precursors to delinquency), and differences in the *individuals' exposure to earlier risk factors* (e.g., prenatal exposure to toxins or child abuse during the preschool period) *and promotive factors* (e.g., a good relationship with an adult). The second understudied area has to do with two aspects of individuals' futures: firstly, the possible course of subsequent delinquent development (or pathways) as examined by longitudinal studies of youths who have been followed up into adulthood; and secondly, expected exposure to risk and promotive factors based on the observation of such factors in older populations of youths. Examples of "new" risk factors that may enter individuals' lives include gang membership, victimization, and alcohol intoxication. In summary, we propose that developmental models should benefit from knowledge of pathways and exposure to risk and promotive factors based on past studies which can then provide a framework in which to place the development of specific individuals. In that sense, population data can describe both the stages in pathways to serious delinquency (the latter being the outer, more severe boundary) and the gradual accumulation of risk and protective factors that can maximally take place in populations (another instance of an outer boundary). Knowledge of these two types of outer boundary will make it possible to describe the past history of an individual's antisocial and delinquent behavior, his/her past exposure to risk and protective factors, and possible future exposure to ongoing or new risk and protective factors.

One of the key advantages of such a model is that, in contrast to current statistical models, it is likely to provide valuable information about choices and targets of intervention. This is very much in line with contemporary principles of prevention and intervention, with its focus on behavioral development and an emphasis on reducing exposure to risk factors while at the same time increasing exposure to promotive factors (Slot, 1995; Pollard, Hawkins, & Arthur, 1999).

This chapter argues that an enhanced developmental model incorporating these aspects ideally should represent the following components: behavioral development and the accumulation of risk and promotive factors with development. In addition, we argue that the integration of these components can be best achieved in a three- rather than a two-dimensional model. We also propose that such a model is needed, especially if policymakers, informed lay-persons, and practitioners will find it easier to understand than current multivariate formulae. To construct such a model it is necessary to review five key topics: (i) pathways representing individuals' escalation toward serious property offences and violence; (ii) differences between individuals in their exposure to risk and promotive factors at birth (called start-up factors) and subsequently during childhood, adolescence, and early adulthood; (iii) developmental accumulation of risk and promotive factors over time; (iv) the existence of a dose–response relationship between the number of risk/promotive factors and later serious delinquency and violence; and (v) additive and compensatory effects of promotive and risk factors. Finally, we integrate these five aspects into a single, three-dimensional cumulative developmental model.

Escalation and the formulation of developmental pathways

Youths who commit acts of violence or serious theft rarely do so *de novo*. Instead, many criminologists, child psychologists, and psychiatrists agree that the majority of youth who commit acts of violence or serious theft practiced less serious forms of delinquency earlier in life (e.g., Loeber *et al.*, 1992; Loeber, Wung *et al.*, 1993; Elliott, 1994; Elliott & Menard (1996); Rutter, Giller, & Hagell, 1998; Le Blanc, 2002; Warr,

2002). Thus, the onset of violence is usually preceded by a history of escalation in the severity of aggression, which often, but not always, starts in childhood (Loeber *et al.*, 1998; Moffitt, 1993). Research shows that for some offenders, early involvement in status offences and delinquency are stepping stones on pathways to serious, violent, and chronic offending. About a quarter to a third of those children who engage in non-delinquent disruptive behavior are at risk of escalating to minor delinquent acts. About a third to a half of child delinquents are at risk of escalating to serious delinquency (Loeber & Farrington, 2001).

A key issue in criminology is whether individuals' development to serious delinquency fits a hierarchical, developmental model that can represent individuals' escalation from minor to serious antisocial acts. Le Blanc (2002) reviewed the extensive literature on methods and findings pertaining to escalation processes in delinquency (such as transition matrices, dynamic classification strategies, cluster analyses, semi-parametric or mixed Poisson regression analyses, and developmental sequence strategies) and found substantial evidence for developmental sequences from minor to more serious forms of delinquency (e.g., Loeber, 1988; Elliott, Huizinga, & Menard, 1989; Le Blanc, Côté, & Loeber, 1991; Elliott, 1994).

The findings of several studies (e.g., Elliott, 1994) focus on a single escalation pathway. However Loeber, Wung *et al.* (1993) challenged this and tested a triple pathway model (Figure 5.1), which better fitted the data. The three-pathway model has been subsequently replicated across two other samples in the Pittsburgh Youth Study (Loeber, Wung *et al.*, 1993; Loeber *et al.*, 1998). The pathways are: (i) an *authority conflict pathway* prior to the age of 12, that starts with stubborn behavior, has defiance as a second stage, and authority avoidance (e.g., truancy) as a third stage; (ii) a *covert pathway* prior to age 15 which starts with minor covert acts, has property damage as a second stage, and moderate to serious delinquency as a third stage; and (iii) an *overt pathway* that starts with minor aggression, has physical fighting as a second stage, and more severe violence as a third stage. It is possible that within this last stage, homicide constitutes a separate, and most serious, component. Recent longitudinal research on the Pittsburgh Youth Study (Loeber *et al.*, 2005) indicates that 94 percent of later homicide offenders have displayed violence earlier in life. The pathways are hierarchical in that those who have advanced to the most serious behavior in each of the pathways have usually displayed persistent problem behavior characteristics at the earlier stages in each pathway. The pathways are also related to neighborhoods. For example, a higher percentage of youth in the most disadvantaged neighborhoods escalates from minor

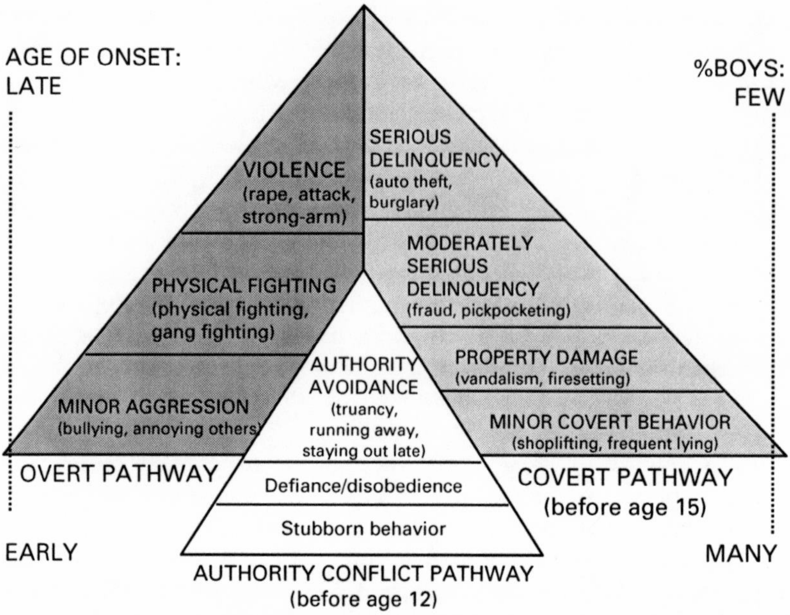

Figure 5.1. Developmental pathways to serious delinquency and violence

aggression to violence than youth living in more advantaged neighborhoods (Loeber & Wikström, 1993).

Tolan, Gorman-Smith, and Loeber (2000) have also demonstrated empirical support for the triple-pathway model in a sample of African American and Hispanic male adolescents in Chicago and in a nationally representative US sample of adolescents. Further, the Denver Youth Survey and the Rochester Youth Development Study have also largely replicated earlier findings (Loeber *et al.*, 1999). Finally, recent analysis has shown that the pathway model also mostly fits the development of antisocial behavior in girls (Gorman-Smith & Loeber, in press).

The above studies, that have focused primarily on males, show that with age a proportion of boys progress on two or three pathways, indicating an increasing variety of problem behavior over time (Kelley *et al.*, 1997; Loeber, Keenan, & Zhang, 1997; Loeber, Wung *et al.*, 1993). Also, Loeber, Wung *et al.* (1993) found evidence that development in multiple pathways is not interchangeable, in that boys who escalate in the overt pathway are more likely to escalate in the covert pathway as well, compared to a lower probability of boys in the covert pathway escalating in the overt pathway. Thus, aggressive boys are particularly at risk of committing covert acts, whereas boys engaging in covert acts are less likely to develop aggressive behaviors. Further, escalation in either the overt or covert pathway is often preceded by boys' escalation in the authority conflict pathway (Loeber, Wung *et al.*, 1993). In other words, conflict with authority figures is either a precursor or a concomitant of boys' escalation in overt or covert acts. Also, an early age of onset of problem behavior or delinquency, compared to onset at a later age, is associated with boys' escalation to more serious behaviors in the pathways (Tolan *et al.*, 2000). The pathway model accounts for the majority of the most seriously affected boys, that is the self-reported high-rate offenders (Loeber, Wung *et al.*, 1993; Loeber, Keenan, & Zhang, 1997) and court-reported delinquents (Loeber, Keenan, & Zhang, 1997). Evidence for the escalation of antisocial behaviors according to pathways also fits findings in psychiatry of a hierarchical, escalation model in disruptive behavior disorders (American Psychiatric Association, 1994). Research findings support the notion that a proportion of boys who qualify for oppositional defiant disorder are at risk of developing conduct disorder over time, whereas a proportion of conduct-disordered boys are at risk of developing antisocial personality disorder[1] (Loeber, Burke, & Lahey, 2002; Lahey *et al.*, in press). In summary, developmental pathways in antisocial behavior/delinquency and developmental transitions between different disruptive diagnoses share a conceptualization of escalation in the severity of antisocial behaviors with development in certain individuals. By a process of selection, increasingly smaller groups of youth become at risk for the more serious behaviors.

It should be kept in mind that the formulation and tests of the above pathway model are limited in that they use retrospective information prior to age 7, which is not known to be consistently reliable. Keenan and Shaw (2003) formulated a dual-stage escalation model for the preschool period. One pathway, called *pathway to reactive antisocial behavior*, starts with irritable behavior during infancy. Children displaying persistent irritability are at risk of developing emotional difficulties as toddlers (low frustration tolerance, overactivity, and being demanding), and, in turn, are at risk of developing disruptive angry behavior as preschoolers. A second pathway, called *pathway to proactive antisocial behavior*, starts with children displaying under-arousal (i.e., they are under-responsive to stimulation) who appear at risk of developing behavior difficulties as toddlers (as demonstrated by persistent unresponsiveness to punishment, and high sensation-seeking), and, in turn, are at risk of developing callous unemotional behavior later (demonstrated by stealing, lying, deliberate fighting, and violation of

[1] Even when controlling for the APD criterion of conduct disorder having been present prior to age 16 (American Psychiatric Association, 1994).

rules). The two pathways in early childhood postulated by Keenan and Shaw (2003) clearly need substantiation, but can eventually be linked to the first two steps in the authority conflict pathway in our pathway model (stubborn behavior and defiance/disobedience; Figure 5.1). Such an addition would enhance a future model of the development of antisocial behavior from early childhood to early adulthood.

Both the Loeber and the Keenan pathway models have in common the operation of selection processes, starting with a broad base of children with age-normative problem behaviors. From that group a select proportion of children advances to the next stage, and from that group, an even smaller select group advances to the next, more serious stage of problem behavior. This incremental selection process, as children advance through deviancy pathways, can be conceptualized as a shift in the distribution of youth. Whereas at the initial level of age-normative problem behavior the distribution is usually normal, as children advance through pathways the distribution becomes increasingly skewed as it increasingly represents the more deviant youth.

The specification of developmental pathways can be contrasted with the identification of *developmental trajectories*, which are defined as the classification of individuals according to their behavior *over time*. The assumption is that a population of individuals "is composed of a mixture of groups with distinct developmental trajectories" (Nagin & Tremblay, 2001: 21). Typically, trajectory analyses have been based on repeated measurements of a single indicator of problem behavior. Usually, the results of trajectory analyses have identified young males whose problem behavior remains high over time, those whose problem behavior remains low, those whose problem behavior increases, and those whose problem behavior decreases between childhood and early adulthood (e.g., Maughan *et al.*, 2000; Broidy *et al.*, 2003; Bushway, Thornberry, & Krohn, 2003; Lacourse *et al.*, 2003; Shaw & Nagin, 2003; Nagin & Tremblay, in press). Although the trajectory approach has provided new insights into the development of antisocial and delinquent behavior, it has not usually illuminated heterotypic continuity of different categories of problem behaviors and, therefore, has not yet described escalation processes from less to more serious forms of delinquency in terms of timing of behavior changes, emergence of high-rate serious offenders, and transition probabilities between less and more serious forms of antisocial acts. In addition, all attempts at trajectory analyses to date are postdictive rather than predictive in that assignment of individuals to specific trajectories is only possible when all longitudinal data is used. Instead, practitioners and researchers need developmental models that can illustrate selection processes and the slow incremental nature within individuals of heterotypic transformations of different forms of antisocial behavior and delinquency from childhood to adulthood.

Risk factors

The majority of theories about the causes of crime and antisocial behavior are generally based on risk factors alone, although different terms for such factors have been used (e.g., Elliott *et al.*, 1985; Wilson & Herrnstein, 1985; Le Blanc & Fréchette, 1989; Gottfredson & Hirschi, 1990; Moffitt, 1993; Farrington, 1996). Risk factors can be distinguished according to the different domains and contexts in which they operate. Overall, researchers and theoreticians agree (with some variation) to distinguish risk factors in the following domains: individual, family, and peer group. In addition, some risk factors are associated with children's exposure to risk factors in specific contexts, including characteristics of the school attended and the neighborhood in which the children reside or spend their time (Loeber *et al.*, 1998; Howell, 2003; Stouthamer-Loeber *et al.*, 2002). Data from prediction studies indicate that risk factors from each of the domains (individual, family, peers, schools, and neighborhoods) contribute to the explanation of why some individuals and not others progress from minor problem behavior such as bullying, to physical fighting, to violence (e.g., Farrington, 1997; Hawkins *et al.*, 1998; Lipsey & Derzon, 1998, Loeber *et al.*, in press). Individuals' exposure to an accumulation of risk factors in multiple domains rather than in a single domain heightens the probability of later adverse outcomes (Rutter, Tizard, & Whitemore, 1970). For example, Deater-Deckard *et al.* (1998) reported that four domains (child characteristics, socio-cultural, parent, and peer experiences) each contributed to the prediction of externalizing problems.

Many researchers have been relatively silent about the developmental saliency and priority of different domains of risk factor (individual, family, peer, etc.), other than noting that children's exposure to family factors usually precedes their exposure to peer factors (e.g., Loeber, 1985). However, another way of looking at development (instead of linked to developmental periods, such as early, middle, and late childhood) is to examine the relative saliency of risk domains as an explanation of why some individuals escalate from minor problem behaviors to very serious forms of delinquency. No single domain is thought fully to explain this pattern of development. Instead, the data suggest that risk factors from all three domains (individual, family, and peers) and the two contexts (schools and neighborhoods) contribute to the explanation of delinquency escalation processes. Figure 5.2

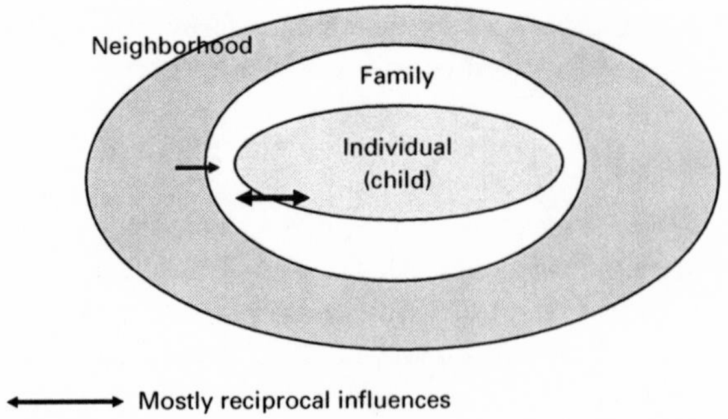

Figure 5.2. Nested domains of influences on children (toddler period)
Source: Based on Bronfenbrenner, 1979.

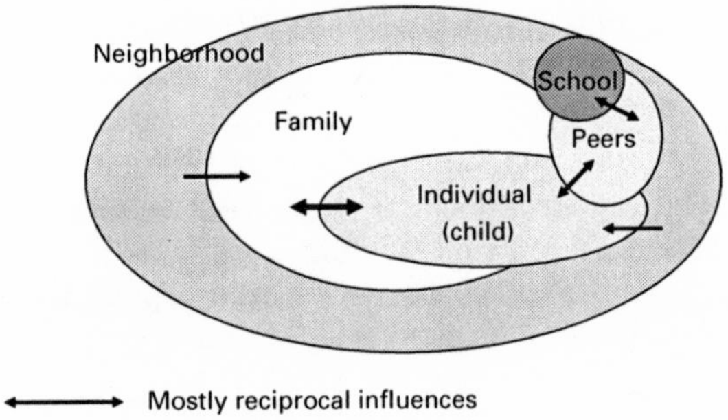

Figure 5.3. Changes in nested domains of influences on children from middle childhood onward.

shows the typical thinking about the nesting of risk factors (based on Bronfenbrenner's [1979] model; for another variant, see Lerner & Castellino, 2002) in which, at a young age, the individual (child) is mostly affected by family factors, which in turn are affected by neighborhood factors. In this conceptualization, the child is only indirectly affected by neighborhood factors through the family. As children develop, this nesting of problem behaviors changes, with children becoming more mobile and also becoming more active in selecting settings with their own risk and promotive factors (Wikström, 2005). This is represented in Figure 5.3, when children become exposed to risk and promotive factors of peers, school, and, eventually, work. Thus, with development, there is a reconfiguration of risk domains with new domains being introduced over time.

Developmentally graded risk factors. Among the risk factors, some are thought to be present at birth or to become manifest shortly afterwards, while other risk factors emerge later in individuals' lives. Before discussing each category of risk factor, our overall strategy is to view risk factors from a developmental angle in that children's exposure to different risk factors is gradual, that with development, children's exposure to different risk domains increases, and that many risk factors persist over time and, consequently, are "stacked" over time. It would be clearly untenable to insist that all the risk and promotive factors mentioned in the preceding section are present in juveniles' lives from a very young age onward. Instead, it is much more likely that selection processes operate in which certain categories of children and youth are incrementally exposed to certain risk and promotive factors as they grow into adults.

Table 5.1 summarizes our knowledge of risk factors in each of the different domains as children grow into adults (largely based on Loeber, 1990; Hawkins *et al.*, 1998; Lipsey & Derzon, 1998; Howell, 2003). To structure the review of the risk factors, we distinguish between different developmental periods, starting with risk factors present at birth and continuing with those emerging during the following periods: preschool, elementary school, middle/high school, and early adulthood. Emergence is defined as the probable earliest exposure of children to risk factors. Systematic knowledge in this respect is still wanting, and as a result we have made estimates (knowing that some of the onset of risk factors, such as in the case of poor executive functioning, partly depends on the state of measurement in that area). Note that emergence should not be taken too literally and may apply differently from one child to another. However, we maintain that an accumulation of risk factors may take place over many years, and that risk factors at birth (e.g., low IQ, negative emotionality), may be followed by exposure to "new" risk factors emerging during early childhood, such as language problems, which in turn may be followed by other novel risk factors emerging during middle to late childhood, such as poor social skills, or poor academic achievement. During adolescence, novel risk factors may consist of heavy substance use or delinquent victimization. These examples are risk factors in the individual domain, but Table 5.1 shows that a similar accumulation of new risk factors may occur in other domains as well, such as the family, peers, schools, and neighborhood (including work). It should be noted that, to some extent, risk factors emerging in one life period may persist across another life period and that even when they are time-limited (e.g., child abuse) they may influence the probability of serious delinquency in a cumulative manner.

What developmental shifts in the saliency and accumulation of risk and promotive factors take place over time? Figure 5.4, based on

Table 5.1. *Emergence of risk factors*

Domain	At birth	Early childhood	Mid to late childhood	Adolescence	Early adulthood
Individual	Low IQ	CONTINUITY OF EARLIER INDIVIDUAL FACTORS +	CONTINUITY OF EARLIER INDIVIDUAL FACTORS +	CONTINUITY OF EARLIER INDIVIDUAL FACTORS +	CONTINUITY OF EARLIER INDIVIDUAL FACTORS +
	Negative emotionality	NEW FACTORS Developmental delays	CONTINUITY OF EARLIER INDIVIDUAL FACTORS +	CONTINUITY OF EARLIER INDIVIDUAL FACTORS +	CONTINUITY OF EARLIER INDIVIDUAL FACTORS +
	Prenatal exposure to toxins	Language problems	NEW FACTORS Withdrawn behavior	CONTINUITY OF EARLIER INDIVIDUAL FACTORS +	CONTINUITY OF EARLIER INDIVIDUAL FACTORS +
	Pregnancy/birth complications	Lack of guilt	Poor social skills	NEW FACTORS Heavy substance use	CONTINUITY OF EARLIER INDIVIDUAL FACTORS +
	Perinatal problems	Callous/ unemotional behavior	Cognitive attributional bias pertaining to aggression	Drug-dealing	Unemployment
		Positive attitude to behavior problems	Poor academic achievement	Weapon use	
		Impulsivity/ daringness	Low school motivation	Delinquent victimization	
		Attention problems	Positive attitude to delinquency		
		Poor executive functioning	Positive attitude to substance use		

		Counter control (child acts up more when disciplined)	Negative life events		
			Poor ability to plan for the future		
			Early puberty/ maturation (especially in girls)		
Family	Low SES	CONTINUITY OF EARLIER FAMILY FACTORS +	CONTINUITY OF EARLIER FAMILY FACTORS +	CONTINUITY OF EARLIER FAMILY FACTORS +	CONTINUITY OF EARLIER FAMILY FACTORS +
	Large family	NEW FACTORS Inconsistent discipline	CONTINUITY OF EARLIER FAMILY FACTORS +	CONTINUITY OF EARLIER FAMILY FACTORS +	CONTINUITY OF EARLIER FAMILY FACTORS +
	Parental unemployment	Physical punishment	NEW FACTORS Poor parent–child relationship	CONTINUITY OF EARLIER FAMILY FACTORS +	CONTINUITY OF EARLIER FAMILY FACTORS +
	Welfare	Child abuse	Poor communication		
	Family delinquency	Neglect	Poor supervision		
	Parent psychopathology	Deviant siblings	Low aspirations for child		
	Parent substance abuse	No. of caretaker changes			
	Poor education of parent(s)	High parental stress			
	Teenage motherhood	Social isolation			
	Single parenthood	Poor relationship with partner			

Table 5.1. *(Cont.)*

Domain	At birth	Early childhood	Mid to late childhood	Adolescence	Early adulthood
		Parental positive attitude to child problem behavior			
Peers		NEW FACTORS Peer rejection	CONTINUITY OF EARLIER PEER FACTORS +	CONTINUITY OF EARLIER PEER FACTORS +	CONTINUITY OF EARLIER PEER FACTORS +
		Victimization (bullying)	NEW FACTORS Peer delinquency	CONTINUITY OF EARLIER PEER FACTORS +	CONTINUITY OF EARLIER PEER FACTORS +
			Peer substance use	NEW FACTORS Neighborhood gangs	CONTINUITY OF EARLIER PEER FACTORS +
School			NEW FACTORS	CONTINUITY OF EARLIER SCHOOL FACTORS +	
			High school deviancy level		
			Poorly organized school		
Neighbor-hood			NEW FACTORS Disadvantaged neighborhood	CONTINUITY OF EARLIER NEIGHBOR-HOOD FACTORS +	CONTINUITY OF EARLIER NEIGHBORHOOD FACTORS +
			High neighborhood crime		

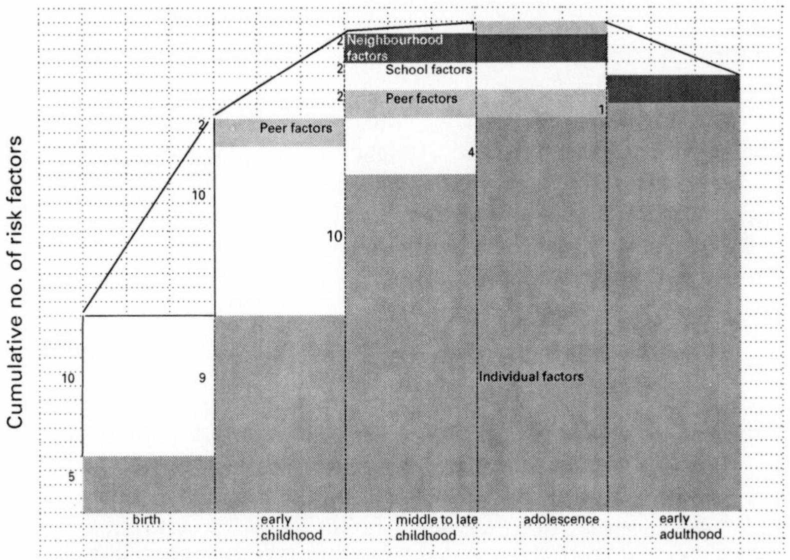

Figure 5.4. Developmental model of onset, accumulation, and continuity of risk factors

Table 5.1, shows that the total number of risk factors associated with antisocial behavior and delinquency to which children can be exposed is about the same at or close to birth (15), emerging in the preschool years (12), and emerging in the elementary school years (18). A much lower number of risk factors probably first appear during the middle and high school years (5). Thus, the most salient risk window of children's exposure to risk factors is prior to adolescence. This must be true for early-onset cases of antisocial behavior and delinquency. Even within the category of early-onset cases, the model is flexible in that we assume that none of the early risk factors is necessary for the emergence of antisocial behavior and delinquency. In that sense, there can be some substitution of risk factors that apply to some and not to other early-onset cases. This important point can be investigated by the examination of risk patterns for different categories of offenders.

The emergence of later-onset cases of antisocial behavior/delinquency can be explained in at least three ways: (i) the absence (or limited number) of risk factors early in life; (ii) children's exposure to risk factors at that later age; and/or (iii) the accumulation of risk factors with a later onset. Thus, the explanations of early-onset and later-onset antisocial behavior/delinquency are similar, in that children are likely to be exposed to an accumulation of risk factors rather than any one single risk.

The accumulation of risk factors represented in Figure 5.4 questions a commonly held assumption among practitioners, researchers, and lay-people, namely that individual risk factors manifest themselves mostly during early childhood, and that "nurture" in the form of endogenous risk factors (in the family, peer groups, etc.) would manifest itself more dominantly afterwards. In contrast to this notion, however, Figure 5.4 suggests that individual risk factors continue to increase in number after childhood and constitute a substantial proportion of all known risk factors after early childhood.

Dose–response relationship between risk factors and delinquency

In the field of epidemiology, there are many examples of diseases and other negative outcomes that become more likely the higher the number of risk factors that are present in individuals' lives. Typically in epidemiological research, risk factors are dichotomized and the presence of each risk factor is counted as one. A summary score is then computed representing the number of known risk factors to which an individual is exposed (this is usually called the Burgess method of computing future risk). A key reason we emphasize the Burgess method rather than a multivariate approach is that the former method is more suitable for the computation of false positive and false negative errors, which are essential pieces of information for the design and evaluation of screening devices to establish the future risk of delinquency (and escalation to serious offending) for each individual. The computation of relative improvement over chance (ROC) curves based on sensitivity and specificity is a further aid in determining the optimal cut-off to use in such a screening score (e.g., Farrington & Loeber, 1989).

Studies agree that the higher the number of risk factors, the greater the likelihood that individuals will be affected by a disease or other deviant behavior such as serious delinquency. This association is usually called a dose–response relationship and has been demonstrated for the full range of indicators of antisocial behavior: sociopathy (Robins, 1966), externalizing problems (Deater-Decker *et al.*, 1998), conduct problems (Sameroff *et al.*, 1998; Fergusson & Woodward, 2000; but see Gerard & Buehler, 2004), serious delinquency (Smith *et al.*, 1994), and violence (Farrington, 1997; Loeber *et al.*, 2005).

Figure 5.5 shows results from longitudinal analyses by Farrington (1997) on the data of the Cambridge Study on Delinquent Development. An index of seven factors measured at ages 8–10, consisting of troublesomeness, conduct disorder by age 13, acting out, social handicap,

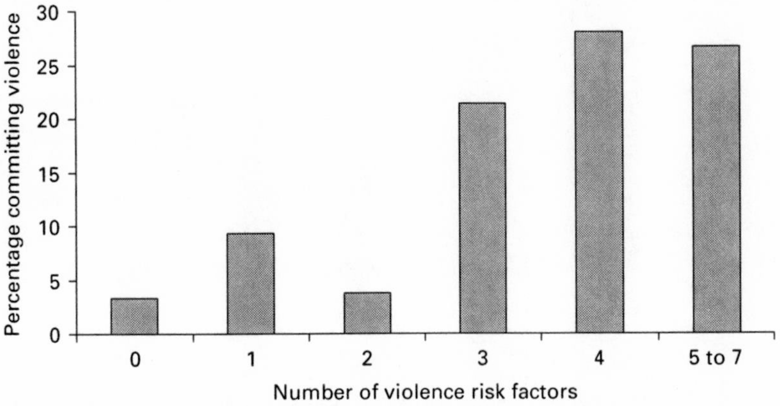

Figure 5.5. The prediction of violence in a London sample
Source: Farrington, 1997.

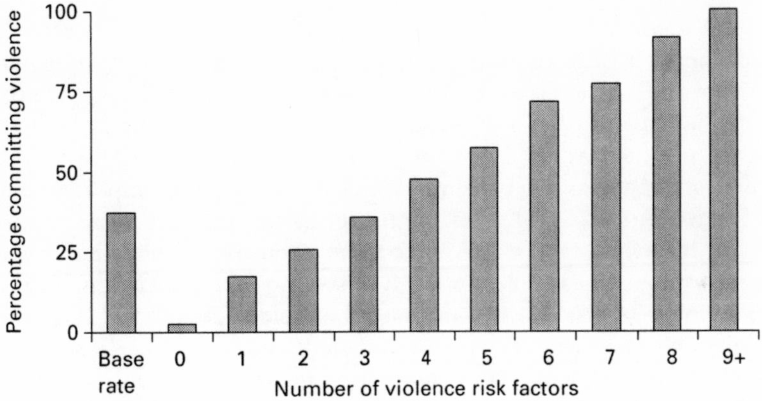

Figure 5.6. Proportion of boys committing violent offences for different levels of risk
Source: Based on Loeber *et al.*, 2005.

convicted parent, low non-verbal intelligence, and poor parental child-rearing behavior. This index predicts conviction for violence up to age 20 (odds ratio [OR] = 4.7). As another example (Figure 5.6), a prediction index in the Pittsburgh Youth Study was constructed on the basis of the eleven strongest predictors of violence (Loeber *et al.*, 2005): truancy, low school motivation, onset of delinquency before age 10, cruelty to people, depressed mood, physical aggression, callous/unemotional behavior, low family socio-economic status, family on welfare, high parental stress, and bad (i.e., disadvantaged) neighborhood

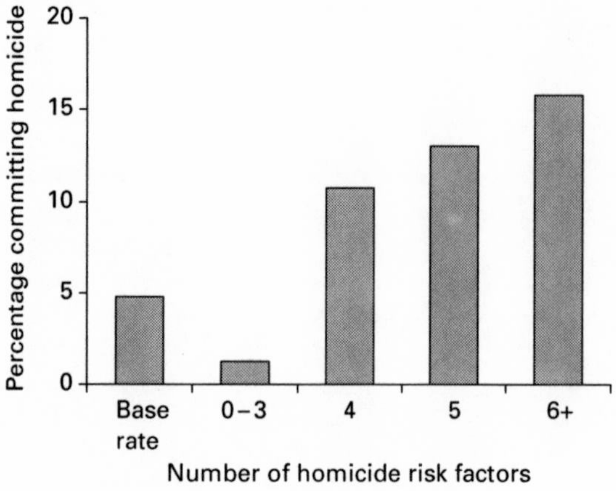

Figure 5.7. Proportion of violent boys convicted of homicide for different levels of risk
Source: Based on Loeber *et al.*, 2005.

(parent report). Figure 5.6 also shows that the dose–response relationship applies to the number of predictors and the probability of later violence (OR = 6.0 for four or more risk factors). Remarkably, the range of probabilities in the Pittsburgh data is from 3 percent at zero risk factors to 100 percent at eleven or more risk factors (that is, a much wider range than in Farrington's [1997] study). Another important issue to be determined is whether homicide, as the most extreme form of violent behavior, can be predicted among violent offenders, and whether, in this case as well, there is a dose–response association between the number of risk factors and later homicide. Figure 5.7 shows the prediction of homicide among the violent offenders (Loeber *et al.*, 2005) based on the following risk factors: high risk score (of antisocial behavior) at screening, positive attitude to substance use, conduct disorder by age 13, carrying a weapon, gang-fighting, selling hard drugs, peer delinquency, being held back in school, and family on welfare. Figure 5.7 shows that the higher the number of risk factors, the higher the probability of homicide. The probability of homicide is low for zero to three risk factors, but after that it increases almost linearly to about 15 percent at six or more risk factors. The OR is high (14.5, based on four or more risk factors). In summary, these results (and those of several other studies) indicate a robust association between the number of risk factors and the probability of later violence. Remarkably, the association holds even when slightly different risk factors are measured from study to study.

The dose–response relationship has also been demonstrated between risk factors and several other areas of functioning and maladjustment, including intelligence (Sameroff *et al.*, 1993), some psychiatric disorders (Rutter, 1979), internalizing problems (e.g., Atzaba-Poria, Pike, & Deater-Deckard, 2004), attention-deficit hyperactivity disorder (Biederman *et al.*, 1995), and substance use (Bry, McKeon, & Pandina, 1982; Smith *et al.*, 1994). The dose–response relationship appears robust in that it applies to both genders (e.g., Sameroff *et al.*, 1998; Fergusson & Woodward, 2000), different ethnic or racial groups (Sameroff *et al.*, 1998; Atzaba-Poria, Pike, & Deater-Deckard, 2004; Loeber & Farrington, 2004), households with different income levels, single-parent or two-parent families (Sameroff *et al.*, 1998), and different neighborhoods (Wikström & Loeber, 2000). Thus, the dose–response relationship between risk factors and later negative outcomes is well replicated, robust across different populations, and also applies to antisocial and delinquent behavior.

Against the backdrop of the replication of the dose–response relationship across different outcomes and populations, one should recognize that the strength of the association is not the same across studies and that the percentage of false positive and false negative errors varies greatly from study to study even where the same outcome is considered (e.g., Farrington, 1997; Loeber *et al.*, 2005). This has partly to do with different prevalence rates of outcomes (rarer outcomes are more difficult to predict) and different prevalence levels of the predictors (e.g., Deater-Deckard *et al.*, 1998). The results are not related only to the Burgess method, but are also apparent when multiple regression analyses are done, showing significant increments in R^2 (e.g., Shaw & Emery, 1988; Atzaba-Poria, Pike, & Deater-Deckard, 2004).

It is important to know whether children whose exposure to risk factors decreases over time will have a lower probability of a negative outcome than those exposed to persistent risk factors. Sameroff *et al.* (1998) examine this in their follow-up of adolescents from age 4 to ages 13 and 18, and found that those children who were in a high-risk group at age 4, but had moved to a low-risk group by age 13, demonstrated an improvement in their IQ of 13 points (i.e., more than one standard deviation). In contrast, those who were in a low-risk group at age 4, but had moved to a high-risk group at age 13, saw a drop in their IQ of 15 points. It is our impression that positive or negative changes in exposure to risk factors over time similarly influences the probability of serious delinquency, but, as far as we know, research in this area is currently lacking.

Figure 5.6, and to some extent Figure 5.7, suggest a linear association between the number of risk factors and the probability of later deviance. However, some studies have found a positively accelerating relationship (e.g., Rutter, 1979). The possible reasons behind divergent findings remain to be investigated. Several reasons may present themselves, including non-equivalence of risk factors (where the presence of certain risk factors disproportionally increases the risk of a later negative outcome) or threshold effects (where there is a low impact in the presence of few risk factors, but a substantial impact in the presence of one or more additional risk factors).

Stability. Implied in Table 5.1 is that some risk factors may persist over time. Investigations of risk factors often ignore the fact that such factors, similar to the outcomes that they purportedly predict, may vary in their temporal stability over time. For instance, children's direct exposure to conflict and aggression between parents may decrease dramatically or stop completely once the parents separate and divorce, while heavy substance use by parents may be more persistent over time. On the other hand, exposure to some risk factors (such as familial crime) may be associated with a heightened risk of delinquency in the offspring that may have an impact that lasts from childhood at least until the adolescent period. Another category of risk factors, such as exposure to the physiological effects of the mother's smoking during pregnancy, may occur during a sensitive period (in this case, that of brain development). Yet few studies have addressed the issue of stability of risk factors. An exception is Sameroff *et al.* (1998), who found that environmental risk factors correlate 0.77 over a five-year period (ages 13 to 18), which is about the same level of stability as intelligence. Loeber *et al.* (2000) found that the year-to-year stability coefficient for the interactions between parents and their boys between ages 6 and 18 averages 0.66 for bad parent–child relationship, 0.70 for poor parent–child communication, and lower for poor supervision (0.56) and physical punishment (0.46). Examination of absolute stability reveals that this is higher for bad relationships and poor communication, but decreases with age for poor supervision and physical punishment. It should be noted, however, that despite level changes in risk factors with development, many of the known risk factors continue to predict later negative outcomes, including delinquency, at different ages of children (e.g., Loeber *et al.*, 1998; Loeber *et al.*, in press).

It is plausible that the presence of some risk factors sets in motion a cascade of other risk factors (Conger, Patterson, & Ge, 1995). For example, the toxic teratogenic effect of maternal smoking may increase the probability of several other risk factors in the offspring, including poor executive functioning, poor academic achievement in school, low motivation to attend school, truancy, and, subsequently, delinquency. As another example, the presence of several risk factors (e.g., parents' exposure to enduring stress and parents' substance abuse) may increase the chance of antisocial behavior in the offspring at home, which in turn may set the scene for heightened risk of problem behavior outside of the home. Yet, as Howell (2003: 110) points out, it remains to be seen when and how risk factors operate in a "sequential causal chain." It is clearer that the prevalence of different risk factors is higher in disadvantaged compared to advantaged neighborhoods (Wikström & Loeber, 2000; Stouthamer-Loeber *et al.*, 2002).

Promotive factors

Most criminology and psychopathology studies with a public health slant have routinely neglected the study of promotive factors (Lösel & Bender, 2003). Promotive factors are associated with the likelihood of reduced antisocial behavior/delinquency and/or increased positive outcomes, including positive adjustment and positive mental health. Some authors refer to variables as if they are either uniquely promotive or uniquely risk-related (e.g., Rae-Grant *et al.*, 1989). Others emphasize that (i) some promotive and risk factors are merely opposite ends of the same variable, (ii) that the promotive and risk end of variables need not be just mirror images of each other but may differ in the magnitude of their relationship to an outcome, and (iii) that there are unique promotive factors without a risk equivalent (Stouthamer-Loeber *et al.*, 1993, 2002, 2004). Finally, promotive factors have been conceptualized as processes that play a special role in the presence of risk (Rutter, 1990), reflecting interaction effects where the effect of a promotive (or protective) factor is greater when risk is high than when risk is low. Our own approach (Stouthamer-Loeber *et al.*, 1993, 2002, 2004) is to advance the investigation of promotive factors first as main effects, similar to the search for the main effects of risk factors, and then investigate the interaction effects between promotive and risk factors.

Developmentally graded promotive factors. There is an increasing body of research on promotive factors (see the review by Lösel & Bender, 2003), but that body is still minuscule in comparison to the number of publications on risk factors pertaining to antisocial behavior and delinquency. In particular, we know very little about the developmental aspects of the accumulation of promotive factors through the life course. However, the framework proposed by Hawkins and colleagues (Catalano & Hawkins, 1996) and ourselves (Stouthamer-Loeber *et al.*, 2002) is unusual in criminology because each postulates changes within promotive factors to explain individual differences in the development of offending. At the risk of being speculative, we postulate that some promotive factors, like risk factors, may be present at birth, but that other factors emerge during the first decades of life. Table 5.2 shows

Table 5.2. *Emergence of promotive factors*

Domain	At birth	Early childhood	Middle to late childhood	Adolescence	Early adulthood
Individual	Normal to high IQ	CONTINUITY OF EARLIER INDIVIDUAL FACTORS +	CONTINUITY OF EARLIER INDIVIDUAL FACTORS +	CONTINUITY OF EARLIER INDIVIDUAL FACTORS +	CONTINUITY OF EARLIER INDIVIDUAL FACTORS +
	Easy temperament	NEW FACTORS No developmental delays	CONTINUITY OF EARLIER INDIVIDUAL FACTORS +	CONTINUITY OF EARLIER INDIVIDUAL FACTORS +	CONTINUITY OF EARLIER INDIVIDUAL FACTORS +
	No prenatal exposure to toxins	No language problems	NEW FACTORS Not withdrawn behavior	CONTINUITY OF EARLIER INDIVIDUAL FACTORS +	CONTINUITY OF EARLIER INDIVIDUAL FACTORS +
	No pregnancy/birth complications	Presence of guilt feelings	Good social skills	NEW FACTORS Believes likely to be caught if delinquent	CONTINUITY OF EARLIER INDIVIDUAL FACTORS +
	No perinatal problems	No callous/ unemotional behavior	No cognitive attributional bias pertaining to aggression	Many skills for getting a job	NEW FACTORS Being employed or in school
		Negative attitude to behavior problems	Good academic achievement		Military service
		No impulsivity/ daringness	High school motivation		Move away from disadvantaged neighborhoods

		No attention problems	Negative attitude to delinquency		Positive relationship with partner
		Good executive functioning	Negative attitude to substance use		
		No counter control (child does not act up more when disciplined)	Positive life events		
		Emergent skills/ talent			
		Ability of plan for the future			
Family	Medium to high SES	CONTINUITY OF EARLIER FAMILY FACTORS +	CONTINUITY OF EARLIER FAMILY FACTORS +	CONTINUITY OF EARLIER FAMILY FACTORS +	CONTINUITY OF EARLIER FAMILY FACTORS +
	Small family	NEW FACTORS Consistent discipline	CONTINUITY OF EARLIER FAMILY FACTORS +	CONTINUITY OF EARLIER FAMILY FACTORS +	CONTINUITY OF EARLIER FAMILY FACTORS +
	No parental unemployment	Low physical punishment	NEW FACTORS Mentoring by adults	CONTINUITY OF EARLIER FAMILY FACTORS +	CONTINUITY OF EARLIER FAMILY FACTORS +
	No welfare	No child abuse			CONTINUITY OF EARLIER FAMILY FACTORS +
	No family delinquency	No neglect			
	No parent psychopathology	No deviant siblings			
	No parent substance abuse	Few or no caretaker changes			

Table 5.2. *(Cont.)*

Domain	At birth	Early childhood	Middle to late childhood	Adolescence	Early adulthood
	Moderate to good education of parent(s)	Low parental stress			
	No teenage motherhood	Social engagement			
	Two-parent family	Good relationship with partner Parental negative attitude to child problem behavior Availability of supportive adults other than parents			
Peers		NEW FACTORS Good relationship with peers	CONTINUITY OF EARLIER PEER FACTORS +	CONTINUITY OF EARLIER PEER FACTORS +	CONTINUITY OF EARLIER PEER FACTORS +
		No victimization (bullying)	NEW FACTORS Low peer delinquency	CONTINUITY OF EARLIER PEER FACTORS +	CONTINUITY OF EARLIER PEER FACTORS +
			Low peer substance use	NEW FACTORS Most friends attend school	CONTINUITY OF EARLIER PEER FACTORS +
				Not gangs	NEW FACTORS Marriage to prosocial partner

			Low number of sexual partners
School	NEW FACTORS Low school deviancy level Well-organized school	CONTINUITY OF EARLIER SCHOOL FACTORS +	
Neighborhood	NEW FACTORS Advantaged neighborhood Low neighborhood crime Move to a better neighborhood	CONTINUITY OF EARLIER NEIGHBOR-HOOD FACTORS +	CONTINUITY OF EARLIER NEIGHBOR-HOOD FACTORS +

promotive factors mentioned in the research literature (or factors that are probably promotive according to our view) as being relevant to antisocial behavior and delinquency (based on Bachman, O'Malley, & Johnston, 1978; West, 1982; Kandel *et al.*, 1988; Sampson & Laub, 1990; Stouthamer-Loeber *et al.*, 1993, 2002, 2004; Farrington, 1994; Smith *et al.*, 1994; Pollard, Hawkins, & Arthur, 1999; Arthur *et al.*, 2002; Lösel & Bender, 2003). Where research appears wanting, we have inserted factors that we think are probable promotive factors. Most of the promotive factors are the inverse of risk factors, in that many, but not all, of the promotive factors represent the other pole of risk factors. However, we do not argue that promotive factors are the complete inverse of risk factors (see Stouthamer-Loeber *et al.*, 1993, 2004 for details). Research shows that there are several promotive factors that do not have a risk factor equivalent. Examples of these unique promotive factors are having many skills for getting a job, engagement in military service, belief in the likelihood of being caught if delinquent, etc. As with the development of risk factors, we assume that there is a developmentally graded emergence of promotive factors (see Table 5.2). Some of the promotive factors are thought to be present at birth (e.g., moderate to high intelligence, absence of prenatal exposure to toxins), while other factors become manifest later. It is also thought that there is a high degree of temporal stability of protective factors, although the data on this have not yet been reported. In the Pittsburgh Youth Study (Stouthamer-Loeber *et al.*, 2002), accountability, perceived likelihood of getting caught for delinquent acts, and low physical punishment, are recurring factors that are associated with desistance in persistent serious delinquency at different ages. Relatively little is known about increases in protective factors with development. Stouthamer-Loeber *et al.* (1993) found that the proportion of significant associations between promotive factors and delinquency increases with age. This conclusion, however, is provisional for the reason that the age comparisons are based on different cohorts, and, therefore, require replication to be proven.

It is likely that promotive factors, such as risk factors, are correlated, in that one promotive factor may set the scene for another promotive factor to emerge. For instance, association with prosocial peers may generate new prosocial behavior, which, once adopted by an individual child, may further decrease the probability that that child will engage in delinquent acts. Hawkins (2003) and his colleagues are among the few who have specified prosocial pathways in the delinquency research that can be conceptualized as a string of promotive factors. They postulate that opportunities for prosocial behavior set the scene for interpersonal involvement, which in turn produces rewards, improving bonding to others and promoting belief in a moral order. Research shows that the prevalence of different promotive factors is highest in the most advantaged neighborhoods (Stouthamer-Loeber *et al.*, 2002; Wikström, 2005).

Inverse dose–response relationship between promotive factors and delinquency

Is there an inverse dose–response relationship between the number of promotive factors and later deviance (the higher the number of promotive factors, the lower the probability of deviance)? There are very few research studies addressing this question. Outside the area of delinquency, Sameroff *et al.* (1998: 172) found that the higher the number of promotive factors, the lower the probability of behavior problems, with the results mirroring the results of the risk factors: "The more risk factors, the worse the outcomes; the more promotive factors, the better the outcomes." Smith *et al.* (1994) also found that the higher the number of protective factors, the higher was the probability of resilience to delinquency (i.e., the higher the percentage of non-offenders or those not seriously delinquent). For example, in the presence of five or fewer promotive factors, only 18.9% of the youth are not seriously delinquent. The proportion of non-delinquent adolescents rises to 32.4% in the presence of six to seven promotive factors, and 75.5% for those exposed to eight or more promotive factors. In summary, those youth with many promotive factors "were four times more likely to be resilient than youth with few protective factors" (Smith *et al.*, 1994: 235). Similar results have been reported by Wikström and Loeber (2000), thus lending support to the notion that the accumulation of promotive factors in juveniles' lives counters the likelihood of later delinquent involvement.

Do promotive factors offset the impact of risk factors?

What is the evidence that promotive factors buffer the risk for later antisocial behavior and delinquency? Research findings are sparse, but the data indicate that the additive mixture of risk and promotive factors predicts later deviance. For instance, Stouthamer-Loeber *et al.* (2002) showed that even at the level of the number of risk or promotive domains (child behaviors, child attitudes, school, peers, family, demographic characteristics), the sum of risk and promotive domains (where

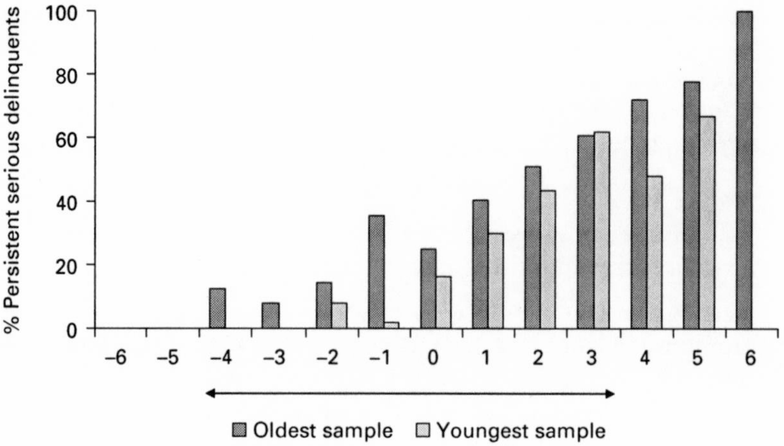

Figure 5.8. The higher the number of risk domains (and the lower the number of promotive domains), the higher the risk of later persistent serious delinquency
Source: Stouthamer-Loeber *et al.*, 2002.

the number of promotive domains is deducted from the number of risk domains) linearly predicts persistent serious delinquency (Figure 5.8). The higher the number of risk domains to which a youth is exposed and the lower his/her exposure to promotive domains, the greater the likelihood of later persistent serious delinquency. Conversely, the higher the number of promotive domains and the lower the number of risk domains, the smaller the likelihood of later persistent serious delinquency. This was replicated for the youngest and oldest samples; for different degrees of neighborhood advantage and disadvantage; for specific risk and promotive factors; and for early and late onset forms of delinquency (Wikström & Loeber, 2000; Stouthamer-Loeber *et al.*, 2002). Not all researchers, however, have found that the relationship between risk and promotive factors is linear. For example, Pollard *et al.* (1999), studying such diverse outcomes as substance use, arrest, and attack to hurt, found a non-linear effect with the effect of risk factors greater as the level of risk increased. However, it is plausible that once neighborhood context is taken into account non-linear associations occur. For example, Wikström & Loeber (2000: 1130) report that "the overwhelming majority of boys with a high risk score were involved in serious offending regardless of the socioeconomic context of their neighbourhood." However, neighborhood matters greatly for those with a balanced score of risk and promotive factors.

Toward a three-dimensional model of developmental pathways and developmentally graded risk and promotive factors

Let us summarize the preceding discussion. Firstly, we have reviewed developmental pathways from minor to serious delinquent behavior (Figure 5.1). Secondly, we have discussed developmentally graded, cumulative onset of risk factors (Table 5.1; Figure 5.4) and developmentally graded, cumulative onset of promotive factors (Table 5.2). Thirdly, we have seen that there are dose–response relationships between the number of risk factors and the probability of later delinquency and violence (Figures 5.5–5.7), and an inverse dose–response relationship between the number of promotive factors and the reduced probability of later delinquency and violence. Finally, we have seen that knowledge of the proportion of risk and promotive factors is more important than knowledge of either (Figure 5.8). The question then is how to bring these different strands of evidence together? At this point we want to take a rather unconventional route. In science, the verification of models is usually accomplished by mathematical formulae. We are not aware of formulae that describe the different aspects that we have stressed. An alternative, or rather a step toward such a composite model, is to display the above interrelationships visually (for another example of a visual model, see Muchisky *et al.*, 1996).

To achieve a composite model, we have rejected the notion that it should be two-dimensional, because it would be too limiting and would not be able to represent simultaneously the co-development of individuals' progression from minor to serious delinquency as a function of the accumulation of risk and promotive factors. Instead, we have constructed a three-dimensional model. Before discussing this, we will present each component. Figure 5.9 shows a version of two of the pathways depicted in Figure 5.1, which has been reoriented into the horizontal plane. These two pathways are overt and covert behavior (leaving aside for the moment the authority conflict pathway), with the overt pathway triangle superimposed on the covert pathway triangle. Figure 5.10 represents the developmentally graded, cumulative onset of risk factors in a number of vertical panels, each of the same shape, but with ribs of different sizes, representing different degrees of individuals' exposure to risk factors, so they would fit on the horizontal pathway picture (Figure 5.9). In the central and highest risk rib, the number of risk factors present at birth is thought to be higher than in the adjoining ribs, the accumulation of risk factors is highest, and the length of the rib is shown to be longest to represent the higher degree of severity of

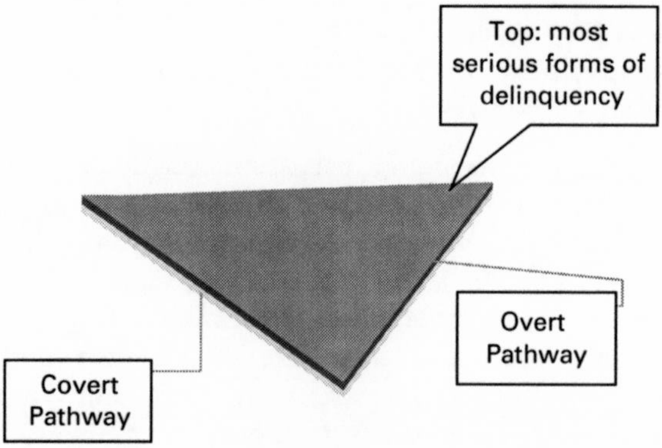

Figure 5.9. Pathway model flipped horizontally (overt pathway on the top and covert pathway underneath)

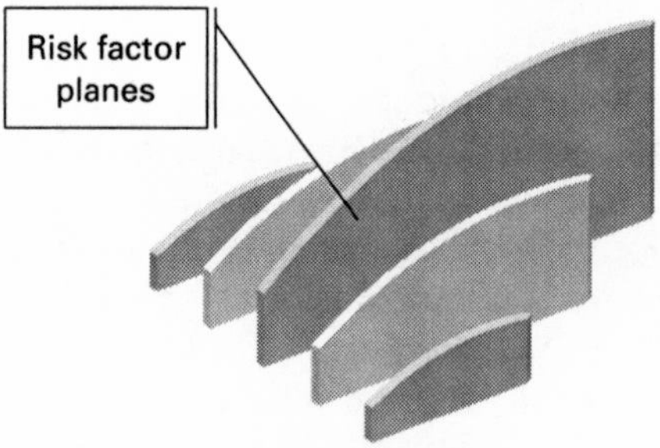

Figure 5.10. Accumulation of risk factors at different levels of accumulation

delinquency. In contrast, the adjoining smaller ribs represent fewer risk factors at birth and a smaller accumulation of later risk factors. Figure 5.11 represents the distribution of "start-up" risk factors at birth in the form of a long triangle. The central top of that triangle indicates a category of children with the highest number of risk factors at birth and at the extremes are those with the fewest number of risk factors at that time. Figure 5.11 represents developmental rather than chronological time.

Figure 5.12 represents ribs of the accumulation of promotive factors in an inverse way to the risk factors. However, the central rib is the least tall because those who advance to the most serious acts are usually exposed to the lowest number of promotive factors. In contrast, individuals who do not advance to serious delinquency outcomes tend to start out in life with, and accumulate more, promotive factors than those

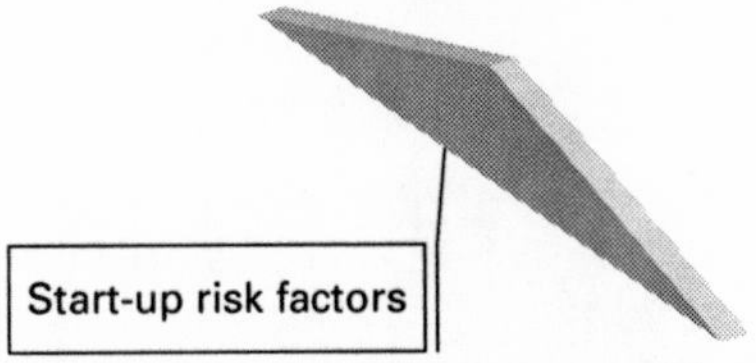

Figure 5.11. Distribution of risk factors at birth (start-up risk factors)

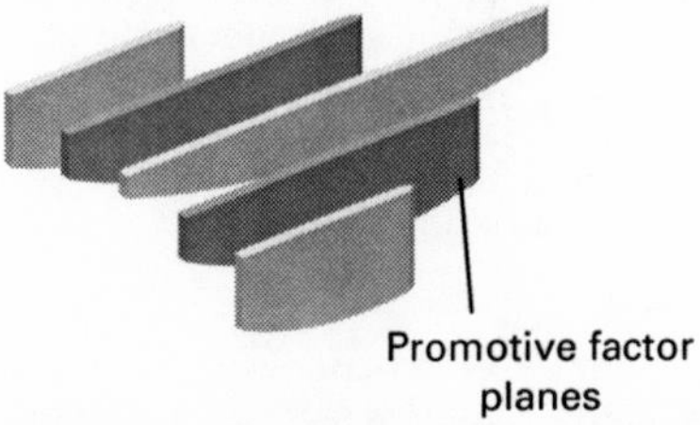

Figure 5.12. Accumulation of promotive factors at different levels of accumulation

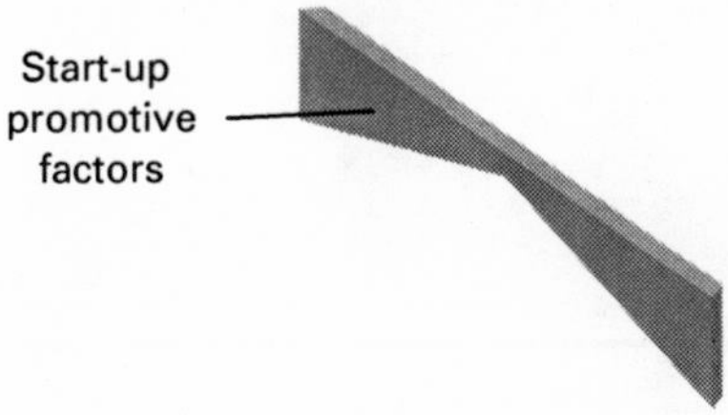

Figure 5.13. Distribution of promotive factors at birth (start-up promotive factors)

in the central rib. Figure 5.13, in the form of half a butterfly, may clarify the "start-up" promotive factors which are thought to be lowest in the centre and highest at the extremes.

Finally, Figure 5.14 shows how each of the above elements are put together. Individuals who advance to the most serious delinquent acts on the horizontal pathways (the flat, double triangle) are thought to be exposed to the highest number of risk factors over time *and* the lowest number of promotive factors over time. At birth, they also tend to have the highest number of risk factors (see the start-up risk panel) and the lowest number of promotive factors (see the start-up promotive factors). To clarify this cumulative, developmental model, Figure 5.15 shows how it looks from the front, while Figure 5.16 shows how it looks from underneath.

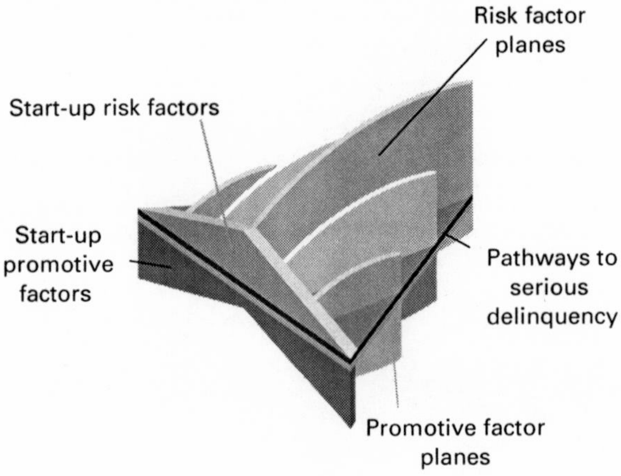

Figure 5.14. The full model of developmental pathways as a function of the accumulation of risk and promotive factors (shown from above)

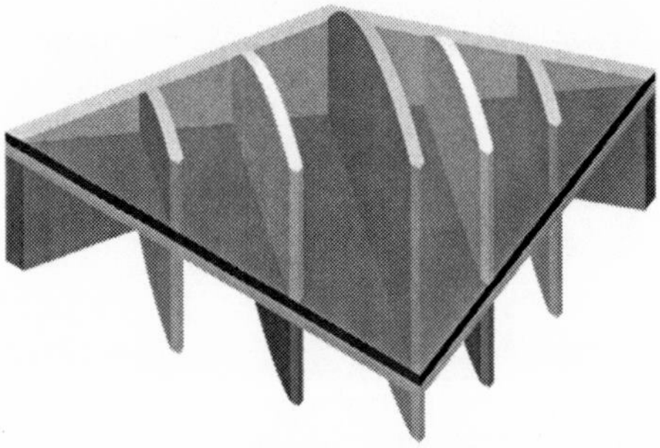

Figure 5.15. The full model of developmental pathways as a function of the accumulation of risk and promotive factors (shown from the front)

Relevance of the model for assessments and interventions

What is the relevance of the cumulative, developmental model for assessment and the evaluation of preventive and remedial interventions?

Assessments. Advances have been made in the past decades in the area of more precise assessment of juveniles' problem behavior in terms of the types of behavior, their severity, and prognostic validity. In addition, screening instruments are now available to go beyond the range of problem behaviors of juveniles to include the past history of risk factors to which juveniles have been exposed (e.g., Koegl, Webster, & Levens,

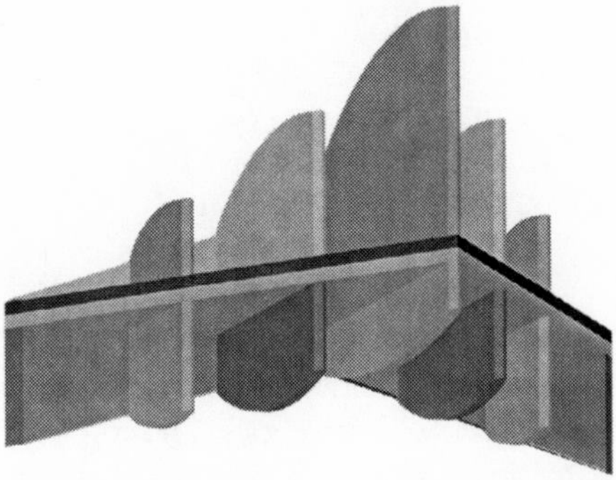

Figure 5.16. The full model of developmental pathways as a function of the accumulation of risk and promotive factors (shown from underneath)

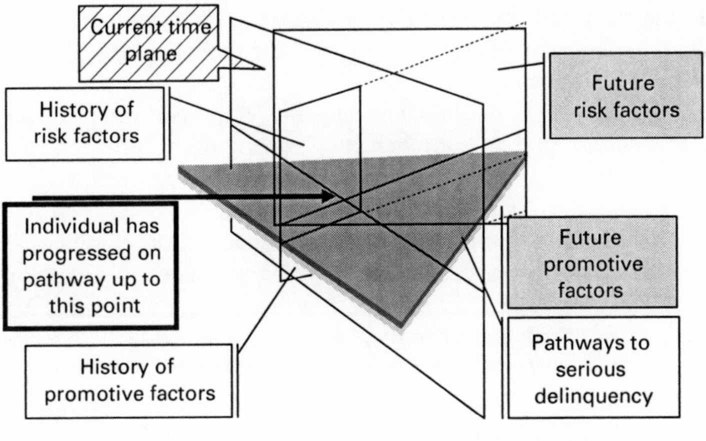

Figure 5.17. Position of an individual on the pathway showing actual exposure to risk and promotive factors (in front of vertical current time plane) and potential exposure to these factors (behind vertical current time plane)

2001). Based on the information provided in this chapter, we argue, however, that assessments can probably benefit from two other components (see Figure 5.17). The first is an appraisal of current and past promotive factors to which juveniles are exposed, because it is the mixture of risk and promotive effects that appears most crucial in determining the future risk of serious offending as well as the probability of full desistance or lower-level offending. The second is an appraisal of juveniles' expected future exposure to risk and promotive factors based on knowledge from longitudinal survey studies. Specifically, assessments of developmentally graded exposure to risk factors, based on longitudinal survey studies, could be employed to calculate the probability that juveniles will be exposed in the future to risk and promotive factors typically emerging for that age group.

One might argue that cross-sectional studies contain such information. There are several reasons why this is not the case. Firstly, in contrast to cross-sectional studies, longitudinal studies have the power to specify selection processes determining which groups of youth are most likely to be exposed to future risk and promotive factors. The second reason has to do with promotive factors associated with stable non-offending or a de-escalation from serious to minor or offending-nonoffending. Since juveniles' engagement in delinquency varies from year to year, it is important to establish which promotive factors are associated with persistent non-offending or, alternatively, with a stable de-escalation in the severity of offending. Longitudinal studies, rather than cross-sectional studies, are the best methods by which to identify promotive factors.

Preventive and remedial interventions. We agree with Howell (2003) that a developmental approach to offending needs a reconceptualization of when interventions, preventive or remedial, can best take place. He has been a primary proponent of the influential Comprehensive Strategy that addresses the full continuum of antisocial development, with two foci for implementing change: prevention and early intervention, and graduated sanctions. We believe that this orientation, which is based on knowledge of risk and promotive factors (called protective factors in this case), can also greatly benefit from the assessment of future risk through developmentally graded expectations of exposure to risk and protective factors. We argue that this is especially important because of the fact that even the most effective interventions do not reduce the risk of recidivism by more than 40 percent (Lipsey & Wilson, 1998) and that the reoffending rate of high-risk populations of youth still remains extraordinary high (Loeber & Farrington, 1998).

It should be understood that knowledge of risk and promotive factors, as listed in Tables 5.1 and 5.2, does not mean that we have available the tools to change each of them, and of course some are not malleable (e.g., single parenthood). However, we hope that our lists of the risk and promotive factors and our model will stimulate the development of other forms of intervention that can augment the overall efficacy of interventions currently available. It is our impression that most treatment programs lack components that focus on increasing or strengthening promotive factors. We foresee that interventions that mobilize or enhance promotive factors (together with the reduction of risk factors) eventually are likely to improve treatment efficacy and, possibly, the maintenance of treatment effects. We agree, however, with Pollard *et al.* (1999) that a sole focus on interventions enhancing promotive factors only, because of the compensatory function of risk and promotive factors, is likely to be inadequate. Another possible beneficial result of our model specification is the further individualization of interventions tailored to an individual's past, present, and possible future exposure to risk and promotive factors.

Finally, we should stress that our design of a three-dimensional model of antisocial behavior has certain limitations. Firstly, we are mostly focusing on the cumulative processes of risk and promotive factors rather than the specifics of mediation and moderation within and between risk and promotive factors. Also, we do not focus on possible reciprocal processes between risk and protective factors and negative or positive child behaviors, or the fact that as children's mobility in the community increases with age, they become more able to select settings and situations in which novel risk and protective factors may present themselves. We are also aware that our model may have different components depending on the subject population of study (girls vs. boys, different ethnic groups), but we think it is generic enough to serve as a model to explain a range of forms of maladjustment other than serious delinquency. The model depicts escalation in the severity of antisocial behavior better than de-escalation to lower severity levels, but de-escalation could perhaps be incorporated in the next iteration of the model. Also, there is a need to transfer the basic mathematical properties of our model into future model-testing. It is clear that many tasks await, and we hope that this chapter will inspire others to improve on where we are at this point.

References

American Psychiatric Association (1994). *Diagnostic and Statistical Manual of Mental Disorders*, 4th edn. Washington, DC.

Arthur, M. W., Hawkins, J. D., Pollard, J. A., Catalano, R. F., & Baglioni, A. J., Jr. (2002). "Measuring risk and protective factors for substance use, delinquency, and other adolescent problem behaviors: The Communities that Care Youth Survey." *Evaluation Review* 26: 575–601.

Atzaba-Poria, N., Pike, A., & Barrett, M. (2004). "Internalising and externalising problems in middle childhood: a study of Indian (ethnic minority) and English (ethnic majority) children living in Britain." *International Journal of Behavioral Development* 28: 449–460.

Atzaba-Poria, N., Pike, A., & Deater-Deckard, K. (2004). "Do risk factors for problem behavior act in a cumulative manner? An examination of ethnic minority and majority children through an ecological perspective." *Journal of Child Psychology and Psychiatry and Allied Disciplines* 12: 707–718.

Bachman, J. G., O'Malley, P. M., & Johnston, J. (1978). *Youth in Transition*, vol. VI. Ann Arbor, MI: University of Michigan Institute for Social Research.

Biederman, J., Milberger, S., Faraone, S. V., Kiely, K., Guite, J., Mick, E., Ablon, S., Warburton, R., & Reed, E. 1995. "Family environment risk factors for attention-deficit hyperactivity disorder: a test of Rutter's indicators of adversity." *Archives of General Psychiatry* 52: 464–470.

Broidy, L. M., Nagin, D. S., Tremblay, R. E., Bates, J. E., Brame, B., Dodge, K. A., Fergusson, D., Horwood, J. L., Loeber, R., Laird, R., Lynam, D. R., Moffitt, T. E., & Pettit, G. S. (2003). "Developmental trajectories of childhood disruptive behavior and adolescent delinquency: a six-site, cross-national study." *Developmental Psychology* 39: 222–245.

Bronfenbrenner, U. (1979). *The Ecology of Human Development*. Cambridge, MA: Harvard University Press.

Bry, B. H., McKeon, P., & Pandina, R. J. (1982). "Extent of drug use as a function of number of risk factors." *Journal of Abnormal Psychology* 91: 273–279.

Bushway, S. D., Thornberry, T. P., & Krohn, M. S. (2003). "Desistance as a developmental process: a comparison of static and dynamic approaches." *Journal of Quantitative Criminology* 19: 129–153.

Catalano, R. F. & Hawkins, J. D. (1996). "The social development model: a theory of antisocial behavior." In J. D. Hawkins (ed.), *Delinquency and Crime: Current Theories*. New York: Cambridge University Press.

Conger, R. D., Patterson, G. R., & Ge, X. (1995). "It takes two to replicate: a mediational model for the impact of parents' stress on the adolescent adjustment." *Child Development* 66: 80–97.

Deater-Deckard, K., Dodge, K. A., Bates, J. E., & Pettit, G. S. (1998). "Multiple risk factors in the development of externalizing behavior problems: group and individual differences." *Development and Psychopathology* 10: 469–493.

Elliott, D. S. (1994). "Longitudinal research in criminology: promise and practice." In E. G. M. Weitekamp & H. J. Kerner (eds.), *Cross-national Longitudinal Research on Human Development and Criminal Behavior*. Dordrecht: Kluwer.

Elliott, D. S., Huizinga, D., & Ageton, S. S. (1985). *Explaining Delinquency and Drug Use*. Beverly Hills, CA: Sage.

Elliot, D. S., Huizinga, D., & Menard, S. (1989). *Multiple Problem Youth: Delinquency, Substance Use, and Mental Health Problems*. New York: Springer Verlag.

Elliott, D. S. & Menard, S. (1996). "Delinquent friends and delinquent behavior: temporal and developmental patterns." In D. Hawkins (ed.), *Delinquency and Crime: Current Theories*. Cambridge: Cambridge University Press.

Farrington, D. P. (1986). "Age and crime." In M. Tonry & N. Morris (eds.), *Crime and Justice: An Annual Review of Research*. Chicago: University of Chicago Press.

(1994). "Interactions between individual and contextual factors in the development of offending." In R. K. Silbereisen, & E. Todt (eds.), *Adolescence in Context: The Interplay of Family, School, Peers and Work in Adjustment*. New York: Springer Verlag.

(1996). "Individual, family and peer factors in the development of delinquency." In C. R. Hollin & K. Howells (eds.), *Clinical Approaches to Working with Young*. Chichester, UK: Wiley.

(1997). "Early prediction of violent and non-violent youthful offending." *European Journal on Criminal Policy and Research* 5: 51–66.

Farrington, D. P., ed. (2005). *Integrated Developmental and Life-Course Theories of Offending*. Advances in Criminological Theory 14. New Brunswick, NJ: Transaction.

Farrington, D. P. & Loeber, R. (1989). "Relative improvement over chance (RIOC) and phis as measures of predictive efficiency and strength of association in 2 × 2 tables." *Journal of Quantitative Criminology* 5: 201–213.

Fergusson, D. M. & Woodward, L. J. (2000). "Educational, psychosocial, and sexual outcomes of girls with conduct problems in early adolescence." *Journal of Child Psychology and Psychiatry and Allied Disciplines* 41: 779–792.

Gerard, J. M. & Buehler, C. (2004). "Cumulative environmental risk and youth maladjustment: the role of youth attributes." *Child Development* 75: 1832–1849.

Gorman-Smith, D. & Loeber, R. (in press). "Are developmental pathways in disruptive behaviors the same for girls and boys?" *Journal of Child and Family Studies*.

Gottfredson, M. R. & Hirshi, T. (1990). *A General Theory of Crime*. Stanford: Stanford University Press.

Hawkins, D., ed. (2003). *Violent Crime: Assessing Race and Ethnic Differences*. Cambridge: Cambridge University Press.

Hawkins, J. D., Herrenkohl, T., Farrington, D. P., Brewer, D., Catalano, R. F., & Harachi. T. W. (1998). "A review of predictors of youth violence." In R. Loeber & D. P. Farrington (eds.), *Serious and Violent Juvenile Offenders: Risk Factors and Successful Interventions*. Thousand Oaks, CA: Sage.

Howell, J. C. (2003). *Preventing and Reducing Juvenile Delinquency. A Comprehensive Framework*. Thousand Oaks, CA: Sage.

Huizinga, D., Weiher, A. W., Espirutu, R., & Esbensen, F. (2003). "Delinquency and crime. Some highlights from the Denver Youth Survey." In T. P. Thornberry & M. D. Krohn (eds.), *Taking Stock of Delinquency: an Overview of Findings from Longitudinal Studies*. New York: Kluwer/Plenum.

Kandel, E., Mednick, S. A., Kirkegaard-Sorensen, L., Hutchings, B., Knop, J., Rosenberg, R., & Schulsinger, F. (1988). "IQ as a protective factor for subjects at high risk for antisocial behavior." *Journal of Consulting and Clinical Psychology* 56: 224–226.

Keenan, K. & Shaw, D. D. (2003) "Development of conduct problems during the preschool years." In B. B. Lahey, T. E. Moffitt, & A. Caspi (eds.), *Causes of Conduct Disorder and Juvenile Delinquency*. New York: Guilford Press.

Kelley, B. T., Loeber, R., Keenan, K., & DeLamatre, M. (1997). "Developmental pathways in boys' disruptive and delinquent behavior." *OJJDP Juvenile Justice Bulletin*. http://www.ncjrs.org/.

Koegl, C. J., Webster, C. D., & Levens, K. S. (2001). *Early Assessment Risk List for Boys: RL–20B*, version 2. Toronto: Earlscourt Child and Family Centre.

Lacourse, E., Nagin, D., Tremblay, R., Vitaro, F., & Claes, M. (2003). "Developmental trajectories of boys' delinquent group membership and facilitation of violent behaviors during adolescence." *Developmental Psychopathology* 15: 183–97.

Lahey, B. B., Loeber, R., Burke, J. D., & Applegate, B. (in press). "Predicting future antisocial personality disorder in males from a clinical assessment in childhood." *Journal of Consulting and Clinical Psychology*.

Lahey, B. B., Moffitt, T. E., & Caspi, A., eds. (2003). *Causes of Conduct Disorder and Juvenile Delinquency*. New York: Guilford Press.

Le Blanc, M. (2002). "The offending cycle, escalation and de-escalation in delinquent behavior: a challenge for criminology." *International Journal of Comparative and Applied Criminal Justice* 26: 53–83.

Le Blanc, M., Côté, G., and Loeber, R. (1991). "Temporal paths in delinquency: stability, regression, and progression analyzed with panel data from an adolescent and a delinquent male sample." *Canadian Journal of Criminology* 33: 23–44.

Le Blanc, M. & Fréchette, M. (1989). *Male Criminal Activity from Childhood through Youth: Multilevel and Developmental Perspectives*. New York: Springer Verlag.

Lerner, R. M. & Castellino, D. R. (2002). "Contemporary developmental theory and adolescence: developmental systems and applied developmental science." *Journal of Adolescent Health* 31: 122–135.

Lipsey, M. W. & Derzon, J. H. (1998). "Predictors of violent or serious delinquency in adolescence and early adulthood: a synthesis of longitudinal research." In R. Loeber & D. P. Farrington (eds.), *Serious and Violent Juvenile Offenders: Risk Factors and Successful Interventions*. Thousands Oaks, CA: Sage.

Lipsey, M. W. & Wilson, D. B. (1998). "Effective intervention for serious juvenile offenders: a synthesis of research." In R. Loeber & D. P. Farrington (eds.), *Serious and Violent Juvenile Offenders: Risk Factors and Successful Interventions*. Thousand Oaks, CA: Sage.

Loeber, R. (1985). "Patterns and development of antisocial child behavior." In G. J. Whitehurst (ed.), *Annals of Child Development*. Greenwich, CT: JAI Press.

(1988). "Natural histories of conduct problems, delinquency, and associated substance use: evidence for developmental progressions." In B. B. Lahey & A. E. Kazdin (eds.), *Advances in Clinical Child Psychology*. New York: Plenum.

Loeber, R. (1990). "Development and risk factors of juvenile antisocial behavior and delinquency." *Clinical Psychology Review* 10: 1–41.

Loeber, R., Burke, J. D., & Lahey, B. B. (2002). "What are adolescent antecedents to antisocial personality disorder?" *Criminal Behavior and Mental Health* 12: 24–36.

Loeber, R., DeLamatre, M., Keenan, K., & Zhang, Q. (1998). "A prospective replication of developmental pathways in disruptive and delinquent behavior." In R. Cairns, L. Bergman & J. Kagan (eds.), *Methods and Models for Studying the Individual:* 185–215. Thousand Oaks, CA: Sage.

Loeber, R., Drinkwater, M., Yin, Y., Anderson, S. J., Schmidt, L. C., & Crawford, A. (2000). "Stability of family interactions from ages 6 to 18." *Journal of Abnormal Child Psychology* 28: 353–369.

Loeber, R. & Farrington, D. P. (1998) (eds). *Serious and Violent Juvenile Offenders: Risk Factors and Successful Interventions.* Thousand Oaks, CA: Sage.

(2001) *Child Delinquents: Development, Intervention and Service Needs.* Thousand Oaks, CA: Sage.

Loeber, R. & Farrington, D. P. (2004). "Verschillende oorzaken van delinquentie tussen etnische en national groepen? Longitudinale analyses van criminaliteit onder jonge mannen in Pittsburgh en London [Are between-race and between-country causes of delinquency the same? Longitudinal analyses of young males in Pittsburgh and London]." *Tijdschrift voor Criminologie* 46: 330–346.

Loeber, R., Farrington, D. P., Stouthamer-Loeber, M., White, R. R., Stallings, R., & Joliffe, D. (in press). *Violence and Serious Theft: Origins and Developmental Course from Childhood to Adulthood.* Mahwah, NJ: Lawrence Erlbaum Associates.

Loeber, R., Green, S. M., Lahey, B. B., Christ, M. A. G., & Frick, P. J. (1992). "Developmental sequences in the age of onset of disruptive child behaviors." *Journal of Child and Family Studies* 1: 21–41.

Loeber, R., Homish, D. L., Wei, E. H., Pardini, D., Crawford, A. M., Farrington, D. P., Stouthamer-Loeber, M., Creemers, J., Koehler, S. A., & Rosenfeld, R. (2005). "The prediction of violence and homicide in young males." *Journal of Consulting and Clinical Psychology* 73: 1074–1088.

Loeber, R., Keenan, K., Lahey, B. B., Green, S. M., & Thomas, C. (1993). "Evidence for developmentally based diagnoses of oppositional defiant disorder and conduct disorder." *Journal of Abnormal Child Psychology* 21: 377–410.

Loeber, R., Keenan, K., & Zhang, Q. (1997). "Boys' experimentation and persistence in developmental pathways toward serious delinquency." *Journal of Child and Family Studies* 6: 321–357.

Loeber, R., Wei, E., Stouthamer-Loeber, M., Huizinga, D., & Thornberry, T. (1999). "Behavioral antecedents to serious and violent juvenile offending: joint analyses from the Denver youth survey, Pittsburgh youth study, and the Rochester Development Study." *Studies in Crime and Crime Prevention* 8: 245–263.

Loeber, R. & Wikström, P.-O. (1993). "Individual pathways to crime in different types of neighborhood." In D. P. Farrington, R. J. Sampson, &

P.-O. Wikström (eds.), *Integrating Individual and Ecological Aspects of Crime*. Stockholm: Liber Forlag.

Loeber, R., Wung, P., Keenan, K., Giroux, B., Stouthamer-Loeber, M., Van Kammen, W. B., & Maughan, B. (1993). "Developmental pathways in disruptive child behavior." *Development and Psychopathology* 5: 101–132.

Lösel, F. & Bender, D. (2003). "Protective factors and resilience." In D. P. Farrington & J. Coid (eds.), *Early Prevention of Adult Anti-social Behavior*. Cambridge: Cambridge University Press.

Maughan, B., Pickles, A., Rowe, R., Costello, E. Jane, & Angold, A. (2000). "Developmental trajectories of aggressive and non-aggressive conduct problems." *Journal of Quantitative Criminology* 16: 119–137.

Moffitt, T. E. (1993). "Adolescence-limited and life-cycle-persistent antisocial behavior: a developmental taxonomy." *Psychological Review* 100: 674–701.

Muchisky, M., Gershoff-Stowe, L., & Thelen, E. (1996). "The epigenetic landscape revisited: a dynamic interpretation." In C. Rovec-Collier & L. Lipsett (eds.), *Advances in Infancy Research*, vol. X. Norwood, NJ: Ablex Publishing.

Nagin, D. S. & Tremblay, R. E. (2001). "Developmental trajectories of physical aggression from school entry to late adolescence." *Journal for Child Psychology and Psychiatry* 42: 503–512.

(in press). "Trajectories of boys' physical aggression, opposition, and hyperactivity on the path to physically violent and nonviolent juvenile delinquency." *Child Development*.

Pollard, J. A., Hawkins, J. D., & Arthur, M. W. (1999). "Risk and protection: are both necessary to understand diverse behavioral outcomes in adolescence?" *Social Work Research* 23: 145–158.

Rae-Grant, N., Thomas, B. H., Offord, D. R., & Boyle, M. H. (1989). "Risk, protective factors, and the prevalence of behavioral and emotional disorders in children and adolescents." *Journal of the American Academy of Child and Adolescent Psychiatry* 28: 262–268.

Robins, L. N. (1966). *Deviant Children Grown Up: A Sociological and Psychiatric Study of Sociopathic Personality*. Baltimore: Williams and Wilkins.

Rutter, M. (1979). "Protective factors in children's responses to stress and disadvantage." In J. E. Rolf (ed.), *Primary Prevention of Psychopathology*. Hanover, NH: University Press of New England.

(1985). "Resilience in the face of adversity." *British Journal of Psychiatry* 147: 589–611.

(1990). "Psychosocial resilience and protective mechanisms." In J. E. Rolf, A. S. Masten, D. Cicchetti, K. H. Nuechterlein, & S. Weintraub (eds.), *Risk and Protective Factors in the Development of Psychopathology*. New York: Cambridge University Press.

Rutter, M., Giller, H., & Hagell, A. (1998). *Antisocial Behavior by Young People*. New York: Cambridge University Press.

Rutter, M., Tizard, J., & Whitmore, K. (1970). *Education, Health, and Behavior*. New York: Wiley.

Sameroff, A. J., Bartko, W. T., Baldwin, A., Baldwin, C., & Seifer, R. (1998). "Family and social influences on the development of child competence."

In M. Lewis & C. Feiring (eds.), *Families, Risk, and Competence*. Mahwah, NJ: Lawrence Erlbaum Associates.

Sameroff, A. J., Seifer, R., Baldwin, A., & Baldwin, C. (1993). "Stability of intelligence from preschool to adolescence: the influence of social and family risk factors." *Child Development* 64: 80–97.

Sampson, R. J. & Laub, J. H. (1990). "Crime and deviance over the life course: the salience of adult social bonds." *American Sociological Review* 55: 609–627.

Shaw, D. S. & Emery, R. E. (1988). "Chronic family adversity and school age children's adjustment." *Journal of the American Academy of Child and Adolescent Psychiatry* 27: 200–206.

Shaw, D. S., Gilliom, M., Ingoldsby, E. M., & Nagin, D. S. (2003). "Trajectories leading to school-age conduct problems." *Developmental Psychology* 39: 189–200.

Slot, N. W. (1995). "Competency-based treatment for antisocial youth." In H. P. J. G. van Bilsen, P. C. Kendall, & J. H. Slavenburg (eds.), *Behavioral Approaches for Children and Adolescents*. New York: Plenum.

Smith, C., Lizotte, A. J., Thornberry, T. P., & Krohn, M. D. (1994). "Resilient youth: identifying factors that prevent high-risk youth from engaging in delinquency and drug use." In J. Hagan (ed.), *Delinquency in the Life Course*. Greenwich, CT: JAI Press.

Stouthamer-Loeber, M., Loeber, R., Farrington, D. P., Zhang, Q., Van Kammen, W. B., & Maguin, E. (1993). "The double edge of protective and risk factors for delinquency: inter-relations and developmental patterns." *Development and Psychopathology* 5: 683–701.

Stouthamer-Loeber, M., Loeber, R., Wei, E., Farrington, D. P., & Wikström, P.-O. (2002). "Risk and promotive effects in the explanation of persistent serious delinquency in boys." *Journal of Consulting and Clinical Psychology* 70: 111–123.

Stouthamer-Loeber, M., Wei, E., Loeber, R., & Masten, A. F. (2004). "Desistance from persistent serious delinquency in the transition to adulthood." *Development and Psychopathology* 16: 897–918.

Thornberry, T. P. (1997). *Developmental Theories of Crime and Delinquency*. New Brunswick, NJ: Transaction.

Thornberry, T. P. & Krohn, M. D. (2002). *Taking Stock of Delinquency: An Overview of Findings from Contemporary Longitudinal Studies*. New York: Kluwer.

Tolan, P. H., Gorman-Smith, D., & Loeber, R. (2000). "Developmental timing of onsets of disruptive behaviors and later delinquency of inner-city youth." *Journal of Child and Family Studies* 9: 203–230.

Warr, M. (2002). *Companions in Crime: The Social Aspects of Criminal Conduct*. Cambridge: Cambridge University Press.

West, D. J. (1982). *Delinquency: Its Roots, Careers and Prospects*. London: Heinemann.

Wikström, P.-O. H. (2005). "The social origins of pathways in crime." In D. P. Farrington (ed.), *Integrated Developmental and Life-Course Theories of Offending*. Advances in Criminological Theory 14. New Brunswick, NJ: Transaction.

Wikström, P.-O. & Loeber, R. (2000). "Do disadvantaged neighborhoods cause well-adjusted children to become adolescent delinquents? A study of male juvenile serious offending, risk and protective factors, and neighborhood context." *Criminology* 38: 1109–1141.

Wikström, P.-O. H. & Sampson, R. J. (2003). "Social mechanisms of community influences on crime and pathways in criminality." In B. B. Lahey, T. E. Moffitt, & A. Caspi (eds.), *Causes of Conduct Disorder and Juvenile Delinquency*. New York: Guilford Press.

Wilson, J. Q. & Hernstein, R. J. (1985). *Crime and Human Nature*. New York: Simon and Schuster.

6 Self-control and social control of deviant behavior in context: development and interactions along the life course

Marc Le Blanc

Introduction

Developmental criminology is concerned with the description and explanation of within-individual changes in deviant behavior along the life course. This chapter focuses on individual development in the context of a community environment. Earlier, we proposed an integrated multi-layered control theory of general deviance (Le Blanc, 1997a). This chapter expands this theory with propositions about the developmental interaction between self and social controls. This chapter is not directly concerned with the general deviance syndrome. Elsewhere, we have proposed an analytical paradigm to study its development (Le Blanc & Loeber, 1998), tested an operatationalization of this hierarchical construct (Le Blanc & Bouthillier, 2003), and formulated a theory of its growth and decline using the chaos–order paradigm (Le Blanc, 2005). In this chapter, we keep in mind these theoretical formulations and the empirical facts about within-individual changes in deviant behavior (Le Blanc & Loeber, 1998; Piquero, Farrington, & Blumstein, 2003), but we are particularly concerned with the development of self and social controls in an environmental context.

The Montreal Two-Sample Longitudinal Study (MTSLS) was supported over the years by grants awarded to me by the Social Sciences and Humanities Research Council of Canada (SSHRC), the Fonds pour la Formation des Chercheurs et l'Aide à la Recherche (Fonds FCAR), and the Conseil Québécois de la Recherche Sociale (CQRS).

My understanding of the chaos–order paradigm and its application in criminology was facilitated and enriched by extended discussions with my colleague Michel Janosz, Professor at the School of Psychoeducation of the Université de Montréal. Without his dedicated help, I could not have produced this chapter and other work on developmental theory.

We use the term control according to its third literal definition in Webster's Dictionary: "a mechanism used to regulate and guide the operation of a system." This notion is compatible with Gibbs' (1989: 23) sociological definition of control: "control is *overt* behavior by humans in the belief that (1) the behavior increases the probability of some subsequent condition and (2) the increase or decrease is desirable." This definition is central in psychology (Lytton, 1990) and in the social sciences since Comte (Le Blanc, 2004).

Existing explanatory theories in criminology are structural rather then developmental. They identify the relevant concepts, for example social disorganization, strain, control, and so on. These theories also specify the interactions between their component concepts, for example bonding theory defines the interactions between involvement, attachment, commitment, and beliefs. However, criminological theories do not specify how these explanatory phenomena are built over time; they do not describe the mechanisms by which these phenomena are created, developed, maintained, and transformed along the life course. One exception is differential association or social learning theory (Akers, 1998) that specifies how a favorable definition of delinquency is acquired and maintained, but this theory is concerned only with the beginning of the course of deviant behavior and it does not indicate what are the mechanisms of desistance. On the contrary, developmental psychology offers statements of the processes of psychological development (Lerner, 2002) without a concrete description of how they affect the course of deviant behavior. This chapter applies developmental psychology knowledge to the understanding of the interaction between self and social controls.

Over the last fifty years, criminology has witnessed enormous theoretical activity that took the form of theoretical elaboration, formalization, integration, modeling and testing of theories (Shoemaker, 2005). However, these theories were elaborations of the ideas of nineteenth-century theorists such as Quételet, Durkheim, Marx, Tarde, Lombroso, and Freud. Control theorists accepted the same basic assumptions about human nature (Empey, 1978; Kornhauser, 1978; Shoemaker, 2005). Over the last three decades, social control theory has become the most prominent empirically based criminological theory for the explanation of deviant behavior. Self-control theory is now regularly referred to and is increasingly empirically tested (Platt & Cullen, 2000).

Existing control theories and models are static in nature. They identify the major causes of deviant behavior, such as tenuous bonds and low self-control, and they state some of the interactions between these constructs (Gottfredson & Hirschi, 1990). However, they do not indicate how controls develop during the life span. They do not respond to the following questions: what is the course and what are the processes responsible for continuity and change in controls? Adopting the control perspective, this chapter illustrates ways in which self and social controls interact in a community context along the life course.

Some analytical tools for the description of the developmental course of deviant behavior are identified (Loeber & Le Blanc, 1990; Le Blanc & Loeber, 1998). However, the description of this course does not address the question of how quantitative and qualitative changes are produced. This question introduces the notion of developmental processes. What are the mechanisms that bring about these changes? Borrowing from the dynamical system perspective, we propose ways for conceiving the processes underpinning the course taken by the syndrome of deviant behavior (Le Blanc, 2005). In this chapter, we apply these tools to the understanding of the development of self and social controls and particularly their transactions.

In sum, we will review the literature on the course of self and social control over the life span with particular attention to quantitative and qualitative changes. In addition, we elaborate on the manner in which the interactions between self and social control in an environmental context can be understood using a dynamical system perspective.

A systemic view of control mechanisms

In our generic control theory (Le Blanc, 1997a), there are four mechanisms of personal control: bonding, allocentrism, modeling, and constraining; and two situations that modulate them: social status and biological capacity. They synthesize numerous factors which are identifiable in the empirical literature as having a potential impact on deviant behavior.

Bonding refers to the various ways by which individuals are held together. Its importance rests in the fact that it reflects the primary need of an individual for integration within a group which grounds the individual in a social and cultural milieu. *Allocentrism* is the psychological maturation, the natural growth and differentiation that characterizes self-control or personality over time. *Modeling* is the existence of pro-social patterns that shape conformity and the opportunities that are available to individuals. *Constraining* is the regulation of conformity through various direct and indirect restraints that are imposed by various social institutions: the socializing instruments.

These four mechanisms are active through the process of learning, a change in behavioral potentiality that occurs as a result of reinforced practice. The impact of this learning process on deviant behavior refers to differential association (Sutherland & Cressey, 1960) or social learning (Akers, 1998). The bonding, modeling and constraining mechanisms will be referred to as social control, while the allocentrism mechanism will be designated self-control.

The mechanisms of bonding, modeling, maturing, and constraining interact simultaneously and causally. They have their own life or ontogeneticity. Le Blanc's theory (1997a) is systemic in the sense that it defines a structure, an organization of its components (the position of the boxes representing the mechanisms in Figure 6.1), as well as reciprocal and directional relationships between the components, including feedbacks (the arrows between the boxes in Figure 6.1). It is also dynamic because over time there is continuity and change within the mechanisms as well as because of their direct and indirect impacts (the superimposed boxes for each mechanism in Figure 6.1). The relative position of the mechanisms depends on the principles of prerequisites and on the distinction between continuity and change. The theory states that there are exogenous factors that do not have a direct impact on deviant behavior: the social status and the biological capacity. Two of the mechanisms of control, bonding and self-control, are prerequisites. They are the foundations of the overall control mechanism. Without bonds, models cannot be significant and constraints cannot be operant.

In consequence, an unbounded individual cannot be sensitive to direct controls or influenced by the available models. In addition, since allocentrism refers to a desirable state, it necessarily precedes the influence of available models and constraints. As a consequence, bonding and allocentrism modulate deviant behavior through modeling and constraining. They are proximal causes. Models and constraints are more specific to the space-time dimension. They are not the more permanent dimensions of control such as bonding and allocentrism. In addition, these mechanisms are in a situation of reciprocal causation at a specific moment. Modeling and constraining are in the same situation; a causal order cannot be established. In addition, the four mechanisms of control are in a synergetic relation. They interact to produce an overall level of control of deviant behavior. Empirical tests of this integrative theoretical model have been conducted (Le Blanc & Biron, 1980; Le Blanc, Ouimet, & Tremblay, 1988; Le Blanc, 1997b).

The development of self-control

A developmental self-control theory of crime can be traced back to Quételet (1842: 95): "This fatal propensity appears to be developed in

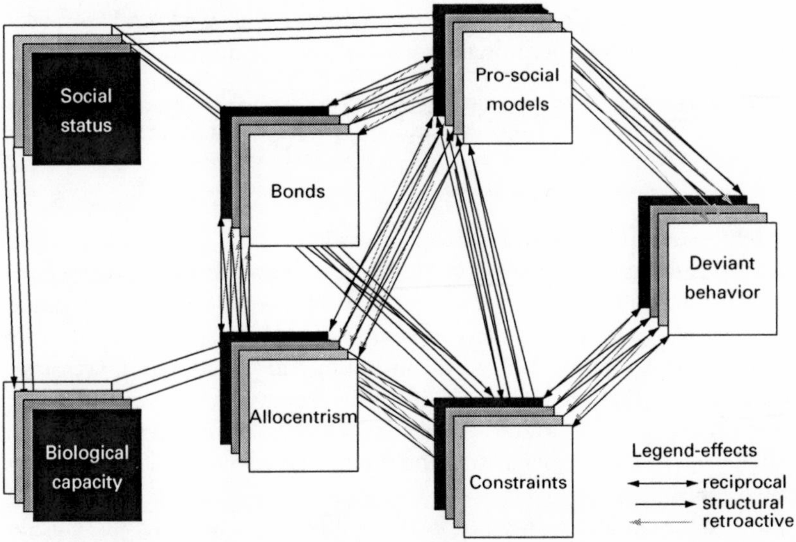

Figure 6.1. The structure of personal control theory
Source: Copyright © (1997) by Transaction Publishers. Reprinted by permission of the publisher.

proportion to the intensity of the physical power & passions of man ... The intellectual and moral development ... subsequently weakens the propensity to crime ... " Thus Quételet formulates a self-control theory composed of three dimensions, biological and psychological characteristics interacting with moral traits, and he employs a language that implies changes over time. Empey (1978) and Shoemaker (2005) view psychoanalysis as part of the control perspective which involves the first two notions proposed by Quételet. According to Freud's control theory, individuals have three personality strata, called the id, the ego, and the superego. The id is the reservoir of basic instinctual drives and motivations, or the libido. The ego, with its conscious and unconscious levels, regulates the libido and manages the adaptation to the external world. The superego is the moral structure, inner restraints derived from fear of sanctions and societal norms. The interactions between these three instances of the personality regulate deviant behavior. These behaviors manifest themselves when there is a conflict between instinctual drives and societal norms. The interactions between the three personality strata, self-control in other words, develops in stages. At the same epoch, Durkheim (1963) was using the terms temperament, intelligence, and personality to refer to one of the components of individual morality called the power of inhibition, a form of self-control.

Later, psychological criminology, based on clinical and empirical research, spoke of a criminal individuality, a criminal personality, or psychopathy to represent the propensity to offend, what is now commonly referred to as low self-control.

The notion of self-control

In 1990, Gottfredson and Hirschi provided a new impetus in criminological research by forcefully restating that the psychological dimension is a crucial explanatory factor of crime. Their theory became a dominant theoretical position and their book the second most cited publication (Cohn & Farrington, 1998). In addition, their theory is increasingly being tested (Platt & Cullen, 2000). This theory has two major postulates: that low self-control is the most important causal factor in explaining antisocial behaviors and that it remains stable in antisocial individuals.

In the psychological literature, there are two definitions of self-control. On one hand, a restricted definition is stated as "the ability to inhibit either impulsive or goal-seeking behavior for the sake of a more inclusive goal" (English, 1958). On the other hand, there is a comprehensive definition that refers to the traits making up the individual as a whole: the "control exercised by the individual over his own feelings, impulses and acts" (Drever, 1969). Gottfredson and Hirschi's (1990) definition of low self-control is primarily a behavioral definition because they stress characteristics that refer to "the vulnerability to the temptation of the moment" such as impulsivity and risk-taking. Throughout their book, it is this aspect of self-control that dominates their argumentation. However, they also include a cognitive dimension: being nonverbal ("...need not possess or value cognitive or academic skills" [89]), short-sighted ("...to be little interested in and unprepared for long term occupational pursuits" [89]), and of low intelligence [89]. They even talk about the characteristic of lack of sensitivity to others: "...tend to be self-centred, indifferent, or insensitive to the suffering and needs of others..." (90) which enlarges their behavioral definition to include the emotional dimension. Finally, they indicate a temperamental dimension to self-control with the following characteristics: physical ("...active and physical" [89]), temper-prone ("...minimum tolerance to frustration and little ability to respond to conflict through verbal rather than physical means" [90]), and insensitive ("...tend to be tolerant to physical pain or to be indifferent to physical discomfort" [90]). All these dimensions clearly correspond to well-known traits composing commonly used structural personality models (Matthews

& Deary, 1998; Clark & Watson, 1999; Miller & Lynam, 2001; Morizot & Le Blanc, 2003a). In general, the first four dimensions could be encompassed within disinhibition, while the last two are part of extraversion. In sum, Gottfredson and Hirschi's definition of self-control is not only a behavioral definition. Because of its temperamental, emotional, and cognitive dimensions, their definition could be viewed as a comprehensive definition of individuality; in line with Drever's (1969) generic definition and even Freud and Durkheim's definitions.

In recent years there have been attempts to assess the construct validity of Gottfredson and Hirschi's notion of low self-control (Grasmick *et al.* 1993; Longshore, Turner, & Stein, 1996; Vazsonyi *et al.* 2001). These studies suggest that self-control is a multi-dimensional construct. Few authors have paid attention to the critical issue of its content validity. Indeed, the fact that low self-control seems multi-dimensional is not surprising because, as we noted, the low self-control dimensions encompass two independent higher-order personality traits: disinhibition and extraversion. Another problem is that Gottfredson and Hirschi's definition of low self-control does not propose any traits related to negative emotionality, even though several studies show that this is one important predictor of antisocial behavior (Krueger, Caspi, & Moffitt, 2000; Miller & Lynam, 2001). Indeed, in the Montreal Two-Sample Longitudinal Study (Morizot & Le Blanc, 2003a) this trait distinguished between representative and adjudicated men across time. In consequence, we can argue that to further explore the issue of self-control is to rest on a replicable structural model of personality traits. This would provide a comprehensive and psychometrically defensible operational definition of individual differences in self-control.

In our personal control theory (Le Blanc, 1997a), we adopt an epigenetic definition of individuality that is represented by the notion of allocentrism. Allocentrism is the movement away from the natural egocentrism of the individual. It manifests itself by a genuine consideration of what surrounds a person; it is the disposition to think about others and to behave in relation to them. This egocentrism–allocentrism axis of the development of humans is present in most of the psychological theories of human development (Lerner, 2002); it often serves to synthesize the psychological dimension that is associated with deviant behavior. The egocentric personality is operationalized by a hierarchical structure that is identifiable through confirmatory factor analysis of longitudinal data on representative and adjudicated samples (Morizot & Le Blanc, 2003a): fifteen primary traits formed six secondary traits and three higher-order traits. These higher-order traits represent a broad description of personality traits comparable to other structural models of personality that have been identified with various personality assessment devices and which are often called the Big-Three (Matthews & Deary, 1998; Clark & Watson, 1999; Miller & Lynam, 2001). They also measure self-control and so an individual high on these traits could be characterized as displaying low self-control.

The course of self-control

The theory of low self-control is increasingly being tested with cross-sectional data (Platt & Cullen, 2000), and once with longitudinal data (Turner & Piquero, 2002). The major dimensions of low self-control are identified but their interactions are rarely uncovered. Moreover, the data do not indicate how low self-control develops during the life course. Since we propose that the course of deviant behavior be looked at in terms of quantitative and qualitative changes and developmental trajectories (Le Blanc & Loeber, 1998), we will apply the same analytical tools to review the development of self-control.

Quantitative changes

Quantitative changes are defined in terms of growth and decline in self-control. Growth is governed by the aging-stability law (Glenn, 1980). According to that law, self-control tends to stabilize and become less likely to change as a person grows older. This law contradicts Gottfredson and Hirschi's postulate that low self-control remains stable. The psychological literature has data which reflects these contradictory positions.

Structural continuity corresponds to the stability of a self-control structure at different ages. Costa and McCrae (1997) conclude that the personality structure seems constant across different ages even if there is a lack of studies testing its invariance with longitudinal data. This type of continuity can be estimated by examining the covariations among personality traits across time through confirmatory factor analysis. Morizot and Le Blanc (2003a) tested a maladaptive hierarchical traits structure on representative and adjudicated samples of men followed up for twenty-five years. They concluded that the structure identified can be assumed to be on the same measurement scale across time, that no major changes occurred in the self-control structure over twenty-five years.

Rank-order continuity refers to the stability of individual differences within a group. A strong correlation indicates that individuals remain in the same position within their group across time. Roberts and DelVecchio (2000), in a meta-analysis, observe that the mean correlation coefficient becomes linearly stronger as the individuals' age increased. In addition, Morizot and Le Blanc (2003a) find that this observation also applies to adjudicated adolescents and these men show the highest mean correlations. Therefore, the adjudicated men, as compared with representative individuals, tend to maintain, at a higher degree, their rank order in their group during adolescence as well as during adulthood. Their low self-control seems stable as Gottfredson and Hirschi (1990) postulate, and more stable than in the general population.

Mean-level continuity refers to the stability in the quantity of a personality trait across time. Allport (1961) suggests that with age, personality traits tend to change in the direction of greater maturity. Many cross-sectional and longitudinal studies using various personality assessment devices and samples reveal that when personality is first assessed in adolescence or early adulthood, significant mean-level changes in traits typically occur in the direction of growth (Costa & McCrae, 1997; Caspi & Roberts, 1999; Helson, Kwan, John, & Jones, 2002; Roberts *et al.*, in press). McCrae *et al.* (2000) add that the maturational trend in personality traits observed from adolescence to early adulthood is also observable after the age of 30, although the rate seems to be lower. Morizot and Le Blanc's (2003a) analysis confirms that the adjudicated men display higher scores in nearly every maladaptive personality trait from adolescence to midlife, although they manifest better self-control.

In summary, these results suggest that both stability and change are observable in the development of self-control. On the one hand, the magnitude of the rank-order continuity estimates show that individual differences in self-control tend to be more stable across time. On the other hand, the mean-level continuity assessment reveals a non-trivial maturational trend toward a better psychological adjustment. This indicates that self-control traits are not developmentally static predispositions. Moreover, measurement invariance across groups and across time suggests that a personality structure is a meaningful instrument for studying very different types of individuals. However, adjudicated males and men in the general population show clear differences in personality development. In consequence, Gottfredson and Hirschi's (1990) position that low self-control remains stable across the life course is a gross statement of its development toward allocentrism.

Qualitative changes

Qualitative changes refer to something new and more complex according to the ontogenetic principle. These changes in nature are subdivided into a developmental sequence of hierarchical stages.

Concerning self-control and its direction toward allocentrism, numerous theories postulate that stages of human development exist. There are psychosexual (Freud, 1905), cognitive (Piaget, 1967), moral (Kohlberg, 1976), psychosocial (Erickson, 1972), ego (Loevinger, 1976), and interpersonal (Sullivan, Grant, & Grant, 1957) developmental sequences of stages. Even if the results of the quantitative change studies support the hypothesis of a normative maturation in the direction of allocentrism, they do not commend stage-based theories because no evidence for discrete stages can be drawn from these data. However, the marked slowing of the maturation rate after age 30 may be an indication that these men have reached some sort of qualitatively distinct psychological adaptation. It is plausible that this phenomenon is more closely associated with the fact that by age 30 the majority of these men have desisted from the typical adolescent lifestyle (Arnett, 1999) and gained new social bonds through involvement in adult social roles (Caspi, 1993, 1998; Sampson & Laub, 1993).

Developmental trajectories

Quantitative and qualitative changes and the course of self-control form a general trajectory. Reviews of typological studies of personality conclude that despite the fact that individuals differ in age, gender, ethnicity, language, culture, historical period, and geographic region, three replicable personality types are identifiable: Adjusted, Overcontrolled, and Undercontrolled (Caspi, 1998; Robins, John, & Caspi, 1998; Asendorpf *et al.*, 2001). A number of cross-sectional and longitudinal studies examined the antecedents, concurrent correlates, and consequences of these personality types. They revealed that the types display differentiated profiles in personality traits and in important cognitive, behavioral, and social adjustment variables (York & John, 1992; Caspi & Silva, 1995; Pulkkinen, 1996; Robins *et al.*, 1996; Hart *et al.*, 1997; Asendorpf & van Aken, 1999; Chang Weir & Gjerde, 2002; van Aken *et al.*, 2002). In addition, some studies showed that the three types are identifiable at different periods of the life course, but that type membership is not stable across time (Asendorpf & van Aken, 1999). The scientific community has paid very little attention to the task of identifying trajectories of personality development even though two studies illustrate the developmental trajectory perspective (Block, 1971; Tubman *et al.*, 1992).

Morizot and Le Blanc (2005), using a representative sample of men, are able to identify four self-control developmental trajectories. The level of antisocial behavior increases from the better to the less mature trajectories. In addition, Morizot and Le Blanc (2003b) identify similar self-control developmental trajectories in the adjudicated sample of men and each of them relates differentially to antisocial behavior across time. These trajectory results are less supportive of Gottfredson and Hirschi's general theory of antisocial behavior. Indeed, our results with antisocial men, that can be assumed to be a persistent low self-control group as compared with normative individuals, show that different personality types are differentially related to antisocial behavior trajectories. Firstly, the Overcontrolled tend to be those who are the most highly involved in antisocial behavior across time. At first glance, the identification of such a personality type supports Gottfredson and Hirschi's claims. However, the Undercontrolled tend to be as highly involved in antisocial behavior as the Overcontrolled during adolescence while, contrary to the Overcontrolled, whose problems remain stable, the Undercontrolled's antisocial behavior desistance parallels their psychological maturation. The general theory of antisocial behavior does not account for such a trajectory. Moreover, the Resilients displayed a normative personality profile in adolescence followed by a personality maturation until midlife. These men are the least involved in antisocial behavior across time. Again, a general theory of antisocial behavior would not have predicted such a trajectory. Finally, the Anomics displayed a very unstable personality trajectory across time. They display high levels of antisocial behavior during the worsening phases of their trajectory. Once more, the general theory would not predict such a trajectory. In a nutshell, the identification of trajectories suggests that the role of self-control in the explanation of antisocial behavior would arguably require a more specific formulation according to different developmental types of self-control.

In conclusion, the data reported in this section on the development of self-control suggests that there is ample knowledge on the quantitative and qualitative changes in self-control and that there is emerging knowledge on the trajectories of self-control in general and for groups with low self-control. All these data challenge seriously Gottfredson and Hirschi's (1990) postulate that low self-control remains stable across the life course for antisocial individuals. In Figure 6.1, the propensity mechanism is represented by the interactions between the biological capacity and self-control.

The development of social controls

Social control emphasizes the notions of power, authority, and influence. Comte used this term in this manner in 1826 (Le Blanc, 2004b). However, Durkheim (1963) was the first to formulate a theory of social control. He proposed two mechanisms of social control: attachment to the group and social constraints. For Durkheim, socialization has attachment to the group as its base, a form of identification of the individual with their family, corporation, country, and humanity. This type of attachment necessitates the attachment to persons, which, in turn, is a source of commitment to the morality of an individual's group. If attachment is the first mechanism of socialization, the individual needs the help of social constraints for socialization to be effective. They are forces that impose restraints and limits on the behavior of individuals. These forces are coercive because they apply to behaviors that are prohibited and that could be sanctioned by the authorities. These forces manifest themselves as rules that dictate appropriate behaviors and by sanctions that are applied when rules are violated. For Durkheim, the individual adhesion to norms and the probability of being sanctioned create an obligation to behave according to social rules.

American criminology has been redefining Durkheim's two fundamental notions for a century. For example, Nye (1958) elaborated the notion of social constraints by distinguishing forms of controls: direct and indirect, internal and external, and formal and informal. Hirschi (1969) developed the notion of bond (attachment, commitment, involvement, and beliefs) to elaborate Durkheim's notions of attachment to a group. More recently, Sampson and Laub (1993) used the notion of social capital to refer to bonds and the notion of social control in Nye fashion.

The notion of social control

Our integrative theory of personal control (Le Blanc, 1997a) distinguishes among three forms of social control: bonds, constraints, and models. Following Hirschi (1969), the replications of his theory (Kempf, 1993), and its formalization (Le Blanc & Caplan, 1993), we stated that an individual's bond with society manifests itself in relation to several institutions constituting the different spheres of the person's world. Four institutions are important for adolescents: family, school, peers, and religion. For adults, the main institutions are marriage, work, children, peers, and religion. The person relates to these institutions through two avenues: attachment to persons and commitment to institutions. A person's level of attachment to parents determines their level of attachment to peers and to other persons. The cumulative impact of these attachments protects the person against deviant influences and discourages deviant behavior. The second element of the bond is the commitment to institutions. Commitment refers to an affective investment in education, work, religion, and so on. In addition, the person is committed not only by their present investments but also by what they hope to achieve. Therefore, when a person faces the temptation to commit a deviant act, they must evaluate the costs of their behavior relative to the investment they have made.

Following Durkheim's (1895, 1934) classic distinction between norms, defined as rules of law and moral values, and discipline, circumscribed as monitoring and punishment, we propose that there are two major sources of restraint when an individual envisages a deviant behavior: internal and external constraints (Le Blanc, 1994b). Labeling theorists elaborated the formal external constraint construct (Shoemaker, 1990), while bonding theorists developed the informal social reaction point of view (Le Blanc & Caplan, 1993). Furthermore, bonding theorists elaborated the notion of internal constraint under the notion of beliefs (Hirschi, 1969) and deterrence theorists proposed the notion of perceived certainty and severity of sanctions (Paternoster, 1987). Durkheim had already identified these notions.

While bonds and constraints can define social control in Durkheim fashion, we now know that we have to take into account opportunities. Tarde (1924) introduced a modeling explanation of delinquency, which was then developed by Sutherland (Sutherland & Cressey, 1960; Akers, 1998). Modeling, particularly by peers, is an important cause of adolescent delinquency according to numerous studies (Warr, 2002). In the formulation of low self-control theory, Gottfredson and Hirschi (1990) suggest that low self-control leads to street life and to the membership of a deviant group. These factors, in turn, lead to more frequent deviant behavior. In a recent restatement of their theory, these authors bring back Cloward and Ohlin's (1960) notion of legitimate and illegitimate opportunities. In our theory, these opportunities are models of two types: models in terms of people, parents, peers and other significant people; or in terms of deviant lifestyle or routine activities. Each form of the models can be prosocial or deviant. When deviant models and routine activities outnumber their prosocial counterparts, deviant behavior will increase.

In sum, our notion of social control involves three constructs that are modulated by social status: bonds to society, internal and external constraints, and models and lifestyles. Le Blanc's theory (1997a) specifies the relative position of these mechanisms (Figure 6.1). Social status is an indirect explanation of deviant behavior. It influences the degree of a person's bonding, which, in turn, affects the appropriateness of constraints and the person's receptivity to prosocial models. The interactions between the bonds, the constraints, and the model constitute the social control mechanism. The social control mechanism is composed of two submechanisms: socialization, which involves the interactions between bonds, and constraints and learning (differential association) that result from the interactions of bonds and models.

The course of social control

Social control theory is the most tested theory in criminology (Kempf, 1993). However, these tests are narrow and static. They identify one or a few constructs and they test some interactions between them. A test of a comprehensive model is rare (Le Blanc, Ouimet, & Tremblay, 1988; Le Blanc, 1997b). However, compared to the numerous tests of social control theory, very few studies address the question of how social control develops during the life course.

Quantitative changes

Quantitative changes in social control refer to variations over time of social status, bonds, constraints, and models. Their growth is governed by the aging-stability law (Glenn, 1980). According to that law, controls are more important during adolescence and tend to stabilize and become less likely to change as a person grows older. In addition, these changes are in the direction of greater conformity (Jessor & Jessor, 1977; Le Blanc *et al.*, 1980; Jessor, Donovan, & Costa, 1991; Le Blanc, 1992, 1994a). We will therefore limit ourselves to adolescence and young adulthood since thereafter there are very few studies that deal with this age group except those by Sampson and Laub (1993).

We do not know of many growth curves for *bonds*. However, a meta-analysis by Laursen, Coy, and Collins (1998) concludes that the frequency of parent–child conflict decreases from early adolescence to mid-adolescence and from there to late adolescence, while the conflict effect increases during puberty and with age during adolescence. Loeber *et al.* (2000) present data for the 6- to 18-year-old span. They show that poor communication and a disadvantaged relationship between parent and child does not materially change during that age range. However, single parents and teenage mothers experience significantly worse interactions with their sons over time. Using a cross-lagged design, Le Blanc *et al.* (1980) show that, for representative and adjudicated samples, there is no change in the attachment to parents between early and late adolescence, but there is an improvement of the attachment to other figures. Commitment to schooling and work also improves.

Turning to *models*, there are also some striking age trends in everyday life activities (Larson & Richards, 1989; Larson & Verma, 1999; Osgood

& Lee, 1993). Le Blanc *et al.* (1980) show that involvement in leisure activities and participation in activities with family members was increasing. In addition, they found a decrease in loitering, particularly in the adjudicated sample. The same tendency was observed for routine activities favoring deviant behavior (unstructured socializing, activities outside the home, and at-home activities) (Osgood *et al.*, 1996). Concerning deviant peers, Le Blanc *et al.* (1980) found a decrease in attachment over this period. Elliott and Menard (1996) observed that during late adolescence the percentage of youths in less delinquent groups increases and the percentage of individuals in more delinquent groups declines. However, there is a considerable stability in the type of group with whom adolescents affiliated from one year to the next and, when change occurred, it was a gradual transition from one peer-group type to a type not too dissimilar. Finally, these authors observed an increase in levels of isolation as adolescents approached adulthood and entered into monogamous relationship. In addition, the relevance of peers decreases during adolescence (the importance of peers, time spent in their company, and loyalty to peers). In addition, there are changes in the exposure to delinquent peers which rises during late childhood and early adolescence (Stoolmiller, 1994), and falls during a relatively brief period around mid-adolescence (Warr, 1993). The Jessor study shows an increase in the importance of friends' models for drinking (Jessor & Jessor, 1977) and for drugs use (Jessor, Donovan, & Costa, 1991). If the relevance of peers decreases during adolescence, the importance of intimates increases (Buhrmester, 1996). In addition, there are age-related changes in the definition of friendship (Aboud & Mendelson, 1996). During preadolescence, there is a move from looking exclusively for a stimulating companionship to exchanging intimacies; later on, the nature of friendship centers more on emotional support, autonomy, and the needs of, or the need for, friends.

Finally, there are quite a few indications of changes for external *constraints*, but not many for internal constraints. Jessor and Jessor (1977) note a decrease in perceived parental control during adolescence. This tendency is confirmed by Le Blanc *et al.* (1980). For their representative sample, parental monitoring and discipline as well as school sanctions decline. However, there are no such changes in their adjudicated sample. Loeber *et al.* (2000) report that physical punishment decreases, while poor supervision and low-level positive parenting increases between ages 6 and 18 years. Internal controls also vary during adolescence. Tolerance to deviance increases during adolescence (Jessor & Jessor, 1977), but decreases during youth (Jessor, Donovan, & Costa 1991). Le Blanc *et al.* (1980) confirm the first tendency for conventional adolescents, while the second tendency happens during the second half of adolescence in the adjudicated sample. In addition, Zhang, Loeber, and Stouthamer-Loeber (1997) confirm that delinquent attitudes progress during adolescence, particularly toward serious violence and minor and serious theft. Whatever the level of the changes, the stability of beliefs is impressive in the Thornberry *et al.* (1994) and Elliott and Menard (1996) models.

In addition to the growth curves reported in the literature, some studies use cross-lagged analysis with two or more waves of data during adolescence and variables that could operationalize some of the constructs of our social control theory. For example, the Rochester group has produced a number of publications with four to six variables and two to five data waves (Thornberry *et al.* 1991, 1994; Krohn *et al.* 1996; Thornberry, 1996), while we worked with two waves (Le Blanc *et al.*, 1980; Le Blanc, 1992; Le Blanc, 1994b; 1997a). The National Youth Study, among other data sets, has also generated many such analyses. In all of these models, we find firstly that the effect of a particular variable on itself at a subsequent point in time is higher than its impact on other control variables or deviant behavior at the same point in time or another moment. Secondly, a causal sequence emerges in which deviant peers and attitudes display a stronger direct effect on offending than family or school bonding and constraints variables. Thirdly, the studies make clear that a deterioration of prosocial, and an increase of antisocial, social controls amplify offending. For example, in a recent study, Simons *et al.* (1998) observed that a decrease in quality of parenting and school commitment or an increase of deviant peers will produce a statistically significant increase in self-reported conduct problems, holding constant the level of earlier oppositional/defiant behavior. Fourthly, Le Blanc (1993) reports that with deceleration of offending, conventional and adjudicated adolescents strengthen their bonds to conventional society (family and school) and distance themselves from unconventional bonds (delinquent peers), even if external constraints are less stringent (parental discipline and social reaction). Although this general tendency is evident for the two samples of adolescents, sequential covariation does not always show the same intensity or direction. The adolescents in the representative sample were more mature or grown up, while the adolescents of the adjudicated sample showed some, but not outstanding, maturational improvement.

Qualitative changes and trajectories

There are some indications of continuity and change in social controls during the life course. Bonds, models, and constraints evolve according to the maturational hypothesis. However, there is little evidence of developmental sequences except for peer relations (Oden, 1988), external control (Durkheim, 1934), and play (Berk, 1989).

In reviewing the literature on offending trajectories, Le Blanc (2002) was able to identify a good number of studies using the dynamic classification perspective and the quantitative change strategy. In a previous section, we saw that some developmental trajectories of self-control were identified by longitudinal studies. However, we were not able to identify trajectories of social control in general, neither for bonds, constraints, nor models.

In sum, criminology has made considerable conceptual efforts in defining social controls and studying their interactions in relation to deviant behavior. However, knowledge is scant about the quantitative changes and virtually non-existent concerning qualitative changes and trajectories.

The interaction of self and social controls

Freud (1963) and Durkheim (1963) proposed interactions between self and social controls. For Freud, the interactions between the ego and the superego regulate deviant behavior. For Durkheim, there are three interacting instances that produce morality: the power of inhibition (temperament, intelligence, personality), the attachment to a group, and social constraints. Reiss (1951) was the first criminologist to test that deviant behavior is the joint result of deficient social and personal controls. We follow that road with our theory (Le Blanc, 1997a) and empirical models (Le Blanc & Biron, 1980; Le Blanc, Ouimet, & Tremblay, 1988; Le Blanc, 1997b). Let's start by reviewing the most discussed integrative theory of the last decade.

Gottfredson and Hirschi's integrative theory

Gottfredson and Hirschi (1990) state an integrative control theory. Social control in terms of bonding, through attachment, commitment, and involvement, and social constraint processes, by way of beliefs, supervision, and discipline, is no longer the major cause of offending as was the case in the 1969 version of control theory (Hirschi, 1969). Low self-control is the principal cause. "The major cause of low self-control thus appears to be ineffective child-rearing" (Hirschi, 1969: 97) and it is a cause of criminal behavior that is moderated by criminal opportunities. However, Gottfredson and Hirschi suggest that "parental concern for the welfare or behavior of the child is a necessary condition for successful child-rearing" (Hirschi 1969: 98). Internal and external constraints intervene between self-control and offending because "supervision presumably prevents criminal and analogous acts" (Hirschi, 1969: 99). Situational factors also mediate the impact of low self-control: "the link between self-control and crime is not deterministic, but probabilistic, affected by opportunities and other constraints" (Gottfredson & Hirschi, 1990: 53) (see also their restatement [Gottfredson & Hirschi, 2003]). These opportunities may be routine activities, deviant opportunities, or the exposure to deviant role models and delinquent peers. This statement indicates two intervening mechanisms between self-control and offending: situations and constraints. In sum, Gottfredson and Hirschi are proposing the following causal model, that is also described by Figure 6.1. A tenuous bond to society accompanied by ineffective child-rearing practices favors the maintenance of low self-control, which, in turn, will support offending if constraints are ineffective and if the situation is favorable to deviance.

Some studies of adults examine the intervening impact of some of these constructs. Grasmick *et al.* (1993) show that self-control does not display a direct effect on criminality whereas criminal opportunities do, but their interaction is significant (Deng, 1994; Nagin & Paternoster, 1994; Piquero & Tibbets, 1994). Gibbs, Giever, and Kerr (1994) show that self-control mediates the impact of parental management. Some studies with representative samples of adolescents examine some components of Gottfredson and Hirschi's theory. Mak (1990) adds that the impact of belief in laws is much more important then self-control. Brownfield and Sorenson (1993) find that self-control does not display a direct relationship with self-reported delinquency, but, with peer delinquency, it is the most significant direct link with official delinquency. Wood, Pfefferbaum, and Arneklev (1993) find that low self-control is the best direct explanation of theft, vandalism, interindividual delinquency, legal and illegal substance use, and imprudent behavior. Polakowski (1994) concludes that self-control is more powerful than social control variables in explaining conviction and self-reported delinquency at the middle of adolescence and up to 21 years of age. Peter, Lagrange, and Silverman (2003) conclude that both self-control and strain are more important contributors to delinquency than delinquent peers, but in an additive not in an interactive way. Longshore *et al.* (2004) show for a sample of adults that drug use is not directly explained by low self-control but that its effect is mediated by internal constraints (beliefs) and differential association variables. However, low self-control is associated with tenuous bonds (attachment and involvement). Finally, Pratt, Turner, and Piquero (2004) show that for whites, self-control is predicted cross-sectionally and longitudinally by parental constraints (supervision and discipline).

In sum, the range of constructs is limited in each particular study. However, they support some of the links of Gottfredson and Hirschi's integrative control theory. When using a more comprehensive set of constructs, such as those in Figure 6.1, we can report data that confirms that structure, cross-sectionally and longitudinally, with a representative sample (Le Blanc, Ouimet, & Tremblay, 1988) and with an adjudicated sample (Le Blanc, 1997b). However, controlling for all constructs, the model domain of variables displays the most important direct effect followed, in turn, by the constraint, the self-control, and the bonding domains of variables. However, such integrative theory and tests are structural and static. They specify the structure, the relations between the notions, but they do not state the dynamics of the interactions between them. Let's state these interactions in a developmental perspective.

Interactions between self and social controls and deviant behavior

The development of deviant behavior

The key phenomenon to be explained by criminology is the course of conformity to conventional standards of behavior (Le Blanc, 2005). This notion is represented by the construct of general deviance that we have delimited with four subconstructs: covert, overt, and authority conflict, and reckless behaviors. They are composed of twelve forms of deviant behavior (Le Blanc & Bouthillier, 2003). The notion of conformity to conventional standards is circumscribed by population behavioral norms for a particular society in a specific historical period. Laws define many of these norms and custom the others. All these behaviors can be measured through a self-reported instrument and many of them with official records.

General deviance manifests itself in different ways during the lifespan. It is a heterotypic phenomenon. During infancy, it takes the form of authority conflicts and physical aggression (Loeber & Hay, 1997). During childhood, these behaviors change in seriousness and diversity and, in addition, the authority conflict manifests itself at school and covert behaviors are added (Loeber & Hay, 1997). With adolescence, the syndrome is diversified in terms of covert, overt, and authority conflict, and reckless behaviors are added (Le Blanc & Bouthillier, 2003). During adulthood some criminal behaviors gradually stop and new forms of offending are introduced (tax evasion and family violence), school authority conflict is replaced by problems at work, and there are new forms of reckless behavior (compulsive gambling).

Our developmental theory states that the course of deviant behavior takes the form of a reverse U-shape for every individual during their life course (Le Blanc, 2005). Individuals vary in the timing, height, and length of their reverse U-shape trajectory of deviant behavior. The description of the course of deviant behavior can be easily accomplished with the tools of the developmental paradigm (Le Blanc & Loeber, 1998). However, these measures of quantitative and qualitative changes do not describe the processes that characterize the course of deviant behavior.

Three complementary perspectives on development

As a starting point, we accept the orthogenic principle stated by Werner (1957: 126): "whenever development occurs it proceeds from a state of relative globality and lack of differentiation to a state of increasing differentiation, articulation, and hierarchic integration." This principle is compatible with the contextual theoretical perspective in developmental psychology and the chaos–order perspective. The contextual perspective states that every phenomenon is historic. Constant changes at all level of analysis characterize life, and embeddedness of each level with all others is a particularity of all human phenomena. In the contextual perspective, development is also probabilistic. This means that the influence of the changing context on the trajectory of development is partly uncertain and that development must be defined in terms of "organism-context reciprocal, or dynamic-interactional relations" (Lerner, 1986: 69). However, the organization and the internal coherence of the organism limit the probabilities of different trajectories. The chaos–order view acknowledges that type of contextuality for every phenomenon (Briggs & Peat, 1989).

The commonsense definition of the term chaos refers to a state "in which chance is supreme", "confusion" and an "unorganized state" according to Webster's Dictionary. In hard science, chaos refers to a relative state of disorder, uncertainty, non-linearity, and unpredictability and it talks about open systems, complex systems, the fractal nature of systems, self-organization, conservation of energy, structured randomness, non-linear dynamics, inner rhythms and sensitivity to the initial condition. Notions that are present in one way or another in developmental psychology (see, for example, Thelen and Smith [1998] on a dynamic system theory of human development). However, the confusion that is involved in a chaotic state is never pure randomness and chance. In the chaos–order perspective, "statements clarifying the limits and likelihood of future behaviors can still be made for a chaotic process" (Peak & Frame, 1994: 158). Chaos refers to a state where there are low probabilities of many types of deviant behavior, in consequence there is a high level of uncertainty about which deviant behavior will occur. This situation is particularly common in the domain of deviant behavior during adolescence and for chronic offenders.

These perspectives are compatible with the interactional view of development. This interactional synergy is the result of at least four types of quantitative relationships between contexts, controls, and deviant behavior. Firstly, each of them is state-dependent. Secondly, there are reciprocal relations between them at a specific point in time. Thirdly, the directional relations between contexts, controls, and deviant behavior are such that they will become alternately independent and dependent variables along the life course. Fourthly, there are retroactive effects between them, deviant behavior at time one will reduce the impact of some controls at time two. This interactional synergy is also the result of qualitative transition along the life course. Among others, there can be sleeper effects (Kagan & Moss, 1962); a change in a control variable will only manifest itself much later than it occurred and there can be abrupt changes (Flavell, 1971); deviant behavior may increase dramatically after a change in a control variable; there can be a ceiling effect (Le Blanc & Fréchette, 1989); and deviant behavior may stay transitory.

The developmental interaction between self and social controls

As we did for the interaction between controls and deviant behavior, we postulate that there is a dynamical interaction between the two general mechanisms of control, that is, self-control and social control. They interact, according to the principles of the above theoretical perspectives, to produce an overall level of control of deviant behavior. We will use two instruments to illustrate the construction of the dynamical interaction of self and social controls: Lewin's (1946) psychological space landscapes and Briggs and Peat's (1989) phase space map. These instruments and the underlying system thinking are metaphors that may help us understand the interconnected development of self and social controls.

Self and social control landscape

According to Lewin's topological field theory, different forces have to be distinguished. Figure 6.2 represents these forces as three parallel spaces. The deviant behavior, self-control, and social control layers of these forces are specific systems. These life spaces need to be represented in their particular setting and within a specific situation. Forces in a field may compete, conflict, overlap, sum, or interact. These fields of forces are also conceived as mutually interdependent because they are state-dependent and interacting (the lines connecting the fields, Figure 6.2).

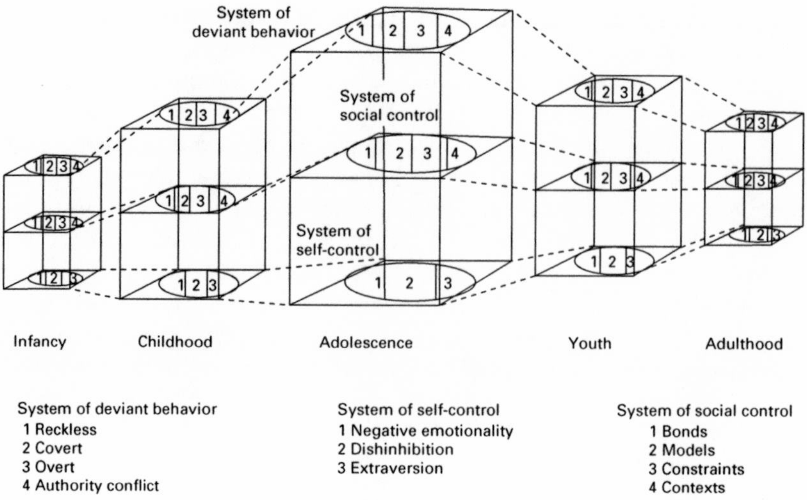

Figure 6.2. The landscape of self and social control and deviant behavior

The phase space map of self and social controls development

Lewin's topological field theory offers a landscape of the developmental fusion of self and social control but it does not illustrate what may happen when they interact. The phase space map may help us understand when self and social control are changing in synergy. Figure 6.3 presents such a map for the development of controls and their interactions with deviant behavior.

Attractors and bifurcations. An *attractor* is a sort of magnetic point that structures a phenomenon, in our case contexts, self and social controls, and deviant behavior. Their magnetic nature is represented by the tendency of a phenomenon, once initiated, to repeat. This state dependency has been amply documented for deviant behavior (Le Blanc & Loeber, 1998). Deviant behaviors do not operate as attractors at the same age for each individual or necessarily in the same sequence (Le Blanc, 2005). Attractors exist in various forms in the self and social control systems.

Concerning the bond control system, there are two subsystems, attachment to persons and commitment to institutions (Le Blanc & Caplan, 1993; Le Blanc, 1997a). These subsystems are attractors in the bonding system, but we can easily think of attractors in each of these subsystems. As an example, we can list some of the attractors in the attachment subsystem: mother, father, siblings, teacher, coach,

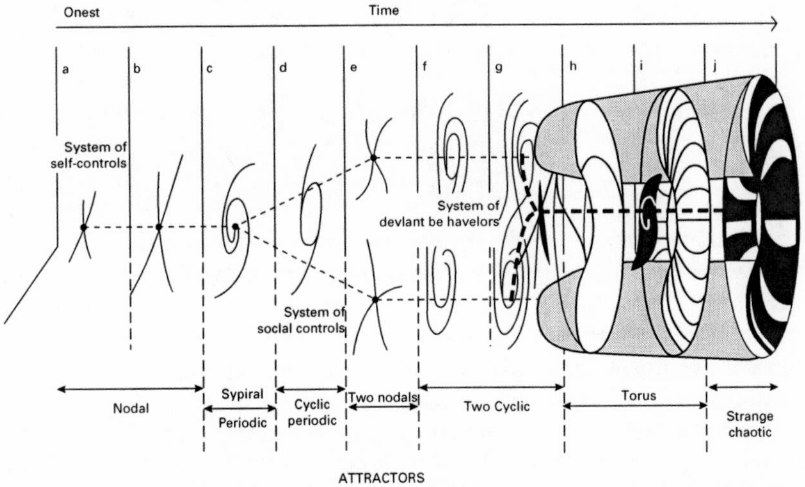

Figure 6.3. The development of self and social controls from a chaos point of view

neighbor, intimate friend, girl friend, wife, and so on. In the self-control system, there are three major subsystems or attractors if we refer to Morizot and Le Blanc's (2003a) hierarchical structure of personality: disinhibition, negative emotionality, and extraversion; each of them is a system in itself since they are composed of two traits that comprise many other traits. In the constraints domain, there are external and internal subsystems; external constraints could be formal attractors (expulsion from school, arrest, and conviction) or informal attractors (reactions of parents, peers, teachers, to deviant attitudes and behaviors); while internal constraints are the legitimacy of parental and school rules, the beliefs, the perception of risks of formal sanctions, and so on (Le Blanc, 1994a; 1997a). Finally, in the model's system of control, there are two major subsystems, routine activities favoring deviance and the availability of persons or groups involved in deviance (Le Blanc, 1997a).

Each attractor is normative. Most individuals have the opportunity to attach to a mother, a father, a friend, or a teacher, etc. They have the opportunity to commit themselves to school, work, sport, etc. Most individuals will encounter various types of prosocial and antisocial models and will participate in various routine activities. In addition, they will develop internal constraints and they will be submitted to many types of external constraint. Moreover, all the self and social control systems and subsystems are age-graded by society whereas bonds, models, and constraints are heterotypic phenomena.

In summary, we can represent the components of self and social controls as attractors, magnetic points that concur to their own construction. In Figure 6.3, this is represented by the self-control nodal attractor in section (a) that develops into a stronger attractor in section (b) or the social control attractor in section (e) that develops into a stronger attractor in section (f), or the same of the deviant behavior system in sections (h) and (i). Their magnetic nature is reflected by their constant capacity to duplicate themselves. In addition, they are normative in the sense that these risk and protective factors are absent or present in a certain quantity or quality from time to time. Finally, the pull of each control is dependent on changes in its own system parameters (characteristics of particular control: nature, quantity, frequency) and degrees of freedom (number of ways the control subsystems have the ability to move trajectories for example), but particularly on modifications of the parameters of the components of the self and social control systems, the numerous independent variables.

Some phenomena may also be *repellors* (Abraham, 1995). For example, the opportunity to use a hard drug may be a repellor for most adolescents. The repellent value of hard drugs is high for most adolescents and also for most drug users. Some self and social controls could be repellors. For example, the fear of arrest could be a repellor. In the attachment subsystem, some attachment figures may be repellors; the fourth-grade teacher, a bantam hockey coach, or a gay friend, for example, could be repellors. In sum, all systems and subsystems of control have their own attractors and repellors. The attractors or repellors in the personal control system and subsystems can produce disequilibrium or chaos in their own system. In Figure 6.3, this disequilibrium is represented by the interactions between the self-control and the social control systems in sections (f) and (g) and subsequent ones. Hanging around with a delinquent friend (the model box in Figure 6.1) or being intercepted by a police officer in a park (the constraints box in Figure 6.1) are other examples of nodal attractors. They are experiences that could be reinforced. If the adolescent hangs out more often with his delinquent friends, the pull of the attractor is amplified (section b of Figure 6.3). A periodic attractor consists of a series of repeated states. A periodic attractor can represent the association with more then one delinquent friend. It can be pictured as a spiral attractor (section c of Figure 6.3) or a cyclic attractor (section d of Figure 6.3) depending on the number of delinquent friends or the time spent with them.

All attractors produce positive and negative feedbacks. Positive feedbacks can come from the delinquent peers system itself; for example, the number of delinquent peers, one of the parameters of this subsystem, introduces the adolescent to numerous good experiences. Or positive feedbacks can come from other components of the self and social control system, for example inappropriate parental management techniques or negative emotionality. It is the same for negative feedbacks; they can originate from the peer subsystem, such as losing an intimate prosocial friend, or from other components of the self and social control system, such as increased parental supervision or alienation. As age increases, opportunities and controls are modified; affiliation to a gang, for example, may be added to the delinquent peers subsystem. Association with delinquent peers and affiliation to a delinquent gang are then two attractors (section e of Figure 6.3). If the association with delinquent peers and the affiliation with a delinquent gang becomes solid, we then have two cyclic attractors (sections f and g of Figure 6.3). The difference in the number of cycles between sections (f) and (g) represents the increasing degree of affiliation. Later, the system will go through different phases of uncertainty. The system is the torus attractor situation in sections (h) and (i) of Figure 6.3. A strong attachment to delinquent friends and affiliation with a delinquent gang become cyclic attractors and they interact. Their interactions form a torus attractor, or a high turbulence, as represented in Figure 6.3. There is then an increased unpredictability in the peer subsystem. Because of this trajectory, a high level of unpredictability can result in deviant behavior and we then have a strange attractor. The dark portion of section (j) Figure 6.3 represents this type of attractor. This situation of chaos happens when a person has only delinquent friends and is a member of the core group of a gang. Then the peer system loses its ability to regulate itself toward a normative situation and association with prosocial peers. This example can be reformulated with all the components of self and social controls.

It should be noted that some attractors are only minor nodal attractors, while others are major nodal attractors. For example, in the bonding subsystem, parents are probably major nodal attractors while a neighbor of the same age that a child plays with once in a while would be a minor nodal attractor; some figures would be cyclic, for example a friend who is constant for many years. Some other attachment figures could be chaotic; for example, if the attachment to the mother is very insecure the child will have difficulties in relating to other figures of the attachment subsystem. The nature of the attractor is a parameter of the system evolution.

As age and as opportunities increase, controls are transformed and the system goes through different phases of uncertainty. This situation is represented by the torus attractor in sections (h) and (i) and subsequent sections of Figure 6.3. Self-control, social control, and deviant behavior thereby become cyclic attractors and, in addition, they *interact.* The interactions form a torus attractor and high turbulence exists in the person control system. The coupled motion of the interactions between the self and social control and deviant behavior systems wraps the coupled motion around the surface of a torus. There is then increased unpredictability in the person system of control of deviant behavior. In addition, their interactions will cause perturbations in the initial conditions of these systems; the result will then be an amplification of the key parameters. Because of this evolution, a high level of unpredictability can result and we have then a strange attractor. Section (j) of Figure 6.3 represents this type of attractor. This situation of chaos could happen when a person offends frequently and regularly, when self-control is low, and when social controls are tenuous. The situation of chaos characterizes adolescence in general when deviant behavior and most offences display their highest participation rates. But it also describes the situation when a particular adolescent has a high frequency of offending. In this case, the system loses its ability to regulate itself toward conventional behavior and this comorbid extreme situation is called the persistent-offending trajectory.

As we have shown (Le Blanc & Loeber, 1998) in the previous section of this chapter, there are quantitative and qualitative changes in the course of deviant behavior and growth and escalation in self and social controls. Nevertheless, there is also decline and de-escalation. Figure 6.4 illustrates the processes by which high levels of deviant behavior are replaced by conforming behavior. Studies support the idea of increased complexity and increased uncertainty in deviant behavior (Le Blanc & Loeber, 1998), but very few studies describe the de-escalation process (Le Blanc, 2002). This observation applies particularly to the development of self and social controls. In Figure 6.4, the level of uncertainty decreases in the systems of control; the self-control and the social control systems are moving toward an increased conformity and maturation. This is represented by the decrease in darkness between sections (a) and (c). The consequence of these quantitative and qualitative changes is a de-escalation in deviant behavior. The individual moves from a high frequency of offending and serious offences to less numerous and serious crimes as age increases (Le Blanc & Fréchette, 1989; Le Blanc & Loeber, 1998). This is represented by sections (d) to (j) in Figure 6.4.

The growth and decline of the systems of self and social control can be characterized quantitatively and qualitatively as indicated in our review of the course of deviant behavior (Le Blanc, 2005) and our reviews above of the course of self and social controls. In turn, the

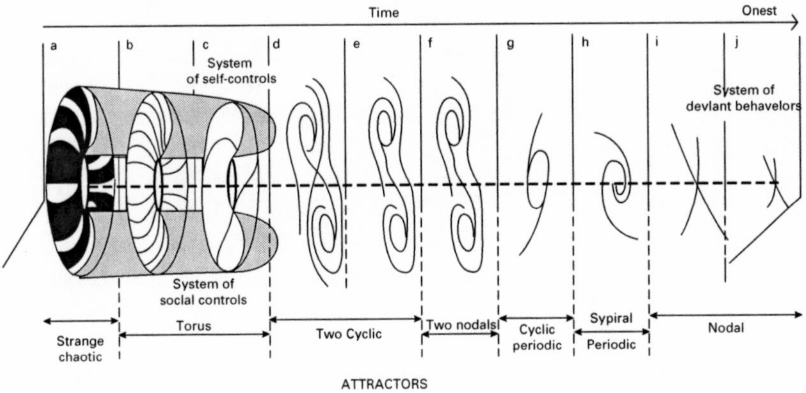

Figure 6.4. The development of self and social controls from a chaos point of view

consequence of the presence of these changes is the appearance of critical periods at the intersections of these stages, periods when the systems of deviant behavior and self and social control are in a state of disequilibrium. Classical developmentalists call these periods "transitions" (Lerner, 2002). Some criminologists refer to "turning points" to indicate these periods (Sampson & Laub, 1993); others use the notions of "drift" (Matza, 1957) or "strain" (Cohen, 1955). Behaviorists define these transitions as learnings that represent a change in the behavioral repertoire of an organism (Lerner, 2002). Chaos theorists call these transitions "bifurcations" (Gleick, 1987; Briggs & Peat, 1989). For all these authors, a varying level of turbulence and chaos characterizes these critical periods. The course of development, because of the difficulty or ease of the transitions, can manifest sleeper effects (Kagan & Moss, 1962), abrupt changes (Flavell, 1971), ceiling effects (Le Blanc & Fréchette, 1989); or there may be other non-conceptualized effects. A *bifurcation* is a forking or a splitting due to a change in one or more parameter that regulates an attractor. It happens when a system changes in a major way (Abraham, 1995). In section (e) and section (h) of Figure 6.3, the splitting of a system could be caused by the presence of a new attachment figure, going to day-care or attending elementary school. Attachment to the mother has attained a certain level and attachment to a day-care worker becomes a possibility. We are here referring to changes in internal parameters of the attachment subsystem. In section (h), the commission of the first deviant act is a fork that results from the state of the personal control system. The forking is necessarily reinforced by changes in components of the parameters of the self and social control systems. Figure 6.3 also illustrates the fractal nature of these systems. When there is a bifurcation in a system, the attractor basin increases as well as the degrees of freedom and the parameters. Consequently, the uncertainty level and turbulence also increases. Abraham (1995) proposes many types of bifurcation for a phase space map (Le Blanc & Janosz, 1998).

Self-organization and interdependence. Self-organization is a characteristic of systems, as well as of all living and human beings. It is a basic principle of developmental theories (Lerner, 2002). Developmentalists recognize the importance of the self-regulating process when they state that the individual is active in his development. The individual gives form to his experience by activating or deactivating environments. In the social control system, as in all its components, this principle implies that individuals can modify the parameters by altering the quantity and the nature of the attachment to parents, for example. Individuals are not obliged to attach to other adult figures even if they are attached to their parents which can cause a possible bifurcation in the attachment subsystem. Individuals can learn from their experiences; they can stop being attached to a particular deviant friend after an especially bad experience. Whatever the relative importance of this self-organization process for the influence of the overall control system, a subsystem, such as the attachment subsystem, has a tendency to become more complex, as illustrated by sections (a) to (j) in Figure 6.3. This complexity can take the form of chaos or a strange attractor. There are at least two major types of chaos according to Briggs and Peat (1989), the far-from-equilibrium chaos and the equilibrium-thermal chaos (Le Blanc & Janosz, 1998). The first type of chaos is a spontaneous emergence of order, for example the reversible system in which offending will dissipate in the transitory offending trajectory, or the attachment to a deviant friend that has ceased. The second type of chaos, the equilibrium-thermal chaos, is a conservative system, which represents when offending is irreversible for a long period of time, shown, for example, by a persistent offending trajectory or an enduring insecure attachment to the mother.

The self and social control systems, as with all the components of their subsystems, are subject to interactions; they are *interdependent*. In the chaos–order paradigm, interactions are feedback loops represented in Figures 6.3 and 6.4. These feedback loops are governed by the autopoetic paradox according to Briggs and Peat (1989). This paradox says that the degree of autonomy of a system is a function of the number of feedback loops that maintain the system. However, the number of feedback loops thus increases opportunities for other systems to enter in the movement. In the model subsystem of social control for example, we could say the frequency of contact with deviant friends preserves the

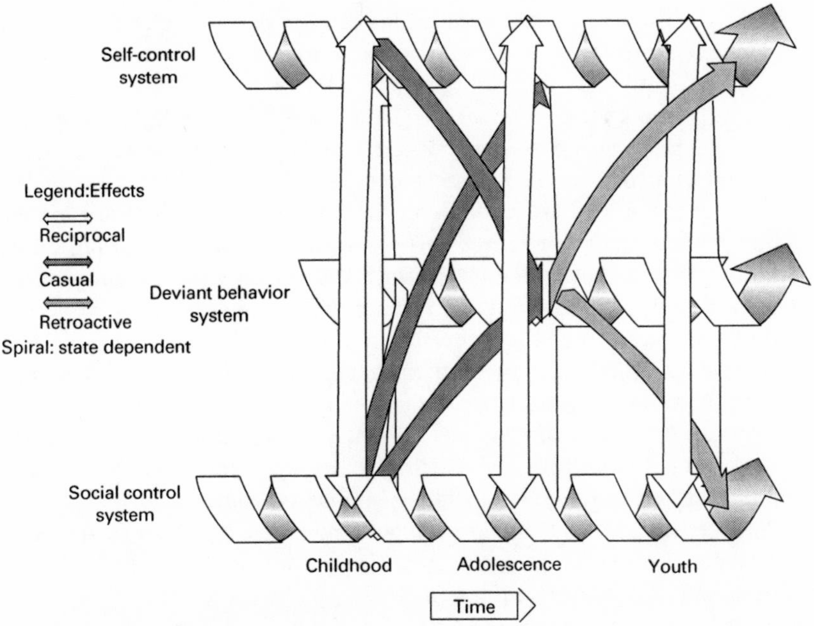

Figure 6.5. The personal control of deviant behavior
Source: Copyright © (1997) by Transaction Publishers. Reprinted by permission of the publisher.

habit of associating with such peers. In this case, each additional activity with deviant peers is a supplementary positive feedback loop. These feedback loops will open avenues for affiliation with a delinquent gang. In the bond subsystem of social control for example, we could imagine that the quality of the attachment with prosocial adults will reinforce the bonding of the individual, thereby providing additional positive feedback loops. They will permit an intimate attachment to a person of the opposite sex. The same sequence could be represented for all the subsystems of self and social control.

Figure 6.5 represents the overall dynamics of the personal control system of deviant behavior, that is, interdependence. The figure integrates the mechanisms of the developmental course of controls and deviant behavior, their developmental processes, and their dynamical interactions. It shows the combined action of continuity and change in each subsystem (co-evolution), and the interlocking of the subsystems with each other (interaction). Firstly, Figure 6.5 represents continuity and change over time. The figure must be read from left to right to follow the development of deviant behavior and personal controls. Secondly,

Figure 6.5 also shows the interactions between deviant behavior and self and social controls. In this case, the figure must be read vertically.

The horizontal reading of Figure 6.5 implies that we think in terms of continuity and change (the arrow at the bottom of the figure indicates time). Each spiral represents a system – deviant behavior, self-control, or social control – or a subsystem because of the fractal nature of the world. These spirals are metaphors that represent the mechanisms we propose and specify the course and processes of their development. The time dimension that is associated with the spirals shows orthogenesis. The beginning of the spirals represents the initial condition, while the rest of the spirals introduces the sensitivity to the initial condition. The independent spirals are there to indicate that each system is a self-organizing phenomenon. Co-evolution is indicated by the placement of the spirals on three dimensions. Finally, along each spiral there are probabilistic quantitative and qualitative changes, and trajectories. Each spiral could be described by a figure similar to Figure 6.3.

The vertical reading of Figure 6.5 implies that we think in terms of interdependencies between the systems and subsystems. The embeddedness and the reciprocal relations between the three principal systems manifest these interdependencies. In Figure 6.5, embeddedness is represented by the fact that each system spiral is part of the general personal control system. As an example, attachment to persons is a subsystem of the bonding subsystem, which in turn is a subsystem of the social control system, which in turn is a subsystem of the personal control system. In Figure 6.5, the white arrows show these interactions at different phases of the life course, in this case childhood, adolescence, and youth. Figure 6.5 also represents the synergistic perspective when we look simultaneously at the vertical and the horizontal perspectives. As indicated earlier on, there are various types of relations: reciprocal, causal, state-dependent, and retroactive. White arrows indicate reciprocal relations, while dark arrows show some causal relations and gray arrows some retroactive effects. These dark and gray arrows emerge from intersections in the spirals to indicate critical periods in the course of deviant behavior and personal control. Notwithstanding these relationships between systems and subsystems, there are also some independent changes relative to the initial condition. The use of spirals implies state-dependency. In sum, a change in a person's level of deviant behavior will alter the subsequent level of self-control and level of social control. A change in self-control will also affect the subsequent level of deviant behavior and social control, and so on. In Figure 6.5, the reciprocal and causal relationships, state-dependencies, and retroactive effects are represented for three specific moments. In fact, these interactions exist all along the time dimension, in periods, years, months, weeks, days, hours, minutes, seconds. Synergy exists at all points along the time dimension and, therefore, the control system of deviant behavior looks like a torus attractor such as described in Figure 6.3. Figure 6.5 represents the overall dynamics of the personal control system of deviant behavior. The figure integrates the mechanisms of the developmental course of controls and deviant behavior and their interactions. The beginnings of behavior and control systems represent the initial condition, while the rest of the course is state-dependent. The independent systems are there to indicate that each is a self-organizing phenomenon. In addition, in each system there are probabilistic quantitative and qualitative changes. Figure 6.5 shows the combined action of continuity and change in each subsystem, (co-evolution) and the interlocking with each other (interaction). The changes in each subsystem are described earlier in this chapter. In Figures 6.3 and 6.4, co-evolution is represented by the changes on each side of the horizontal line dividing the planes of the figure, that is, the changes in deviant behavior and the changes in personal controls.

Figure 6.3 also illustrates that personal controls are progressively constructed (sections a and b). Criminologists associate that period of the course of personal control with the creation of a criminal propensity that is called low self-control by Gottfredson and Hirschi (1990). At some point a bifurcation is encountered, an offence is committed (section c of Figure 6.3). This offence, according to our understanding of the processes, is probably precipitated by antisocial models (exposure to deviant friends or particular routine activities). The interdependence of the course of personal control and the course of deviant behavior is synergistic. The synergy is manifested by the relationships between the two attractors, the personal control system and the deviant behavior system; these interactions are illustrated in sections (d) to (j) in Figure 6.3. This synergy is the result of three underlying phenomena. Firstly, there are the reciprocal relationships between these two systems; at a specific point in time the level of self-control influences the level of deviant behavior reciprocally. Secondly, there are directional relationships between the two systems; changes in the personal control system will subsequently introduce changes in the deviant behavior system. Thirdly, there are retroactive effects between the two systems; changes in the deviant behavior system will subsequently produce new adaptations in the personal control system. In fact, these interactions exist all along the time dimension, the life span.

The environmental context of self and social control: the community

Le Blanc's multi-layered generic control theory (1997a) states that community control explains the rate of deviance, personal controls explicate the deviant activity, and event control does or does not facilitate the deviant event. He states that deviant events are embedded in an individual's deviant activity (or career) and the deviancy rate of their community. His theory of community control proposes that a high rate of conformity to conventional standards of behavior persists in a community when the social organization is sound and the cultural organization robust, when direct controls are efficient, and when there are sufficient legitimate opportunities. Therefore, the regulation of conformity is conditional on the quality of the setting and on the position of the community in the social structure. The event control theory assumes that conformity to conventional standards of behavior in a specific situation occurs when routine activities are conventional, when situational self-control is high, when there is no occasion for the perpetration of a deviant act, and when guardianship is reliable. Therefore, the regulation of conformity is conditional on the quality of community controls and personal controls. If we were to illustrate this generic control theory of deviant behavior, we could add a layer to the three layers in Figure 6.2 based on Lewin's topological theory. The four layers would then be deviant behavior, event control, personal control, and community control.

With these statements, we adopt the same position as Wikström (this volume, ch. 3) (see also Wikström and Sampson, 2003; Wikström, 2004, 2005), that the interaction between the individual and the community happens in specific situations. We state that the individual level of control mediates the impact of community control on a deviant event. Consequently, the convergence of a particular level of community control with a specific level of personal control creates a situation that renders a deviant act possible, specifically if there is an occasion to perform a deviant act. With these statements, we also choose to follow the dominant position in developmental psychology (Lerner, 2002). This position states the environment never has a direct effect on behavior; rather, that it is always mediated by the individual who is stimulated or limited by the environment, or conversely by the individual who activates or deactivates the environment. In developmental psychology, the last decade has produced a variety of models illustrating the developmental interaction between the context and the individual (Gottlieb, Magnusson, Thelen and Smith, Wapner and Demick, Ford and Lerner: see Lerner, 2002).

In criminology, very few theoretical statements have proposed interdependencies between community controls and personal controls. Kornhauser (1978: 69) synthesizes Shaw and McKay's theory in a graph where social disorganization implies weak controls and, on the basis of these weak controls, youths become delinquent with or without the influence of organized crime and delinquent companions. Kornhauser then elaborates her theory by adding that cultural disorganization implies a loss of direct external control by the family, and the resulting defective socialization will produce weaker direct internal control. She also indicates that social disorganization implies that the attachment and commitment of the child, as well as the instrumental bond to institutions, will be attenuated and, as a consequence, direct control will suffer at school and in the family. Twenty years later, Elliott *et al.* (1996) rightly observed that the theoretical discussion of the neighborhood effects is rudimentary.

Some empirical studies, such as Simcha-Fagan and Schwartz (1986), Gottfredson, McNeil, & Gottfredson (1991), and Lizotte *et al.* (1993), conclude that the direct impact of community variables on individual offending is marginal. In addition, very few studies have tried to disentangle the effects of community and individual variables (Reiss & Rhodes, 1961; Loeber & Wikström, 1993; Kupersmidt *et al.* 1995; Wikström & Loeber, 2000). However, there is a clear indication that the community structural characteristics are mediated by dimensions of community organization (Sampson, Raudenbush, & Earls, 1997). In addition, there are good indications that social disorganization variables have an indirect impact on offending. For example, Sampson (1993) shows that community-level differences in social cohesion and indirect controls do have significant effects, through family management techniques, on individual-level variations in offending, deviant attitude, and association with delinquent peers (see also Bursik & Grasmick, 1993; Chase-Lansdale *et al.*, 1997; Pratt, Turner, & Piquero, 2004).

With this knowledge in mind, our theory (Le Blanc, 1997a) adopts a theoretical unification perspective for the understanding of the interactions between community and personal controls. Figure 6.6 illustrates these relationships. There are six categories of factors that are represented for each type of control: the grounds (setting, biological capacity), the milieus (social position of the community, social status of the individual or his family), the expectations (cultural organization, allocentrism), the social conditions (social organization or collective efficacy, social bonds), the restraints (direct controls, internal and external constraints), and the situation (legitimate opportunities, prosocial influences). In Figure 6.6, the position of these factors is structured according to the layer of control, community and personal, and to their proximity to the dependent variable for each level of control (the light gray arrows).

Consequently, Figure 6.6 describes certain theoretical statements of interdependencies between community-level and individual-level constructs. The general statement is that the constructs of the community layer directly induce the range of variation of the construct of the self and social control layer (the double-line arrows).

When this is considered in detail, the following statements may be made. Firstly, the quality of the community setting (space, quality of air, and so on) affects the biological capacity of individuals. In a community with a high level of lead in the air, the children will display specific biological difficulties.

Secondly, the social structure of the community limits the range of individual and family social and ethnic status in a particular community. This phenomenon of structural homogeneity is well known in social ecology (Bursik & Grasmick, 1993).

Thirdly, the level of social organization of the community entails the level of individual social bonding; this proposition was suggested by Kornhauser (1978) and is supported by Sampson (1993) and others. In addition, social disorganization narrows the possibilities of individual development and maturation of self-control; this proposition by Wikström and Sampson (2003) is empirically supported, cross-sectionally and longitudinally, by Pratt, Turner, & Piquero (2004). Furthermore, social disorganization implies a wider range of antisocial models and, as a consequence, more adolescents in a community that displays traits of social disorganization will have increased opportunities to associate with delinquent peers and gangs. The mediating role of models between social disorganization and deviant behavior is proposed by Kornhauser (1978) and supported by Sampson (1993). It is also well known that the level of social organization of a community will limit the level of internal and external constraints placed on individuals. Social organization should be related to offending through internal control (Kornhauser, 1978) and parental management (Sampson, 1993). This is effectively the case for parental management (Chase-Lansdale *et al.*, 1997; Pratt, Turner, & Piquero 2004).

Fourthly, the community level of cultural organization restricts expectations for the development of the individual in terms of the social bond and self-control. Kornhauser (1978) proposes that cultural disorganization attenuates individual bonding; however, we do not know of

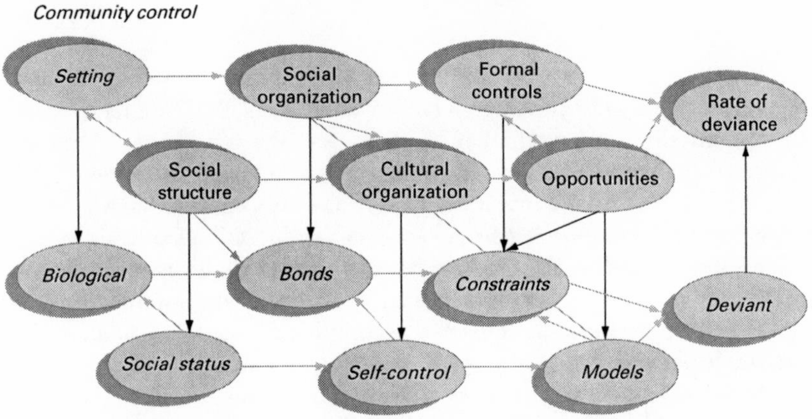

Figure 6.6. Personal control. Interdependencies between community control and personal control

any study supporting that proposition. Cultural expectations and opportunities mould internal constraints while external constraints depend on the quality of the social organization and the nature of direct controls in the community.

Fifthly, Figure 6.6 proposes that the level of formal control in a community will influence the level of internal and external constraints on individuals, i.e., parental management, perception of risk of arrest, attitude toward authority, school discipline, and so on. This link between community control and personal control seems legitimate but it is not mentioned in the literature to our knowledge.

Sixthly, in Figure 6.6 the available antisocial and prosocial influences which the individual chooses depend on the range of legitimate and illegitimate opportunities in the community and on the level of social and cultural organization in the community. These links between community and personal control are still hypothetical to our knowledge.

In sum, community-level constructs are contextual factors of individual-level constructs; they modulate the individual explanation, self and social controls, of deviant behavior. In what way does community control interact with personal control? Because of the fractal nature of the world in the chaos–order paradigm, the developmental process that describes Figure 6.3 applies to the interdependency between community control and self and social control. In Figure 6.3, we could replace self-control by community control and social control by personal control to illustrate their interaction over time.

Conclusion

Criminology has been very creative and productive in delimiting and measuring the syndrome of general deviance and describing its course – the quantitative and qualitative changes and the trajectories along the life course. Criminology has also been highly imaginative in identifying and elaborating its explanatory concepts and subconcepts such as those of self and social control. Moreover, it has been very effective in operationalizing their ensuing constructs and extremely fruitful in testing models of various degrees of complexity. Notwithstanding this intensive scientific activity, criminology has accomplished very little concerning the description of the course of self and social controls and offers only generalities about the developmental transactions between self and social controls and with deviant behavior, particularly in the context of a community.

In this chapter, we have tried to illustrate how the tools of field theory and the chaos–order paradigm could help us to map the interdependent development of self and social controls in interaction with deviant behavior in a community context. Developmental criminology, with its paradigm and its large body of data on the continuity and change of general deviance, offers meaningful tools to describe the course of the personal control of deviant behavior along the life course. However, we have argued that it does not help us to gain a genuine understanding of the processes that support continuity and change. With the tools of the chaos–order paradigm, we have tried to show how these processes happen. We did so for the course of deviant behavior (Le Blanc, 2005) and, in this chapter, we have applied the same tools to self and social controls. The phase space map of the chaos–order paradigm is a way to describe their development as a dynamical process. In consequence, moving from the analysis of the course of these phenomena to the examination of their underlying processes is the next challenge for the developmental criminology of the twenty-first century. This is the case because the development and the explanation of general deviance are characterized by complexity. Criminologists now accept that the syndrome of general deviance is the result of multiple influences: biological, psychological, social, cultural, and so on. However, our ability to understand and describe how these influences interact is limited. There are large gaps between our perception of the complexities of these interactions, our discursive statements about these phenomena, our operational models describing them, and the results of the empirical tests of these models. The discursive statements and the empirical models of criminology are characterized by oversimplification.

Until recently, most of the discursive theoretical statements and the quantitative models in criminology have been dominated by linear thinking. On one hand, human development, as stressed by developmentalists (Lerner, 2002), is only partially the result of a linear process; linearity is only part of the puzzle. The dominant theoretical statements of the 1990s, low self-control (Gottfredson & Hirschi, 1990) and general strain (Agnew, 1992), adopt linear thinking and terminology. They remain linear even if they are called interactional and recursive (Thornberry, 1996) or if they consider multiple levels of explanation (Le Blanc, 1997a). All of them do not take completely into account numerous and complex interactions and the random component that is part of development. On the other hand, studies have showed us repeatedly that our theories and models are reductionist. One blunt example of such simplification is that integrative explanatory models rarely attain 50 percent of explained variance. They are inefficient because they are incomplete; our constructs are badly operationalized; and our measures are deficient, and the strategies and methods of analysis are inadequate. In sum, our theories and models still suffer from two difficulties: considering the maximum possible number of interactions that can be perceived, and integrating a random component in the development of general deviance and self and social controls.

In this chapter, we have explored a different way of overcoming these difficulties. We have tried to show that some tools of the chaos–order paradigm can help us describe the complexity of the development of personal control and general deviance. After applying these tools, we are convinced of their heuristic utility. We believe that the obtained description of the developmental processes of self and social controls is an improvement on existing knowledge in the social and behavioral sciences. In particular, we have shown that principles such as continuity–discontinuity, equilibrium–disequilibrium, probabilistic determinism, and self-organization are compatible with developmental theories in psychology, sociology, and criminology. The chaos–order paradigm is another way of stressing and reinforcing the consensus between the developmental theories of different disciplines. In addition, the chaos–order paradigm opens a new avenue of investigation for the improvement of our perceptions, theoretical statements, and empirical models. We can more fully consider the complexities of the interactional development of self and social controls and deviant behavior. It offers a new way of thinking about the probabilistic nature of development and with the notion of fractality it draws our attention to the possibility that structures are reproduced at the multiple levels of explanation of the phenomenon of deviance. The chaos–order paradigm is not a miraculous solution to our difficulties in understanding the complexity of development; it is only a possible avenue of research.

References

Aboud, F. E. & Mendelson, M. J. (1996). "Determinants of friendship selection and quality: developmental perspectives." In W. B. Bukowski, A. F. Newcomb, & W. W. Hartup (eds.), *The Company They Keep.* New York: Cambridge University Press.

Abraham, F. D. (1995). "Introduction to dynamics: a basic language; a basic metamodeling strategy." In F. D. Abraham & A. R. Gilgen (eds.), *Chaos Theory in Psychology.* Westport, CT: Greenwood Press.

Agnew, R. (1992). "Foundation for a general strain theory of crime and delinquency." *Criminology* 30: 47–87.

Akers, R. L. (1998). *Social Learning and Social Structure: A General Theory of Crime and Deviance.* Boston. Northeastern University Press.

Allport, G. W. (1961). *Pattern and Growth in Personality.* New York: Holt, Rinehart, & Winston.

Andrews, D. A. & Bonta, J. (1998). *The Psychology of Criminal Conduct*, 2nd edn. Cincinnati, OH: Anderson Publishing.

Arnett, J. J. (1999). "Adolescent storm and stress reconsidered." *American Psychologist* 54: 317–326.

Asendorpf, J. B., Borkenau, P., Ostendorf, F., & van Aken, M. A. G. (2001). "Carving personality description at its joint: confirmation of three replicable personality prototypes for both children and adults." *European Journal of Personality* 15: 169–198.

Asendorpf, J. B. & van Aken, M. A. G. (1999). "Resilient, overcontrolled, and undercontrolled personality prototypes in childhood: replicability, predictive power, and trait-type issue." *Journal of Personality and Social Psychology* 77: 815–832.

Berk, L. (1989). *Child Development.* Boston: Allyn and Bacon.

Blackburn, R. (1993). *The Psychology of Criminal Conduct: Theory, Research and Practice.* Toronto: Wiley.

Block, J. (1971). *Lives through Time.* Berkeley, CA: Bancroft.

Boudon, R. (1984). *La place du désordre.* Paris: Presses Universitaires de France.

Briggs, J. & Peat, F. D. (1989). *Turbulent Mirror.* New York: Harper and Row.

Brownfield, D. & Sorenson, A. M. (1993). "Self-control and juvenile delinquency: theoretical issues and empirical assessment of selected elements of a general theory of crime." *Deviant Behavior* 14: 243–264.

Buhrmester, D. (1996). "Need fulfillment, interpersonal competence, and the developmental contexts of early adolescent friendship." In W. M. Bukowski, A. F. Newcomb, and W. W. Hartup (eds.), *The Company They Keep: Friendship in Childhood and Adolescence.* Cambridge: Cambridge University Press.

Bursik, R. J. (1986). "Ecological stability and the dynamics of delinquency." In A. J. Reiss & M. Tonry (eds.), *Crime and Justice: An Annual Review*. Chicago: University of Chicago Press.

Bursik, R. J. & Grasmick, H. G. (1993). *The Dimensions of Effective Community Control*. New York: Lexington Books.

Buss, D. M. (1994). "Personality evoked: the evolutionary psychology of stability and change." In T. F. Heatherton & J. L. Weinberger (eds.), *Can Personality Change*. Washington, DC: American Psychological Association.

Caplow, T. (1988). "The comparative charting of social change in advanced industrial societies." *European Studies Newsletter* 5: 1–6.

Caspi, A. (1993). "Why maladaptive behaviors persist: sources of continuity and change across the life course." In D. C Funder, R. D. Parke, C. Tomlinson-Keasy, & K. Widaman (eds.), *Studying Lives through Times: Personality and Development*. Washington, DC: American Psychological Association.

(1998). "Personality development across the life course." In W. Damon (ser. ed.) & N. Eisenberg (vol. ed.), *Handbook of Child Psychology, vol. III: Social, Emotional, and Personality Development*. New York: Wiley.

Caspi, A. & Roberts, B. W. (1999). "Personality continuity and change across the life course." In L. A. Pervin & O. P. John (eds.), *Handbook of Personality: Theory and Research*. New York: Guilford Press.

Caspi, A. & Silva, P. A. (1995). "Temperamental qualities at age 3 predicts personality traits in young adulthood: longitudinal evidence from a birth cohort." *Child Development* 66: 486–498.

Chang Weir, R. & Gjerde, P. F. (2002). "Preschool personality prototypes: internal coherence, cross-study replicability, and developmental outcomes in adolescence." *Personality and Social Psychology Bulletin* 28: 1229–1241.

Chase-Lansdale, P. L., Gordon, R. A., Brooks-Gunn, J., & Klebanov, P. K. (1997). "Neighbourhood and family influences on the intellectual and behavioral competence of preschool and early school-aged children." In J. Brooks-Gunn, G. J. Duncan, & J. Larence (eds.), *Neighbourhood Poverty, vol. I: Context and Consequences for Children*. New York: Russell Sage.

Clark, L. A. & Watson, D. (1999). "Temperament: a new paradigm for trait psychology." In L. A. Pervin & O. P. John (eds.), *Handbook of Personality: Theory and Research*. New York: Guilford Press.

Cloward, R. A. & Ohlin, L. E. (1960). *Delinquency and Opportunity: A Theory of Delinquent Gangs*. New York: Free Press.

Cohen, A. K. (1955). *Delinquent Boys: The Culture of the Gang*. New York: The Free Press.

Cohn, E. G. & Farrington, D. P. (1998). "Changes in the most cited scholars in major American criminology and criminal justice journals between 1986–1990 and 1991–1995." *Journal of Criminal Justice* 26: 99–116.

Costa, P. T. & McCrae, R. R. (1997). "Longitudinal stability of adult personality." In R. Hogan, J. Johnson, & S. Briggs (eds.), *Handbook of Personality Psychology*. San Diego, CA: Academic Press.

Deng, X. (1994). "Toward more understanding of crime: an integrated model of rational choice and self-control theories." Paper presented at the Annual Meeting of the American Society of Criminology, Miami.

Drever J. (1969). *A Dictionary of Psychology*. Baltimore: Penguin Books.

Dunford, F. W. & Elliott, D. S. (1984). "Identifying career offenders using self-reported data." *Journal of Research in Crime and Delinquency* 21(1): 57–86.

Durkheim, E. (1895). *Les règles de la méthode sociologique*. Paris: Alcan (1960 edition, Presses Universitaires de France).

Durkheim, E. (1934). *De l'éducation morale*. Paris: Alcan (1963 edition, Presses Universitaires de France).

Elliott, D. S., Huizinga, D., & Ageton, S. S. (1985). *Explaining Delinquency and Drug Use*. Beverly Hills, CA: Sage.

Elliott, D. S., Huizinga, D., & Menard, S. (1989). *Multiple Problem Youth: Delinquency, Substance Abuse, and Mental Health Problems*. New York: Springer Verlag.

Elliott, D. S. & Menard, S. (1996). "Delinquent friends and delinquent behavior: temporal and developmental patterns." In J. D. Hawkins (ed.), *Delinquency and Crime: Current Theories*. New York: Cambridge University Press.

Elliott, D. S., Wilson, W. J., Huizinga, D. Sampson, R. J., Elliott, A., & Rankin, B. (1996). "The effects of neighborhood disadvantage on adolescent development." *Journal of Research in Crime and Delinquency* 33: 389–426.

Empey, L. T. (1978). *American Delinquency*. Homewood, IL: Dorsey Press.

Erickson, E. H. (1972). *Adolescence et crise, la quête de l'identité*. Paris: Flammarion.

Eysenck, H. J. (1989). "Personality and criminality: a dispositional analysis." *Advances in Criminological Theory* 1: 89–111.

Fararo, T. J. (1989). *The Meaning of General Theoretical Sociology: Tradition and Formalization*. New York: Cambridge University Press.

Feldman, M. P. (1978). *Criminal Behavior: A Psychological Analysis*. New York: Wiley.

Flavell, J. H. (1971). "Stage related properties of cognitive development." *Cognitive Psychology* 2: 421–453.

Fréchette, M. & Le Blanc, M. (1987). *Délinquances et délinquants*. Montreal: Gaétan Morin.

Freud, S. (1905). *Trois essais sur la théorie de la sexualité*. Paris: Gallimard (1964).
(1963). *An Outline of Psychoanalysis*. New York: Norton.

Gibbs, J. J., Giever, D. & Kerr, J. S. (1994). "Parental management and self-control: an empirical test of Gottfredson and Hirschi's general theory." Paper presented at the Annual Meeting of the American Society of Criminology, Miami.

Gibbs, J. P. (1989). *Control Sociology's Central Notion*. Chicago: University of Illinois Press.

Gleick, J. (1987). *Chaos: Making of a New Science*. New York: Viking Penguin.

Glenn, N. D. (1980). "Values, attitudes, and beliefs." In O. G. Brim & J. Kagan (eds.), *Constancy and Change in Human Development*. Cambridge, MA: Harvard University Press.

Gottfredson, M. R. & Hirschi, T. (1990). *A General Theory of Crime*. Stanford: Stanford University Press.

(2003). "Self-control and opportunity." In C. L. Britt & M. R. Gottfredson (eds.), *Control Theories of Crime and Delinquency*. Advances in Theoretical Criminology 12. New Brunswick, NJ: Transaction.

Gottfredson, D. C., McNeil, R. J., & Gottfredson, G. D. (1991). "Social areas' influences on delinquency: a multilevel analysis." *Journal of Research in Crime and Delinquency* 28: 197–226.

Grasmick, H. G., Tittle, C. R., Bursik, R. J., & Arneklev, B. J. (1993). "Testing the core implications of Gottfredson and Hirschi's general theory of crime." *Journal of Research in Crime and Delinquency* 30: 5–29.

Harpur, T. J. & Hare, R. D. (1994). "Assessment of psychopathy as a function of age." *Journal of Abnormal Psychology* 103: 604–609.

Hart, D., Hofmann, V., Edelstein, W., & Keller, M. (1997). "The relation of childhood personality types to adolescent behavior and development: a longitudinal study of Icelandic children." *Developmental Psychology* 33: 195–205.

Helson, R., Kwan, V. S. Y., John, O. P., & Jones, C. (2002). "The growing evidence of personality change in adulthood: findings from research with personality inventories." *Journal of Research in Personality* 36: 287–306.

Hirschi, T. (1969). *Causes of Delinquency*. Berkeley, CA: University of California Press.

Jessor, R., Donovan, J. E., & Costa, F. M. (1991). *Beyond Adolescence: Problem Behavior and Young Adult Development*. New York: Cambridge University Press.

Jessor, R. & Jessor, S. L. (1977). *Problem Behavior and Psychological Development: A Longitudinal Study*. New York: Academic Press.

Kagan, J. & Moss, H. (1962). *Birth to Maturity*. New York: Wiley.

Kempf, K. (1993). "Hirschi's theory of social control: is it fecund but not yet fertile?" *Advances in Theoretical Criminology* 4: 143–186.

Kohlberg, L. (1976). "Moral stages and moralization: the cognitive-developmental approach." In T. Lickong (ed.), *Moral Development and Behavior*. New York: Holt, Rinehart, and Winston.

Kornhauser, R. R. (1978). *Social Sources of Delinquency: An Appraisal of Analytic Models*. Chicago: University of Chicago Press.

Krohn, M. D., Lizotte, A. J., Thornberry, T. P., Smith, C., & McDowall, D. (1996). "Reciprocal causal relationships among drug use, peers, and belief: a five waves panel model." *Journal of Drug Issues* 2: 405–426.

Krueger, R. F., Caspi, A., & Moffitt, T. E. (2000). "Epidemiological personology: the unifying role of personality in population-based research on problem behaviors." *Journal of Personality* 68: 967–998.

Kupersmidt, J. B., Griesler, P. C., Derosier, M. E., Patterson, C. J., & Davis, P. W. (1995). "Childhood aggression and peer relations in the context of family and neighborhood factors." *Child Development* 66: 356–375.

Larson, R. & Bradley, M. H. (1991). "Daily companionship in late childhood and early adolescence: changing developmental contexts." *Child Development* 62: 284–300.

Larson, R. W. & Richards, M. H. (1989). "Introduction: the changing life space of early adolescence." *Journal of Youth and Adolescence* 18: 501–509.

Larson, R. W. & Verma, S. (1999). "How children and adolescents spend time across the world: work, play, and developmental opportunities." *Psychological Bulletin* 125: 701–736.

Laursen, B., Coy, K. C., & Collins, W. A. (1998). "Reconsidering changes in parent–child conflict across adolescence. a meta-analysis." *Child Development* 69: 817–832.

Le Blanc, M. (1983). "Delinquency as an epiphenomenon of adolescence." In R. Corrado, M. Le Blanc, & J. Trépanier (eds.), *Current Issues in Juvenile Justice*. Toronto: Butterworths.

(1992). "Family dynamics, adolescent delinquency and adult criminality." *Psychiatry* 55: 236–253.

(1993). "Prevention of adolescent delinquency: an integrative multilayered theoretically based perspective." In D. P. Farrington, R. Sampson, & P.-O. Wikström (eds.), *Linking Community and Individual Levels Explanations of Crime*. Stockholm: National Council on Crime Prevention.

(1994a). "Measures of escalation and their personal and social predictors." In H. J. Kerner & E. Weitekamp (eds.), *Longitudinal Research on Human Development and Criminal Behavior*. Amsterdam: Kluwer.

(1994b). "The relative importance of internal and external constraints in the explanation of late adolescence delinquency and adult criminality." In J. McCord (ed.), *Coercion and Punishment in Long-term Perspectives*. Cambridge: Cambridge University Press.

(1997a). "A generic control theory of the criminal phenomenon, the structural and the dynamical statements of an integrative multilayered control theory." *Advances in Theoretical Criminology* 7: 215–286.

(1997b). "Socialization or propensity: a test of an integrative control theory with adjudicated boys." *Studies in Crime and Crime Prevention* 6 (2): 200–224.

(2002). "The offending cycle, escalation and de-escalation in delinquent behavior: a challenge for criminology." *International Journal of Comparative and Applied Criminal Justice* 26 (1): 53–84.

(2004). "Théories de la régulation de la déviance." In D. Jolivet, G. Lopez, & S. Tiztzis (eds.), *Dictionnaire critique des sciences criminelles*. Paris: Dalloz.

(2005). "An integrative personal control theory of deviant behavior answers to contemporary empirical and theoretical developmental criminology issues." *Advances in Theoretical Criminology* 14: 125–163.

Le Blanc, M. & Biron, L. (1980). *Vers une théorie intégrative de la régulation de la conduite délinquante des garçons*. Montreal: Groupe de recherche sur l'inadaptation juvénile, Université de Montréal.

Le Blanc, M. & Bouthillier, C. (2003). "A developmental test of the general deviance syndrome with adjudicated girls and boys using hierarchical confirmatory factor analysis." *Criminal Behavior and Mental Health* 13: 81–105.

Le Blanc, M. & Caplan, A. (1993). "Theoretical formalization, a necessity: the example of Hirschi's bonding theory." *Advances in Theoretical Criminology* 4: 239–343.

Le Blanc, M., Charland, R., Cote, G., & Pronovost, L. (1980). *Développement psycho-social et évolution de la délinquance au cours de l'adolescence.* Montreal: Groupe de recherche sur l'inadaptation juvénile, Université de Montréal.

Le Blanc, M. & Fréchette, M. (1989). *Male Criminal Activity from Childhood through Youth: Multilevel and Developmental Perspectives.* New York: Springer Verlag.

Le Blanc, M. & Janosz, M. (1998). "The development of problem behavior, course and processes." Paper presented at the Life History Research Society, Montreal, May 6–9.

Le Blanc, M. & Loeber, R. (1998). "Developmental criminology upgraded." In M. Tonry (ed.), *Crime and Justice Handbook.* Chicago: University of Chicago Press.

Le Blanc, M., Ouimet, M., & Tremblay, R. E. (1988). "An integrative control theory of delinquent behavior: a validation 1976–1985." *Psychiatry* 51: 164–176.

Le Blanc, M., Vallières, E., & McDuff, P. (1992). "Adolescents' school experience and self-reported offending: a longitudinal test of a social control theory." *International Journal of Youth and Adolescence* 8: 197–247.

Lerner, R. M. (2002). *Concepts and Theories of Human Development.* New York: Random House.

Lewin, K. (1946). "Behavior and development as a function of the total situation." In L. Carmichael (ed.), *Manual of Child Psychology.* New York: Wiley.

Lizotte, A. J., Thornberry, T. P., Krohn, M. D., & Chard-Weirscheim, D. (1993). "Neighbourhood context and delinquency: a longitudinal analysis." In H. J. Kerner & E. Weitekamp (eds.), *Cross-national Longitudinal Research on Human Development and Criminal Behavior.* Dordrecht: Kluwer.

Loeber, R., Drinkwater, M., Yin, Y., Anderson, S. J., Schmidt, L. C., & Crawlord, A. (2000). "Stability of family interactions from age 6 to 18." *Journal of Abnormal Child Psychology* 28: 353–359.

Loeber, R. & Hay, D. (1997). "Key issues in the development of aggression and violence from childhood to early adulthood." *Annual Review in Psychology* 48: 371–410.

Loeber, R. & Le Blanc, M. (1990). "Toward a developmental criminology." In M. Tonry & N. Morris (eds.), *Crime and Justice: An Annual Review.* Chicago: University of Chicago Press.

Loeber, R. & Wikström, P.-O. (1993). "Individual pathways to crime in different types of neighborhoods." In D. P. Farrington, R. J. Sampson, & P.-O. Wikström (eds.), *Integration of Individual and Ecological Aspects of Crime.* Stockholm: Allmänanna Förlaget.

Loevinger, J. (1976). *Ego Development: Conceptions and Theories.* San Francisco: Jossey-Bass.

Longshore, D., Chang, E., Hsieh, S-C., & Messina, N. (2004). "Self-control and social bonds: a combined control perspective on deviance." *Crime and Delinquency* 50: 542–564.

Longshore, D., Turner, S., & Stein, J. (1996). "Self-control in a criminal sample: an examination of construct validity." *Criminology* 3: 209–228.

Lytton, H. (1990). "Child and parent effects in boys' conduct disorder: a reinterpretation." *Developmental Psychology* 26: 683–697.

Mak, A. S. (1990). "Testing a psychosocial control theory of delinquency." *Criminal Justice and Behavior* 17: 215–230.

Matthews, G. & Deary, I. J. (1998). *Personality Traits*. New York: Cambridge University Press.

Matza, D. (1957). *Delinquency and Drift*. New York: Wiley.

McCrae, R. R., Costa, P. T., Ostendorf, F., Angleitner, A., Hrebickova, M., Avia, M. D., Sanz, J., Sanchez-Bernardos, M. L., Kusdil, M. E., Woodfield, R., Saunders, P. R., & Smith, P. B. (2000). "Nature over nurture: temperament, personality, and the life span development." *Journal of Personality and Social Psychology* 78: 173–186.

Miller, J. D. & Lynam, D. (2001). "Structural models of personality and their relation to antisocial behavior: a meta-analytic review." *Criminology* 39: 765–798.

Moffitt, T. E. (1993). "'Life-course-persistent' and 'adolescent-limited' antisocial behavior: a developmental taxonomy." *Psychological Review* 100: 674–701.

Morizot, J. & Le Blanc, M. (2003a). "Continuity and change in personality from adolescence to midlife: a 25-year longitudinal study comparing representative and adjudicated men." *Journal of Personality* 71(5): 705–755.

—— (2003b). "Searching for a developmental typology of personality in an adjudicated men's sample and its relations to antisocial behavior: a longitudinal study of an adjudicated men sample." *Criminal Behavior and Mental Health* 13(4): 241–277.

—— (2005). "Searching for a developmental typology of personality and its relations to antisocial behavior: a longitudinal study of a representative sample of men." *Journal of Personality* 73(1): 139–182.

Nagin, D. S. & Paternoster, R. (1994). "Individual capital and social control: the deterrence implications of a theory of individual differences in criminal offending." *Criminology* 32: 581–606.

Nye, F. I. (1958). *Family Relationships and Delinquent Behavior*. New York: Wiley.

Oden, S. (1988). "Alternative perspectives on children's peer relationships." In T. D. Yawkey & J. E. Johnson (eds.), *Integrative Process and Socialization: Early to Middle Childhood*. Hillsdale: Erlbaum.

Osgood, D. & Lee, H. (1993). "Leisure activities, age and adult roles across the lifespan." *Society and Leisure* 16(1): 181–208.

Osgood, D. W., Wilson, J. K., O'Malley, P. M., Bachman, J. G., & Johnston, L. D. (1996). "Routine activities and individual deviant behavior." *American Sociological review* 61: 635–655.

Paternoster, R. (1987). "The deterrent effect of the perceived certainty and severity of punishment: a review of the evidence and issues." *Justice Quarterly* 4: 173.

Patterson, G. R., Reid, J. B., & Dishion, T. J. (1992). *Antisocial Boys*. Eugene: Castalia.

Peak, D. & Frame, M. (1994). *Chaos under Control*. New York: Freeman.

Peter, T., Lagrange T. C., & Silverman, R. A. (2003). "Investigating the interdependence of strain and self-control." *Canadian Journal of Criminology and Criminal Justice* 45: 431–464.

Piaget, J. (1967). *La psychologie de l'intelligence*. Paris: Armand Colin.

Piquero, A. R., Farrington, D. P., & Blumstein, A. (2003). "The criminal career paradigm." *Crime and Justice* 30: 359–506.

Piquero, A. & Tibbets, S. (1994). "Specifying low self-control and situational factors in offender decision-making." Paper presented at the Annual Meeting of the American Society of Criminology, Miami.

Platt, T. C. & Cullen, F. C. (2000). "The empirical status of Gottfredson and Hirschi's general theory of crime: meta-analysis." *Criminology* 38: 932–964.

Polakowski, M. (1994). "Linking self and social control with deviance: illuminating the structure underlying a general theory of crime and its relation to deviant activity." *Journal of Quantitative Criminology* 10(1): 41–76.

Pratt, T. C., Turner, M. G., & Piquero, A. R. (2004). "Parental socialization and community context: a longitudinal analysis of the structural sources of low self-control." *Journal of Research in Crime and Delinquency* 41: 219–243.

Pulkkinen, L. (1996). "Female and male personality styles: a typological and developmental analysis." *Journal of Personality and Social Psychology* 70: 1288–1306.

Quetelet, A. (1835). *Sur l'homme et le développement de ses facultés, ou essai de physique sociale*. Paris: Bachelier.

Reckless, W. C. (1961). "A new theory of delinquency and crime." *Federal Probation* 25 (December): 42–46.

Reiss, A. J. (1951). "Delinquency as a failure of individual and social controls." *American Sociological Review* 16: 196–207.

Reiss, A. J. & Rhodes, A. L. (1961). "The distribution of juvenile delinquency in the social class structure." *American Sociological Review* 26: 720–732.

Roberts, B. W. & Del Vecchio, W. F. (2000). "The rank-order consistency of personality traits from childhood to old age: a quantitative review of longitudinal studies." *Psychological Bulletin* 126(1): 3–25.

Roberts, B. W., Robins, R. W., Caspi, A., & Trzesniewski, K. H. (in press). "Personality trait development in adulthood." In J. L. Mortimer & M. Shanahan (eds.), *Handbook of the Life Course*. New York: Plenum.

Robins, R. W., John, O. P., & Caspi, A. (1998). "The typological approach to studying personality." In R. B. Cairns, L. R. Bergman, & J. Kagan (eds.), *Methods and Models for Studying the Individual*. Thousand Oaks, CA: Sage.

Robins, R. W., John, O. P., Caspi, A., Moffitt, T. E., & Stouthamer-Loeber, M. (1996). "Resilient, overcontrolled, and undercontrolled boys: three replicable personality types." *Journal of Personality and Social Psychology* 70: 157–171.

Rutter, M., Giller, H., & Hagell, A. (1998). *Antisocial Behavior by Young People*. New York: Cambridge University Press.

Sampson, R. J. (1993). "Family and community-level influences on crime." In D. P. Farrington, R. J. Sampson, & P.-O. Wikström (eds.), *Integration of Individual and Ecological Aspects of Crime*. Stockholm: Allmänanna Förlaget.

Sampson, R. J. & Laub, J. H. (1993). *Crime in the Making: Pathways and Turning Points through Life*. Cambridge, MA: Harvard University Press.

Sampson, R. J., Raudenbush, J. D., & Earls, F. (1997). "Neighborhoods and violent crime: a multilevel study of collective efficacy." *Science* 277: 918–924.

Schuerman, L. A. & Kobrin, S. (1986). "Community careers in crime." In A. J. Reiss & M. Tonry (eds.), *Crime and Justice: An Annual Review*. Chicago: University of Chicago Press.

Shoemaker, D. J. (2005). *Theories of Delinquency: An Examination of Explanations of Delinquent Behavior*. New York: Oxford University Press.

Simcha-Fagan, O. & Schwartz, J. E. (1986). "Neighbourhood and delinquency: an assessment of contextual effects." *Criminology* 24: 667–703.

Simons, R. L., Johnson, R. D., Conger, V. D., & Elder, G. (1998). "A test of a latent trait versus a life course perspective on the stability of adolescent antisocial behavior." *Criminology* 36: 217–243.

Steinberg, L. (1996). *Adolescence*. Toronto: McGraw Hill.

Stoolmiller, M. (1994). "Antisocial behavior, delinquent peer association, and unsupervised wandering for boys: growth and change from childhood to early adolescence." *Multivariate Behavioral Research* 29: 263–288.

Sullivan, D. E., Grant, M. W., and Grant, J. D. (1957). "The development of interpersonal maturity: application to delinquency." *Psychiatry* 20 (4).

Sutherland, E. H. & Cressey, D. R. (1960). *Principles of Criminology*, 6th edn. Chicago: Lippincott.

Tarde, G. (1924). *La criminalité comparée*. Paris: Alcan.

Tarter, R. E., Vanykov, M. M., Giancola, P., Dawes, M. A., Blackson, T., Mezzich, A., & Clark, D. (1999). "Etiology of early age onset substance use disorder: a maturational perspective." *Development and Psychopathology* 11: 657–683.

Thelen, E. & Smith, L. B. (1998). "Dynamic system theories." In W. Damon & R. M. Lerner (eds.), *Handbook of Child Psychology*, vol. I: *Theoretical Models of Human Development*. New York: Wiley.

Thornberry, T. P. (1987). Toward an interactional theory of delinquency. *Criminology* 25(4): 963–892.

(1996). "Empirical support for interactional theory: a review of the literature." In J. D. Hawkins (ed.), *Delinquency and Crime: Current Theories*. New York: Cambridge University Press.

Thornberry, T. P., Krohn, M. D., Lizotte, A. J., Smith, C., & Tobin, K. (2003). *Gangs and Delinquency in Developmental Perspective*. Cambridge: Cambridge University Press.

Thornberry, T. P., Lizotte, A. J., Krohn, M. D., & Farnworth, M. (1994). "Delinquent peers, beliefs, and delinquent behavior: a longitudinal test of interactional theory." *Criminology* 32 (1): 47–84.

Thornberry, T. P., Lizotte, A. J., Krohn, M. D., Farnworth, M., & Jang, S. J. (1991). "Testing interactional theory: an examination of reciprocal causal relationship among family, school and delinquency." *Journal of Criminal Law and Criminology* 82: 3–33.

Thrasher, F. M. (1927). *The Gang*. Chicago: University of Chicago Press.

Tubman, J. G., Lerner, R. M., Lerner, J. V., & von Eye, A. (1992). "Temperament and adjustment in young adulthood: a 15-year longitudinal analysis." *American Journal of Orthopsychiatry* 62: 564–574.

Turner, M. G. & Piquero, A. R. (2002). "The stability of self-control." *Journal of Criminal Justice* 30: 457–471.

Van Aken, M. A. G., van Lieshout, C. F. M., Scholte, R. H. J., & Haselager, G. J. T. (2002). "Personality types in childhood and adolescence: main effects and person–relationship transactions." In L. Pulkkinen & A. Caspi (eds.), *Paths to Successful Development: Personality in the Life*. New York: Cambridge University Press.

Vazsonyi, A. T., Pickering, L. E., Junger, M., & Hessing, D. (2001). "An empirical test of a general theory of crime: a four-nation comparative study of self-control and the prediction of deviance." *Journal of Research in Crime and Delinquency* 38: 91–131.

Warr, M. (1993). "Age, peers, and delinquency." *Criminology* 31: 17–40.

(2002). *Companions in Crime: The Social Aspect of Criminal Conduct*. Cambridge: Cambridge University Press.

Werner, H. (1957). "The concept of development from a comparative and organismic point of view." In D. B. Harris (ed.), *The Concept of Development*. Minneapolis: University of Minnesota Press.

Wikström, P.-O. (2004). "Crime as alternative: towards a cross-level situational action theory of crime causation." In J. McCord (ed.), *Beyond Empiricism: Insitutions and Intentions in the Study of Crime*. Advances in Criminological Theory 13. New Brunswick, NJ: Transaction.

(2005). "The social origins of pathways in crime: towards a developmental ecological action theory of crime involvement and its changes." In D. P. Farrington (ed.), *Integrated Developmental and Life Course Theories of Offending*. Advances in Criminological Theory 14. New Brunswick, NJ: Transaction.

Wikström, P.-O. & Loeber, R. (2000). "Do disadvantaged neighborhoods cause well-adjusted children to become adolescent delinquents?" *Criminology* 38: 1109–1142.

Wikström, P.-O. & Sampson, R. J. (2003). "Social mechanisms of community influences on crime and pathways in criminality." In B. B. Lahey, T. E. Moffitt & A. Caspi. (eds.), *Causes of Conduct Disorder and Juvenile Delinquency*. New York: Guilford Press.

Wills, T. A., Sandy, J. M., & Yaeger, A. (2000). "Temperament and adolescent substance use: an epigenetic approach to risk and protection." *Journal of Personality* 68: 1127–1151.

Wilson, J. Q. & Herrnstein, R. J. (1985). *Crime and Human Nature*. New York: Simon & Schuster.

Wood, P. B., Pfefferbaum, B., & Arneklev, B. J. (1993). "Risk-taking and self-control: social psychological correlates of delinquency." *Journal of Crime and Justice* 16: 111–130.

York, K. L. & John, O. P. (1992). "The four faces of Eve: a typological analysis of women's personality at midlife." *Journal of Personality and Social Psychology* 63: 494–508.

Zhang, Q., Loeber, R., & Stouthamer-Loeber, M. (1997). "Developmental trends of delinquency attitudes and delinquency: replication and synthesis across time and samples." *Journal of Quantitative Criminology* 13: 181–216.

Zucker, R. A. (1987). "The four alcoholisms: a developmental account of the etiologic process." In P. C. Rivers (ed.), *Nebraska Symposium on Motivation: Alcohol and Addictive Behavior*. Lincoln: University of Nebraska Press.

Zucker, R. A., Fitzgerald, H. E., & Moses, H. D. (1995). "Emergence of alcohol problems and the several alcoholisms: a developmental perspective on etiologic theory and life course trajectory." In D. Cicchetti & D. Cohen (eds.), *Developmental Psychopathology*, vol. II: *Risk, Disorder, and Adaptation*. New York: Wiley.

7 Desistance, social bonds, and human agency: a theoretical exploration

Anthony Bottoms

> The I, the I is what is deeply mysterious.
>
> (Wittgenstein, 1915; quoted in Sluga, 1996: 321)

> It is perfectly true, as philosophers say, that life must be understood backwards. But they forget the other proposition, that it must be lived forwards.
>
> (Kierkegaard, 1843; quoted in Wollheim, 1984: 1)

> Criminals are ipso facto beyond the moral community.
>
> (Waddington, 2003: 395)

The SCoPiC Network aims to understand more fully both individuals' pathways into and out of crime, and the social contexts within which those pathways develop. Historically, however, there has been an interesting contrast between analyses of the onset and early development of criminal careers, and analyses of desistance from crime. The former have been predominantly individually and psychologically focused, and only recently has a more socially contextual approach been developed (see, for example, Wikström & Loeber, 2000). Desistance analyses, however, while markedly fewer in number than analyses of onset, have always tended to include at least some discussion of social context. For example, the well-known Cambridge Study in Delinquent Development has analyzed the effects of both locational change (Osborn, 1980) and marriage (Farrington & West, 1995) in relation to persistence in or desistance from crime in adulthood. In the early 1990s, one of the leading research studies on desistance (Sampson & Laub, 1993) also explicitly adopted a "social bonds" theoretical approach, arguing that "the stronger the adult ties to work and family, the less crime and deviance among [former] delinquents" (Laub & Sampson, 2003: 6; see further below). However, in the decade since Sampson and Laub's (1993) path-breaking book, a number of writers, including most recently Laub and Sampson (2003) themselves, have suggested that desistance cannot be fully understood by reference to social bonds alone. Rather, it is argued, we must additionally have regard to the concept of "will" or "human agency," a concept that most writers have interpreted mainly individualistically, with special emphasis on the fact that individual human beings are "*active participants in constructing their lives*" (Laub & Sampson, 2003, emphasis added).

Unfortunately, however, in their important recent contribution Laub and Sampson say relatively little about how, in detail, this concept of "human agency" is to be understood, or how it should be utilized to enrich our understanding of desistance. The main purpose of this chapter is to address these questions, with special reference to some important (if somewhat disparate) recent analyses of human agency by social theorists and philosophers. In pursuing this goal, however, it will also be vital not to lose sight of what I would regard as the established importance of social bonds in relation to desistance. The task of this chapter, therefore, is *to reflect carefully on the theorization of human agency in the context of desistance, while not losing sight of the social context within which agency is exercised.*[1] As that task is pursued, it will, I hope, come to be seen that there is much merit in the quotations from Wittgenstein and Kierkegaard that are placed at the head of this chapter. The quotation from Waddington, however, incorporates a profound error; but, since a similar view is held by a significant number of other people, it is an error with potentially important social consequences.

Recent research on desistance

On the dust-jacket of Shadd Maruna's (2001) book, *Making Good*, Professor John Laub comments that "the topic of desistance from crime has not received the theoretical research and policy attention it deserves." In the four years since then, a good deal has been done to rectify this situation, partly by John Laub himself with his colleague Robert Sampson (Laub & Sampson 2001, 2003), and partly by others

[1] With a group of colleagues at the University of Sheffield, I am currently conducting empirical research on desistance among a sample of male non-occasional offenders, with a starting age of about twenty. We set out the broad theoretical framework for our empirical study in a recent article (Bottoms *et al.*, 2004). This chapter has a different focus, since it concentrates much more fully on the theorization of human agency in the context of desistance; hence the two papers should be read as complementary. I am grateful to my Sheffield colleagues (Andrew Costello, Deborah Holmes, Grant Muir, and, especially, Joanna Shapland) for very useful discussions in the course of writing this chapter. Thanks also to Leo Cheliotis, Andrew von Hirsch, and Per-Olof Wikström of the Cambridge Institute of Criminology for helpful comments on an earlier draft.

(e.g., Farrall, 2002; Giordano, Cernovich & Rudolph, 2002; Burnett & Maruna, 2004; Stouthamer-Loeber *et al.*, 2004; Ezell & Cohen, 2005).

I do not intend here to review this literature comprehensively. Instead I want to focus principally on the findings of just two studies, those of Laub and Sampson (2003) and Stouthamer-Loeber *et al.* (2004). To put these findings in context, however, I shall first examine the recent important text by Ezell and Cohen (2005).

Ezell and Cohen

The subtitle of Ezell and Cohen's book accurately summarizes their main empirical focus, namely "continuity and change in long-term crime patterns of serious chronic offenders." Three samples of serious chronic male offenders were drawn from the files of the California Youth Authority at different dates (1981–1982, 1986–1987, 1991–1992), and their official arrest histories were examined up to June 2000. A main purpose of the analysis was to test, using long-term follow-up data, the empirical claims of three leading criminological theories relating to age and criminality, namely Gottfredson and Hirschi's (1990) "general theory of crime," Moffitt's (1993, 1997) "dual taxonomy theory," and Sampson and Laub's (1993) "age-graded theory of informal social control."[2]

Briefly, Gottfredson and Hirschi's theory proposes (i) that between-group differences in criminality[3] are a function of low or high self-control, and that (with very few exceptions) individuals' relative levels of self-control are stable from the age of about 8–10 onward, and (ii) that the relationship between age and crime is invariant, that is to say, there is indeed a marked age–crime curve, of a pattern familiar to all criminologists (see, e.g., Maruna 2001: 21), but since "*all* individuals commit fewer crimes as they age, then age is actually irrelevant to the study of crime and no sociological, psychological or economic variables that covary with age (e.g., employment, marriage) can explain this 'age effect'" (Ezell & Cohen, 2005: 23, emphasis in original). By contrast, Moffitt (1993, 1997) proposes a typological theory of crime, based on the view that different classes of offenders have different empirical crime

[2] The later work of Laub and Sampson (2003) was not available to Ezell and Cohen (2005) when they wrote the bulk of their book. However, a few comments on this later text are made in Ezell and Cohen's closing chapter (see note 4 below).

[3] "Criminality" in Gottfredson and Hirschi's (1990) work has a special meaning, namely individuals' "propensity to use force and fraud." The book thus deliberately (and controversially) promotes an "explicit consideration of the propensity to crime as distinct from the commission of criminal acts" (4). Additional considerations are then invoked to explain, for example, why propensity is not always turned into criminal acts.

patterns, and that each type of offending pattern has a different explanation. In particular, she distinguishes between "adolescence-limited" offenders and "life course persistent offenders." The former group, it is suggested, does not begin offending until the onset of adolescence, and then confines or limits its offending to the adolescent years, often with only a small number of arrests; but the latter group, as its name implies, begins offending early in life, and its members then consistently engage in criminal and antisocial behaviour throughout their lives. Finally, Sampson and Laub (1993) draw on the life-course perspective within sociology, and propose a more flexible theory than either Gottfredson and Hirschi or Moffitt, suggesting that a principal source of changes in criminality over the life course derives from the strength of informal social control at various given points (see further discussion below).

Ezell and Cohen's analyses of their Californian samples offers little support for the hypotheses of either Gottfredson and Hirschi or (as regards "life-course persisters") Moffitt. Their study, in their own words, reaches three principal conclusions (Ezell & Cohen, 2005: 256–257), of which the third is the most important for present purposes. These conclusions are:

- "Our results clearly indicate that continuity of arrest patterns will be much stronger when the measurement periods are closer together in time. That is, greater stability (including between-group stability) is displayed within shorter (e.g. two years) compared to longer periods of time."
- There was a "significant amount of heterogeneity in the longitudinal arrest patterns of serious youthful offenders ... even in this select extreme segment of the offender population." These results strengthen the contention of Sampson and Laub that "far more heterogeneity exists ... than previously thought," and that this heterogeneity occurs "over extended periods of the life-course."
- "*Large variations in criminal arrest patterns appear during adulthood that cannot be simply argued as the long-term consequences of childhood propensities.*" (Emphasis added.)

Thus, these analyses of official arrest data fail to support *either* the "stable between-group differences in criminality" *or* the age-invariance thesis of Gottfredson and Hirschi; and, among these samples of very persistent adolescent offenders, there was also much less post-adolescence "life-course persistence" than might have been expected from Moffitt's thesis. The evidence of the California study is, the authors conclude, therefore "perhaps most consistent with the predictions implied from

Sampson and Laub's (1993) age-graded social control theory" (Ezell & Cohen, 2005: 259).[4] Putting matters another way, it would seem that officially recorded criminal careers over a longish term are very variable, and a more flexible theory explains such variation better than theories that postulate "invariance" or inevitable "persistence." Moreover, and of potentially crucial importance to our eventual discussion of human agency, given this degree of variance, it seems very hard successfully to predict long-term criminal career patterns from factors present in adolescence, at least using traditional predictive factors. By contrast, short-term recidivism patterns show much greater continuity, and thus greater predictability.

Laub and Sampson

In view of the impressive independent empirical support offered to Laub and Sampson's analyses by Ezell and Cohen's recent work, it is time to take a closer look at the Laub/Sampson *oeuvre.*

All the empirical work of these authors on desistance derives from long-term analyses of a sample of 500 male delinquents (and a matched control sample of non-delinquents) originally studied by Sheldon and Eleanor Glueck (1950) in the 1940s. In Sampson and Laub's (1993) first book, *Crime in the Making*, the Gluecks' extensive data set is reanalyzed up to age 32,[5] using modern data-processing techniques. Figure 7.1, taken from the concluding chapter of *Crime in the Making*, well summarizes the "dynamic theoretical model of criminality over the life-course" that the authors propose. In the center of the diagram, at late adolescence, is the juvenile outcome of "delinquency," which (by comparison with the matched controls) can be seen to result from a complex mix of factors (structural background factors, individual difference constructs, family and school factors, and peer influence).

Thereafter, however, matters are by no means set in stone. In subsequent (adult) developments in individual lives, two factors in particular were found to alter the trajectories that might be thought to have been set during adolescence; these factors are described by Sampson and Laub as weak or strong "labor force attachment" and weak or

[4] They further note that "the results of our study dovetail nicely with some of the results of the recent work of Laub and Sampson (2003)" (Ezell & Cohen, 2005: 261). It should of course be noted that the authors' data consist exclusively of official arrest histories, and the limitations of such data must be borne in mind when considering the results.

[5] There were three data-gathering points, at ages 14, 25, and 32.

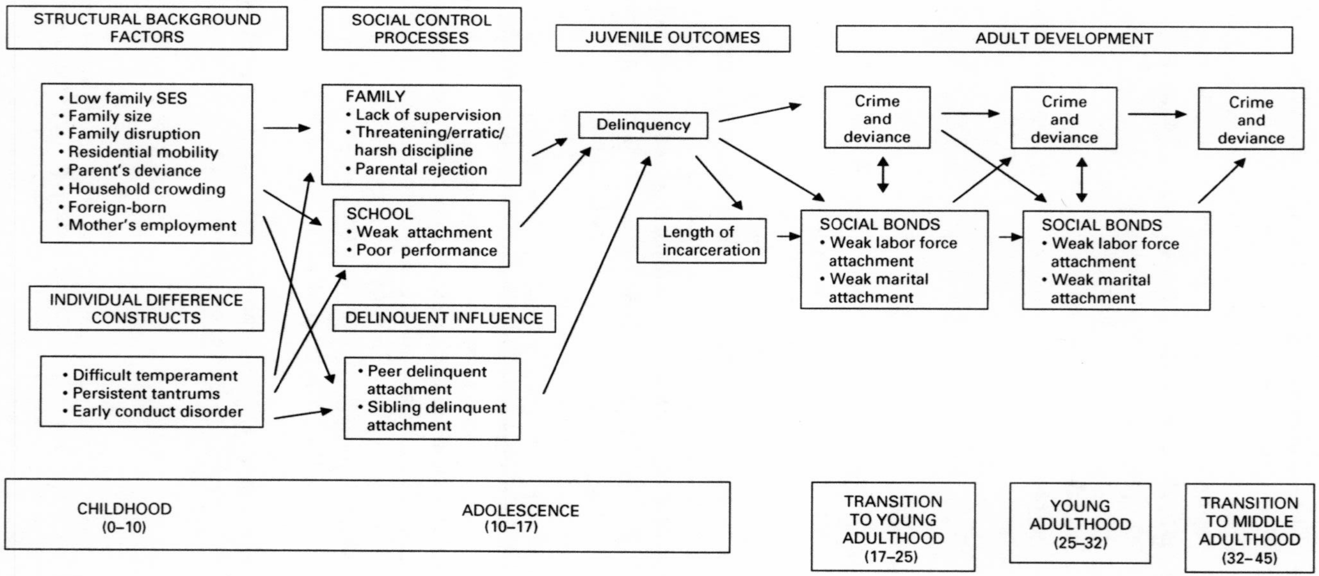

Figure 7.1. Sampson and Laub's "Dynamic theoretical model of criminality over the life course"
Source: Sampson & Laub (1993: 244–245.) Reprinted by permission of the publisher from CRIME IN THE MAKING by Robert Sampson and John Laub, pp. 244–245, Cambridge Mass Harvard University Press,

strong "marital attachment."[6] In other words, the authors present their post-adolescence results as a classic manifestation of control theory (Hirschi, 1969), with an emphasis on *attachment* to the positive social bonding processes provided by stable employment and/or a strong marital attachment.[7] The influence of such events in the men's lives is established by regression models, holding individual differences constant to test the effect of the fresh "attachment."

In their subsequent book, *Shared Beginnings, Divergent Lives*, Laub and Sampson (2003: 6–8) detail a number of criticisms that had been made of their earlier work. They state that, in their opinion, the most important challenge to *Crime in the Making* is presented in a review by John Modell (1994), according to whom: "The authors cannot divorce themselves from a variables focus ... nor are they adept at discerning (or portraying) the inner logic of lives revealed in data such as these." Bravely agreeing with this criticism, Laub and Sampson (2003) set out upon the difficult task of tracing and interviewing a subsample of the Gluecks' original 500 delinquents, in a quest to understand retrospectively the "inner logic of [their] lives." *Shared Beginnings, Divergent Lives* contains rich qualitative data derived from fifty-two interviews with such men, now in their late sixties. (The interviewees included "persisters," "desisters," and those with "zigzag criminal careers"). The book also, however, contains sophisticated quantitative analyses of the official criminal records of the whole original delinquent sample, from age 7 to age 67; and, to the relief of the authors, the results from these analyses "turned out to sit rather well with in-depth narratives and qualitative analyses" (Laub & Sampson, 2003: 293).

The quantitative analyses clearly suggest that "there are important differences in adult criminal career trajectories that cannot be predicted from childhood." This obviously left open the question "what *does* account for these differences?" (Laub & Sampson, 2003: 113, emphasis in original). Following analysis of the qualitative data, the authors, in their concluding chapter, suggest that:

> although there are multiple pathways to desistance, our [qualitative] data suggest that desistance is facilitated by *self-described "turning points" – changes in situational and structural life circumstances like a good marriage or a stable job – in*

[6] A further "turning point" for many of the men was military service in the Second World War era; see, especially, Sampson and Laub (1996).

[7] "Attachment to spouse" was a composite variable derived from interview data. "Weak attachment" was indicated by "signs of incompatibility"; subjects with "strong attachment" generally displayed "close, warm feelings towards their wives, or were compatible in a generally constructive relationship" (Sampson & Laub, 1993: 144). Thus, the variable does not simply measure marriage/non-marriage, but also the quality of conjugal relationships.

combination with individual actions (that is, personal agency). Although age is clearly important in understanding desistance, a focus on age and age alone obfuscates understanding the life course of crime. From our perspective, desistance is best viewed as *a process realized over time*, not a single event. (Laub & Sampson, 2003: 278, emphasis added).

A few pages later, Laub and Sampson (2003: 281) indicate that the theoretical concept which best captures their approach is that of *situated choice*. "Our interest is in the interaction between life-course transitions, macro-level events,[8] situational context, and individual will"; that is, in "the interaction of structure and choice." They see this approach as distinctively different from the "variables focus" of their earlier work, criticized by John Modell (1994). Their new approach is described as moving "away from a strict variable-based approach ... [toward] a person-based approach – *a study of several constructs that, taken as a whole, represent the person*" (Laub & Sampson, 2003: 9, emphasis added).

In adopting this person-based approach, however, Laub and Sampson do not uncritically ally themselves with earlier writers on desistance who have favored an agency-oriented approach. Indeed, they specifically criticize some of them: "Offenders can and do desist without a conscious decision to 'make good' (compare Maruna, 2001), and offenders can and do desist without a 'cognitive transformation' (compare Giordano, Cernovich, & Rudolph, 2002)" (Laub & Sampson, 2003: 279). The authors' interesting suggestion here is that agency can be important in desistance even where, as often happened with the men they studied, desistance could be described as occurring "by default" and as "not necessarily a conscious or deliberate process." Many men apparently made a commitment to go straight without even realizing it, because "before they realized it, they had invested so much in a marriage or a job that they did not want to risk losing their investment" (Laub & Sampson, 2003: 278–279).

The overall argument, then, is that offenders can and do encounter potential "turning points" in their lives, and how they choose to respond to those "turning points" (such as new relationships or new jobs) can have a decisive effect on their subsequent offending. That is so even where the subject, at the time of his response to the "turning point," does not think much, or at all, about the potential consequences of his choice for subsequent criminality. More decisive and explicit

[8] One very important macro-level event for the Laub/Sampson sample was of course the Second World War and its aftermath; so, military service was a "turning point" for some of the men (above, note 6) and the so-called "GI Bill" provided vital financial assistance for post-service training for some (e.g., the case of Bruno, described in Laub & Sampson, 2003: 127–128).

turnings-away from crime can and do occur, but, it is argued, they are not, empirically, a necessary path to desistance. Crucially, however, it is central to Laub and Sampson's (2003) overall argument that even the processes involved in "desistance by default" still involve *choices by offenders in response to potential turning points*.

Nevertheless, as previously indicated, Laub and Sampson (2003) do not provide any very significant elaboration as to how "choice," within an explicitly non-determinist framework (Laub & Sampson, 2003: 34) is to be analysed. Given that all their qualitative interviews took place when their subjects were aged 60+, it is of course unreasonable to expect the authors themselves to have elaborated empirically on this issue, since the inevitable retrospectivity of the men's accounts of their "choices" would mean that such accounts – speaking of events maybe forty years beforehand – would not necessarily be reliable. However, in addition to the empirical issues, significant theoretical issues are raised by the explicit incorporation of "human agency" into a life-course perspective. For example:

- how is the "agency" dimension of the analysis to be distinguished from the more "causal" elements?
- how, theoretically, is the "choice" dimension of the analysis to be related to the "social bonds" dimension?
- how are people's choices related to their overall understandings of themselves (i.e., what is often described as their "sense of self")?

It will be an important part of the task of the present chapter to begin to consider some of these topics, as a way of building on Laub and Sampson's important analysis.

Stouthamer-Loeber et al.

I can deal rather more briefly with the last of the desistance texts to be considered here, which is a paper deriving from the work of the Pittsburgh Youth Study (Stouthamer-Loeber *et al.*, 2004).

This analysis focused on 506 males in the oldest sample within the Pittsburgh Youth Study, and "desisters" were defined as those who were persistent serious offenders in adolescence (i.e., ages 13–19),[9]

[9] "Serious" offences were defined as: auto theft, breaking and entering, strong-arming (robbery), attacking to seriously hurt, and rape/forced sex (all measured by a self-reported delinquency schedule or a teacher's report form). Offenders were classified as "persistent serious offenders in adolescence" if a serious offence was reported for at least two of the seven years from age 13 to age 19.

but who did not commit any serious offence during early adulthood (i.e., ages 20–25).[10] Using these definitions, 190 of the cohort were serious persistent delinquents in adolescence, of whom 101 were persisters and 66 desisters, while the remaining 23 had significant data items missing and so could not be classified.

The authors compared their desistance results with an earlier analysis that had studied the factors that are associated with *becoming* a persistent serious adolescent delinquent (i.e., "onset"). Although for technical reasons they considered that this comparison "should be interpreted with caution," nevertheless the findings are congruent with those of Laub and Sampson (2003), in that the authors "did not find much evidence that the same factors that predict onset also [negatively] predict desistance." Thus, the paper concludes that "onset, acceleration, maintenance and desistance *could have different predictors, reflecting different processes*" (Stouthamer-Loeber *et al.*, 2004: 914, emphasis added).[11]

Moreover, and again congruently with Laub and Sampson's work, many individual factors measured at ages 13–16 did not significantly distinguish between subsequent persisters and desisters. These include various specific behaviors such as hard drug use, frequent alcohol use, high number of sex partners, cruelty to people or animals, and serious delinquency, as well as several beliefs or cognitions such as lack of guilt, attitude toward school, and pro-social self-perception (for a complete list, see Stouthamer-Loeber *et al.*, 2004: 909). On the other hand, a logistic regression analysis showed that there were four so-called "promotive" factors which were measured at ages 13–16 and which did distinguish between desisters and persisters in adulthood (911).[12] These can usefully be divided into two groups,[13] "sanction" factors and

[10] Those who committed non-serious offences in early adulthood were counted as desisters for this purpose. There were thirty-seven in this group, compared with twenty-nine "complete desisters."

[11] On the other hand, in apparent contrast with Laub and Sampson (2003), the Pittsburgh analysis showed that "desisters and persisters were fairly similar in terms of having a steady girlfriend or getting married, the duration of their relationship, and whether they were raising a family together" (Stouthamer-Loeber *et al.*, 2004: 913). However, these findings should be regarded as of limited significance since they do not explicitly measure the quality of the relationship (unlike the Laub/Sampson study); moreover, the authors report that their analyses "did not address the temporal order between the two processes of forming relationships and of desistance" (913).

[12] The combination of these factors correctly predicted 71 percent of the desisters and persisters in early adulthood, and explained about 23 percent of the variance.

[13] A further factor measured at ages 13–16, "being accountable" (i.e., tells parents of whereabouts, actions, etc.), was significantly related to adult desistance on a bivariate basis but did not remain significant in the logistic regression. Risk factors measured at ages 13–16 which were, on a bivariate basis, associated with a *lower* probability of

"peer" factors. Sanction factors comprise (i) greater belief in likelihood of getting caught by police if crimes are committed, and (ii) low use of physical punishment by parents, whilst peer factors comprise (iii) good relationship with peers, and (iv) low participation by peers in alcohol/drug misuse. Of these, subsequent analyses suggest that "low use of physical punishment" is the most influential single predictor of subsequent desistance.

What is of special interest about these results, taken in conjunction with those of Laub and Sampson and others, is as follows. All studies are congruent in suggesting that factors associated with onset and factors associated with desistance are not necessarily the same, and that many "risk factors" associated with onset do not (negatively) predict desistance. Laub and Sampson (2003) especially emphasize *situated choice* (i.e., the interaction of structure and choice) in adulthood as being connected with desistance. Stouthamer-Loeber *et al.* (2004), however, suggest that some factors measurable at ages 13–16 are, at least statistically, "promotive factors" for later desistance; and these "promotive factors" center upon peer relations and sanction factors. The crucial question is, therefore: *Is the Laub/Sampson emphasis on "situated choice" in adulthood compatible with the Stouthamer-Loeber* et al. *emphasis on "promotive factors" already discernible in adolescence?* That is a question that must be returned to at the end of this chapter.

Human agency: an introduction

Although the so-called "structure–agency" question is part of the staple fare of debates in sociological theory, there is remarkably little consensus among sociologists as to how, precisely, "human agency" is to be analyzed. Indeed, it is hard to disagree with the comment of Emirbayer and Mische (1998: 962) that the term agency "has maintained an elusive, albeit resonant, vagueness" in sociological analysis.

As it happens, however, there are a number of recent texts which have sought to throw light on this topic. In this chapter, I have selected three analyses of human agency by sociologists, and one by a philosopher, which I believe can help criminologists to take forward the emerging concern with this concept in the field of desistance studies. A striking feature of these texts is that each has a different emphasis; nevertheless, in my view, something of permanent value can be derived from them all. What follows is, accordingly, a work of exploration and attempted

desistance in adulthood, were: being manipulative, high peer delinquency, and having a positive attitude to delinquency (Stouthamer-Loeber *et al.*, 2004: 909).

synthesis. It is a work of exploration because its task is to explore theoretical texts from adjacent fields of scholarship, in an attempt to see whether these texts can assist criminologists in studying desistance. Inevitably, in pursing this quest, there is also an element of selective (but hopefully not theoretically improper) appropriation. But what follows is also a work of synthesis, made necessary because the principal texts that are analyzed are so different. A key question therefore becomes: can the selected insights from each author be coherently welded together into an appropriate synthesis, which can be constructively utilized by criminologists?[14]

Having tackled these major questions, I shall also in my conclusion return to the challenging further question posed in the preceding subsection, concerning the relationship of the concept of human agency in adult desistance to apparently "promotive" factors already discernible in adolescence.

In the first instance, it is analytically most appropriate to consider each of the four texts separately.

Barry Barnes: Agency, sociability, causation, and responsibility

According to the back cover of Barry Barnes' (2000) *Understanding Agency*, its author (a leading British sociologist) believes that:

> social theory is moving in the wrong direction in its reflections on human freedom and autonomy. It has borrowed notions of "agency" and "choice" from everyday discourse, but increasingly it puts a misconceived individualistic gloss upon them. Against this, Barnes unequivocally identifies human beings as social agents in a profound sense, and emphasises the vital importance of their sociability. Notions of "agency", "freedom" and "choice" have to be understood by reference to their role in communicative interaction ...

Not dissimilarly, the American social psychologist Bernard Malle (2002: 189) tells us in a recent paper that:

> More than any other species, humans develop a high level of self–other differentiation, such as in their goals, beliefs and habits. At the same time, their complex social relations demand a high degree of self–other coordination, particularly during ongoing social interactions. What solves the puzzle of simultaneous differentiation and coordination is human social cognition, which forges integrative representations of self and other in social situations. This integration is made possible in part by the *folk theory of mind and behavior*, which provides a common conceptual framework for the interpretation of information about self

[14] On the difference between synthesis and eclecticism, see Bottoms (2000). The task of synthesis is, in this particular case, made more important by the fact that none of the principal works on agency considered in this chapter cross-references the other works.

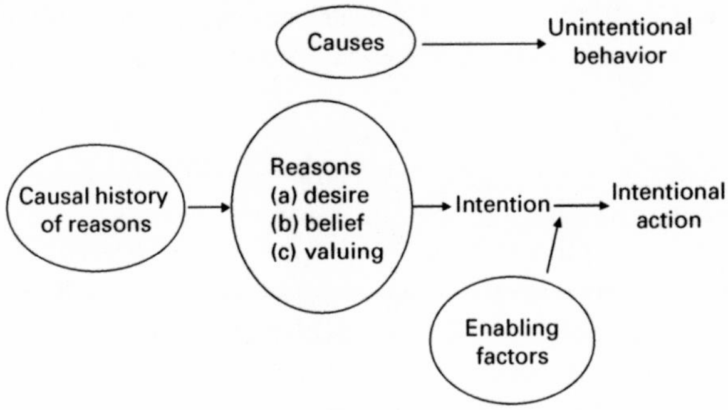

Figure 7.2. Modes of explanation of behavior and action
Source: Malle (2002, with minor adaptation.) Copyright © 2002. From The Social self: Cognitive, Interpersonal and Intergroup Perspectives, edited by Joseph P Forgas and Kipling D. Williams, New York: Psychology Press. Reproduced by permission of Routledge/Taylor and Francis Group, LLC.

and other, centered on such concepts as agency, intentionality, belief and desire (emphasis in original).

So, the sociologist and the social psychologist agree that the concept of agency needs to be located firmly within a framework of "sociability" (Barnes) or "self–other coordination" (Malle). Malle further argues (and Barnes' text concurs) that all of this is linked to a *folk theory of mind and behavior*, which includes concepts like intentionality.

What is this "folk theory" or "commonsense discourse"? Malle (2002: 196) provides a useful basic map of it, which is reproduced here as Figure 7.2. There is, first, *unintentional behavior*, which has a *cause* or *causes*. This behavior may result from a medical condition (e.g., having an epileptic fit), or it may be an accidental act that the person unintentionally causes directly (e.g., knocking over a vase while demonstrating a tennis stroke) or indirectly (e.g., driving a car which skids on an icy road and hits another car).

But there is also *intentional action*, which is normally attributed, in "folk theory," to agents' *reasons* (as opposed to causes). These reasons are of three kinds: a desire ("she changed jobs because she wanted more money"), a belief ("she refused to have an abortion because of her religious beliefs"), or a valuing ("she reads art books because she finds them really interesting"). It is also possible, however for the observer (or, sometimes, an actor) to offer a *causal history of the agent's reasons* (for example, "she's still a Catholic because she's so afraid of her father; that's why she won't have an abortion"); Malle calls this a "CHR" (causal history of reasons) explanation. It is further possible that an intentional action is dependent on an *enabling factor*, without which it would remain a mere intention ("he's wanted to escape from prison for some time, but it was only when the workman left the ladder outside the hut that he was able to").

Barry Barnes, as we have seen, strongly emphasizes the sociability of human beings; he also, however, strongly advocates a version of "ordinary causal explanation in the human realm" (Barnes, 2000: xii). That is to say, for Barnes a "reasons" explanation can in principle always be backed by what Malle would call a CHR explanation; and such an explanation, "while formally voluntaristic, could as well have been causal" (Barnes, 2000: 23; see also Loyal & Barnes, 2001; Loyal, 2003: Ch. 3). Thus, Barnes defends in his book a version of what philosophers call *compatibilism*, that is to say, "the view that the existence of voluntary actions sensibly described as involving will or agency is not inconsistent with determinism" (Barnes, 2000: 32).[15]

The two separate principal elements of Barnes' argument (i.e., sociability and causality) obviously need to be linked if his thesis is to maintain overall coherence; and Barnes also needs to explain why, if causality is as significant as he avows, ordinary lay discourse is so voluntaristic. He, of course, recognizes all this, and offers various arguments to support his case. However, given the main purposes of the present chapter, I shall not pursue these issues here; rather, I shall focus on some of the key implications for desistance research of Barnes' two central emphases.

Taking first the emphasis on sociability, Barnes argues that there is a strong linkage between the concept of agency, understood within the context of human sociability, and the concept of *responsibility*. We can see this if we look at the field of criminal law, which clearly incorporates within it what Malle calls a "folk theory of mind and behavior."[16] Standard criminal law doctrine in most countries is that a crime is not committed unless there is both a criminal act (*actus reus*) *and* the defendant has acted intentionally or recklessly[17] in committing that act

[15] Barnes adds that compatibilism is "often understood as the specific perspective of complete determinists and reductionists, but no position is taken on either of these philosophical doctrines in this book" (32). On compatibilism, see further Van den Beld (2000).

[16] It is an interesting and illuminating point that, among the three main texts by social theorists considered in this chapter, only Barnes makes this link to legal concepts of responsibility.

[17] The term "recklessness" has been given "several different shades of meaning" in recent English law (Ashworth, 2003: 180), but is here used in its core sense of "advertent recklessness," i.e., being aware of the risks of prohibited consequences occurring if an act is committed, but proceeding nevertheless with the act in question.

(*mens rea*). In other words, the criminal law normally both *requires agency*,[18] and *holds people to account* for their wrongful acts, provided that they were intentional or reckless. (Or, in the terms of Figure 7.2, one is held to account by the law for one's *actions* but not one's unintentional *behaviors*.)[19] For Barnes, the concept of agency has to be understood as very closely linked to social responsibility not only in the field of law, but also in everyday discourse. So, agency is not to be considered – as it has been by some writers – simply in individualistic terms ("P chose to act in such-and-such a way"), but additionally and crucially in intersubjective terms ("P chose to act in such-and-such a way in that intersubjective context"), where part of its function is for the actor to be *held responsible* for the good or bad things he or she has done.[20] And much of this is extremely mundane. Voluntary (or "agentic") action, we commonly assume, can in principle be modified by the actor on request – and that is how we can and do assume it to be voluntary. To use Barnes' (2000: 71) examples, there is: "the proposed walk easily adjusted to include a call at the shop (please, would you mind?) [or] the cigarette likely to be put out on request." If the person refuses either request, he is seen as within his rights, but also perhaps as unfriendly or churlish – he is, therefore, seen as intersubjectively responsible for this voluntary but uncooperative act. As in the criminal law, however, there are further factors that might cause us to exempt the refuser from an adverse attribution of responsibility – as where she says of the shop request: "no, sorry, I have to go for a hospital appointment straight after my walk, and I won't have time for the detour" (this is akin to the criminal law defence of necessity).

If all this is correct, then part of the process of becoming a mature and fully socialized adult person is the process of *learning to accept*

[18] And it therefore exempts from criminal liability defendants who can show that they were not capable of acting with full agency (for example, by reason of insanity or infancy), or were placed under severe external pressure (for example, by reason of duress or necessity) and therefore made a "forced choice." See generally Ashworth (2003).

[19] A complex middle category, however, is negligence. Here there is no intention or recklessness, but, where A can be said to owe B a duty of care, and fails to fulfill his/her responsibility, A is held liable by the civil law, and in certain circumstances by the criminal law, for his/her negligence. On the reasons why in such circumstances A can properly be regarded as a wrongdoer despite the absence of intention or recklessness, see Hart (1968: ch. 6).

[20] Barnes provides a useful distinction between *status* and *state*. To hold someone responsible for their actions is to assign to them a *status* of responsibility within that social system. An actor's *state of mind* is in principle a different question. However, we can know very little of what goes on in other people's minds; hence what, in folk theory, is characterized as intention (a state) is, according to Barnes, often in reality a disguised attribution of responsibility (a status).

responsibilities within intersubjective contexts, on a reciprocal basis with others, within a framework of mutual accountability. For example, most adults will belong to a number of smallish groups, within each of which there will be mutual help and support, but also an expectation that each member is responsible for certain tasks, and/or certain standards of behavior. All this is entailed by what Barnes regards as the given sociability of the human condition. In the light of this analysis, it is particularly interesting to note a summary statement by Laub and Sampson (2003: 194) regarding their overall impressions, from their qualitative interviews, of the lives of the men in the Gluecks' sample who had persisted in offending until a relatively late age. According to Laub and Sampson, it was not that these relative "persisters" could be identified by "a single trait like intelligence or even a series of static traits." Rather:

the persistent offender seems devoid of connective structures at each phase of the life course, especially involving relationships that can provide informal social control and social support... Generally, the persistent offenders we interviewed experienced residential, marital, and job instability, failure in the school and the military, and relatively long periods of incarceration. Men who desisted from crime led rather orderly lives, whereas the life of the persistent offender was marked by frequent churning, almost as in adolescence. Surely part of this chaos reflects an inability to forge close attachments or make any connection to anybody or anything. One can view the men as possessing *a distorted sense of autonomy without any commitment or concern for others* (emphasis added).

Putting this in Barnes' language, we could say that the men in question had not fully learned how to engage in responsible reciprocal action within small groups. And, for Barnes, "social life as we know it *requires* responsible agents" (Barnes, 2000: 74, emphasis added). Or, to state the point more fully from Barnes' own helpful summary, his theory:

identifies human beings as complex active creatures, who are, nonetheless, social creatures. That they are social creatures is manifest in their interaction. Firstly, they act toward each other as agents capable of giving an intelligible account of what they are doing and why; and often this is much the same thing as stating why what they are doing is right and justified. *Accountability* is required if agents are to co-ordinate their understandings, sustain a shared sense of what they are likely to do in the future and hold each other to account for the mutually recognised outcomes of what they have done in the past. Secondly, they act toward each other as agents sensitive to symbolically conveyed evaluations of their actions and potentially responsive to them. *Susceptibility* in this sense is necessary for the co-ordination of actions and their coherent ordering around collectively agreed goals. Clearly, susceptibility implies intelligibility, which implies accountability. Accountability and susceptibility are two closely intertwined components of responsibility, and together constitute a necessary basis for social interaction. Social life as we know it requires responsible agents who may be held accountable, and to whom it makes a difference that they have been so held. Of course, there are human beings who fall short of what is required. And there are countless occasions when normal responsible agents fall short of what is necessary in the way of accountability or susceptibility ... (Barnes, 2000: 74, emphasis in original).

Thus "social life as we know it" is, for Barnes, a continual achievement, the achievement of what he calls *collective agency* by sociable humans, with a subtle and always evolving context of susceptibility and accountability.

In my view, this analysis by Barnes, set against Laub and Sampson's summary of the qualities found in the persistent offenders they interviewed, is deeply illuminating. Nevertheless, I can imagine anyone who has read this far being somewhat puzzled. When social scientists talk about "agency," they normally speak of some aspect of the inner life of the individual – for example, the individual "taking a decision" or "exercising choice" or "showing will-power." In Barnes' analysis, there is very little of this "inner life"; and it will be part of my later argument that we need to reinstate such a dimension, alongside the crucial insights about social life to which Barnes has drawn our attention.

What, then, of the second main strand of Barnes' overall analysis, that of *causation*? Here a central point at issue is that of "acting otherwise." Both Roy Bhaskar (1979: 146) and Anthony Giddens (1976: 75) have each independently stated it to be "analytic to the concept" of agency, or an action, that the person acting "could have acted otherwise"; and that is certainly also what is assumed in the lay theory of fully responsible action that underpins the criminal law. Barnes, however, is deeply skeptical about the value of claims that people "could have acted otherwise," at least as regards explanations in the social sciences. It is worth setting out his objections at some length in the present context (Barnes, 2000: 31):

Social theorists have ... no account of how to distinguish actions involving choice or agency from other actions or behaviours. All too often their theories are an eclectic concoction of causal and voluntaristic notions, notions immiscible with each other, but mixed nonetheless, as it were, by shaking hard. And whilst the causal components of the resulting potion may have a useful role, it remains obscure what positive work the voluntaristic notions are supposed to do. An incompatibilist social theory could work if it were based on a conception of free choice as wholly uncaused and unpredictable. Then the distinction of the caused and the chosen could be used to mark the bounds of predictive explanatory science in the human realm. But this is a position rarely taken in the social sciences for the obvious reason that it implies the redundancy of that project. Theorists in the social sciences are bound to become involved, however reluctantly, in predictive and/or explanatory projects ... But once theories become predictive or explanatory it is going to be asked whether they are not "really" causal theories, adorned in a wholly superfluous metaphysics of agency; for our familiar discourse of prediction and explanation is a broadly causal one. And if reply is made that human actions, in the last analysis, "could have been otherwise," that, as it stands, will count merely as another assertion of the metaphysics in question.

Two points are of particular interest about this argument in the context of the desistance literature. Firstly, Laub and Sampson (2003), in introducing agency into their theoretical approach (in *Shared Beginnings, Divergent Lives*), seem very willing to adopt what Barnes describes as the "rarely taken" position regarding the "uncaused and unpredictable" character of agency, and to treat this as a way of marking, precisely, "the bounds of predictive explanatory science in the human realm". Whether that implies "the redundancy of the project" of explanation, as Barnes avers, is, however, extremely doubtful, since Laub and Sampson clearly are willing to introduce causal factors into their analysis; they are therefore happy, it would appear, to accept "the distinction of the caused and the chosen" within their overall explanatory framework. Of course, however, that then raises the further question: "how do we know the difference between the caused and the chosen?," and it will be necessary to return to that difficult question before this chapter is concluded.

Secondly, the question of "acting otherwise" is close to the heart of offenders' everyday understandings of possible paths to desistance. As is well known, in early adulthood many offenders, even those with quite lengthy criminal records, say they would "like to stop"; but they also often say that they are not sure that they will be able to desist in certain specific situations, in the face of various possible temptations or provocations.[21] What they are usually anticipating here is the possibility of what philosophers since Plato have called "weakness of will," or *akrasia*; that is, "the state of mind an agent is said to be in when he performs an intentional act that goes against his better judgement" (Flew 1979: 344).[22] In thinking about possible "weakness of will" situations in the future, real-life offenders certainly assume that, in those situations, they

[21] In the Sheffield desistance study (see note 1), interview comments of this kind are being frequently encountered. The language of "temptations or provocations" is taken from the work of Wikström (2004), to be discussed more fully later. "Temptations" refers particularly to the seductions of property offending (easy money) and/or addictive substances (drugs, alcohol); "provocations" refers particularly to situations that might be interpreted (rightly or wrongly) as requiring some kind of aggressive response.

[22] The word "usually" has been included in this sentence because sometimes offenders may have in mind instead a situation where they may succumb to future offending

will have a real choice between acting in the way that they would (in calmly reflective mode) like to act, and the possibility that they will "do something stupid" (as they often put it) in the heat of the moment (such as deciding to lash out in a fight, or going along with a friend's suggestion of "earning some easy money"). *Existentially*, then, "weakness of will," and some of the tough choices it presents, seems a real enough possibility to many offenders; and if that is the case, then it seems entirely reasonable to ask whether Barnes, in the long quotation above, has got it seriously wrong when he talks about agency possibly constituting "a wholly superfluous metaphysics." Indeed, it is striking that Barnes' analysis hardly mentions the "weakness of will" question, discussing it in half a page, and solely within the framework of rational choice theory.[23] Anyone who is skeptical about the validity of the standard commonsense claim that "s/he could have acted otherwise" surely needs to pay more attention than this to this crucial point; and it is a topic to which I will return later in this chapter.

Both parts of Barnes' analysis (the "sociability" and the "causation" strands) have left us with questions about a possibly missing existential or "inner life" dimension, an omission that appears somewhat similar to that pointed out by Modell (1994) in relation to Sampson and Laub's (1993) earlier work. Barnes is aware of and unapologetic about this feature of his work: at one point, he describes himself as one of a group of social theorists who "have ceased to focus theory on the individual human subject, and [have] stressed the importance of communication between persons" (Barnes, 2000: 78). It is worth explicitly noting, therefore, that such a position is contested and very controversial within sociology. For example, one sociological analyst whose book was written to challenge such views concludes his argument as follows (Campbell, 1996: 161–162):

> Action is best represented as that portion of an individual's conduct which is meaningful to the actor: that is to say, has significance for the actor given his or her current commitments and action state ... All action is ultimately performed alone, undertaken by the individual as the sole agent. No matter whether the action in question is "social" in the sense of occurring in the company of others, or even if it is part of an ongoing system of "interaction," it is still an individual

because of a compulsion such as a drug addiction. On the distinction between weakness of will and compulsion, see further below.

23 See Barnes (2000: 19), discussing Elster (1984). According to Barnes, the "major difficulty" with Elster's view is that it entails "rational human actions powered by will, and non-rational human actions where will has been overpowered by some contingency or other, and it is no longer possible to predict how a person will act simply by working at what it is rational for her to do." This criticism, however, is obviously specific to weakness of will within a framework of rational choice theory.

and largely covert accomplishment. This is because all true actions are the outcome of an "act of will," a covert and personal event which actors can only perform for themselves. Hence understanding action must involve grasping the character and nature of this process of "willing" and whilst recognising that it is not translatable into either metaphysics or biology, appreciate that it centres around the individual's ability to create and manipulate meaning. Those "meanings" which are most pertinent to the occurrence of an act do not stem from any pool of "inter-subjective" understandings or shared typifications, least of all from any social rules and conventions, but are created *de novo* by individuals as and when they are needed to meet the immediate exigencies of their action situation, and although they will probably draw heavily on cultural material, this will probably be closely woven into the actor's past experiences and future hopes to comprise the effective inner "life-world" of the actor. It is these essentially personal, intra-subjectively created meanings which are the immediate and direct "causes" of actions.

The emphasis of this passage, however, almost certainly goes too far in the opposite direction to Barnes; as previously indicated, a more balanced position would simultaneously emphasize *both* agents' "self–other differentiation" *and* "self–other co-ordination" (Malle, 2002). Nevertheless, Campbell is right to draw attention to the fact that there is an element of agency which is "covert and personal," which "centres around the individual's ability to create and manipulate meaning," and which, ultimately, "actors can only perform for themselves." The next two contributions to be considered focus more fully than Barnes on these "inner" and "covert" aspects of agency.

Margaret Archer: Agency, the self, emotions, and the enactment of roles

It is intriguing that in the same calendar year, 2000, two leading British sociologists both published books on agency, with minimal reference to the other's work.

Margaret Archer's (2000) *Being Human: The Problem of Agency* claims to be a "revindication of the concept of humanity, rejecting contemporary social theory that seeks to diminish human properties and powers" (the rejected theories are, principally, rational choice theory and various versions of social constructionism, especially those with a "linguistic turn"). The book is the final volume in a trilogy, the earlier works focusing principally on culture (Archer, 1988) and structure (Archer, 1995); thus, the author's interest in agency lies principally in its linkage to these other elements of social life. Within this framework, when discussing human agency, particular preoccupations for Archer are the concept of *self* and the concept of *identity*, both of which concepts have been under attack in contemporary social theory (see the revealing quotations listed in Archer, 2000: 18–19). The author believes that to understand the decisions made by human subjects, we need to understand fairly fully who they are and how they understand themselves. This involves, certainly, an understanding of social structures, culture, and language, but it also involves "tearing down the privacy sign" on our "inner lives," "because what we are is forged between our potential species powers and our encounters with the world" (Archer, 2000: 317). And a key part of our inner lives is the "internal conversation" in which we all silently engage as we go about our daily business, choosing whether to do this or that, internally commenting on the actions of people around us, and so on.

For Archer, normal human beings have a "continuous sense of self"; a sense, for example, that the person who is writing this chapter is one and the same being (although also markedly different in many ways) as a young boy who was sent to boarding school at the age of eight. Archer further argues that human beings, with their given ontological characteristics, must necessarily operate simultaneously in three separate "orders," namely (Archer, 2000: 198–199):

- The *natural order*, which is concerned with *physical well-being* and *body–environment* relations. This order embraces our physical health, hunger, bodily warmth/coldness, and so on, all of which arise from the *embodiment* of human beings.
- The *practical order*, which is concerned with *performative achievement* and *subject–object relations*. This order embraces our performance of basic tasks such as (in the modern world) cooking, cleaning, gardening, mending broken household gadgets, driving a car, keeping up-to-date with official paperwork coming into our household, and so on. This order arises because "all persons are constrained to live and work, in one way or another, in the practical world" (198); we have to get various practical tasks done ("subject–object relations") in order to be able to fulfill the basic routines of daily life.
- The *discursive* or *social order*, which is concerned with that "sociality [which] is … necessarily the lot of human beings". "We cannot avoid becoming a *subject among subjects*" (emphasis added), which necessarily brings with it some "concerns about our social standing" in various specific situations.

So, normal people have a continuous sense of self, and they continually (although of course in a myriad of ways) find themselves encountering the natural, the practical, and the social orders. For Archer, these are the basic ingredients out of which self-understanding (which in turn underpins agency) is formed. Archer's overall argument on these themes is very elaborate (arguably over-elaborate: Benton, 2001), and I shall not here follow it in all its dimensions. Suffice it to say that the discussion, while not substantively following Wittgenstein, amply supports his view (as expressed in the quotation at the head of this chapter) that the self is elusive and mysterious, although not unanalyzable.

A key element of Margaret Archer's argument concerns emotionality (Archer, 2000: chs. 6 and 7), and Archer divides this human characteristic into what she calls its "first-order" and "second-order" dimensions (195). To begin at the beginning, "different clusters of emotions represent commentaries upon our concerns and are emergent from our human relationships with the natural, practical and discursive orders of reality respectively" (195). Emotions are thus, in the first instance, understood by Archer in Charles Taylor's (1985: 48) sense of "affective modes of awareness of situation"; they are "*relational to something, which is what gives them their emergent character*, and that 'something' is our own concerns which make a situation a matter of non-indifference" (Archer, 2000: 195). It follows that when our concerns are engaged in a given situation, there is an emotional reaction, positive or negative (or a mixture of both); and such emotions are not only experienced at the time, but are also frequently recalled when our "continuous sense of self" remembers a situation in our past life. These reactive emotions directly relate to the three "orders"; for example, most of us can recall emotions associated with particular situations of physical danger or ill-health; and I can recall complex emotions relating to starting life at boarding school, a sudden transition that had radical implications for daily life in both the practical and the discursive/social orders, each of which was accompanied by a mixture of negative and positive emotional reactions.

But all this is what Archer calls first-order emotionality. There is also, she argues, another kind of emotionality ("second-order" emotionality), which "entails a shift from the inarticulate to the articulate, from the less adequate to the more adequate characterisation, and from initial evaluation to transvaluation" (Archer, 2000: 227).[24] Those interested in literature may, in considering this concept, find a useful linkage to

[24] On transvaluation, see Taylor (1985: 63–64), quoted in Archer (2000: 226): "Our feelings incorporate a certain articulation of our situation, that is, they presuppose that we characterise our situation in certain terms. But at the same time they admit of – and very often we feel that they call for – further articulation, the elaboration of finer terms permitting more penetrating characterisation. *And this further articulation can in turn transform the feelings*" (emphasis added). So, according to Archer, transvaluation entails "progressive articulations of our first-order emotions" which result in "a real emotional elaboration which is very different from … action-replay" (Archer, 2000: 226).

William Wordsworth's (1802: 740) characterization of poetry (a highly ordered choice and placement of words) as taking its origin "from emotion recollected in tranquillity."[25] However, rather than follow Archer's "first-order/second-order" terminology, I shall refer to the two designated kinds of emotionality as "reactive" and "reflective" respectively.[26]

For Archer, one issue of particular concern is what she calls the emergence of "personal identity," which, she argues, comes about through persons making a particular "pattern of commitments" which defines who they are. Leaving aside here the controversial issue of the definition of "personal identity,"[27] we can instead focus upon Archer's interesting argument that *genuine commitments necessarily entail some element of transvaluation of emotions*, and that this reflective emotionality can sometimes conflict with reactive emotions. So, as she explains it (using her "first-order" terminology):

> if one of our ultimate concerns is wife and family, the emotional commentary arising from an attractive occasion for infidelity will not just be the first-order desire for the liaison, but emotionally we will also feel it as a threat, as a potential betrayal of something which we value more. Its emotional impact is literally that of a *liaison dangereuse*. In an important sense, we are no longer *capable* of the simplicity of a purely first-order response: reactions to relevant events are emotionally transmuted by our ultimate concerns (Archer, 2000: 242, emphasis in original).

For the criminological scholar interested in desistance, this quotation has immediate resonance as a potentially valuable development of the "social bonds" theoretical tradition, in a way that links it more fully to emotional concerns.

We can take matters a little further by reference to Archer's discussion of *roles*. Again, her theoretical discussion on this topic is complex, but we can perhaps encapsulate its essence, without oversimplification, through

[25] More fully: "Poetry … takes its origin from emotion recollected in tranquillity: the emotion is contemplated till, by a species of reaction, the tranquillity gradually disappears, and an emotion, kindred to that which was before the subject of contemplation, is gradually produced … In this mood successful composition generally begins … "

[26] This is in order to avoid any implication that reflective emotionality is of a "higher order" (and hence superior) to reactive emotionality.

[27] For Archer (2000: 10), "whereas self-identity, the possession of a continuous sense of self, [is] held to be universal to human beings, personal identity is an *achievement*. It comes only at maturity, *but is not attained by all*: it can be lost, yet re-established" (emphasis added). But how, empirically, one distinguishes between someone who has "attained personal identity," and another who has not, remains extremely unclear; and for me at least this raises serious questions about the sustainability of Archer's particular version of the concept of "personal identity."

comments on a few paragraphs from the end of her book where Archer speaks partly in autobiographical mode (Archer, 2000: 293–294). First, there is the initial "dipping of the toe" into the role:

> Any social role makes its demands on time, energy and commitment. Those who have experienced enough of it to wish to make some of its associated interests their own have also changed, to the extent that they now *know* ... that they do indeed find these things interesting ... they now see their self-worth as being constituted by role occupancy [in this particular role] (emphasis in original).

Several things are important here. First, the social role is, of course, socially defined: we have some idea, from living in that society, of *what it means* to adopt the role of a parent, a shop worker, a member of a pub darts team, or whatever. But "toe-dipping" into the role produces at least a minimal degree of change in the person doing the experimenting; there is a genuine personal–social interaction between the individual and the social expectations of the role.

But, Archer goes on, "most roles are greedy consumers," making significant demands on the role-holder who is committed to the role. Many people hold several roles simultaneously – Margaret Archer herself, for example, tells us that she is an academic, a parent, and a churchgoer. But if all these roles are "greedy," "then who or what moderates between their demands?" The answer has to be, of course, the person within the roles; and, indeed, the person makes each role his or her own through his/her fulfillment of it.[28] But Archer (2000: 294) wants us to note the overall consequences of all this:

> in determining *how much* of themselves anyone will put into their various ultimate concerns, they are simultaneously deciding *what* they will put in. This arises because in arriving at their concerns and deeming some ultimate and others as subordinate (and thus to be accommodated to the former), they define themselves ... It is this *overall* personal identity that they will bring to executing any particular component of their concerns (emphasis in original).

Thus, in the end, social role expectations and personal identity are linked in a very complex overall interaction.[29] That interaction,

[28] Thus, "through choosing (and being chosen) to be Professor of Sociology at Warwick University, I personify the role in my own fashion which makes me distinct from all others who hold the same job contract. My obligations I accept as mine, but their execution, far from swamping me, are used to define me myself" (Archer, 2000: 76).

[29] Archer is, of course, here using the concept of "personal identity" according to her own definition of the term (see note 27 above). However, in this context a different concept of personal identity, as more widely used in social identity theory (see later discussion) would arrive at a similar result. Notice also that, in the process here described by Archer, the substance of an individual's "personal identity" may change. (That is, since individuals "define themselves" by reference to various external role expectations, it

however, can have severely practical consequences. In the field of desistance, for example, it is clear that many young male recidivist offenders find significantly conflicting demands on their time, and on their "ultimate concerns," from, on the one hand, their girlfriend/partner pressing them to adopt the role of caring partner, and, on the other hand, their delinquent friends pressing them to continue in their role as delinquent group member (see, e.g., Warr, 2002). In deciding, as Archer puts it, "how much of themselves" they will put in to these conflicting and often "time-greedy" demands, the young men are ultimately, in a real sense, deciding *who they are*.[30] That is why Laub and Sampson's (2003) language of "turning points" seems so apt in this kind of situation. Overall, also, Archer's subtle theoretical framework certainly helps us to see more fully how it could come about that, for Laub and Sampson's subjects, "desistance was not necessarily a conscious or deliberate process." For, on Archer's analysis, the men in the Gluecks' sample could easily have made "a commitment to going straight without even realising it," through the gradual adoption of roles and their associated emotional commitments and readjustments.[31]

Two further issues arise from this discussion. The first relates to *adulthood*. Criminologists interested in desistance are acutely aware that the age–crime curve of criminal involvement moves most rapidly downward from about age 19 to age 25.[32] For many young people, this is of course the time of the adoption of various facets of adulthood and adult roles, and it might indeed not be a coincidence that the onset of adulthood and of desistance are so often concurrent (Bottoms *et al.*,

follows that they may "define themselves differently" if one of the roles comes to seem more important to them.) Thus "personal identity," in Archer's discussion, turns out to be a somewhat more dynamic concept than the author's initial statements (see note 27 above) might seem to suggest.

30 There are obvious links here to the now large body of literature in social psychology on social identity theory and self-categorization theory (see, e.g., Capozza & Brown, 2000; Forgas & Williams, 2002, part III), though these theories are not discussed by Archer. This literature is potentially also of considerable relevance to criminological studies of desistance, because of the accepted importance of "social bonds" in this field; however, it would distort the balance of this chapter to discuss social identity/self-categorization theory here.

31 What is implied here is gradual normative change through the adoption of certain commitments, a view that raises potential connections to a more explicitly normative literature on so-called "agent-centered morality," either broadly Kantian or broadly Aristotelian: see Harris (1999).

32 This has been known for many years in circumstances where the age–crime curve is calculated using an *offender-based* method, but such a procedure of course gives special prominence to one-off adolescent offenders. Hence the importance of Laub and Sampson's (2003: 86) recent demonstration that, among the Gluecks' sample of institutionalized juvenile offenders, the lifetime incidence of *offences* committed by the sample followed exactly the same age–crime trajectory.

2004). Certainly, in early interviews in the Sheffield desistance study (see note 1 above), the research team have often found offenders' initial thoughts of desistance linked to comments like "I'm growing up," "I'm more mature now," and so forth. It is at the moment no more than a hypothesis, but reading such comments through the theoretical framework of Margaret Archer's work, one might suggest *first*, that desistance entails some adoption of the expectations of various adult roles, and, in Barnes' terms, a willingness to accept adult responsibilities in various small-group contexts; and *secondly*, that the adoption of various commitments (to girlfriend, job, etc.) might have a "transvaluing" emotional effect, in a way that could start to affect other decisions that one might be tempted to make (as with Archer's *liaison dangereuse* example – and for "volume offenders" *liaisons dangereuses* do not have to be sexual, but can include, for example, the lure of a mate offering an opportunity for easy money). We can potentially again see Laub and Sampson's concept of "situated choice" here, but with the added dimensions of a deeper understanding of the onset of adulthood in relation to selfhood and reflective emotionality.

Secondly, what if anything can be said about *persisters* from Archer's analysis? Of course, Archer does not discuss persistent offenders as such, but when discussing emotionality, she has an insightful passage about those who "drift from job to job, place to place and relationship to relationship" perhaps in a "spiral of homelessness and addiction" (Archer, 2000: 247). Such contexts, Archer contends, require individuals to be "pre-occupied with the satisfaction of first-order [emotional] commentaries – the next night and the next fix." She adds, rightly, that reversal of such life situations is possible, but argues that while they last they can stunt the growth of reflective emotionality precisely because the demands of daily living in a relatively unstructured environment impose a preoccupation with short-term needs which tends to be accompanied by the insistent "pushes and pulls" of reactive emotions. This, again, seems to be a valuable insight, and an issue well worth further empirical investigation in the context of the study of desistance and persistence.

Emirbayer and Mische: Agency as a temporally embedded process of social engagement

We turn now from British sources to a lengthy American article on agency by Mustafa Emirbayer and Ann Mische (1998). This contribution has some similarities to that of Margaret Archer, notably in its emphasis on daily practices (though these are approached from a different philosophical starting point)[33] and on the inner world of the agent ("we ground this capacity for human agency in the structures and processes of the human self, conceived of as an internal conversation possessing analytic autonomy": 974). As with Barry Barnes (2000), however, there is also an emphasis on the "intrinsically social and relational" features of agency, while nevertheless taking the view (congruently with Campbell, 1996) that "transpersonal contexts ... cannot themselves serve as the point of origin of agentic possibilities, which must reside, one level down (so to speak), at the level of self-dynamics" (Emirbayer & Mische, 1998: 973–974).

The most distinctive feature of Emirbayer and Mische's approach to agency is its strongly stated emphasis on *temporality*: "we argue ... that agentic processes can *only* be understood if they are linked intrinsically to the changing temporal orientations of situated actors" (Emirbayer & Mische, 1998: 967, emphasis added).[34] Drawing on the work of George Herbert Mead (1932), Emirbayer and Mische (1998: 968–969) suggest that "as actors respond to changing environments, they must continually reconstruct their view of the past in an attempt to understand the causal conditioning of the emergent present, while using this understanding to control and shape their responses in the arising future." Here the authors are very close to a source that they do not cite, namely Kierkegaard's aphorism, as quoted at the beginning of this chapter. But Kierkegaard's formulation perhaps captures the existential dilemma embedded in the temporal approach to agency more sharply than do Emirbayer and Mische; for the central existential problem is that, however much we understand of our past, in Kierkegaard's words, "life ... must be lived forwards," so there is always an element of uncertainty about it, particularly when we are embarking on a new chapter of life, or reach a "turning point." As we have seen, such issues are highly relevant to the study of desistance.

According to Emirbayer and Mische (1998: 971), there are three principal "dimensions" of human agency, which they label the *iterational*, the *projective*, and the *practical-evaluative* dimensions; or, alternatively

[33] Emirbayer and Mische (1998: 967) ground their work in the philosophical approach of American pragmatism (whose advocates "insist that action not be perceived as the pursuit of pre-established ends, but rather that ends and means develop coterminously within contexts that are themselves ever changing"). Margaret Archer (2000: 1–2) identifies herself as part of a school of "Social Realism," based on the work of philosophers such as Roy Bhaskar (1989) and Roger Trigg (1989).

[34] This sentence occurs as part of a passage where the authors emphasize their strong indebtedness to the pioneering work of Jeffrey Alexander (1988), while nevertheless regretting that Alexander "neglects to situate his analysis of agency within a specifically temporal framework."

stated, the dimensions of *routine*, *purpose*, and *judgment* (963). There is, it is said, an important "dynamic interplay" (963) among these three dimensions, so that "all three ... are to be found, in varying degrees, within any concrete empirical instance of action" (972). So, overall, Emirbayer and Mische (1998: 963) see human agency as "a temporally embedded process of social engagement, informed by the past (in its habitual aspect), but also oriented toward the future (as a capacity to imagine alternative possibilities) and toward the present (as a capacity to contextualize past habits and future projects within the contingencies of the moment)." The human agent, it is argued, always stands at the conjunction of these three dimensions, but of course the flow of time continually sweeps onward, so that today's present is tomorrow's past, and there are always new futures to be considered in the light of unexpected fresh events. An additional complication is that actors are, in different social contexts, often embedded within several different temporal-relational flows at once (e.g., at home and in the workplace), so that their agency might "exhibit [a primarily] projective orientation" within one context, "even as they exhibit [a primarily] iterational orientation within another" (Emirbayer & Mische, 1998: 972).

As should be clear from the preceding sentence, in Emirbayer and Mische's analysis the three postulated agentic dimensions of routine, purpose, and judgment are not simply identified with the past, the future, and the present. Rather, these are, in the strict sense, *dimensions of currently-exercised agency*, and in a given situational context one or other dimension might, in empirical reality, be dominant.

What, then, in more detail, can be understood about the three proposed dimensions of agency? The *iterational* dimension refers to: "the selective reactivation by actors of past patterns of thought and action, as routinely incorporated in practical activity, thereby giving stability and order to social universes and helping to sustain identities, interactions and institutions over time" (971). This obviously has strong connotations of *habit* and *repetition* (see Wikström, this volume: ch. 3). I will return later to the reasons why Emirbayer and Mische insist that iteration is correctly identified as an element of agency.

The second dimension of agency is *projective*, and, according to Emirbayer and Mische (1998: 971), it can be defined as: "the imaginative generation by actors of possible future trajectories of action, in which received structures of thought and action may be creatively reconfigured in relation to actors' hopes, fears and desires for the future." Although, inevitably, they are immersed in their current context, agents may thus "move 'beyond themselves' ... and construct changing images of where they ... want to go, and how they can get there" (984). The projective dimension, then, refers to the longer-term plans or hopes of the agent, the desire to move toward a different future in a particular sphere of his or her life. Since such plans and hopes are often about possible future *commitments*, there are important links here to Margaret Archer's analysis, not least at the emotional level (an aspect that is reflected in the final works of Emirbayer and Mische's initial statement above).[35]

Finally, there is the *practical-evaluative* dimension of agency, which, according to Emirbayer and Mische (1998: 971) entails: "the capacity of actors to make practical and normative judgements among alternative possible trajectories of action, in response to the emerging demands, dilemmas and ambiguities of presently evolving situations." In other words, this is the element of *current choice* in agency, although it is, say the authors, important not to misunderstand this concept. A choice can, on occasion, of course be a "highly discrete" event, but on other occasions a choice "blends indiscriminately into the flow of practical activity, and is only clearly perceived after the fact" (Emirbayer & Mische, 1998: 999). Each of these possibilities requires brief elaboration. In relation, first, to the more "discrete" kinds of current choice, the authors additionally claim that "*through deliberation with others* (or sometimes, self-reflexively, with themselves) about the pragmatic and normative exigencies of lived situations, actors *gain in the capacity to make considered decisions that may challenge received patterns of action*" (Emirbayer & Mische, 1998: 994, emphasis added). I shall return to the significance of this claim shortly. Secondly, and in relation to less "discrete" choices, Emirbayer and Mische emphasize that choices do not have to be "the product of articulable explicit reasoning," but can be much more subconscious, "a matter of tacit adjustment or adaptation to changing contingencies – including feedbacks from experience" (999). This is, in my view, an important point that can be used to develop the argument of those, such as Laub and Sampson (2003), who argue that offenders can make a commitment to go straight without even realizing it, perhaps because "before they realized it, they had invested so much in a marriage or a job that they did not want to risk losing their investment" (278–279).

[35] In an interesting comment, Emirbayer and Mische (1998: 991) also suggest that in "much of empirical sociology . . . the notion of projects has largely been ignored, due in part to its perceived subjective nature and the apparent incompatibility of 'imaginative' phenomena with behavioral observation, survey techniques and macrostructural analysis." The authors rightly call for projectivity to be "put to use in empirical research."

There is, in my judgment, much merit in Emirbayer and Mische's (1998) approach to agency as "a temporally embedded process of social engagement." The explicitly temporal orientation – prefigured in Kierkegaard's aphorism 150 years previously – highlights the fact that human beings are always taking decisions within a flow of time where they are simultaneously building on past events (perhaps in a pattern of continuity, perhaps in a pattern of attempted change) and, at least potentially, projecting future possibilities. Such an understanding of agency quite well captures some of the dilemmas of desistance from offending among recidivists. So, for example, the young men we are currently interviewing in Sheffield (see note 1 above) often speak, in interviews, about their anxieties in facing the future, and the fact that, even when they really want to change, there may be formidable social forces that may potentially press them back into old patterns of behavior, instead of in the new directions that they hope for.

There are two particular features of Emirbayer and Mische's (1998) analysis that we can usefully examine a little more closely. The first of these is the element of habit, routine, or repetition within the iterative dimension, which is "the most difficult to conceive of in properly agentic terms" (975). However, the scholarly approach that has regarded habit as "little more than a matter of stimulus and response" is seen by the authors as unfortunate (976). Rather, while the mental activity in question is considered to take place "at a low level of conscious reflection," agents are still required to "selectively recognize, locate and implement" schemas of social experience in particular social contexts, and thus this kind of activity is, in the authors' view, properly described as agentic. To support this view, Emirbayer and Mische note the tradition of "virtue ethics" of Aristotle and Aquinas, and Aristotle's inclusion of *hexis* ("any settled disposition or state leading to action") within virtue ethics. "Habits could not form the basis for virtue if they were merely automatic activity" (Emirbayer & Mische, 1998: 976), but Aristotle regarded *hexis* as different from mechanical behavior, since the former entails a settled disposition toward a given course of action. So, Driver A might always drive within speed limits on motorways; Driver B might normally "allow herself" 10 m.p.h. above the speed limit; and Driver C might "allow himself" up to 30 m.p.h. above the limit if he thinks he can get away with it. These are fairly *settled* moral choices, which repeated observation of the driving of A, B, and C would confirm. The action of motorway driving at a certain speed on a certain day then becomes, in effect, pre-programmed and habitual for A, B, and C, but – Emirbayer and Mische insist – in each case the actor is properly described as exercising agency, having long ago decided his/her general approach to the speed limits on motorways, and then, at a low level of consciousness, "selectively implementing" this pattern of behaviour in the car on the day in question.

All of this is considered to be conceptually crucial by Emirbayer and Mische because they regard the iterational dimension of agency as strongly linked to the other dimensions, as a key background feature. For them, "both the projective and the practical-evaluative dimensions are deeply grounded in habitual, unreflected and mostly unproblematic patterns of action by which we orient our efforts in the greater part of our daily lives" (Emirbayer & Mische, 1998: 975). That is to say, our habitual patterns of action form the starting point for projective hypothesizations and conscious practical-evaluative choices; "the formation of projects," for example, "is always an interactive, culturally embedded process by which social actors negotiate their way toward the future, ... [attempting] to reconfigure received schemas by generating alternative possible responses to the problematic situations they confront in their lives" (Emirbayer & Mische, 1998: 984). This seems to be a good way of conceptualizing the hesitant progress toward desistance from crime described by several authors who have taken a qualitative research approach to this topic (e.g., Maruna, 2001; Laub & Sampson, 2003).

The second main substantive feature that I want to consider from Emirbayer and Mische's theorization concerns what the authors describe as the possibility of agents "increas[ing] or decreas[ing] their capacity for invention, choice and transformative impact" (1003). A quite similar idea has been put forward in an article on developmental criminology by Per-Olof Wikström (2005), though Wikström's main emphasis is on a "stronger agency" with increased age.[36] The basic idea of Emirbayer and Mische's formulation is that in some contexts the iterational dimension of agency may be dominant, but that, "by subjecting their own agentic orientations to imaginative recomposition and critical judgement, actors can loosen themselves from past patterns of interaction and reframe their relationships to existing constraints" (1010). This "critical judgement," of course, may be assisted by discussions with others (see earlier quotation). Thus, we are here centrally in the territory of the relationship of agency to social bonds, a matter that also preoccupies Archer (2000). Emirbayer and Mische's (1998: 1004) general approach to this issue is that empirical social action is

[36] Wikström (2005: 224) argues that, at the start of their lives individuals have "practically no agency," but as they age and develop they acquire "a greater potential to influence their activity field (a stronger agency) ... This is partly a consequence of organismic change (e.g. biological maturation) and partly a consequence of increased experiences and (culturally age-defined) increases in social independence."

"never … completely determined or structured," but that, as agency is always exercised in specific structural and cultural contexts, "there is no hypothetical moment at which agency actually gets 'free' of structure … [in] some pure Kantian transcendental will." However, critical reflection, especially in conjunction with trusted others, can lead actors, in the words of the quotation above, to "loosen themselves from past patterns of interaction." There is obviously a significant truth here, but we also need to be cautious. Following Barnes' analysis of agency and sociability, we need to be aware of the deep connections between agency and being "held responsible"; and we noted also, from Laub and Sampson's (2003: 194) analysis, the perception that persistent offenders had "a distorted sense of autonomy without any commitment or concern for others." How, in life-change situations, one "loosens oneself from past patterns of interaction" whilst also finding oneself fulfilled agentically and responsibly in new small-group situations, remains an intriguing question. Or, as Emirbayer and Mische (1998: 1005) put it, an important challenge for empirical research in the future is "that of locating, comparing and predicting the relationship between different kinds of agentic processes and particular structuring contexts of action."

Jeanette Kennett: Weakness of will and self-control

As we turn to the last of the four main texts on agency to be considered in this chapter, we also engage with a different academic discipline. Jeanette Kennett is an Australian philosopher, and in her book *Agency and Responsibility* (Kennett, 2001) she offers a sustained analysis of the philosophical debates surrounding the "weakness of will" issue, a topic that was briefly raised when discussing Barnes' work. Essentially, Kennett seeks to provide a sophisticated philosophical defence for the "commonsense moral psychology" (or "folk theory") that underpins everyday lay discourse and the criminal law on issues of responsibility.

In a useful review of Kennett's book, Daniel Cohen (2003) points out that, for Kennett, there are two cross-cutting typologies at work when discussing moral failures. They are, first, the distinction between "evaluative failures" (when an agent forms a mistaken judgment about what he/she ought to do) and "practical failures" (when an agent fails to act in the way that, all things considered, he/she judges that one ought to act in a given situation). The second typology distinguishes between responsible action and non-responsible action, where the standard commonsense judgment is applied that one is responsible only where "he/she could have acted otherwise." Putting these two typologies together, one obtains the simple classification set out in Figure 7.3.

	Responsible action	Non-responsible action
Evaluative moral failure	Recklessness	"Evaluative compulsion"
Practical moral failure	Weakness of will	Compulsion

Figure 7.3. Categories of moral failure in Kennett's analysis
Source: Cohen (2003, after Kennett, 2001.)

Kennett's principal concern is with "weakness of will," that is, where A intentionally performs an act (such as taking hard drugs) even though he has said he intends in future to avoid that class of act (because, perhaps, he knows that his wife would be really upset if he became addicted again). Some philosophers have argued that "weakness of will" cannot be sustained as a coherent separate conceptual possibility, but must in the final analysis always collapse into one of two other states. These are, using the language of Figure 7.3, either *recklessness* (that is, the action was one of evaluative moral failure, not practical moral failure, and the actor has shown by his action that he was never really committed to abstinence from hard drugs); or *compulsion* (that is, the actor's drug-taking results from an addiction that he cannot resist). At the beginning of her book, Kennett spells out the consequences of such claims:

> If we assimilate weakness [of will] to recklessness then, though we hold on to the idea that the weak-willed are responsible for what they do, we must think that they do not really judge to be best the actions that they say they judge best ... [that is, they] are often insincere in their public pronouncements. On the other hand, if we assimilate weakness [of will] to compulsion then, though we retain the idea that the weak really do judge it to be better to act in one way while in fact acting in another, we must then think that the weak are not really responsible for what they do. (Kennett, 2001: 5)

In everyday language, "weakness of will" is a standard formulation – the person who says he genuinely wants to control his temper, or wants to stop smoking, but in a "moment of weakness" succumbs intentionally to the temptation to hit out, or have "just one" cigarette, is an obvious case in point. As previously noted, it is also standard for criminologists to meet offenders in early adulthood who say they want to desist from crime but are not sure if they can. In all of these very practical instances, if the philosophical skeptics are right then, as Kennett points out, we either have to say that the agent did not really mean it when s/he said s/he wanted to stop smoking/offending (because the very fact of continuation, according to the skeptics, shows that cessation was not what s/he most wanted); or alternatively, that s/he did really mean it but *had* to do what s/he did (commit crime, resume smoking) because of a compulsion. The second of these options perhaps looks, in most circumstances,[37] to be the more plausible, but as Kennett points it has its own costs in terms of exempting the person from responsibility for the act in question.[38]

A further necessary corollary of all this is that, as Kennett points out, there is no place for the idea of self-control if we abandon the concept of weakness of will:

> Common sense does not hold that simply knowing what is best is sufficient to ensure that we do what is best ... [It] recognizes that Jane may have a struggle on her hands if she judges that she ought not to eat cream cakes, yet desires, albeit not overwhelmingly [i.e., not obviously compulsively] to do so ... The revisionary accounts cannot make sense of Jane's struggles at all since they cannot, or cannot fully, acknowledge that they occur. (Kennett, 2001: 5)

In my view, Figure 7.3 offers some very useful conceptual distinctions, of considerable relevance to criminologists interested in desistance. Moreover, Kennett certainly succeeds in her aim of providing a plausible philosophical defence of the commonsense distinctions, and hence of the possibility of someone acting intentionally with "weakness of will." However, whether she has succeeded in overcoming all the philosophical obstacles to a successful defence, it is ultimately impossible for a non-philosopher to say.

The purpose of including a discussion of Kennett's work in the present chapter is twofold. First, it highlights the importance of the "weakness of will" issue for the general discussion of agency (by contrast with Barnes, who, as suggested earlier, understates the significance of this issue). Secondly, this chapter is specifically about desistance from crime, and there is little doubt that "weakness of will" and "self-control" are of considerable significance for desistance studies, a point that must now be elaborated.

Three questions about self-control in relation to desistance can usefully be explored here. First, what exactly *is* self-control? The most well-known use of this concept in criminology is by Gottfredson and Hirschi (1990), according to whom, as we saw at the beginning of this chapter,

[37] Although the first option is certainly not unimaginable as a plausible possibility in some empirical circumstances, e.g., in the case of someone who continually says he really wants to stop drinking, but nevertheless consumes eight pints each night for several years.

[38] For an interesting early example of this kind of reasoning, see the comments by St. Paul: "The good which I want to do, I fail to do, but what I do is the wrong which is against my will; and if what I do is against my will, clearly it is no longer I who am the agent, but sin that has its dwelling in me" (Romans 7: 19–20, Revised English Bible translation).

between-group differences in criminality are a function of low or high self-control, and (with very few exceptions) individuals' relative levels of self-control are stable from an early age. Hence, for Gottfredson and Hirschi (1990: 91) self-control is a generalized propensity, a "stable construct useful in the explanation of crime"; and people who lack self-control "tend to be impulsive, insensitive, physical (as opposed to mental), risk-taking, short-sighted and nonverbal" (90). A different, and so far less well-known, formulation has however recently been offered by Per-Olof Wikström (2004) who differentiates self-control from morality, within a more dynamic conception of propensity.[39] For Wikström (2004), morality and self-control are "the key *individual* causal mechanisms that impact on individuals' perceptions of alternatives and process of choice relevant to engagement in crime" (Wikström, 2004: 8, emphasis added).[40] Wikström further suggests, however, that "morality is more basic than self-control" in this respect, and that self-control "only becomes relevant as a (part) cause of crime at the stage when the person considers to act upon a temptation or provocation in ways that are defined as illegal *and conflict with his or her own morals*. At this stage a person's degree of self-control will be crucial . . . " (Wikström, 2004: 17, emphasis added). The italicized phrase is, of course, remarkably similar to Kennett's philosophical characterization of "weakness of will" (see Figure 7.3).[41] It is notable, however, that Wikström speaks of a person's "degree of self-control." A fully agentic approach to self-control might

[39] For Wikström (2004: 13) the general concept of *propensity* refers to "individual differences in seeing alternatives and making choices in particular settings. Propensity is thus not individual characteristics (which cause propensity), and it is not action (which is the outcome), but it is the process that links the two (the seeing and choosing, emerging from the individual characteristics and resulting in certain actions)." Within this framework, *crime propensity* is defined as "the generalized tendency to see crime as an option and to choose that action," and the key causal mechanisms involved in crime propensity are considered to be morality and self-control.

[40] But, one must emphasize, Wikström (2004) also sees other (non-individual) causal mechanisms as relevant to whether a crime is actually committed, for example the "temptations and provocations," and the perceived deterrence, in the *setting*. See, for example, Wikström (2004: fig. 1.1).

[41] Strictly speaking, Kennett (2001: 132) distinguishes between a broad and a narrow conception of what she calls "orthonomy" ("the rule of the right"), against which moral failure (see Figure 7.3) is adjudged. In the broad conception, "not only are [the agent's] desires and actions appropriately responsive to her *beliefs* about what is desirable, but also those very beliefs and desires accord with the facts about what is *truly* desirable: that is, about the facts about what she would stably desire that she do at the ideal limit of information, rational reflection, and dialogue with others" (emphasis in original). In the narrow version of orthonomy, the agent's moral wishes "are desirable at least by her own lights"; that is, she "acts in accordance with her beliefs about what she has most reason to do." Clearly, using this distinction, Wikström (2004) is referring to the narrow conception of orthonomy.

frame this concept in a somewhat different way, as we shall see shortly when considering Jeanette Kennett's discussion of "varieties of self-control."

A second very important question concerns the way in which, in detail, "weakness of will," or "lack of self-control," differs from recklessness (see Figure 7.3), and whether this distinction has criminological as well as philosophical significance. To explore this issue, it is useful to note that, for Kennett (2001: 171–180), there are three types of recklessness, of which the third type is "most central to both common-sense and legal conceptions of reckless action." This type of recklessness

> is rooted in a fundamental indifference to the reasons provided by the legitimate claims and concerns of others. These agents are not blinded either by desire or by ideology, as [the first two types] are. Rather, their actions manifest indifference to, not (culpable) ignorance of, the reasons for refraining from actions [causing] ... bad consequences to others ... The problem is that these agents, *unlike straightforwardly weak agents, are not governed by the deliberative norms revealed in the conversational stance*[42] ... in reaching their practical judgements or actions. They are more narrowly concerned that the desires they act upon be the desires they want to act on ... (Kennett, 2001: 177–178, emphasis added)

Thus, there is a significant difference between reckless agents and weak-willed agents, even if both commit the same act. The reckless agent (of the third type) is "fundamentally indifferent" to the moral claims of others. The weak-willed person recognizes (at least to some extent) those claims, but then fails – when it comes to the crunch – to act in accordance with his/her own moral understandings.

It is again interesting to link this analysis to that of Laub and Sampson (2003), which I previously considered when discussing the work of Barnes (in its "sociability" aspect). A key phrase that Laub and Sampson (2003: 194) use when describing persistent offenders is that they possess "a distorted sense of autonomy without any commitment or concern for others." The potential linkage here with Kennett on recklessness is obvious. However, it is also important to recall that the persistent offenders in Laub and Sampson's study could not be easily

[42] On "the conversational stance," see Kennett (2001: 100ff.); the concept is derived from Pettit and Smith (1996). Its basic idea is "that reason is not wholly self-contained or self-referential. Reasoning is something that we must do together. Both practical and theoretical evaluations can be conversationally interrogated and there are norms governing such a conversation ... we must presuppose that we are engaged in [what Pettit and Smith call] 'a common world-directed enterprise ... of trying to determine what, in the light of the facts, the agent is required to desire and do'" (Kennett, 2001: 100–101).

predicted from factors measurable in adolescence (see earlier section). Hence we have to face the possibility that the apparent recklessness of these men could, in some cases, be a result of adult social experience and not (*pace* Gottfredson and Hirschi) a life-long propensity. Laub and Sampson (2003: 280) add support to that possibility when they say:

> For those without permanent addresses, steady jobs, spouses and other rooted forms of life, crime and deviance is an unsurprising result – *even for those possessing so-called prosocial traits*. As a consequence of chaotic and unstructured routines, one has increased contact with those individuals who are similarly situated . . . [so] we find in our narrative data that the influence of deviant peers and criminal networks is particularly salient in the lives of persistent offenders (emphasis added).[43]

Without wishing to cast doubt on the observed importance of "deviant peers and criminal networks" for persisters, there is another dimension that is worth considering here, and this returns us to Margaret Archer's (2000) distinction between reactive and reflective emotionality. On Archer's analysis, among people lacking "rooted forms of life" and living, day-to-day, with "chaotic and unstructured routines," reactive emotionality is inevitably dominant, and there is little opportunity to develop more reflective, commitment-oriented dimensions of emotionality. Such an absence of reflective emotionality could, obviously, reinforce attitudes and practices based on "fundamental indifference" to the claims and concerns of others; that is, recklessness rather than self-control.

The philosophical distinction between recklessness and weakness of will, among those continuing in crime in early adulthood, would seem to merit greater attention than it has received, either from criminologists or in debates on criminal policy. Both these groups of offenders are recidivists, but the second group shows an element of moral commitment lacking (at least for the time being) in the first; and this important difference is something upon which those wishing to promote rehabilitation could potentially build. The very existence of "weakness of will" among at least some young recidivists shows also how fundamentally mistaken Waddington (2003) is in claiming that offenders, *by definition*, are not part of the moral community (see the quotation at the head of this chapter).[44] To a greater extent than has often been recognized

[43] Laub and Sampson (2003: 280) note that actual co-offending reduces with age, but, for persisters, the influence of deviant peers does not, because "one has increased contact with those who are similarly situated," that is, "similarly unattached and free from nurturing, social capital or support, and informal social control."

[44] To be fair, Waddington's point is made *en passant*, in the context of a chapter that is focused upon public-order policing in circumstances of political contention. The

(especially in political and media debates), some of them self-define in precisely the opposite manner, as persons who do want to go straight and to be part of the ordinary moral community, but are afraid that they might "do something stupid" (see earlier discussion). Whatever her success in the strictly philosophical debate, Jeanette Kennett (2001) has therefore done criminology a service by drawing to our attention the significance of the "weakness of will" category of action, and the importance of differentiating it from the greater callousness (moral indifference) of the reckless.

The third and final issue about self-control to be raised here concerns *varieties of self-control.* Kennett (2001) devotes a whole chapter (ch. 5) to this topic, raising many philosophical issues that are not of concern for present purposes. But part of her discussion is severely practical, and is certainly of relevance to our current concerns. For example, Kennett (2001: 134–135) draws attention to the fact that self-control does not have to occur simultaneously with the temptation or provocation ("synchronic self-control"); rather, *diachronic self-control* (self-control across time) can also be exercised. Suppose D has decided he really wants to desist from crime; suppose further that he has some delinquent friends whose company he genuinely enjoys. D might nevertheless deliberately decide (and cases of this sort are certainly not unknown: see Kerner, 2005) to stop seeing his friends, because he is afraid that if he goes out with them he will inevitably get caught up in situations where he will find himself drawn into committing crimes with them. He has, therefore, taken a prior decision of diachronic self-control, to try to preempt a later temptation. Or again, in a more synchronic situation, agents might be able to bolster simple self-control by what Kennett (2001: 142) calls "*expansion and aggregation of... motives.*" Suppose that E, a heroin addict, is detoxified in prison and decides to try to desist. Suppose further that, on a particular occasion, he is tempted to go back onto hard drugs. As well as trying to refocus his attention on the original reasons for his commitment to desist (synchronic cognitive self-control), E might also summon up additional arguments, such as reminding himself of the money he will save if he rejects the (strong) temptation to resume his habit. Although perhaps "none of these considerations taken alone" would have the effect of creating self-control in the face of severe temptation, "taken together they provide the incentive [the tempted

argument is that the policing of political dissidents motivated by ideals is quite different from the policing of "ordinary criminals" because of the more contested legitimacy of police action in the former context. That point can be readily conceded; but the way in which Waddington chooses to make his point is both unnecessarily sweeping and extremely unfortunate.

agent] needs" (Kennett 2001: 142); that is, "expansion and aggregation of motives" allows self-control to be reasserted.

These severely practical examples are of great interest to criminology, because they help us to see that self-control is not simply a generalized propensity, as Gottfredson and Hirschi (1990) would have it, but can also be a matter of active decision-making. "Weakness of will" is a category very familiar to those who are trying to desist; and there are active tactics that can be deployed to try to maximize self-control in a situation where the agent believes he might be overwhelmed by "weakness of will." In short, and perhaps paradoxically, paying careful attention to a strictly philosophical analysis has helped us to restore a more fully agential element of self-control into criminological discourse.

Discussion and synthesis

Having considered all the four main texts, we can now turn to discussion and synthesis. A useful place to begin is with the three questions raised at the end of our initial discussion of the work of Laub and Sampson (2003), namely:

- how is the "agency" dimension of the analysis to be distinguished from the more "causal" elements?
- how, theoretically, is the "choice" dimension of the analysis to be related to the "social bonds" dimension?
- how are people's choices related to their overall understandings of themselves (i.e., what is often described as their "sense of self")?

The first of these questions might seem to remain troublesome. In part this is because of the spectre raised by Barry Barnes (2000: 33) that the adoption of a non-determinist perspective (as embraced, for example, by Laub and Sampson (2003)) must "mark the bounds of predictive explanatory science in the human realm." But additionally, if we adopt a caused/uncaused distinction, how – in a social scientific analysis – do we know what is "caused" and what is "uncaused"?

At the level of everyday social science, these issues can seem less daunting than they are to philosophers or social theorists. Let us assume that P, an ex-prisoner, has decided to try to desist for the sake of the future of his newborn child, but one day some of his former criminal associates offer him the opportunity to join in the planning for what looks to be a promising factory break-in, potentially yielding large rewards. Let us further (and, undoubtedly, with more philosophical difficulty) assume that P is truly free to accept or reject this offer; that is, that whichever option he chooses he will afterwards be able genuinely to say, "I could have acted otherwise." In *explanatory* terms, it is actually not at all difficult for us to explain whichever choice he makes. We know why P has decided to try to desist, so if he says "no" to his criminal associates, we can explain that decision as a natural consequence of the prior desistance decision. But we also know that the lure of the money, a desire for his friends' esteem, and so on, might indeed constitute a real temptation to join their enterprise; so if P does say "yes" to his friends, we can explain that decision as well. In other words, and using the framework of Figure 7.2, P has potentially genuine *reasons* for either choice, and some social pressures backing up either option. While these are *reasons* rather than *causes*, the explanatory analysis is (as Barnes correctly points out) fundamentally similar; we can explain either decision. Thus, *for the purposes of explanation*, in ordinary social science there is little purpose in troubling ourselves with the philosophical distinction between the "reasons" and "causes", the "uncaused" and the "caused".[45]

What is difficult for the social scientist, in circumstances such as these, is in fact not explanation, but the *prediction* of which choice P will make. It is, however, perfectly possible to envisage a version of social science that says it *cannot* effectively predict such decisions, though *ex post facto* it can explain. This does not entail the "redundancy of [the social science] project" as Barry Barnes (2000: 33) suggested, but it does suggest limits to the predictive power of that project. This, if I understand them correctly, is what Laub and Sampson's (2003) position now commits them to. It is, of course, a position that is buttressed by the now strong empirical evidence of substantial heterogeneity in criminal careers, and the difficulties of prediction, as summarized at the beginning of this chapter.

When we turn to the second and third key questions set out in the bullet-points at the beginning of this section, we are more centrally in the territory analyzed by the four main writings on agency examined in this chapter. To begin a synthesis of these writings, let us return to the comment by Malle (2002) that human beings routinely display *both* "a high level of self–other differentiation" *and* "a high degree of self–other co-ordination." In my view, the concept of agency is best understood by taking seriously both parts of this claim, and by bringing them together to form a complete picture.

Let us begin with "self–other differentiation," and remind ourselves, with Campbell (1996: 161) that action always has "an individual and largely covert" dimension, a dimension that – if we wish to analyze

[45] For a similar point from the realist perspective, see Archer (2000: 13).

it – requires us to "tear down the privacy sign" (Archer, 2000: 317) and enter the "inner lives of subjects." The writings examined in this chapter that best illuminate and develop this aspect of agency are those by Archer and by Emirbayer and Mische. From Archer (2000) we have especially learned the following:

- that "the continuous self" (and "self-understanding") constitutes an important background element to agentic decision-making – decisions are made by particular individuals, with their unique past histories, their own self-understandings, and so on;
- that emotions constitute an important element in "the self," not only in the sense of emotional reactions to events in the natural, the practical, and the social orders, but also in terms of the "transvaluation" of emotions, based on our social commitments, which can importantly shape the way we see particular situations (as in Archer's *liaison dangereuse* example);
- that the adoption of a role (such as becoming a spouse, a parent, or a regular jobholder) is a complex process involving an interaction between the individual (and his/her self-understanding) and the social expectations of the role; in stepping into and continuing to play various roles, over time individuals in a real sense "define themselves";
- that the transition to adulthood (a subject of great interest to desistance scholars) is closely linked to role transition, and, probably, to a more reflective emotionality. Each of these matters is capable of being utilized in our understanding of desistance, and in prospective empirical research on that topic.

From Emirbayer and Mische (1998) the primary lessons that we can learn seem to be:

- that we need to pay serious attention to the temporal dimension of agency, a dimension so well encapsulated in Kierkegaard's early nineteenth-century aphorism about only ever properly *understanding* our past lives, but nevertheless constantly needing to move forward;
- that true action can sometimes be habitual (a point that is of some importance in relation to what Laub and Sampson (2003) call "desistance by default"), and that habitual patterns of iteration constitute an important background against which agents sometimes make deliberate future projections and current practical-evaluative decisions which attempt to break away from these iterative patterns;
- that individuals are able "to increase their capacity for invention, choice and transformative impact" (1003), especially by processes of

self-critical judgment and discussion with others. By contrast, and linking here with Archer's analysis, those (such as the homeless and the poor) who are necessarily preoccupied with the immediate (the next meal; where shall I sleep tonight?) are much less likely to be able to think "projectively" into "future trajectories of action" where "received structures of thought and action may be creatively reconfigured" (Emirbayer & Mische, 1998: 971).

Once again, it is not difficult to see how each of these lessons might be taken forward in empirical research. Taking Emirbayer and Mische's analysis together with that of Archer, we also obtain a very good sense of how the "choice" dimension of agency is very intimately connected to the "social bonds" dimension, in the process that Laub and Sampson (2003) well describe as "situated choice." In such choices, Emirbayer and Mische (1998: 1004) are surely right to emphasize that "there is no hypothetical moment at which agency actually gets 'free' of structure... [in] some pure Kantian transcendental will."[46]

A final lesson in the area of "self–other differentiation" can be derived from Jeanette Kennett's (2001) analysis of the "varieties of self-control," in particular her distinction between diachronic and synchronic self-control, and the possibility, within synchronic self-control, of adopting the tactic of "expansion and aggregation of motives." This analysis helps us to realize how central everyday practical tactics can be to the concepts of agency and of self-control; and they too are empirically researchable. Future research needs to take account of such everyday matters, as well as more complex and "mysterious" (to quote Wittgenstein) matters such as the nature of the self.

Malle (2002) rightly enjoins us, when analyzing human lives, to have regard not only to self–other differentiation, but also to humans' "high degree of self–other co-ordination." It is Barry Barnes' (2000) major achievement to have shown how central the concept of responsible agency is to self–other coordination, and a juxtaposition of Barnes' analysis with that of Laub and Sampson (2003) demonstrates how the long-term persistent offenders in the Gluecks' sample were, as individuals, relatively lacking in precisely this quality of self–other social and moral coordination. (The men possessed "a distorted sense of

[46] This comment, of course, directly raises the structure–agency debate in social theory. But acceptance of the comment does not solve this problem, because among those who take such a view there is still an important difference between adherents of Giddens' (1984) structuration theory, and those who favor Archer's (1995) "morphogenetic approach." It is not necessary to enter this territory for present purposes.

autonomy without any commitment or concern for others": Laub & Sampson, 2003: 194.) Clearly, then, this is a central issue for future studies of desistance, social bonds, and human agency, and it needs to be sensitively married to those other aspects of agency which are, in Campbell's words, more "individual" and "covert."

The topic of "agency and responsibility," however, necessarily requires one to enter difficult debates in moral philosophy, particularly concerning whether agents "could have acted otherwise," and whether "weakness of will" can be adequately distinguished from recklessness, on the one hand, and compulsion, on the other. These two debates (i.e., on "acting otherwise" and on "weakness of will") are linked, and those who are skeptical of the philosophical possibility of "acting otherwise" in a given situation need to pay close attention to the "weakness of will" issue. The weakness of will issue also has real practical bite in the context of the study of desistance, because many young adult offenders wish to desist, but are very aware of the possibility of intentionally "doing something stupid" in a given situation. The distinction between acting with "weakness of will," and acting in a reckless manner, also merits closer criminological attention than it has received. The fact that many young recidivists have very "ordinary" social and moral ambitions – such as getting married, a steady job, and living in a "decent" area (Bottoms *et al.*, 2004) – shows unequivocally that, in self-definitional terms, such offenders are, *pace* Waddington (see the introduction to this chapter), in significant ways very much part of the social and moral community. It is, surely, to society's advantage to recognize this fact, and to encourage them to strengthen their links with the mainstream moral community.

In that connection, one should finally note, of course, that many would-be desisters face formidable social-structural disadvantages; to take only one example, a significant criminal record is hardly an advantage in the employment market. (Indeed, it might be regarded as surprising that there is as much desistance as there is among recidivists, given some of the structural blockages that they face.) It has not been the purpose of this chapter to examine these macro-structural issues, but, in studying agency, one should emphatically not forget Laub and Sampson's (2003: 281) correct prescription that criminologists considering desistance need to consider "the interaction between life-course transitions, situational context and individual will."

If the analysis of the preceding pages is correct, then a coherent synthesis of the insights of the four main texts considered in this chapter can indeed be achieved, with only the explicitly "causal" dimension of Barnes' work having to be rejected in such a synthesis. Moreover, it can,

I believe, reasonably be claimed that the synthesis of the different insights on human agency offered by these very different writers offers rather more than the sum of the parts. That is to say, because the different texts focus on different aspects of human agency, and each text covers issues that the others do not (or do not fully) consider, bringing them together in a coherent synthesis gives us a much richer overall view of the multi-faceted character of human agency than can be gleaned from more partial analyses. Moreover, as I hope the preceding pages have adequately indicated, such a synthesis can be directly and creatively used to enrich desistance studies.

"Situated choice" and "promotive factors"

I turn finally to a question that arose at the end of the initial discussion of desistance studies, namely: "Is the Laub/Sampson (2003) emphasis on 'situated choice' in adulthood compatible with the findings of Stouthamer-Loeber *et al.* on 'promotive factors' for desistance, given that the promotive factors are already discernible in early adolescence?"

At first sight, the logic of these two scholarly approaches appears to be very different. Laub and Sampson place emphasis on the lack of congruence between factors associated with the onset of delinquency and with desistance from crime, and their "situated choice" approach is very much based on a non-deterministic social science that focuses on their subjects' active responses to key "turning points" that presented themselves in adulthood. Stouthamer-Loeber *et al.*, on the other hand, adopt the more traditional "risk-factor" and "predictive" approach (an approach which is obviously compatible with determinism), and they have identified some factors in adolescence that, although not associated with adolescent criminality or its absence, nevertheless seem (through what has been described as a "sleeper effect") in some way to be predictive of desistance a decade later. The time-focus of the two approaches is very different (Laub/Sampson focusing on the immediate "situated choice"; Stouthamer-Loeber *et al.* on possible long-term "sleeper effects"), as are the mechanisms that are emphasized ("choice" versus "risk factors"). So, on the surface the degree of compatibility of the two studies seems to be quite low.

Before abandoning the quest for compatibility, however, let us re-examine more closely the exact character of the "sleeper factors" for desistance that were uncovered in the Stouthamer-Loeber *et al.* analysis. As we saw earlier, these could be divided into two groups: first, "sanction factors" (low use of physical punishment by parents; and greater belief by adolescents in the likelihood of getting caught if crimes were committed), and secondly, "peer factors" (good relationship with peers; and low participation by peers in substance misuse). Given the limitations of the presently available data, no definitive comments are possible, but the nature of these particular "promotive" factors does raise some intriguing issues.

Take first the question of peers. In analyses of the Tübingen Criminal Behavior Development Study, one of the factors that sharply divided "persisters" from "desisters" during the period when the sample was aged between 25 and 35 was "cutting off contacts with problematic peers or with the 'milieu'" (Kerner, 2005) – almost certainly primarily by using tactics of "diachronic self-control" (Kennett, 2001). It might not be too fanciful to suggest that those who, in adolescence, had "good relationships with peers" might be able more maturely to handle peer pressures at key turning points in early adulthood. Similarly with "sanction factors": it is perhaps not implausible to suggest that those who, in adolescence, received less physical punishment from parents (and therefore, presumably, more reasoned dialog) might be better placed to make well-reasoned judgments (or what Laub and Sampson might call good "situated choices") in early adulthood. In other words, the "sleeper factors" for desistance identified by Stouthamer-Loeber *et al.* in the Pittsburgh Youth Study might plausibly be reinterpreted as "promotive factors for the exercise of responsible agency." And if that is correct, then the apparent tension between this study and that of Laub and Sampson (2003) is largely dissolved. There is, inevitably, a significant element of speculation in this suggestion, but the suggestion itself is, hopefully, of potential interest to future researchers.

Conclusion

The aim of this chapter has been to reflect carefully on the theorization of human agency, while not losing sight of the social context within which agency is exercised; and, in the light of this analysis, to enrich our understanding of desistance from crime, and consider additional possibilities for the future empirical study of agency in the context of desistance. By its nature, an analysis of this kind is primarily exploratory, and so it has to finish in a somewhat open-ended way – possibilities have been raised, but how they will work out when subsequently applied in an empirical context, or subjected to further theoretical analysis, remains to be seen. Nevertheless, it is hoped that enough fresh possibilities have been explored to be of constructive value to future scholars of desistance.

References

Alexander, J. C. (1988). *Action and its Environments*. New York: Columbia University Press.

Archer, M. S. (1988). *Culture and Agency*. Cambridge: Cambridge University Press.

(1995). *Realist Social Theory: The Morphogenetic Approach*. Cambridge: Cambridge University Press.

(2000). *Being Human: The Problem of Agency*. Cambridge: Cambridge University Press.

Ashworth, A. J. (2003). *Principles of Criminal Law*, 4th edn. Oxford: Oxford University Press.

Barnes, B. (2000). *Understanding Agency: Social Theory and Responsible Action*. London: Sage.

Benton, T. (2001). "A stratified ontology of selfhood." *Journal of Critical Realism* 4: 36–38.

Bhaskar, R. (1979). *The Possibility of Naturalism*. Brighton: Harvester.

(1989). *Reclaiming Reality*. London: Verso.

Bottoms, A. E. (2000) "The relationship between theory and research in criminology." In R. D. King & E. Wincup (eds.), *Doing Research in Crime and Justice*. Oxford: Oxford University Press.

Bottoms, A. E., Shapland, J., Costello, A., Holmes, D., & Muir, G.(2004). "Towards desistance: theoretical underpinnings for an empirical study." *Howard Journal* 43: 368–389.

Burnett, R. & Maruna, S. (2004). "So 'prison works' does it? The criminal careers of 130 men released from prison under Home Secretary Michael Howard." *Howard Journal* 43: 390–404.

Campbell, C. (1996). *The Myth of Social Action*. Cambridge: Cambridge University Press.

Capozza, D. & Brown, R., eds. (2000). *Social Identity Processes*. London: Sage.

Cohen, D. (2003). "Review of *Agency and Responsibility* by Jeanette Kennett." *Australian Journal of Philosophy* 81: 444–445.

Elster, J. (1984). *Ulysses and the Sirens*. Cambridge: Cambridge University Press.

Emirbayer, M. & Mische, A. (1998). "What is agency?" *American Journal of Sociology* 103: 962–1023.

Ezell, M. E. & Cohen, L. E. (2005). *Desisting from Crime: Continuity and Change in Long-Term Crime Patterns of Serious Chronic Offenders*. Oxford: Oxford University Press.

Farrall, S. (2002). *Rethinking What Works with Offenders: Probation, Social Context and Desistance from Crime*. Cullompton, UK: Willan.

Farrington, D. P. & West, D. J. (1995). "Effects of marriage, separation and children on offending by adult males." In Z. S. Blan & J. Hogan (eds.), *Delinquency and Disrepute in the Life Course*. Greenwich, CT: JAI Press.

Flew, A., ed. (1979). *A Dictionary of Philosophy*. New York: St. Martin's Press.

Forgas, J. P. & Williams, K. D., eds. (2002). *The Social Self: Cognitive, Interpersonal and Intergroup Perspectives*. New York: Psychology Press.

Giddens, A. (1976). *New Rules of Sociological Method*. London: Hutchinson.

(1984). *The Constitution of Society*. Cambridge: Polity Press.

Giordano, P. C., Cernovich, S. A., & Rudolph, J. L. (2002). "Gender, crime and desistance: toward a theory of cognitive transformation." *American Journal of Sociology* 107: 990–1064.

Glueck, S. & Glueck, E. T. (1950). *Unravelling Juvenile Delinquency*. New York: Commonwealth Fund.

Gottfredson, M. R. & Hirschi, T. (1990). *A General Theory of Crime*. Stanford: Stanford University Press.

Harris, G. W. (1999). *Agent-Centered Morality: An Aristotelian Alternative to Kantian Internalism*. Berkeley: University of California Press.

Hart, H. L. A. (1968). *Punishment and Responsibility*. Oxford: Clarendon Press.

Hirschi, T. (1969). *Causes of Delinquency*. Berkeley: University of California Press.

Kennett, J. (2001). *Agency and Responsibility: A Common-sense Moral Psychology*. Oxford: Clarendon Press.

Kerner, H. J. (2005). "Crime prevention, prospects and problems: the case of effective institutional versus community-based treatment programs for prevention of recidivism among youthful offenders." Lecture to 129th International Senior Seminar, United Nations Asia and Far East Institute for the Prevention of Crime and the Treatment of Offenders, Tokyo (to be published in the Proceedings of the Senior Seminar).

Laub, J. H. & Sampson, R. J. (2001). "Understanding desistance from crime." In M. Tonry (ed.), *Crime and Justice: A Review of Research* 28: 1–69.

(2003). *Shared Beginnings, Divergent Lives: Delinquent Boys to Age 70*. Cambridge, MA: Harvard University Press.

Loyal, S. (2003). *The Sociology of Anthony Giddens*. London: Pluto Press.

Loyal, S. & Barnes, B. (2001). "Agency as a red herring in social theory." *Philosophy of Science* 31: 507–524.

Malle, B. F. (2002). "The social self and the social other: actor–observer asymmetries in making sense of behavior." In J. P. Forgas & K. D. Williams (eds.), *The Social Self: Cognitive, Interpersonal and Intergroup Perspectives*. New York: Psychology Press.

Maruna, S. (2001). *Making Good: How Ex-convicts Reform and Rebuild their Lives*. Washington DC: American Psychological Association.

Mead, G. H. (1932). *The Philosophy of the Present*. Chicago: University of Chicago Press.

Modell, J. (1994). "Review of *Crime in the Making*." *American Journal of Sociology* 99: 1389–1391.

Moffitt, T. E. (1993). "Adolescence-limited and life-course-persistent antisocial behaviour: a developmental taxonomy." *Psychological Review* 100: 674–701.

(1997). "Adolescence-limited and life-course-persistent offending: a complementary pair of developmental theories." In T. P. Thornberry (ed.), *Developmental Theories of Crime and Delinquency*. Advances in Criminological Theory 7. New Brunswick, NJ: Transaction.

Osborn, S. G. (1980). "Moving home, leaving London and delinquent trends." *British Journal of Criminology* 20: 54–61.

Pettit, P. & Smith, M. (1996). "Freedom in belief and desire." *Journal of Philosophy* 93: 429–449.

Sampson, R. J. & Laub, J. H. (1993). *Crime in the Making: Pathways and Turning Points through Life.* Cambridge, MA: Harvard University Press.

(1996). "Socioeconomic achievement in the life course of disadvantaged men: military service as a turning point, circa 1940–1965." *American Sociological Review* 61: 347–367.

Sluga, H. (1996). " 'Whose house is that?' Wittgenstein on the self." In H. Sluga & D. G. Stern (eds.), *Cambridge Companion to Wittgenstein.* Cambridge: Cambridge University Press.

Stouthamer-Loeber, M., Wei, E., Loeber, R., & Master, A. S. (2004). "Desistance from persistent serious delinquency in the transition to adulthood." *Development and Psychopathology* 16: 897–918.

Taylor, C. (1985). *Human Agency and Language.* Cambridge: Cambridge University Press.

Trigg, R. (1989). *Reality at Risk.* London: Harvester Wheatsheaf.

Van den Beld, T., ed. (2000). *Moral Responsibility and Ontology.* Dordrecht: Kluwer.

Waddington, P. A. J. (2003). "Policing, public order and political contention." In T. Newburn (ed.), *Handbook of Policing.* Cullompton, UK: Willan.

Warr, M. (2002). *Companions in Crime: The Social Aspects of Criminal Conduct.* Cambridge: Cambridge University Press.

Wikström, P.-O. (2004). "Crime as alternative: towards a cross-level situational action theory of crime causation." In J. McCord (ed.), *Beyond Empiricism: Institutions and Intentions in the Study of Crime.* Advances in Criminological Theory 13. New Brunswick, NJ: Transaction.

(2005). "The social origins of pathways in crime: towards a developmental ecological action theory of crime involvement and its changes." In D. P. Farrington (ed.), *Integrated Development and Life Course Theories of Offending.* Advances in Criminological Theory 14. New Brunswick, NJ: Transaction.

Wikström, P.-O. H. & Loeber, R. (2000). "Do disadvantaged neighborhoods cause well-adjusted children to become adolescent delinquents? A study of male juvenile serious offending, individual risk and protective factors, and neighborhood context." *Criminology* 38(4): 1109–1142.

Wollheim, R. (1984). *The Thread of Life.* Cambridge: Cambridge University Press.

Wordsworth, W. (1802). "Preface to the Second Edition of 'Lyrical Ballads' ". In T. Hutchinson (ed.), *The Poetical Works of Wordsworth (1936).* London: Oxford University Press.

Index

N.B. Numbers in bold refer to figures and tables.

Printed in the United States
154340LV00003B/21/P